In this, his major work to date, Herbert Clark sets out the thesis that language use is really a form of joint action. A joint action is one that is carried out by an ensemble of people acting in coordination with each other. Language use is thus more than the sum of a speaker speaking and a listener listening. It is the joint action that emerges when speakers and listeners – writers and readers – perform their individual actions in coordination, as ensembles. In contrast to work within the cognitive sciences, which has seen language use as an individual process, and to work within the social sciences, which has seen it as a social process, the author argues strongly that language use embodies both individual and social processes.

This book will be essential reading for all students and researchers interested in the ways in which language operates in its human and social context.

Using language

Using language

HERBERT H. CLARK | *Department of Psychology, Stanford University*

CAMBRIDGE
UNIVERSITY PRESS

Published by the Press Syndicate of the University of Cambridge
The Pitt Building, Trumpington Street, Cambridge CB2 1RP
40 West 20th Street, New York, NY 10011–4211, USA
10 Stamford Road, Oakleigh, Melbourne 3166, Australia

First published 1996

Printed in Great Britain at the University Press, Cambridge
Set in Monotype Imprint and Monotype Grotesque

A catalogue record for this book is available from the British Library

Library of Congress cataloguing in publication data applied for

ISBN 0 521 56158 2 hardback
ISBN 0 521 56745 9 paperback

TAG

Contents

Preface

Writing a book can be like visiting a famous old city. You arrive with a copy of the *Guide Michelin* and begin touring the recommended sights. But as you walk from one landmark to the next, you discover the city beyond the *Guide*. Some features don't have the beauty or authenticity described in the *Guide*, and others aren't in the *Guide* at all. In one district, you find an exciting new style of architecture, and in another, an experiment in urban ecology. In still another, you come upon a new community of immigrants, complete with its own markets, restaurants, and religious activities. As you go from place to place, you meet more and more residents, who seduce you into extending your stay. By the time you leave, you realize that the city is just not what you expected. It is richer, more sophisticated, more diverse, and it took your visit to discover that.

Writing this book has been just such an experience. I am indebted to many for making it such an exciting, constructive, pleasurable, and prolonged experience. I wish to thank a great many collaborators for guiding me through new areas and expanding my horizons: Bridget Bly, Susan Brennan, Sam Buttrick, Stuart Card, Thomas Carlson, Jean Fox Tree, Ellen Francik, Wade French, Richard Gerrig, Ellen Isaacs, Barbara Malt, Catherine Marshall, Daniel Morrow, Gregory Murphy, Gisela Redeker, Edward Schaefer, Michael Schober, Robert Schreuder, Elizabeth Shriberg, Dale Schunk, Vicki Smith, Heather Stark, Elizabeth Wade, Thomas Wasow, Steve Whittaker, Deanna Wilkes-Gibbs. I owe a special debt to Randi Engle, Pim Levelt, Gisela Redeker, and Michael Schober for commenting on an earlier draft of the book and instigating fundamental changes in it. I credit Michael Schober with implanting the ideas that delayed the book the longest. Finally, the book wouldn't be what it is without Eve Clark, who has been the ideal companion on all my travels.

For the preparation of this book, I am indebted financially to the National Science Foundation, the Advanced Research Projects Agency, the Center for the Study of Language and Information at Stanford University, and, especially, the Max Planck Institute for Psycholinguistics, Nijmegen, the Netherlands.

Note on examples

A book about language use wouldn't be comprehensible without examples of spontaneous speech, so I have appealed to authentic examples wherever I could. Most of them are from the London–Lund corpus, a corpus of British English conversation collected and transcribed by Jan Svartvik, Randolph Quirk, and the Survey of English Usage at University College London and the Survey of Spoken English at the University of Lund (Svartvik and Quirk, 1980).[1] I have identified these examples by their text numbers (e.g., 1.1) and tone unit numbers (e.g., 245) like this: (1.1.245). The original transcripts represent tone units, intonation, overlapping speech, pauses, and many other features of spontaneous conversation. For readability, I have retained only some of these features, as illustrated here (1.1.245):

Reynard:　so it's not until - next year that *the job will be advertised,*
Sam:　　 *January I suppose there* may be an interview round
　　　　　about January,
Reynard:　yeah, - u:m you heard anything about this, .
Sam:　　 nothing at all yet, - -

This example contains the five special symbols:

Feature	Symbol	Example
End of tone unit	,	yeah,
Brief pause (of one light foot)	.	about this, . nothing
Unit pause (of one stress unit)	-	until - next year
Overlapping speech	*x* *y*	*the job will be advertised*
		January I suppose there
Elongated vowel	:	u:m

Overlapping speech, for example, is represented by two stretches of text enclosed by pairs of asterisks. Sam's "January I suppose there" overlaps with Reynard's "the job will be advertised." When there might be confusion, overlapping speech is enclosed in double asterisks, as in "**yeah**". Speech that was inaudible, or almost inaudible, to the transcriber is enclosed in double parentheses, as in "((3 or 4 sylls.))" or "((where are you))". Other noises are enclosed in single parentheses, as in "(- snorts)". In examples cited from other investigators, I have retained

[1] For analyses based on this corpus, see Erman (1987), Garnham, Shillcock, Brown, Mill, and Cutler (1982), Geluykens (1992), Oreström (1983), Stenström (1984), and Svartvik (1980).

the original notation, though sometimes in simplified form. On occasion I have highlighted the features of interest in boldface.

It is impossible to write about using language without mentioning the users themselves. In life, these users aren't generic speakers and addressees, but real people, with identities, genders, histories, personalities, and names. I have tried to keep this point in the foreground by giving the people in my examples names – their actual names whenever possible and fictitious names otherwise. The names serve to remind us of the subject matter of this book – that language is used by individuals at particular times and places for particular purposes.

PART I

Introduction

1 | Language use

Language is used for doing things. People use it in everyday conversation for transacting business, planning meals and vacations, debating politics, gossiping. Teachers use it for instructing students, preachers for preaching to parishioners, and comedians for amusing audiences. Lawyers, judges, juries, and witnesses use it in carrying out trials, diplomats in negotiating treaties, and actors in performing Shakespeare. Novelists, reporters, and scientists rely on the written word to entertain, inform, and persuade. All these are instances of *language use* – activities in which people do things with language. And language use is what this book is about.

The thesis of the book is this: Language use is really a form of *joint action*. A joint action is one that is carried out by an ensemble of people acting in coordination with each other. As simple examples, think of two people waltzing, paddling a canoe, playing a piano duet, or making love. When Fred Astaire and Ginger Rogers waltz, they each move around the ballroom in a special way. But waltzing is different from the sum of their individual actions – imagine Astaire and Rogers doing the same steps but in separate rooms or at separate times. Waltzing is the joint action that emerges as Astaire and Rogers do their individual steps in coordination, as a couple. Doing things with language is likewise different from the sum of a speaker speaking and a listener listening. It is the joint action that emerges when speakers and listeners – or writers and readers – perform their individual actions in coordination, as ensembles.

Language use, therefore, embodies both individual and social processes. Speakers and listeners, writers and readers, must carry out actions as individuals if they are to succeed in their use of language. But they must also work together as participants in the social units I have called ensembles. Astaire and Rogers perform both individual actions, moving their bodies, arms, and legs, and joint actions, coordinating these movements, as they create the waltz. In some quarters, language use has been studied as if it were entirely an individual process, as if it lay wholly within the cognitive sciences – cognitive psychology, linguistics, computer science, philosophy. In other quarters, it has been studied as if it were entirely a social process, as if it lay wholly within the social sciences – social psychology, sociology, sociolinguistics, anthropology. I suggest that it belongs to both. We cannot hope to understand language use without viewing it as joint actions built on individual actions. The challenge is to explain how all these actions work.

The goal of this chapter is to make a preliminary case for the thesis. To do this, I will take a tour through the settings of language use, the people who play roles in these settings, and the way joint actions emerge from individual actions. It will take the rest of the book to fill out the picture and develop principles to account for how language use is a joint action.

Settings of language use

Over the years, when I have asked people for instances of language use, they have offered such examples as "conversation," "reading a novel," "policemen interrogating a suspect," "putting on a play," "talking to oneself," and dozens more. These answers are remarkable for their range. To get a sense of that range, let us look at the answers classified by scene and medium. The scene is where the language use takes place.[1] The medium is whether the language use is spoken or signed or gestural, or written or printed, or mixed. I will use *setting* for the scene and medium combined and divide the media simply into *spoken* and *written* forms.

SPOKEN SETTINGS

The spoken setting mentioned most often is conversation – either face-to-face or on the telephone. Conversations may be devoted to gossip, business transactions, or scientific matters, but they are all characterized by the free exchange of turns among the two or more participants. I will call these *personal settings*. In monologues, in contrast, one person speaks with little or no opportunity for interruption or turns by members of the audience. Monologues come in many varieties

---

[1] See Hymes (1974, pp. 55-56) for a related use of setting and scene.

too, as when a professor lectures to a class, a preacher gives a sermon, or a student relates a recent experience to an entire class. These people speak for themselves, uttering words they formulated themselves for the audience before them, and the audience isn't expected to interrupt. These I will call *nonpersonal settings*.

In *institutional settings*, the participants engage in speech exchanges that resemble ordinary conversation, but are limited by institutional rules. As examples, think of a politician holding a news conference, a lawyer interrogating a witness in court, a mayor chairing a city council meeting, or a professor directing a seminar discussion. In these settings, what is said is more or less spontaneous even though turns at speaking are allocated by a leader, or are restricted in other ways. In *prescriptive settings*, in contrast, there may be exchanges, but the words actually spoken are completely, or largely, fixed beforehand. Think of the members of a church or synagogue reciting responsive readings from a prayer book, or a bride and groom reciting vows in a marriage ceremony, or a basketball referee calling foul. Prescriptive settings can be viewed as a subset of institutional settings.

The person speaking isn't always the one whose intentions are being expressed. The clearest examples are in *fictional settings*: John Gielgud plays Hamlet in a performance of *Hamlet*; Vivien Leigh plays Scarlett O'Hara in *Gone with the Wind*; Frank Sinatra sings a love song in front of a live audience; Paul Robeson sings the title role in the opera *Otello*; or a television pitchman makes a sales pitch to a television audience. The speakers are each vocalizing words prepared by someone else – Shakespeare, Cole Porter, the news department – and are openly pretending to be speakers expressing intentions that aren't necessarily their own.

Related to fictional settings are the *mediated settings* in which there are intermediaries between the person whose intentions are being expressed and the target of those intentions. I dictate a letter for Ed to my secretary Annie; a telephone company recording tells me of the time or weather; a television news reader reads the evening news; a lawyer reads Baker's last will and testament at a hearing; a recording is triggered in a building announcing a fire and describing how to find the fire escape; and a UN interpreter translates a diplomat's French simultaneously into English. When I dictate a letter to my secretary Annie and say "I'll see you Saturday," the person I expect to see on Saturday isn't Annie but the addressee of my letter Ed.

Finally, there are *private settings* in which people speak for themselves without actually addressing anyone else. I might exclaim silently to myself, or talk to myself about solving a mathematics problem, or rehearse what I am about to say in a seminar, or curse at another driver who cannot hear me. What I say isn't intended to be recognized by other people – at least in the way other forms of speaking are.[2] It is only of use to myself.

WRITTEN SETTINGS

When printing, writing, and literacy were introduced, people adapted spoken language to the printed medium, so it is no surprise that written uses have many of the characteristics of spoken ones. The written settings most like conversations are the personal settings, when people write to others they are personally acquainted with, as when I write my sister a letter, or write a colleague a message on the computer. In computer settings where the writing and reading on two terminals are simultaneous, the experience can resemble conversation even more closely.

Many written messages, however, are directed not at individuals known to the writer, but at a type of individual, such as "the reader of the *New York Times*" or "the reader of *Science*." These are *nonpersonal settings*. So a newspaper reporter writes a news story for readers of the *New York Times,* or an essayist writes on Scottish castles for readers of *Country Life,* or a physicist writes a textbook on electricity and magnetism for university undergraduates, or a car owner writes to the service department of Ford Motor Company. The reporter may know a few of the *New York Times'* readers, yet he or she is directing the news story at its general readership. Fiction, too, is usually directed at types of individuals, often defined very broadly, as when Henry James wrote *The Turn of the Screw*, and Edgar Allan Poe wrote "The Masque of the Red Death," and William Shakespeare wrote *Hamlet.* In written fiction, the author is writing for an audience, but as with spoken fiction, the intentions expressed are not his own.

Written settings, like spoken ones, can introduce intermediaries between the person whose intentions are being expressed and the intended audience. These again are mediated settings. Usually, the person actually writing the words is doing so in place of the person who appears to be doing the writing or speaking. Examples: The Brothers Grimm

---

[2] See the discussion of "response cries" (Goffman, 1978) in Chapter 11.

write down the folktale "Aschenputtel"; a translator translates *Hamlet* into French; a ghost writer writes Charlie Chaplin's autobiography; a speech writer writes a speech for the President; my secretary types the letter to Ed from my dictation; and the manuscript editor for this book edits my writing. The President's speech writers, for example, write as if they were the President, who later reads the words as if they were his or her own. We make the pretense that the speech writers weren't even involved in the process. Recorders, translators, ghost writers, secretaries, and manuscript editors, in their different ways, do much the same thing.

In some written settings, the words are selected through an institutional procedure. An advertising firm composes an advertisement for a magazine; a drug company composes the warning label for an aspirin bottle; a food company labels a package as baking soda; the US Senate legislates the wording of a new tax law; and the California legislature decides on the wording of state road signs. Although one person may have composed the words, it is the institution – the ad agency, drug company, or legislature – that is ultimately responsible, approving the wording as faithful to the institution's collective intentions.

Written language is used in private settings as well. I can write in my diary, scribble a reminder to myself, take notes on a lecture, make a grocery list, or work out a mathematics proof on paper. As in the spoken settings, I am writing solely to myself for later use.

What follows are examples of the major types of spoken and written settings, but these types are hardly exhaustive. Humans are creative. For each new technology – writing systems, printing, telegraph, telephones, radio, audio recording, television, video recording, telephone answering machines, interactive computers, and voice recognizers – people have developed new settings. With no end to new technologies, there is no end to the settings they might create. Our interest must be in the principles by which these new forms are created.

	Spoken settings	**Written settings**
Personal	A converses face to face with B	A writes letter to B
Nonpersonal	Professor A lectures to students in class B	Reporter A writes news article for readership B
Institutional	Lawyer A interrogates witness B in court	Manager A writes business correspondence to client B
Prescriptive	Groom A makes ritual promise to bride B in front of witnesses	A signs official forms for B in front of a notary public
Fictional	A performs a play for audience B	Novelist A writes novel for readership B
Mediated	C simultaneously translates for B what A says to B	C ghostwrites a book by A for audience B
Private	A talks to self about plans	A writes note to self about plans

CONVERSATION AS BASIC SETTING

Not all settings are equal. As Charles Fillmore (1981) put it, "the language of face-to-face conversation is the basic and primary use of language, all others being best described in terms of their manner of deviation from that base" (p. 152). If so, the principles of language use may divide mainly into two kinds – those for face-to-face conversation, and those that say how the secondary uses are derived from, or depend on it, or have evolved from it. Language uses are like a theme and variations in music. We look first at the theme, its melody, rhythm, and dynamics, and then try to discover how the variations are derived from it. Fillmore added, "I assume that this position is neither particularly controversial nor in need of explanation." Still, it is worth bringing out what makes face-to-face conversation basic and other settings not.

For a language setting to be basic, it should be universal to human societies. That eliminates written settings, since entire societies, and groups within literate societies, rely solely on the spoken word. One estimate is that about a sixth of the world's people are illiterate. And most languages as we know them evolved before the spread of literacy. We can also eliminate spoken settings that depend on such technologies as radio, telephones, television, and recordings, since these are hardly universal. Most people participate only rarely in nonpersonal, institutional, and prescriptive settings, and even then their participation is usually restricted to certain roles – audiences of lectures, parishioners, court observers. People do often participate in fictional settings, but usually as audience. The commonest setting is face-to-face conversation.

Face-to-face conversation, moreover, is the principal setting that doesn't require special skills. Reading and writing take years of schooling, and many people never do get very good at them. Even among people who know how to write, the most that many ever do is personal letters. Simple essays, to say nothing of news stories, plays, or novels, are beyond them. It also takes instruction to learn how to act, sing, lead seminars, chair meetings, and interrogate witnesses. And most people find it difficult to lecture, tell jokes, or narrate reasonable stories without practice. Almost the only setting that needs no specialized training is talking face to face.

Face-to-face conversation is also the basic setting for children's acquisition of their first language. For the first two or three years, children in both literate and illiterate societies learn language almost solely in conversational settings. Whatever they learn from books also comes in conversational settings, as their caretakers read aloud and check on what they understand. Children may learn some language from other media, but they apparently cannot learn their first language from radio or television alone.[3] In school, the language of peers is influential in the dialect acquired, and that too comes from conversational settings. Face-to-face conversation is the cradle of language use.

NONBASIC SETTINGS

What, then, makes other settings not basic? Let us start with the features of face-to-face conversation listed here (Clark and Brennan, 1991):

1	Copresence	The participants share the same physical environment.
2	Visibility	The participants can see each other.
3	Audibility	The participants can hear each other.
4	Instantaneity	The participants perceive each other's actions at no perceptible delay.
5	Evanescence	The medium is evanescent – it fades quickly.
6	Recordlessness	The participants' actions leave no record or artifact.
7	Simultaneity	The participants can produce and receive at once and simultaneously.

[3] For evidence, see Sachs, Bard, and Johnson (1981) and Snow, Arlman-Rupp, Hassing, Jobse, Joosten, and Vorster (1976).

8	Extemporaneity	The participants formulate and execute their actions extemporaneously, in real time.
9	Self-determination	The participants determine for themselves what actions to take when.
10	Self-expression	The participants take actions as themselves.

If face-to-face settings are basic, people should have to apply special skills or procedures whenever any of these features are missing. The more features are missing, the more specialized the skills and procedures. That is borne out informally.

Features 1 through 4 reflect the *immediacy* of face-to-face conversation. In that setting, the participants can see and hear each other and their surroundings without interference. Telephones take away copresence and visibility, limiting and altering language use in certain ways. Conversations over video hookups lack copresence, making them different too. In lectures and other nonpersonal settings, speakers have restricted access to their addressees, and vice versa, changing how both parties proceed. In written settings, which lack all four features, language use works still differently.

Features 5 through 7 reflect the *medium*. Speech, gestures, and eye gaze are evanescent, but writing isn't, and that has far-reaching effects on the course of language use. Speech isn't ordinarily recorded, but when it is, as on a telephone answering machine, the participants proceed very differently. In contrast, writing is ordinarily relayed by means of a printed record, and that leads to dramatic differences in the way language gets used. With written records and no instantaneity, writers can revise what they write before sending it off, and readers can reread, review, and cite what they have read. Most spoken settings allow the participants to produce and receive simultaneously, but most written settings do not. Being able to speak and listen simultaneously gives people in conversation such useful strategies as interrupting, overlapping their speech, and responding "uh huh," and these are ruled out in most written settings.

Features 8 through 10 have to do with *control* – who controls what gets done and how. In face-to-face conversation, the participants are in full control. They speak for themselves, jointly determine who says what when, and formulate their utterances as they go. In other settings, the participants are restricted in what they can say when. The church, for example, determines the wording of many prayers and responses. In fictional settings, speakers and writers only *make as if* they are taking certain actions – Gielgud is only play-acting his role as Hamlet – and that alters what they do and how they are understood. And in mediated settings, there are really two communications. Wim says "Heeft u honger?" in Dutch, which David translates for Susan as "Are you hungry?" Susan is expected to hear David's utterance knowing it is really Wim who is asking the question. The less control participants have over the formulation, timing, and meaning of their actions, the more specialized techniques they require.

What about private settings? These are sometimes considered the basic setting for language use. We all talk to ourselves, the argument goes, so private settings are surely universal. When we do talk to ourselves, however, the principal medium is the language we have acquired from others. People who know only English use English; people with only Chinese use Chinese; and people with only American Sign Language use American Sign Language. We may develop additional ways of talking to ourselves, but these too are derived from our social ways of talking. In talking to ourselves, we are making as if we were talking to someone else. Private settings are based on conversational settings.

In brief, face-to-face conversation is the basic setting for language use. It is universal, requires no special training, and is essential in acquiring one's first language. Other settings lack the immediacy, medium, or control of face-to-face conversation, so they require special techniques or practices. If we are ever to characterize language use in all its settings, the one setting that should take priority is face-to-face conversation. This is a point I will take for granted in the rest of the book.

Arenas of language use

Language settings are of interest only as arenas of language use – as places where people do things with language. At the center of these arenas are the roles of *speaker* and *addressee*. When Alan is addressing Barbara, he is the speaker and she the addressee. Now, Alan is speaking with the aim of getting Barbara to understand him and to act on that understanding. But he knows he cannot succeed unless she takes her own actions. She must attend to him, listen to his words, take note of his gestures, and try to understand what he means at the very moment he is speaking. Barbara knows all this herself. So Alan and Barbara don't act independently. Not only do they take actions *with respect to each other*, but they *coordinate* these actions with each other. In the term I introduced earlier, they perform joint actions. For a preview of how they manage that, let us start with the notion of background.

MEANING AND UNDERSTANDING

Alan and Barbara begin with a great mass of knowledge, beliefs, and suppositions they believe they share. This I will call their *common ground* (see Chapter 4). Their common ground may be vast. As members of the same cultural communities, they take as common ground such general beliefs as that objects fall when unsupported, that the world is divided into nations, that most cars run on gasoline, that *dog* can mean "canine animal," that Mozart was an eighteenth-century composer. They also take as common ground certain sights and sounds they have jointly experienced or that are accessible at the moment – gestures, facial expressions, and nearby happenings. And, finally, they assume to be common ground what has taken place in conversations they have jointly participated in, including the current conversation so far. The more time Alan and Barbara spend together, the larger their common ground.

Every social activity Alan and Barbara engage in takes place on this common ground (see Chapter 3). Shaking hands, smiling at one another, waltzing, and even walking past each other without bumping all require them to coordinate their actions, and they cannot coordinate their actions without rooting them in their common ground. When language is an essential part of the social activity, as it is in conversation or novel reading or play acting, there is an additional element of coordination between what speakers mean and what addressees understand them to mean – between *speaker's meaning* and *addressee's understanding*.

Suppose Alan points at a nearby sidewalk and says to Barbara "Did you see my dog run by here?" In taking these actions – his utterance, his gesture, his facial expression, his eye gaze – Alan means that Barbara is to say whether or not she saw his dog run by on the sidewalk he is pointing at. This special type of intention is what is called speaker's meaning (see Chapter 5). In doing what he did, Alan intends Barbara to recognize that he wants her to say whether or not she saw his dog run by on the sidewalk, and she is to see this in part by recognizing that intention. The remarkable thing about Alan's intentions is that they involve Barbara's thoughts about those very intentions. To succeed, he must get Barbara to coordinate with him on what he means and what she understands him to mean. That is a type of joint action.

Two essential parts of their joint action are Alan's signals and

Barbara's identification of those signals. I will use the term *signal* for any action by which one person means something for another person. That is, meaning and understanding are created around particular events – with qualifications to come later – that are initiated by speakers for addressees to identify. These events are signals. Alan's signal consists of his utterance, gestures, facial expression, eye gaze, and perhaps other actions, and Barbara identifies this composite in coming to understand what he means (see Chapter 6).

Signals are deliberate actions. Some are performed as parts of conventional languages like English, Dakota, Japanese, or American Sign Language, but any deliberate action can be a signal in the right circumstances. Juliet signaled Romeo that it was safe to visit by hanging a rope ladder from her window. Umpires and referees signal fouls and goals with conventional gestures. Good storytellers signal aspects of their descriptions with nonconventional depictive gestures. We all signal things with deliberate smiles, raised eyebrows, empathetic winces, and other facial gestures. We even signal things by deliberately failing to act where such an action is mutually expected – as with certain pauses and deadpan expressions.[4] So some aspects of signals are conventional, and others are not. Some of the conventional aspects belong to systems of signals such as English or American Sign Language, and others do not. And some signals are performed as parts of intricate sequences, as in conversation or novels, and others are not. When Juliet hung a ladder out for Romeo, she created an isolated signal for a special purpose.

It is impossible for Alan and Barbara to coordinate meaning and understanding without reference to their common ground. When Alan says, "Did you see my dog run by here?" Barbara is to consult the meanings of the words *did, you, see,* etc., and their composition in English sentence constructions. These meanings and constructions are part of Alan and Barbara's common ground because Alan and Barbara are both members of the community of English speakers. To recognize the referents of *my, you, here,* and the time denoted by *did see,* Barbara is to take note of other parts of Alan's signal – that he is gazing at her now and gesturing at a nearby sidewalk. That in turn requires her to consult their

---

[4] A more accurate name for language use might be signal use, since it doesn't suggest an exclusive concern with conventional languages. Unfortunately, such a term is more likely to appeal to generals or engineers than to the rest of us. It would never catch on.

common ground about the immediate situation – that they are facing each other, that the sidewalk is nearby, that Alan is scanning the area in search of something. To identify the referent of *my dog*, she is to consult their common ground for a unique dog associated with him. Common ground is the foundation for all joint actions, and that makes it essential to the creation of speaker's meaning and addressee's understanding as well.

PARTICIPANTS

When Alan asks Barbara about his dog, Connie may also be taking part in the conversation, and Damon may be overhearing from nearby. Alan, Barbara, Connie, and Damon each bear a different relation to Alan's question.

The people around an action like Alan's divide first into those who are truly participating in it and those who are not: *participants* and *non-participants*. For Alan's question, the participants are Alan himself, Barbara, and Connie. These are the people he considers "ratified participants" (Goffman, 1976). They include the speaker and addressees – here Alan and Barbara – as well as others taking part in the conversation but not currently being addressed – here Connie. She is a *side participant*. All other listeners are *overhearers*, who have no rights or responsibilities in it. Overhearers come in two main types. *Bystanders* are those who are openly present but not part of the conversation. *Eavesdroppers* are those who listen in without the speaker's awareness. There are in reality several varieties of overhearers in between.

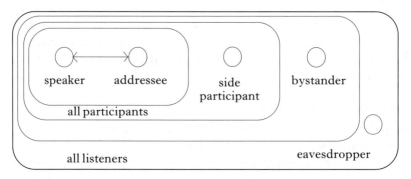

Alan must pay close attention to these distinctions in saying what he says. For one thing, he must distinguish addressees from side participants. When he asks Barbara about his dog and Connie is in the conversation, he must make sure they see that it is Barbara, and not

Connie, who is to answer his question. Yet he must make sure Connie understands what he is asking Barbara (see Chapter 3). He must also take account of overhearers, but because they have no rights or responsibilities in the current conversation, he can treat them as he pleases. He might, for example, try to conceal from Damon what he is asking Barbara by saying "Did you happen to see you-know-what come by here?" It isn't always easy to deal with participants and overhearers at the same time (Clark and Carlson, 1982a; Clark and Schaefer; 1987a, 1992; Schober and Clark, 1989).

So side participants and overhearers help shape how speakers and addressees act toward each other. They also represent different ways of listening and understanding. As an addressee, Barbara can count on Alan having designed his utterance for her to understand, but as an overhearer, Damon cannot. As a result, the two of them go about trying to interpret what Alan says by different means, by different processes. These other roles should help us see more precisely what the roles of speaker and addressee themselves are, and they will.

LAYERS IN LANGUAGE ARENAS

The roles we have met so far, from speaker to eavesdropper, may each enter into a primary setting with a single place, time, and set of participants. In other settings, other agents may take part too, including authors, playwrights, mediators, actors, ghost writers, translators, and interpreters, and they may take part at different places and times. How are we to characterize these other places, times, and roles? What we need, I will suggest, is a notion of layering (Chapter 12).

When someone tells a joke, the other participants must recognize it for what it is – a piece of fiction. Take this stretch of conversation (from Sacks, 1974, in simplified format):

Ken: You wanna hear- My sister told me a story last night.
Roger: I don't wanna hear it. But if you must. (0.7)
Al: What's purple and an island. Grape, Britain. That's what his sister
         told him.
Ken: No. To stun me she says uh, (0.8)
         There were these three girls and they just got married?
         [Continues joke]

When Ken says "My sister told me a story last night," he is making an assertion to Roger and Al in the actual world of the conversation. But when he says "There were these three girls and they just got married," he is making an assertion that is true only in the hypothetical world of the joke. He doesn't really believe there were three actual girls who just got married. He is speaking at that moment as if he, Roger, and Ken were part of the hypothetical joke world, and he was telling them about three actual girls.

What we have here are two *layers of action*. Layer 1 is the primary layer of any conversation, where the participants speak and are addressed then and there as themselves. Layer 2 is built on top of layer 1 and in this example represents a hypothetical world. Each layer is specified by its domain or world – by who and what are in it. When Ken says "My sister told me a story last night," his actions take place entirely in layer 1, the actual domain of their conversation. But when he says "There were these three girls and they just got married," he is both making an assertion in layer 2, the hypothetical domain of the joke, and telling part of a joke in layer 1, the actual domain:

Layer 2   Ken is telling Roger and Al about three actual girls who just got married.
Layer 1   In Los Angeles in 1965, Ken, Roger, and Al jointly pretend that the events in layer 2 are taking place.

We would say that Roger and Al had misunderstood Ken if they thought that the sister was hypothetical and the three girls were actual. Language use requires the primary participants to recognize, however vaguely, all the layers present at each moment.

Layers are like theater stages built one on top of another. In my mind's eye, they look like this:

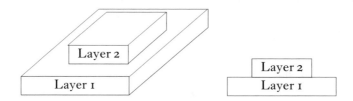

Layer 1 is at ground level, representing the actual world, which is present in all forms of language use. Layer 2 is a temporary stage built on top of layer 1 to represent a second domain. As on a theater stage, characters perform actions in full view of the participants of layer 1. As on a theater stage, these characters cannot know that layer 1 even exists. The three girls have no way of knowing about Ken, Roger, and Al's conversation. In this picture, layer 1 is real, whereas layer 2 is optional and only supported by layer 1. And by recursion there can be higher layers as well.

With layering we can now represent what makes many language settings derivative (see Chapter 12). Face-to-face conversation and personal letters are normally managed in one layer. Jokes, novels, and other pieces of fiction take at least two layers, and when a school teacher reads a piece of fiction aloud, that adds yet another layer. Plays require at least three layers. Dictation also requires two layers. When I dictate a letter for my friend to my secretary, I am talking to my secretary at layer 1 – our actual conversation – yet, simultaneously, speaking to my friend at layer 2. Ghost writing, simultaneous translation, and news reading require still other patterns of layering.

Layering also helps make sense of private uses of language. When George curses at a bad driver who cannot hear him, he deals in two layers. In the privacy of his car (layer 1), he creates in his imagination a domain (layer 2) in which he is actually cursing the driver face to face. When Helen silently exclaims to herself about a beautiful sunset, she does much the same thing. In private, layer 1, she creates an imaginary domain (layer 2) in which she is speaking to her alter ego. With diaries, reminders, and grocery lists, the writers are addressing themselves at a later time and place. This is no different from writing to someone else at a later time and place.

So far, we have seen that language use places people in many roles. In basic settings, there are always speakers and addressees, but there may also be side participants, bystanders, and eavesdroppers. In other settings, there may also be more than one layer of activity, each with its own roles. The primary layer, which I have called layer 1, represents actual people doing actual things. Higher layers represent other domains, often hypothetical, that are created only for the moment. It often takes many different roles, such as actor and stenographer, to create and support them.

Actions of language

What people do in arenas of language use is take actions.[5] At a high level of abstraction, they negotiate deals, gossip, get to know each other. At a lower level, they make assertions, requests, promises, apologies to each other. In doing that, they categorize things, refer to people, and locate

---

[5] By *action*, *act*, and *activity*, I shall always mean doing things *intentionally*. For two views of intention and action, see Bratman (1987, 1990) and Cohen and Levesque (1990).

objects for each other. At yet a lower level, they produce utterances for each other to identify. And at the lowest level, they produce sounds, gestures, writing for each other to attend to, hear, see. These at least are the actions of speakers and addressees in the primary layer of language use. Strikingly, all these actions appear to be joint actions – an ensemble of people doing things in coordination. If we are ever to understand them, we need to know what joint actions are and how they work. That is the topic of Chapter 3. For now, let us look briefly at joint actions and how they are created out of individual actions.

JOINT ACTIONS

When I play a Mozart sonata on the piano, the music I produce reflects certain of my mental and motor processes, from reading the printed music to striking the keys with my fingers. These processes are wholly under my control – as afforded by the piano's mechanics, the printed score, the lighting, and other environmental features. I decide when to begin, how fast to play, when to slow down or speed up, when to play forte and when pianissimo, and how to phrase things. And if my mental and motor processes come off just right, the result will be Mozart.

Something different happens when a friend, Michael, and I play a Mozart duet. This time, my actions depend on his, and his depend on mine. We have to coordinate our individual processes, from reading the notes to striking the keys. Each decision – when to begin, how fast to go, when to slow down or speed up, when to play forte and when pianissimo, how to phrase things – must be a joint one, or the result won't be Mozart. Our performance is best described not as *two individuals* each playing a Mozart piece, but as a *pair of people* playing a Mozart duet.

One contrast here is between *individual* and *joint* actions. A joint action is an action by an ensemble of people. Playing solo is an individual action, but playing a duet is a joint one. We see the same contrast in these comparisons:

Individual action	Joint action
A person paddling a kayak	A pair of people paddling a canoe
A person pushing a car	A quartet of people pushing a car
A lumberjack cutting a log with a saw	A pair of lumberjacks cutting a log with a two-handled saw
A ballerina dancing to a recording	A corps de ballet dancing to a recording
A race-car driver speeding around a track	A set of ten race-car drivers speeding around a track

A person's processes may be very different in individual and joint actions even when they appear identical. Suppose I play my part of the Mozart duet on an electronic keyboard twice – once solo and once with Michael playing his part. If you listened to my part through earphones, you might not notice any difference, yet what I did was very different. In the solo performance I took every action on my own. In the duet I coordinated every action with Michael, and as anyone who has played duets knows, that is no small feat. There are analogous differences between one and two canoe paddlers, one and four auto pushers, one and many dancers, one and two lumberjacks, and one and ten race-car drivers. All these cases illustrate the same point: Performing an individual action solo is not the same as performing the apparently identical action as part of a joint action.

We must therefore distinguish two types of individual actions. When I play the piano solo, I am performing an *autonomous action*. When Michael and I play the piano duet, we are also performing individual actions, but as parts of the duet. These actions are what I will call *participatory actions*: They are individual acts performed only as parts of joint actions. So joint actions such as playing piano duets are constituted from participatory actions. Or, what is the same thing, it takes participatory actions to create joint actions. They are two sides of the same coin:

Type of action	Agents
joint actions	ensemble of participants
participatory actions	individual participants

We can look at any joint action either way – as a whole made up of parts, or as parts making up the whole.

Many joint actions have the participants doing dissimilar things. A driver approaching a crosswalk coordinates with the pedestrian trying to cross it. A ballerina dancing coordinates with the orchestra accompanying her. A clerk slipping a shoe on a woman's foot coordinates with the woman as she extends her foot to accept it. These examples make a second point about joint actions: The participants often perform very different individual actions.

SPEAKING AND LISTENING

Speaking and listening have traditionally been viewed as autonomous actions, like playing a piano solo. One person, say Alan, selects and produces a sentence in speech or on paper, and another person, say

Barbara, receives and interprets it. Using language is then like transmitting telegraph messages. Alan has an idea, encodes it as a message in Morse code, Japanese, or English, and transmits it to Barbara. She receives the message, decodes it, and identifies the idea Alan wanted her to receive.[6] I will argue that speaking and listening are not independent of each other. Rather, they are participatory actions, like the parts of a duet, and the language use they create is a joint action, like the duet itself.

Speaking and listening are themselves composed of actions at several levels. As Erving Goffman (1981a, p. 226) noted, the commonsense notion of speaker subsumes three agents.[7] The *vocalizer* is "the sounding box from which utterances come." (The corresponding role in written settings might be called the *inscriber*.) The *formulator* is "the agent who puts together, composes, or scripts the lines that are uttered." And the *principal* is "the party to whose position, stand, and belief the words attest." The principal is the agent who *means* what is represented by the words, the *I* of the utterance. In Goffman's view, speaking decomposes into three levels of action: meaning, formulating, and vocalizing (see also Levelt, 1989).

In face-to-face conversations, the speaker plays all three roles at the same time — principal, formulator, and vocalizer. When Alan asks Barbara "Did you happen to see my dog run by here?" he selects the meaning he wants to be recognized; he formulates the words to be uttered; and he vocalizes those words. In nonbasic settings, these roles often get decoupled. When a spokeswoman reads a statement by the Secretary of State, she vocalizes the announcement, but it is the Secretary whose meaning she represents, and an aide who formulated them. Ghost writers, to take a different case, formulate and inscribe what they write, but their words represent the meanings of the people they are ghosting for. Much the same goes for translators, speech writers, and copy editors. And in prescriptive settings, meaning and vocalizing get decoupled from formulating. When a bride says "I Margaret take thee Kenneth to my wedded husband" in a marriage ceremony, she refers to herself with *I*,

---

[6] The *message model* implies that Alan's production, and Barbara's reception, can be studied in isolation. It also implies that messages are encoded strings of symbols in a symbol system (say, Japanese or English), so they can be studied in isolation from the processes by which they are produced and received. If speaking and listening are participatory actions, these two implications no longer follow.

[7] To avoid confusion, I have replaced Goffman's terms *animator* and *author* by the terms *vocalizer* and *formulator*.

meaning what she says, but she doesn't formulate what she says. That is prescribed by the church.

Listening, likewise, decomposes into at least three levels of action. When Barbara is asked by Alan "Did you happen to see my dog run by here?" she is first of all *attending* to his vocalizations. She is also *identifying* his words and phrases. And she is the *respondent*, the person who is to recognize what he meant and answer the question he asked. In face-to-face conversations, the addressee plays all three roles at once – respondent, identifier, and attender. But in nonbasic settings, once again, the roles often get decoupled. The main job of copyists, court reporters, and stenographers, for example, is to identify people's utterances, though it is typical for them to try to understand as they do that. Or when Wim, speaking Dutch, says something to Susan through a simultaneous translator speaking English, she may attend to Wim's utterances without identifying or understanding them. And although she attends to, identifies, and understands the translator's English, the only thing she attributes to Wim is the meaning expressed.

The component actions in speaking and listening come in pairs. For each action in speaking, there is a corresponding action in listening:

	Speaking	Listening
1	A vocalizes sounds for B	B attends to A's vocalizations
2	A formulates utterances for B	B identifies A's utterances
3	A means something for B	B understands A's meaning

But the pairing is even tighter than that. Each level consists of two participatory actions – one in speaking and one in listening – that together create a joint action. The overall joint action really decomposes into several levels of joint actions. This is a topic I take up in Chapters 5, 7, 8, and 9.

One of these joint actions is privileged, and it is level 3: speaker's meaning and addressee's understanding. It is privileged, I suggest, because it defines language use. It is the ultimate criterion we use in deciding whether something is or is not an instance of language use. Language use, I assume, is what John Stuart Mill called a *natural kind*.[8] It is a basic category of nature, just as cells, mammals, vision, and learning are, one that affords scientific study in its own right. And what makes it a natural kind is the joint action that creates a speaker's meaning and an addressee's understanding.

---

[8] See, for example, Quine (1970) and Putnam (1970).

EMERGENT PRODUCTS

When we take an action, we foresee, even intend, many of its consequences, but other consequences simply emerge. That is, actions have two broad products: *anticipated products* and *emergent products*. Let us consider some examples.

A friend tells you to print the words *slink, woman, ovate, regal,* and *droll* one below the other, and you do. Then she says, "Now read down the five columns," and you discover, to your amazement, five more words: *sword, lover, imago, natal,* and *knell* (from Augarde, 1986). The down words weren't anything you anticipated. They just emerged. Then you take your discovery to another friend. "Let me print the words *slink, woman, ovate, regal,* and *droll* one below the other. See the words that you get reading down." This time you intend to form the words reading down, so they become an anticipated product.

A twelve-year-old tells you, "Say E," and you say "E." "Say S," and you say "S." "Say X," and you say "X." "Say E," and you say "E." The child says "Now say them all, quickly, three times" and you say "ESXEESXEESXE." And the child retorts "No he isn't!" In producing "ESXE" quickly, you didn't anticipate it would sound as if you were saying "He is sexy." That was an emergent product of your action.

Susan composes a mystery duet for Michael and me to play on two pianos. Our parts are so cleverly devised that neither of us can tell what the duet will sound like. The day we perform it together we discover we are playing "Greensleeves." Later we go to other friends, announce that we are going to play "Greensleeves," and each play our parts. On the first performance, "Greensleeves" was an emergent product of our joint actions, but on the second, it is the anticipated, even intended, product.

When individuals act in proximity to each other, the emergent product of their actions may even go against their desires, a point made by Thomas Schelling (1978). Individuals enter an auditorium one by one. The first arrival sits one third of the way back – not too far forward, but not too far back either. The second and later arrivals, to be polite, choose to sit behind the front-most person. As the auditorium fills, the pattern that emerges has everyone in the rear two thirds of the auditorium. Each individual might prefer the audience to be in the front two thirds of the auditorium, but they have to live with the pattern that emerged.

All actions have anticipated products, and that goes for joint actions too. When Michael and I played our parts of the Mozart duet, we intended to produce the Mozart duet. It was anticipated. Joint actions also have emergent products. When Michael and I played Susan's duet for the first time, we intended to "play a duet," but we didn't intend to "play 'Greensleeves.'" It is simply what emerged. In language use, it is important not to confuse anticipated and emergent products. Many of the regularities that are assumed to be intended or anticipated are really neither, but simply emerge.

SIX PROPOSITIONS

In this chapter I have sketched the approach to language use I will take in this book. Along the way I have introduced several working assumptions.

Proposition 1. Language fundamentally is used for social purposes. People don't just use language. They use language for doing things – gossiping, getting to know each other, planning daily chores, transacting business, debating politics, teaching and learning, entertaining each other, holding trials in court, engaging in diplomacy, and so on. These are social activities, and language is an instrument for helping carry them out. Languages as we know them wouldn't exist if it weren't for the social activities they are instrumental in.

Proposition 2. Language use is a species of joint action. All language use requires a minimum of two agents. These agents may be real or imaginary, either individual people or institutions viewed as individuals. In using language, the agents do more than perform autonomous actions, like a pianist playing solo. They participate in joint actions, like jazz musicians improvising in an ensemble. Joint actions require the coordination of individual actions whether the participants are talking face to face or are writing to each other over vast stretches of time and space.

Proposition 3. Language use always involves speaker's meaning and addressee's understanding. When Alan produces a signal for Barbara to identify, he means something by it: He has certain intentions she is to recognize. In coordination with him, Barbara identifies the signal and understands what he means by it. Much of what we think of as language use deals with the mechanics of doing this effectively. We are not inclined to label actions as language use unless they involve one person meaning something for another person who is in a position to understand what the first person means. Proposition 3 doesn't imply, of course, that language use is nothing more than meaning and understanding. It is a great deal more. It is just that these notions are central, perhaps criterial, to language use.

Proposition 4. The basic setting for language use is face-to-face conversation. For most people conversation is the commonest setting of language use, and for many, it is the only setting. The world's languages have evolved almost entirely in spoken settings. Conversation is also the cradle for children learning their first language. It makes no sense to adopt an approach to language use that cannot account for face-to-face conversation, yet many theorists appear to have done just this. And if conversation is basic, then other settings are derivative in one respect or another.

Proposition 5. Language use often has more than one layer of activity. In many types of discourse – plays, story telling, dictating, television news reading – there is more than one domain of action. Each domain is specified by, among other things, a set of participants, a time, a place, and the actions taken. The actions that story tellers take toward their audience, for example, are in a different layer from the actions that the fictional narrators in their stories take toward their fictional audiences. Conversation, at its simplest, has only one layer of action. The speaker at any moment is the principal, formulator, and vocalizer of what gets said, and the addressees are attenders, identifiers, and respondents. Still, any participant can introduce further layers of action by telling stories or play-acting at being other people. This makes conversation one of the richest settings for language use.

Proposition 6. The study of language use is both a cognitive and a social science. We can view a joint activity such as playing a piano duet from two perspectives. We can focus on the individual pianists and the participatory actions they are each performing. Or we can focus on the pair and the joint action they create as a pair. For a complete picture, we must include both. We cannot discover the properties of playing duets without studying the pianists playing as a pair, and yet we cannot understand what each pianist is doing without recognizing that they are trying to create the duet through their individual actions.

Although the study of language use ought to resemble the study of any other joint activity, it doesn't. Cognitive scientists have tended to study speakers and listeners as individuals. Their theories are typically about the thoughts and actions of lone speakers or lone listeners. Social scientists, on the other hand, have tended to study language use primarily as a joint activity. Their focus has been on the ensemble of people using language to the neglect of the thoughts and actions of the individuals. If language use truly is a species of joint activity, it cannot be understood from either perspective alone. The study of language use must be both a cognitive and a social science.

In this book I combine the two views. In Part II, I take up three foundations of language use: the notion of broad joint activities (Chapter 2), the principles behind joint actions (Chapter 3), and the concept of common ground (Chapter 4). In Part III, I turn to communicative acts themselves, developing the notions of meaning and understanding (Chapter 5) and signaling (Chapter 6). In Part IV, I explicate the notion of levels in joint actions, arguing for a level of joint projects (Chapter 7), meaning and understanding (Chapter 8), presenting and identifying utterances, and executing and attending to behaviors (Chapter 9). In Part V, I take up three broader issues: the joint commitments established in exchanges of goods (Chapter 10); features of conversation (Chapter 11); varieties of layering (Chapter 12). In Part VI, I conclude.

PART II

Foundations

2 | Joint activities

Language use arises in joint activities. You call up your sister for an address, or talk to a friend about what to take on a picnic, or discuss news with a colleague. If you were later asked "What did you do?" you wouldn't describe your acts of speaking. You would describe the joint activities you took part in. "I got an address from my sister." "My friend and I decided what to bring on a picnic." "A colleague and I traded gossip." In each case, you take the joint activity to be primary, and the language you used along the way to be secondary, a means to an end. To account for the language used, we need to understand the joint activities.

A discourse is one type of joint activity – one in which language plays an especially prominent role. Originally the term *discourse* meant conversation or dialogue – literally, a running back and forth – but nowadays it includes lectures, interviews, interrogations, plays, novels, essays, personal letters, and much much more. But if discourses are a type of joint activity, we will never understand how they work until we understand more generally how joint activities work. This, then, is another reason for investigating joint activities.

And just as language use arises in joint activities, these are impossible without using language. Two or more people cannot carry out a joint activity without communicating, and that requires language use in its broadest sense. Yet whenever people use language, they are taking joint actions. Language use and joint activity are inseparable. The conclusion, once again, is that we cannot understand one without the other. We must take what I will call an *action approach* to language use, which has distinct advantages over the more traditional *product approach*.

In this chapter, I take up joint activities and how they work. Although I will focus on those in which language dominates, it is the joint activities *per se* that are of interest. In most the language is merely an emergent product.

Joint activities

What is a joint activity? The approach I will take was inspired by Stephen Levinson's (1979, 1992) notion of *activity type* (1992, p. 69):

> I take the notion of an activity type to refer to a fuzzy category whose focal members are goal-defined, socially constituted, bounded, events with constraints on participants, setting, and so on, but above all on the kinds of allowable contributions. Paradigm examples would be teaching, a job interview, a jural interrogation, a football game, a task in a workshop, a dinner party, and so on.

The notion of activity type, Levinson argued, is preferable to such related notions as "speech event," "episode," "form of life," and Wittgenstein's "language games" "because it refers to any culturally recognized activity, whether or not that activity is coextensive with a period of speech or indeed whether any talk takes place in it at all." For Levinson, an activity type can be either a time-bounded event ("a football game") or an ongoing process ("teaching"). I will call the first *an activity* and the second *activity*. And activity types may have a single participant ("a task in a workshop") or more than one participant ("a dinner party"). My interest is in activities with more than one participant, which are fundamentally different from autonomous activities. I will call them joint activities.

Activity types – hence joint activity types – vary on many dimensions. One is *scriptedness*, the "gradient formed by two polar types, the totally prepackaged activity, on the one hand (e.g., a Roman Mass) and the largely unscripted event on the other (e.g., a chance meeting on the street)" (p. 69). A second dimension is *formality*, ranging from "a highly formal activity on the one hand and a very informal one on the other" (p. 69). A third dimension is *verbalness*, "the degree to which speech is an integral part of each activity" (p. 70):

> On the one hand, we have activities constituted entirely by talk (a telephone conversation, a lecture, for example); on the other, activities where talk is nonoccurring, or if it does occur is incidental (a game of football, for instance). Somewhere in between ... we have the placing of bets, or a Bingo session, or a visit to the grocers.

I would add two more dimensions. One is *cooperativeness*. It ranges from cooperative activities like buying groceries to adversarial, or competitive, activities like playing tennis or cross-examining witnesses in court. The other dimension is *governance*. Quartet playing, chess playing, party planning, and making acquaintance are more or less egalitarian, the participants having roughly equal roles ("A and B did something"). Lecturing to a class, interviewing an applicant, and buying a car are at the autocratic end, with one participant playing a dominant role ("A did something to or for B"). These dimensions are summarized here:

Dimension of variation	From	To
Scripted vs. unscripted	marriage ceremony	chance meeting
Formal vs. informal	city council meeting	gossip session
Verbal vs. nonverbal	telephone call	football game
Cooperative vs. competitive	business transaction	tennis match
Egalitarian vs. autocratic	making acquaintance	class lecture

Because there are still other dimensions of variation, the number of potential activity types is vast.

At first glance, activity types appear to have arbitrary, ad hoc, unprincipled properties, but Levinson argued that that isn't so. These properties "can be seen to follow from a few basic principles, in particular rational organization around a dominant goal" (p. 71), although Levinson didn't say what these principles are. The challenge is to discover these principles – at least for joint activities, especially discourses. We will start on the principles in this chapter, but they will occupy us in various ways for the rest of the book.

EXAMPLE OF A JOINT ACTIVITY

Most joint activities don't come scripted like a marriage ceremony. They emerge in time as two or more people try extemporaneously to accomplish certain ends. Take a conversation I recorded in a California drug store as I was buying a couple of items from a clerk I will call Stone.[1]

Clark walks up to a counter and places two items next to the cash register.
Stone is behind the counter marking off items on an inventory.
Clark, looking at Stone, catches her eye.

---

[1] The transcript here is based on a surreptitious audio recording fleshed out later by my recollection of what occurred. It is incomplete and inaccurate in many respects. Unfortunately, it is difficult to get video records of such exchanges.

Stone, meeting Clark's eyes: "I'll be right there."
Clark: "Okay."
Stone continues marking off items for fifteen seconds, puts the inventory
   aside, turns toward Clark, and manifestly begins to look for the items Clark
   is purchasing.
Clark, noting her search, points at the two items on the counter between them:
   "These two things over here."
Stone nods, takes the items, examines the prices on them, and rings them up on
   the cash register.
Stone: "Twelve seventy-seven."
Clark: "Twelve seventy-seven."
Clark takes out his wallet, extracts a twenty-dollar bill, hands it to Stone, then
   rummages in his coin purse for coins.
Clark: "Let's see that's two pennies I've got two pennies."
Clark hands Stone two pennies.
Stone: "Yeah."
Stone then enters $20.02 in the register, which computes the change.
Stone (handing change to Clark): "Seven twenty-five is your change."
Clark: "Right."
Clark puts the money in his wallet while Stone puts the items and receipt in a bag.
   She hands the bag to Clark, they break eye contact, and he turns and walks
   away.

What Stone and I did was transact a piece of business. I wanted to
buy two items, so she and I exchanged the items for money. Our transaction began when she turned to me and looked for my purchases, and it
ended when we broke eye contact and I left. The transaction got
advanced through a series of joint actions – my catching her eye, our
utterances to each other, her picking up the items, my handing her
money. How does such a rich structure emerge?

PARTICIPANTS AND ROLES
In any joint activity, some people are understood to be taking part, and
others not. When a string quartet plays a Haydn quartet, the four
musicians are the participants. Other musicians may be standing
around, even trying to play along, but unless they are recognized as
ratified participants, they stand outside the playing of the quartet proper
as bystanders, as nonparticipants. People get ratified as participants as
the joint activity gets initiated and carried out. Also, one joint activity can
be embedded within another. When the quartet plays the Haydn piece in
a concert, the quartet playing (one joint activity) is embedded within the

concert performance (another joint activity), and in the concert performance, both musicians and audience are now participants. Likewise,
Stone and I were the participants in our drugstore transaction, and the
nearby customers were nonparticipants. Our transaction was embedded
in a larger joint activity that required Stone and me to coordinate with
other customers vying for her services.

People who take part in a joint activity aren't just participants
simpliciter. They have roles in that activity – *activity roles*. In the quartet
playing, one musician is first violin, another second violin, a third viola,
and a fourth cello. These roles help shape what they each do and are
understood as doing. In the concert performance, other people are
members of the audience, a role that defines still other activities. People in
joint activities get ratified not merely as participants, but as participants
in particular roles.

So it was in the drugstore. Stone was the server, and I was the
customer, roles that helped shape what we did and how we interpreted
each other. When she said "Twelve seventy-seven," I took her to mean I
was to pay her $12.77. It was the server's job at that point to tell me what
I needed to pay. But when I said "Twelve seventy-seven," she didn't take
me to mean that she was to pay me $12.77. That would have violated my
role as customer. The norm for what people do in transactions is partly
defined by their roles. If Stone had later attended a lecture I gave, she and
I would instead be member of the audience and lecturer, roles that
dictate different actions and interpretations. In other joint activities, the
roles might be police officer and citizen, attorney and witness, teacher
and student, supervisor and worker, narrator and audience, priest and
congregation. Indeed, the roles may change from one subactivity to the
next, or emerge only as the nature of the joint activity becomes clear.

The participants in joint activities also have *personal identities*. Stone
and I each had our own identities, beliefs, feelings, and desires, which
also helped shape what we did.

GOALS

People participate in joint activities to achieve certain dominant goals. In
many activities, one person initiates the joint activity with a dominant goal
in mind, and the others join him or her in order to achieve it. I initiated the
business transaction with Stone to buy two items, and she joined me to
complete it. Joint activities can usually be summarized by describing the
dominant goal achieved:

Guide A led tourists B, C, and D through the Eiffel Tower.
Musicians A, B, C, and D played a Haydn string quartet.
A on white and B on black played a game of chess.
Professor A lectured students B, C, D, et al. on labor law.
Caller A got a telephone number from telephone operator B.
Police officer A interrogated witness B about a crime.
Guests A and B at a party got acquainted.
Customer A bought items from server B.

Each description specifies the participants (A, B, et al.), their roles (e.g., guide, tourist), and the goal achieved. Add the words "managed to" to each description – for example, A *managed to* lead B, C, and D through the Eiffel Tower – and we have the same joint activity. That shows that the activity was goal directed, something the participants jointly intended to do. In some joint activities – like a gossip session – the dominant goal may be vague (e.g., "catch up on news"), or it may evolve in the course of the activity.

Although the participants may share the dominant goal, there is usually a division of labor among them. In the tour of the Eiffel Tower, the guide assumes one set of responsibilities, and the tourists another. The two have the same end goal – that the guide lead the tourists through the Eiffel Tower – but differ in what they do in fulfilling the goal. The participants' actions and responsibilities depend on the role they inherited from the activity they are engaged in – e.g., as helper or helped, or guide or guided, or interviewer or interviewee – even in egalitarian activities. In the string quartet, the first violin's responsibilities and actions are very different from the cello's. These are no less joint activities because of the division of labor.

In most joint activities, the participants pursue many goals at once (Brown and Levinson, 1987; Goffman, 1974; Hobbs and Evans, 1980). Their dominant goal, as I have called it, is a *domain goal* – getting their business transacted, the chess game played, the lecture completed, the witness interrogated. But the participants also have *procedural goals*, such as doing all this quickly and efficiently, making clear moves, attending to what is being done. They also have *interpersonal goals*, such as maintaining contact with the other participants, impressing them, being polite, maintaining self-respect. They may also have *private agendas* such as deceiving the others, getting rid of them, or working the situation for personal advantage. These goals are not all alike in their influence on joint activities. They divide at least into public and private goals.

In any joint activity, certain goals become a matter of public record, what the participants are "on record" as doing in the activity. In my terminology, information is *public* in a joint activity if it is openly recognized by all the participants. Some public goals get established explicitly, as when Jack asks Kate to play chess. Others become public without being explicitly agreed to. When I approached Stone in the drugstore, the two of us took it for granted that I was there to buy something. For a goal to be a joint one, as we will see, it must be public, and it is the joint goals that define the joint activity the participants are engaged in. For Jack and Kate to play a game of chess, it must be public that they are doing so. The same goes for me buying the two items from Stone.

Other goals are *private*. Although many of these are innocent enough, others would be self-defeating if they became public. If Duncan is trying to impress Ann with his knowledge of classical music, it wouldn't do to make that goal public. The same goes for being polite and maintaining face and for deceiving or getting rid of others. In competitive activities like chess or tennis, success hinges on keeping private goals private – even deceiving the other participants about them.[2] People's private goals are sometimes in direct conflict with their public goals, making their adherence to the public goals a sham.

So joint activities are influenced by at least two types of goals. Public goals are there for all the participants to see, but private goals are hidden from view. Public and private goals have different consequences.

COORDINATION OF ACTION

Every joint activity requires coordination among its participants. If the four musicians are to play the Haydn quartet, they must coordinate. They must play the same edition in the same key, start together, stick to the same tempo, and finish together. In the drugstore, Stone and I engaged in the same business transaction, and we started, proceeded, and finished together.

How do people manage to coordinate? One way is with conventional procedures. In playing a string quartet, the four musicians exploit conventional procedures for handling their instruments, reading music, setting tempo and loudness, starting and stopping, and much more. In the drugstore, Stone and I used conventional English expressions and

---

[2] When there are more than two participants, as in team sports, there can also be coalitions with private agendas.

applied conventional procedures for specifying the price, exchanging money, bagging the items, and taking them away. But, as we will discover, people also coordinate by means of nonconventional procedures – both in and out of language use. How people coordinate is one of the fundamental issues of language use.

SECTIONS AND BOUNDARIES

Most joint activities get realized as sequences of smaller actions, many of which are themselves joint actions. For the four musicians to play the Haydn quartet, they must play the first, second, and third movements in that order. And to play the first movement, they must play the first section, beginning with the first phrase, beginning with the first measure, beginning with the first note. Playing the quartet divides into sections, or *phases*, each of which divides into subsections or subphases, and so on. What emerges is a hierarchy of joint actions.

So it goes for many unscripted joint activities. When Stone and I transacted our business, the items I wanted had to be identified, their prices identified, the money paid, and the items taken away – and in that order. We might count four main sections, each with its own goal. The identification of the items itself required several subsections, each with its own goal: I showed Stone the items and she identified them as what I wanted to buy. And so on. What emerged, again, was a hierarchy of joint actions. It differed from the Haydn quartet in that its sections and subsections weren't fixed beforehand, but were negotiated as we went along.

One reason joint activities are complicated is two or more people must come to mutually believe that they are participating in the same joint activity. In the drugstore, it wasn't enough for *me* to believe I was in a business transaction with Stone. I had to believe *she* believed the same thing at the same time. Being in the same transaction is like believing we are in the same room at the same time. If I am in the room without Stone, or she without me, neither of us believes we are in the same room at the same time. But once we are both in the room – I can see her, and I can see that she sees me seeing her – we are now doing business together.

Joint activities therefore have boundaries. We can identify three stages of participants A and B with respect to joint activity J:

1. *Entry.* A and B go from not being in J to being in J.
2. *Body.* A and B are in J.
3. *Exit.* A and B go from being in J to not being in J.

In the drugstore, I believed at one point that Stone and I were just entering a business transaction, and at another point that we were just exiting from it. Stone had corresponding beliefs, though they may not have coincided exactly with mine. For me, and for her, the entry and exit defined the boundaries of our transaction.

Entries and exits have to be engineered for each joint action separately. That makes entries and exits especially important features of joint activities. In the drugstore, I tried to engineer Stone's and my entry into the business transaction by standing at the counter and catching her eye, but she put me off ("I'll be right there" "Okay") to go on with her inventory. Only once she began looking for my items did I think we had entered the transaction proper. Our exit was simpler. After paying, I took the bag she offered, turned, and walked away, assuming that she would take this as completing our transaction.

Since the sections of a joint activity are themselves joint activities or joint actions, they too each have an entry, body, and exit. In the drugstore, specifying the items I wanted to buy was a brief joint action: We entered it when I showed Stone the items ("These two things over here"), and we exited from it when she acknowledged them by picking them up. Then came identification of the price to be paid, the payment, and the transfer of goods, three other joint actions.

Joint activities don't always emerge as neatly as these examples suggest. Two joint activities can be simultaneous, as when Jack and Kate gossip while playing cards, canoeing, or cleaning the yard together. A single joint activity can also be intermittent, as when Jack and Kate, in the car, talk, lapse into silence, talk, and lapse into silence in cycles. Joint activities may also divide, as when a single conversation among four people breaks into two conversations (see, e.g., Sacks, Schegloff, and Jefferson, 1974). And they may expand and contract as new participants enter and old participants leave. The challenge is how to describe these dynamics.

Let us draw these observations together into some general claims about joint activities:

Participants	A joint activity is carried out by two or more participants.
Activity roles	The participants in a joint activity assume public roles that help determine their division of labor.
Public goals	The participants in a joint activity try to establish and achieve joint public goals.
Private goals	The participants in a joint activity may try individually to achieve private goals.

Hierarchies	A joint activity ordinarily emerges as a hierarchy of joint actions or joint activities.
Procedures	The participants in a joint activity may exploit both conventional and nonconventional procedures.
Boundaries	A successful joint activity has an entry and exit jointly engineered by the participants.
Dynamics	Joint activities may be simultaneous or intermittent, and may expand, contract, or divide in their personnel.

These claims, of course, need fuller justification, and that will come as we proceed. For now we will take them as a place to start.

Advancement in joint activities

Joint activities advance one increment at a time. My transaction with Stone, for example, emerged in steps. To know what to charge me, she needed to know what I wanted to buy, so we established that first. To know what to pay, I needed to know what she was charging me, so we established that next. To know how much change to give me, she had to know how much money I was giving her, so we established that next. And so on. Each joint action added incrementally to reaching our public goals. What we did in pursuit of those goals depended on what we had done so far.

If joint activities are cumulative, what accumulates? I will argue that it is the common ground of the participants about that activity – the knowledge, beliefs, and suppositions they believe they share about the activity (Chapter 4). Although accumulation of common ground has been studied in discourse (Clark and Haviland, 1974, 1977; Clark and Marshall, 1978, 1981; Gazdar, 1979; Lewis, 1979; Stalnaker, 1978), it occurs in all joint activities.

ACCUMULATION IN DISCOURSE

When people take part in conversations, they bring with them certain prior knowledge, beliefs, assumptions, and other information. Part of this information Robert Stalnaker (1978) called their common ground:

Roughly speaking, the presuppositions of a speaker are the propositions whose truth he takes for granted as part of the background of the conversation...Presuppositions are what is taken by the speaker to be the common ground of the participants in the conversation, what is treated as their common knowledge or mutual knowledge. (p. 320, Stalnaker's emphases)

The participants each have their own presuppositions about the conversation, but as Stalnaker argued, "It is part of the concept of presupposition that the speaker assumes that the members of his audience presuppose everything that he presupposes" (p. 321). They may, of course, be mistaken, but they realize this and have systematic strategies for resolving such discrepancies (see Chapters 7, 8, 9).

The common ground of the participants about their conversation changes as the conversation proceeds. As David Lewis (1979) put it:

Presuppositions can be created or destroyed in the course of a conversation. This change is rule-governed, at least up to a point. The presuppositions at time t′ depend, in a way about which at least some general principles can be laid down, on the presuppositions at an earlier time t and on the course of the conversation (and nearby events) between t and t′. (p. 339)

These changes lead to increments to common ground. We can say that the common ground of the participants about the conversation *accumulates* in the course of that conversation.[3]

Assertions are prototypical linguistic actions for incrementing common ground. As Stalnaker argued, "the essential effect of an assertion is to change the presuppositions in the conversation by adding the content of what is asserted to what is presupposed. This effect is avoided only if the assertion itself is rejected." At one point in the drugstore transaction, Stone and I presupposed that I didn't know the total price of the items I was buying. She tried to change that presupposition by asserting that the price was \$12.77, "Twelve seventy-seven," which I ratified by repeating "Twelve seventy-seven." With the assertion completed, we added to our common ground the presupposition that the price was \$12.77. Other communicative acts – promises, questions, apologies, requests, declarations – increment common ground in other ways.

Accumulation of common ground occurs in all joint activities. To see how, let us begin with a rather formal joint activity, a game of chess. We can then return to the messier, spontaneous business transaction between Stone and me.

---

[3] The common ground may also get restructured as new information accumulates.

STATES AND TRACES

In 1859 Paul Morphy and Adolph Anderssen, two master chess players of their era, met for a game of chess. They began with the chess board in its initial state SA_0 (SA stands for "state of the activity"). Playing white, Morphy made the first move, M_1, displacing his king's pawn (the pawn in front of his king) by two squares (to the square called "king 4"). In doing that, he changed the state of the activity from SA_0 to SA_1. What Morphy did was *increment* the state of the activity, which I will write this way: $SA_0 + M_1 = SA_1$. Next it was Anderssen's turn, and he displaced his queen's pawn to the square called "queen 4." He made the move, M_2, not as an increment to the initial state of the game SA_0, but as an increment to the state as it was after Morphy's move, SA_1. The result was SA_2.

Morphy and Anderssen's game was cumulative in this special sense. Each move, M_i, added an increment to the just prior state, SA_{i-1}, to produce a new state, SA_i. In symbols: $SA_{i-1} + M_i = SA_i$. The game accumulated this way:

Time	Move	State of activity
0	Open game	SA_0
1	M_1	SA_1
2	M_2	SA_2
3	M_3	SA_3
...	...	...
n	M_n	SA_n

Put another way, each state SA_i was the cumulative result of the first i moves of the game, M_1 through M_i, whether made by Morphy or Anderssen. So the official course of the game for the first n moves can be represented by either of these two sequences:

States of the activity: $SA_1, SA_2, SA_3, ..., SA_n$
Trace of the activity: $M_1, M_2, M_3, ..., M_n$

The states of the game are represented by successive configurations of the chess board, and the trace, by moves that relate each two successive configurations. Given SA_0, if you know one sequence, you can figure out the other.

Stone's and my business transaction was cumulative in much the same way. Our transaction began with an initial state SA_0. In approaching the counter, I made the first move, M_1, catching her eye, adding an increment to SA_0 to produce SA_1. She made the second move, M_2, saying

"I'll be right there." Her move incremented not the initial state SA_0, but the state of activity SA_1 after I had caught her eye. As in chess, each move M_i added an increment to the just prior state SA_{i-1} to produce a new state SA_i. In symbols: $SA_{i-1} + M_i = SA_i$.

The current state of Stone's and my transaction was incremented not just by what we did, but by each event we jointly recognized as advancing our joint activity. When Stone entered the two prices on the cash register, it rang a bell when it had the total. Once Stone and I jointly heard the bell, we mutually knew the total was available, so she could assume I would understand what she meant by "Twelve seventy-seven."[4] So our business transaction accumulated this way:

Time	Joint event	State of activity
0	Open transaction	SA_0
1	E_1	SA_1
2	E_2	SA_2
3	E_3	SA_3
...	...	...
n	E_n	SA_n

As with the chess game, we can represent the official course of the business transaction through the first n moves either (1) by the states of joint activity SA_1 through SA_n or (2) by a trace of the joint activity E_1 through E_n.

OFFICIAL AND UNOFFICIAL

In most joint activities, the states and events that become public – mutually known to the participants – divide into those that are officially part of the activity and those that aren't. The division is clear in chess. Chess moves M_i are official parts of the game because they are added to the official trace, alter the official board, and advance the game. In fact, a trace, or record, of the moves is all we formally need to know about a game; it is what is reproduced in chess books and studied by chess aficionados. Other actions may become public even though they play no official role in the game. When Morphy adjusted a piece on the board, moaned over a blunder, sipped water, or took a long time on a move, these were added to Morphy's and Anderssen's common ground, but as information outside the game proper. Chess players are careful

---

[4] In craps, the count on the dice on any throw is outside the players' control, yet it is a joint event that advances the game.

to distinguish the official from the nonofficial at every point in their game.

Stone and I made much the same distinctions in the drugstore. We viewed some of the public events around us as part of the transaction proper, and others as outside it – as when she marked off her inventory, and I dropped several coins. Keeping track of which public states and events are official and which aren't is essential to the orderly advancement of any joint activity.

TIME

Like any idealization, this model of joint activities is incomplete in many ways. One way is time. It assumes that events occur in sequence, and otherwise time doesn't matter. But when actions are simultaneous or continuous, their interpretation can be affected by the passage of time.

Many actions in joint activities aren't sequential, as the model suggests, but simultaneous or overlapping in time. In the drugstore, while I was saying "These two things over here," Stone was following my gesture with her eyes, and I took her as having understood me when her eyes lit on the two items I was pointing at. If she hadn't followed my gesture, or if her eyes had lit on the wrong objects, I would have continued "Over here" or "No, over here." Indeed, simultaneity is the rule for one of the commonest linguistic actions in discourse – acknowledgments like North American "uh huh" and "yeah" and British "m." These often overlap with what they acknowledge or they wouldn't work as intended (see Chapter 8).

Also, many actions in joint activities aren't discrete, bounded events, as the model suggests, but continuous actions in real time. Suppose in the drugstore I had wanted two items on a shelf behind Stone, and I had said, pointing, "Those two things [pause] right [pause] over a little more [pause] there," timing "there" to coincide with her hand reaching the correct items. In referring to the two items, I exploited the continuity of her attention and hand movement and the continuity of my utterance. Demonstrative references with "this," "that," "here," "now," and "just" often depend crucially on the continuity of such actions (see Chapters 6, 8, 11).

Often, what is important to actions is timing and not just sequence as the model has it. Take the exchange:

Stone, meeting Clark's eyes: I'll be right there.
Clark: Okay.

If I had produced "Okay" with no delay, I would have meant "I accept without conditions," but if I had let one second pass first, I would have shown impatience and meant "I accept only reluctantly." One of our goals must be to account for simultaneity, continuity, and the timing of events – to bring time into models of joint activity.

These observations give us a first picture of how joint activities work. The official course of a joint activity starts in an initial state SA_0 and the activity advances with each joint event E_i that adds to the previous state SA_{i-1} to form the current state SA_i. Other states and events become public but are not officially part of the joint activity proper.

Representations of common ground

What accumulates in a joint activity, I have argued, is the common ground of the participants. For most activities, the common ground at any moment divides into three parts:

1. *Initial common ground.* This is the set of background facts, assumptions, and beliefs the participants presupposed when they entered the joint activity.
2. *Current state of the joint activity.* This is what the participants presuppose to be the state of the activity at the moment.
3. *Public events so far.* These are the events the participants presuppose have occurred in public leading up to the current state.

It is worthwhile looking at these divisions, because they will help us understand a number of phenomena in language use. It is easier, however, to identify these divisions in chess than in other joint activities, so let us take up chess before returning to Stone's and my transaction in the drugstore.

INITIAL COMMON GROUND

When Morphy and Anderssen entered their chess game, they each presupposed a vast amount of common ground. They presupposed the rules for chess – how the pieces move and capture, how the two players take turns, who begins, what constitutes a check, mate, and draw. They presupposed how to interpret the chess board and the pieces on it – who is attacking whom, what are the possible next moves. They presupposed the etiquette for chess playing – who sits where, when to keep silent, where to keep score. They presupposed a great deal about the strategies, tactics, and effective procedures in chess – e.g., opening gambits, deceptive moves, end game tactics. Having played each other before, they presupposed something about each other's personal strategies, strengths, weaknesses, practices, habits. And so on. All this formed the starting context of their game – their *initial common ground* CG_0.

Stone and I presupposed much the same type of information as the initial common ground CG_0 for our business transaction. We presupposed the standard procedures in American culture for exchanging money for goods – particularly in drugstores of this type. (Other businesses, even other types of drugstores, work differently.) These procedures have sometimes been called scripts or frames, and they specify what happens in standard situations of this cultural type (see, e.g., Minsky, 1975; Schank and Abelson, 1975). Among other things, they specify the roles and responsibilities of server and customer, actions for establishing the price, actions for exchanging money for goods, and actions for releasing the goods to the customer. Stone and I also presupposed that we both spoke English, that I had enough money, and other such things.

The point is this. People entering a joint activity presuppose a great deal about carrying out that activity. That information is represented in chess as rules, regulations, and etiquette. The analogous information is no less important in the drugstore even though it is represented in uncodified scripts or frames.

CURRENT STATE OF THE ACTIVITY

One part of the initial common ground of the participants in a joint activity is the initial state of the activity SA_0. For Morphy and Anderssen's chess game, the initial state was represented by the chess board in its starting configuration. After ten moves, the current state was represented as shown in the illustration.

Anderssen (black)

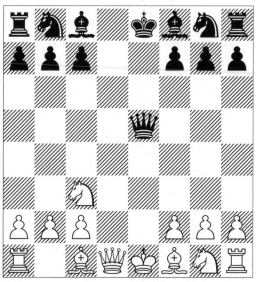

Morphy (white)

What is remarkable about chess – indeed about most games – is that the current state of the activity is represented in quite a concrete form. The chess board and its pieces are an *external representation* of the current state.[5]

External representations are particularly useful. Take Morphy and Anderssen's chess board after their tenth move. Morphy and Anderssen could see at a glance where each piece resided at that point and, by elimination, which pieces had already been captured. They could see that the black queen was threatening the white king – a "check" – and that there were several pieces Morphy could move to defend it. The chess board is the representation in which most rules of chess are stated – how each piece moves and captures, what constitutes checks and mates. So for Morphy and Anderssen, the chess board and chess pieces weren't mere patches of color and lumps of wood, but were elements of a scene they interpreted according to a highly developed understanding of the game.

Stone and I had an external representation of the current state of our business transaction too, and it was the scene around us. We entered the transaction with the scene in an initial configuration, but by the time I

---

[5] I am indebted to Stuart Card for discussions about external representations.

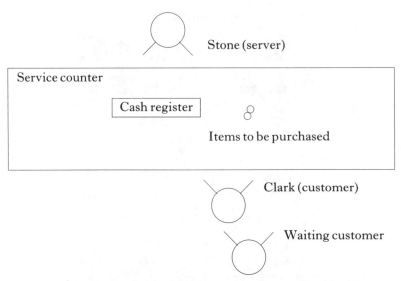

had said "These two things over here," the scene looked something like the bird's-eye-view illustration. At a glance, Stone and I could see that she was the server and I the current customer, that the items I was referring to were those on the counter, that she had yet to ring them up on the cash register, and so on. The scene helped us keep track of where we were in our transaction. So for Stone and me, the scene wasn't simply a set of brute objects. It was a scene we interpreted according to a highly developed understanding of how things work in such transactions.

External representations are more important to joint activities than is usually supposed. The chess board and drugstore scene illustrate some of their properties:

1. *Physical model.* The chess board and drugstore scene are physical models: They can be viewed, touched, and manipulated. Football fields, tennis courts, craps tables, courtrooms, classrooms, churches, and their contents are particularly useful because they too can be viewed, touched, manipulated.

2. *Markers.* External representations contain markers that denote elements of the joint activity. The squares on the chess board are markers for physical locations, and the chess pieces are markers for imaginary objects – such as kings and bishops – that can move, capture, and be captured. In the drugstore, the money and the receipt were markers for elements in the business transaction. Markers range from cards in card games and positions in queues to altars in churches and witness stands in courtrooms.

3. *Locational interpretation.* The markers are interpreted in part by their spatial location with respect to other markers. Anderssen's queen is interpreted as on his king 4 and in position to capture Morphy's king.

4. *Manipulability.* Some markers can be moved or altered, and the participants interpret these changes by the locations and forms that result. Move a wooden marker on a chess board, and you move the queen and change who she is threatening and is threatened by. Hand a twenty-dollar bill to a server, and you change who's in possession of the money.

5. *Simultaneous and parallel accessibility.* External representations are ordinarily accessible to all participants at the same time and in parallel. Morphy and Anderssen could study any part of their board simultaneously, and Stone and I could check out any part of the scene simultaneously.

It is hard to exaggerate the value of these representations. First, they are highly reliable representations of the current state of the activity. The chess board shows precisely where Anderssen's queen is, and because the board is simultaneously accessible to both players, they can both assume it to be part of their common ground. It is hard to dispute the position of a piece. This reliability is especially important in adversarial and business activities. Tennis, basketball, and football have scoreboards, gin rummy has counters, and business transactions have money, cash registers, and receipts, all to prevent disputes about the current state of the activity. And second, external representations are a particularly effective memory aid and medium for imagining moves. The chess board surely helped Morphy and Anderssen recall what they had just done and imagine what they should do next. The drugstore scene helped Stone and me recall our past actions and anticipate our future ones.

External representations are especially valuable as a medium for the actions themselves. Morphy and Anderssen played chess in part by displacing the pieces on the chess board. Stone and I transacted our business in part by manipulating the money, goods, cash register, receipts, and paper bags in the drugstore scene. Many joint activities would seem impossible with such representations.

PUBLIC EVENTS SO FAR

People also keep track of a third division of common ground: the public events since the beginning of their joint activity. In chess, the principal public events are the players' moves, as represented in a record of the game so far. Here, for example, is the official record of Morphy and Anderssen's first ten moves (in so-called descriptive notation):

	White (Morphy)	Black (Anderssen)
1.	P – K4	P – Q4
2.	P×P	Q×P
3.	Kt – QB3	Q – QR4
4.	P – Q4	P – K4
5.	P×P	Q×Pch

Each line denotes a move by white (e.g., "P – K4" or "Pawn to king 4") then one by black (e.g., "P – Q4" or "Pawn to queen 4"). Simple moves are denoted by "–", captures by "X," and checks by "ch." The record will eventually end with a mate, draw, or resignation. As master players, Morphy and Anderssen presumably took much of this record as part of their common ground.

Morphy and Anderssen, however, presumably improved on this bare record to form what I will call an *annotated record*. (1) They almost certainly represented the purpose of each move as "attacking the knight," "pinning the rook," and "defending the queen." (2) They probably also grouped moves into purposeful sequences. Certain opening moves, for example, are called the Ruy Lopez, *Giuoco Piano*, and the Sicilian defense, and Morphy and Anderssen would have presupposed such interpretations. Master players divide games into such sequences in recalling them (Chase and Simon, 1973), and surely represent these groupings during games as well. (3) Morphy and Anderssen probably also interpreted certain moves as "blunders," "bold moves," "surprises." (4) They may also have noted unusually delayed or fast moves as evidence of which moves were difficult and which were easy.

Morphy and Anderssen might also have abstracted away from the annotated trace to form what I will call an *outline record*. They might have represented the first ten moves this way: "We opened by exchanging pawns; Anderssen brought his queen out; we exchanged pawns again; and Anderssen's queen put Morphy in check." Details are left out, but the main thrust of what occurred is clear.

In the drugstore, Stone and I kept track of much the same type of record. At the point when Stone said "Seven twenty-five is your change," she and I presupposed a sequence of public events so far: I had caught her attention; I had specified the items to be bought; she had rung them up; I had handed her a twenty-dollar bill and then two pennies; and she had computed the change. As in chess, we formed an annotated record. I hadn't merely handed her a twenty-dollar bill, but had given her money to pay for the items I was buying. And so on. How we annotated these events was determined by our expectations of what should have happened, on the frame or script for buying items in a drugstore (see Bower, Black, and Turner, 1979). Stone and I probably also abstracted away from many details to form an outline record.

DISCREPANCIES IN COMMON GROUND

As Stone and I talked, we each kept track of our own representations of common ground. She and I were, after all, individual agents with individual beliefs, judgments, and perceptions. Still, the very reason I kept track of our common ground was to have a representation I believed was identical to Stone's – at least to a certain degree of accuracy. I represented my beliefs about our common ground, and any piece of information I thought wasn't part of their common ground wasn't part of it. It is something like the two of us watching a tennis match and each keeping a log of the score, the net balls, the faults, and other such things. We expect our logs to be identical to a certain degree of accuracy.

Despite our best efforts, Stone's and my representations of our common ground were discrepant. Most of these discrepancies went undetected. Other times they might have become obvious to Stone or me or both. If I had detected a discrepancy, I would have had two main options. I could have brought it up and corrected it, or let it go and lived with the consequences. The discrepancy might be so slight that it wouldn't be worth my while to correct it. But I must keep track of every discrepancy I leave uncorrected. I must realize that Stone's representation of our common ground differs from mine in that one piece of information. For this reason it is often more efficient to correct a discrepancy immediately, and that is just what people tend to do (Chapters 8 and 9).

In brief, what the participants take to be common ground in a joint activity falls into three main parts – what they presupposed on entering the activity, the current state of the activity, and the public events that led up to the current state. Each of these parts divides further into the information that is officially part of the joint activity and the information that isn't. What is striking is how this common ground is represented. The current state of the activity, in particular, is often carried in an external representation, like a chess board or drugstore scene, that plays a central role in the course of that activity.

Discourse as a joint activity

What, then, is a discourse? I suggest it is simply a joint activity in which conventional language plays a prominent role. If it is, everything we have learned about joint activities should apply, and I will argue that it does. Can we in principle distinguish discourses from other types of joint activities? The answer, I believe, is no. All joint activities depend on signals or communicative acts – on language in its more general sense. If so, the distinction may be otiose, even misleading.

LANGUAGE IN DISCOURSE

Joint activities vary a great deal in how heavily they rely on conventional language. They lie on what I will call a *discourse continuum*, as illustrated here:

Mostly linguistic	1	telephone conversations, newspaper items, radio reports, novels
	2	face-to-face conversations, tabloid items, television reports, science texts
	3	business transactions, plays, movies, coaching demonstrations, apprenticeship lessons, bridge games
	4	basketball games, tennis matches, two people moving furniture, making love
Mostly nonlinguistic	5	playing a string quartet, waltzing, playing catch

In category 1, almost everything is done by means of conventional language. In the next category, much of what is done requires conventional language, but much also relies on gestures, pictures, video sequences, graphs, and diagrams, without which the language would be incomprehensible. In the middle category, the linguistic and nonlinguistic actions are more balanced and interdependent. In category 4, the focus is on physical actions, the conventional language being largely incidental. At the bottom end, finally, we arrive at joint activities that may take no conventional language at all.

If discourse is a distinct type of joint activity, where on this continuum do we draw the line? The items in categories 1 and 2 are clear examples of discourses, but so are most of the items in category 3. If we draw the line after category 3, how are we to treat the talk that does arise in categories 4 and 5? The yelling among players in a basketball game bears a relation to the ongoing activity even if it isn't essential to it (Levinson, 1992). Throughout the continuum, the conventional language used cannot be understood without viewing it against the joint activity it is part of.

To see this, consider one traditional approach to discourse – sometimes called text linguistics – in which discourses are treated as purely linguistic objects, as *texts*. We ordinarily think of texts as written records of what is uttered in conversations, speeches, or story tellings, but in this tradition they are more abstract. In Halliday and Hasan's (1976) approach, a text is any sequence of sentences that can be given a coherent interpretation. It doesn't matter how or why it was created. The important thing to explain is why it is well or ill formed, just as grammars try to explain why a sentence is grammatical or ungrammatical (van Dijk, 1972, 1977). In this tradition, texts are assumed to be complete in themselves, characterizable independently of surrounding events.

The notion of text, however, makes no sense across most of the discourse continuum. In all but category 1, the text of a joint activity is patently incomplete, no matter how we view language use. Take the text of Stone's and my transaction in the drugstore:

Stone:	I'll be right there.
Clark:	Okay.
Clark:	These two things over here.
Stone:	Twelve seventy-seven.
Clark:	Twelve seventy-seven.
Clark:	Let's see that's two pennies I've got two pennies.
Stone:	Yeah.
Stone:	Seven twenty-five is your change.
Clark:	Right.

To know what "I'll be right there" meant, we need to know that I had just caught her eye and was waiting to be served. To know what Stone's "Twelve seventy-seven" meant, we need to know that she had just rung up my two items on the cash register. To account for each line of text, we need to know where the participants were in the larger joint activity (see Morgan and Sellner, 1980). This holds for all texts in categories 2 through 5. Many of these lack textual coherence even though they are entirely coherent in the joint activity.

The fundamental issue is what to include in language use. If we include any signal – any communicative act – then language use is present across the entire discourse continuum. When Morphy moved his king's pawn, he was really communicating with Anderssen. Normally, chess players communicate by displacing chess pieces on a shared board for their opponents to see, but that isn't essential. In correspondence chess, the players send each other post cards with messages like "Pawn to king

4" and "Pawn captures pawn.," and in blindfold chess, they do much the same thing. Chess moves are a type of communicative act, and the game advances entirely by means of these acts. In this sense, a game of chess belongs in category 1 of the discourse continuum, even though it doesn't rely on a conventional language like English.

The official moves in the drugstore transaction were all communicative acts as well – though some were more than that. My catching Stone's eye was just as much a request for service as her "I'll be right there" was a promise to serve me. Other moves were composite actions. When I handed Stone a twenty-dollar bill, at one level we accomplished the joint physical act of moving the piece of paper from my hand to hers. At another level, we accomplished the joint act of changing the twenty dollars from my possession to hers – an act necessary for our transaction. To accomplish this, I had to communicate what I was doing – I might have intended Stone to hold the bill for a moment, to change it for two tens, or to check whether it was a forgery. By manifestly handing it to Stone at that state of our transaction, I was declaring that it was payment for the articles I was buying, and in taking my money, she accepted that declaration (see Chapters 5 and 6). Our transaction cannot be accounted for without including all communicative acts.

Discourses, then, are not a distinct type of joint activity, at least if we include all communicative acts, as we must in a full account of language use (Chapters 5 through 9). I will use the term when I want to emphasize the language being used.

MODELS OF DISCOURSE

How do people represent the accumulating common ground in a discourse? If a discourse is a joint activity, they should represent (1) the initial common ground, (2) the current state of the activity, and (3) the public events so far. They should also distinguish between those public events that are official to the discourse and those that are not. Most theories of discourse have focused on categories (2) and (3) and then only on the official parts.[6] I will follow this tradition as far as it goes, but add distinctions when needed.

The idea is that the participants in a discourse keep track of a *discourse representation*, which has two main parts. One part is the *textual*

---

[6] For discourse models in this tradition, see van Dijk and Kintsch (1983) and Johnson-Laird (1983), among others.

representation, a representation of the language and other signals used during the discourse. The other is the *situational representation*, a representation of the situation being talked about. The picture is this:

Total common ground

The participants in a discourse need to keep track of the utterances and other signals they have used during the discourse, and they do this in a textual representation. Take the moment just after Stone and I had completed this exchange in the drugstore:

Stone: I'll be right there.
Clark: Okay.

If we understood each other completely, we each would have represented, as part of our common ground, at least these aspects of our signals: (1) the sounds produced; (2) the utterances issued; (3) the words, phrases, and sentences uttered, and their syntactic arrangement; (4) the meanings of the words, phrases, and sentences uttered; and (5) the two turns as constituting the exchange. These are things Stone and I had in our textual representations – but only for a brief time after our utterances. These include all aspects of the signals we needed for producing and understanding what we said.

The participants in a discourse also keep track of the situation they are talking about, and that they do in a situational representation. It represents such elements as: (1) the participants, time, place, and pertinent surroundings; (2) the referents of all expressions used by the participants (e.g., the referents of "I," "will be," "right," and "there"); (3) the social commitments established by what the participants said (e.g., Stone's promise and my acceptance); (4) the piece of the larger transaction accomplished in the exchange. As we saw earlier, part of the situational representation takes the form of an external representation, like the scene in the drugstore, a type of information ignored in most situational representations. With these elements, Stone and I knew what was going on and could decide what to do next. In this view, situational representations represent what the participants have been doing, and textual representations, the communicative devices for taking those actions.

Part of the discourse representation has a privileged status, what I will call the *discourse record*. It represents the official states and events in the current joint activity. These are considered *on record*, as having advanced the joint activity. In chess, the discourse record would contain all of the chess moves, and in the drugstore, all of Stone's and my public actions that advanced our transaction. What is on record stands in contrast to those public states and events that are considered *off record* and not official parts of the joint action. With the addition of the discourse record, the picture now looks like this:

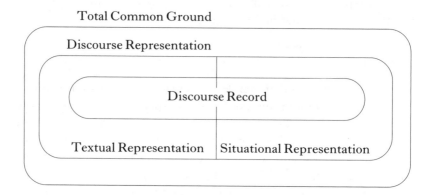

INCREMENTS TO DISCOURSE

People add to discourses mainly through communicative acts, or signals, especially linguistic utterances. Since our interest is in language use, we will want to understand how these work. As before, it is instructive to begin with chess.

A chess move is really a speech act called a declaration (see Chapter 5). When Morphy displaced the pawn on his first move in his game with Anderssen, it was as if he had said to Anderssen, "I hereby declare to you that my king's pawn moves to my king four." In the notation developed in chess for these declarations, Morphy's move is expressed as "P – K4." Let us suppose that Morphy and Anderssen were playing correspondence chess, and that Morphy sent "P – K4" on a post card to Anderssen. In doing so, he presupposed that he and Anderssen shared a *vocabulary* in which P denoted "pawn," K "king," and – "moves to," and a *syntax* in which "P" denoted the subject, "–" the verb or relation, and "K4" the object. These are parts of a conventional language. In English translation, Morphy's statement was "Pawn moves to king 4."

But these elements aren't enough. Which pawn and whose king 4 was Morphy referring to? Morphy had to presuppose that he and Anderssen shared not only the language system, but two other pieces of knowledge. One was the current state of the game, SA_i. For "P – K4," the pieces were in their starting position, and it was Morphy's move. The second was the set of potential moves $\{M_{i+1}\}$ at this juncture – e.g., all of Morphy's pawns could move one or two squares forward. Given SA_i, the pawn Morphy was referring to must be one that could move to K4. Given $\{M_{i+1}\}$, the only pawn in the right position was a king's pawn, and because it was Morphy's turn, it must have been Morphy's king's pawn, and K4 must have been Morphy's king 4.

A more telling example is "P × P," or "Pawn captures pawn." Although Morphy used "P × P" for both his second and his fifth moves, he meant quite different things on the two occasions. The first time he meant "My king's pawn (on my king 4) captures your queen's pawn (on your queen 4)," and the second time, "My queen's pawn (on my queen 4) captures your king's pawn (on your king 4)." What he meant depended on the current state of the game and the ways he could advance it. It depended on how it could increment the game.

Chess expressions like "P × P" illustrate an important property of communicative acts: *efficiency of expression*. In this notation, each expression includes no more information than is necessary to select the intended move out of all possible moves $\{M_{i+1}\}$ given SA_i. In Morphy's second and fifth statements "P × P", the captured piece needed to be specified only as a pawn "P" because it was uniquely identifiable by that description. In Morphy's twenty second statement "R × KBP," the captured piece was also a pawn, but it had to be specified as the king's bishop's pawn "KBP" to distinguish it from other pawns that a rook R could have captured. The efficiency of expression, then, is this: Participants in a joint activity try to express no more than they need to express for their joint efficiency in advancing the current purposes of that activity (see Chapter 5).[7]

Efficiency of expression applies just as readily to English. Here is one of Stone's and my exchanges in the drugstore:

Stone: Twelve seventy-seven.
Clark: Twelve seventy-seven.

,Here again we find the same expression with two different uses. Stone meant "The cost of the items you want to buy is $12.77," and I meant "I am confirming that the amount is $12.77." What Stone meant depended on the current state of our transaction (she had just entered the prices of the two items on the cash register) and the potential next moves. She expressed no more than she needed to. She could presuppose I expected her to specify the cost of the items at that point, and that it would be expressed in dollars. And I expressed no more than I needed to to confirm the precise dollar amount. Note that our utterances weren't sentences, but nominal phrases. If Stone and I were trying to be efficient, these are just what we should expect. Phrasal utterances are common in spontaneous talk.

APPROACHES TO LANGUAGE USE

Language use has been studied in two broad traditions. The *product tradition* grew out of the linguistic study of sentences, words, and speech sounds – the products of language use. It was strongly influenced by the work on generative grammars by Noam Chomsky and his colleagues. The *action tradition*, in contrast, grew out of the philosophical and sociological investigation of intentions and social actions.[8]

In the product tradition, sentences, words, and phonetic segments are treated as linguistic types abstracted away from speakers, times, places, and circumstances in which they might have been produced. Sentences have a syntactic structure; words have a phonological and morphological structure; segments have a phonetic structure; and words

---

[7] For an extreme example, see von Savigny's (1983) discussion of headlight blinking on European roads.

[8] One line of this tradition was developed by such philosophers as Austin (1962), Grice (1957, 1968, 1975, 1978), and Searle(1969, 1975a, 1975b, 1978, 1980), and another, by such sociologists as Goffman (1967, 1971, 1974, 1976, 1978, 1981a), Sacks and Schegloff (1979), Sacks et al. (1974), Schegloff (1968, 1972, 1979, 1982) and Jefferson (1972, 1973, 1978).

have conventional meanings that combine by certain rules of combination. The structure of these items determines only their *potential* uses. To specify an *actual* use, we have to fill in what is missing from "context." For Stone's utterance of the sentence *I'll be right there*, we must note the circumstances – who was speaking, when she was speaking, what she was pointing at, etc. – and fill in the person referred to by *I*, the place referred to by *there*, and the time referred to by *will be* and *right*. We must also look to the "context" to decide whether the speaker was using the sentence to make an assertion, a threat, an apology, or what. The approach is product-centered: You start with the products – the sentences, words, and phonetic segments abstracted away from the circumstances – and fill in the missing content from the actual circumstances.

The product approach has several drawbacks. As we have seen, theories of language structure cannot be extended to cover discourse structure, so the approach has to be fitted out with an entirely different type of analysis to handle discourse. Theories of language structure deliberately abstract away from speakers, listeners, times, places, and the circumstances of utterance, so when these theories are extended to language use, the participants, times, places, and circumstances tend to be relegated to secondary roles and given short shrift. In this approach, sentences, words, and phonetic segments tend to be treated as static timeless objects, whereas utterances play out in real time and, as we have seen, their continuity, simultaneity, and timing count. Also, theories of language structure are concerned solely with conventional languages like English, Japanese, or American Sign Language, so the communicative acts in discourse that are *not* part of conventional languages – eye gaze, gestures, nods, smiles, and manifest actions such as my handing Stone a twenty-dollar bill – are excluded on principle and then ignored.

Perhaps the greatest drawback of the product approach is its attitude toward "context." In logic, the object of study is well-formed formulas, such as "p implies not q," and the rules by which they can be used to make inferences. These theories are exclusively syntactic: They don't depend on the referents of p and q. When logics like this were taken as models for sentence meaning and, later, language use, it was hard to shake the attitude that the referents of utterances were of only secondary interest. The stricture seemed to be that theories of language use shouldn't appeal to "context" until they were forced to. One result is that there has been little investigation within the product tradition of the "context" that does get appealed to.

In the action tradition, the focus from the beginning has been on what people do with language. Discourse isn't merely a linguistic structure. Speakers, listeners, times, places, and the circumstances of utterance are taken into account, and in at least part of the tradition, so are the continuity, simultaneity, and timing of utterances and other actions. Attention is paid to the gamut of communicative acts, from utterances to eye gaze. "Context" is generally given the prominence it deserves and is not treated as the refuge of last resort.

The difference between the two approaches may at first seem slight, but it is fundamental, for it leads to radically different theories of language use. Although we must appeal to results from both traditions, it is the action tradition that will set us off in the right direction.

Conclusions

When people use language, it is generally as part of a joint activity. Now, joint activities range from planning a party or transacting business to playing chess or playing in a string quartet, and they have properties all their own. They take the coordinated actions of two or more participants in particular roles. They each have an entry and an exit, and most emerge in sections and subsections. Most establish a dominant goal, and the participants advance toward that goal one increment at a time. Each of these increments adds to the common ground of the participants, changing what they take to be the current state of the activity.

The argument is that joint activities are the basic category, and what are called discourses are simply joint activities in which conventional language plays a prominent role. If we take language use to include such communicative acts as eye gaze, iconic gestures, pointing, smiles, and head nods – and we must – then all joint activities rely on language use. Chess may appear to be nonlinguistic, but every chess move is really a communicative act, and every chess game a discourse.

Joint activities advance largely through identifiable joint actions by the participants. What are joint actions, and how do they work? These are questions for Chapter 3.

3 | Joint actions

Joint activities advance mostly through joint actions. In buying items in a drugstore, a customer joins a server in opening the transaction, settling on the items wanted, establishing the price, exchanging money, and closing. In a chess game, the players join in specifying discrete moves from the opening of the game to the checkmate. Joint actions like these belong to an extended family of actions that also includes moving together in waltzing, playing notes together in a string quartet, paddling in unison in a canoe, and passing a ball in soccer or basketball. It also includes asking questions, making requests, making assertions, making references – much of what we think of as language use.

What makes an action a joint one, ultimately, is the coordination of individual actions by two or more people. There is coordination of both *content*, what the participants intend to do, and *processes*, the physical and mental systems they recruit in carrying out those intentions. When Ann and Ben paddle a canoe together, they coordinate on their plans – the content of what they do. Overall, they aim to reach the spit of land on the other side of the lake as efficiently as possible, with Ann in front and Ben in the rear. At any moment, they aim to stay on course, with Ann pulling on one side and Ben on the other. Ann and Ben also coordinate on their physical and mental processes. They pull their paddles in rhythm and with a force adjusted to keep them on course; if Ann changes sides, so does Ben; if Ann stops, so does Ben. In joint actions, the processes recruited depend on the plans, and the plans chosen depend on the processes available. If a log drifts in front of their canoe, Ann and Ben both adjust their processes to avoid it, then return to their course. Joint actions cannot be accounted for without understanding the interplay between content and process, and their place in overall joint activities.

Joint actions with language are no different. They too require the coordination of actions – with all that that requires. Although this may be a truism, it is a truism widely ignored. Some of the basic principles of language use are really general principles of joint action, and to understand language use, we must look to the broader principles.

Individual and joint actions

Joint actions pose a paradox. Recall that intentional actions divide into two types-individual and joint actions (Chapter 1). Ann is performing individual actions when she plays a flute, paddles a kayak, or shakes a stick. Ann and Ben are performing joint actions when they play a flute–piano duet, paddle a canoe together, or shake hands. Individual actions are performed by individual people, and joint actions, by ensembles of people. Clearly, there is no agent named Ann-and-Ben who decides "Ah, I am now going to play this duet" and then plays it. Ensembles of people don't intend to do things. Only individuals do (Clark and Carlson, 1982a, b). Yet ensembles of people play duets, paddle canoes, shake hands, and do other things individuals cannot do alone. The paradox is this: An ensemble can do things that it cannot intend to do.

The paradox dissolves once we see that joint actions have individual actions as parts. In Ann and Ben's flute and piano duet, there are three distinct actions:

0.   the ensemble Ann-and-Ben plays the duet (a joint action)
1.   Ann plays the flute part as part of 0 (an individual action by Ann)
2.   Ben plays the piano part as part of 0 (an individual action by Ben)

The joint action in 0 is performed by means of the individual actions in 1 and 2. These individual actions are of a special type (Chapter 1). When Ann plays alone in the privacy of her living room, she doesn't coordinate her actions with anyone else. They are *autonomous actions*. But when she plays the flute part as part of the duet, as in 1, she performs actions as a means of participating with Ben in playing the duet. These I have called *participatory actions*. Joint actions can only be performed by means of participatory actions – by the individual participants each doing their parts. So we can denote a joint action by A and B as a joining of two participatory actions, $part_1(A)$ and $part_2(B)$, as here:

joint[$part_1$(A), $part_2$(B)]

Ann and Ben's duet becomes: joint[Ann plays flute part, Ben plays piano part].

Autonomous and participatory actions are distinguished by the intentions behind them. Here is one way to characterize individual actions:

Individual A is doing individual action *k* if and only if:
   0.   the action *k* includes 1;
   1.   A intends to be doing *k* and believes that 0.

For Ann to be playing a flute piece alone in her living room, she must intend to be playing that piece and believe she has those intentions. Joint actions look different:

Ensemble A-and-B is doing joint action *k* if and only if:
   0.   the action *k* includes 1 and 2;
   1.   A intends to be doing A's part of *k* and believes that 0;
   2.   B intends to be doing B's part of *k* and believes that 0.

For Ann to be playing her part of the flute–piano duet, she must intend to be playing her part, and believe she has these intentions and that Ben has the parallel intentions and beliefs. With participatory acts, Ann does what she does only in the continuing belief that Ben is intending to do his part.[1]

Joint actions must be distinguished from *adaptive* and *deceptive* actions. Consider this series of actions:

   1.   In a dart game, A throws a dart at a stationary dart board B.
   2.   In an arcade game, A shoots a pellet at a moving mechanical duck B.
   3.   As a spy, A shadows an unwary B through San Francisco.
   4.   In a game of catch, A throws a ball for B to catch.
   5.   In tennis, A tries to hit a ball past B.

In all five descriptions, A takes actions with respect to B based on where she predicts B will be. In 1 and 2, her prediction is based on the mechanical properties of dart boards and mechanical ducks. In 3, it is based on what B would do autonomously. In 4, it is based on what B would do in trying to coordinate with A. And in 5, it is based on what B would do believing he thought she was trying to deceive him. Of these, only 4 is a genuine joint action, in which A and B converge on a mutually desired outcome.

---

[1] For discussions of intentions in joint actions, see Grosz and Sidner (1990), Searle (1990), Tuomela (1996), Tuomela and Miller (1988).

In 3, spy A adapts unilaterally to B's actions, and in 5, tennis player A actively deceives her opponent B – a type of anti-coordination. Coordination is different from both adaptation and deception. Our primary concern is coordination.

Coordination

Joint actions are created when people coordinate with each other. Why should they coordinate? The reason, according to Thomas Schelling (1960), is to solve *coordination problems*. Two people have a coordination problem whenever they have common interests, or goals, and each person's actions depend on the actions of the other. To reach their goals, they have to coordinate their individual actions in a joint action. In this view, joint actions are created from the goal backward. Two people realize they have common goals, realize their actions are interdependent, and work backward to find a way of coordinating their actions in a joint action that will reach those goals. It was David Lewis' (1969) insight that language use is really people solving coordination problems. In our terms, it is a complex of joint activities. If Lewis is right, we should learn a great deal about language use from studying these problems. Let us begin with Schelling's analysis.

SCHELLING GAMES

There are many situations in which two people's actions are interdependent and their interests, or goals, are identical. Schelling studied these situations by devising a variety of one-shot problems I will call Schelling games. In each game, two people give their solutions to the same problem, but without consulting each other. Here are four Schelling games:

1. *Coin*. Name "heads" or "tails." If you and your partner name the same, you both win a prize.

2. *Numbers*. Circle one of the numbers listed here. You win if you both succeed in circling the same number:

7   100   13   261   99   555

3. *Meeting*. You are to meet somebody in New York City. You have not been instructed where to meet; you have no prior understanding with the person on where to meet; and you cannot communicate with each other. You are simply told that you will have to guess where to meet and that he is being told the same thing and that you will just have to try to make your guesses coincide. You were

told the date but not the hour of the meeting; the two of you must guess the exact minute of the day for the meeting. At what time will you appear at the meeting place that you elected?

4. *Money.* You are to divide $100 into two piles, labeled A and B. Your partner is to divide another $100 into two piles labeled A and B. If you allot the same amounts to A and B, respectively, that your partner does, each of you gets $100; if your amounts differ from his, neither of you gets anything.

When Schelling got about forty people to play these games, there was a surprising agreement in their responses. For the coin game, 86 percent of them said "heads." For the numbers game, 90 percent selected one of the first three numbers; 7 and 100 were the most popular. For the meeting game – the players were all from New Haven – "an absolute majority" suggested the information booth at Grand Central Station, and "virtually all" would go there at noon. For the money game, 88 percent of the players put $50 in pile A and $50 in pile B. As Schelling pointed out, the players in each game had little to go on: In principle, any solution was as good as any other. Still, they managed to win most of the time.

These are problems of *pure coordination*, where the two partners' interests coincide completely. But, as Schelling argued, the same factors apply even when the two partners' interests diverge, so long as they don't diverge too much. Here are two more Schelling games:

1'. *Unequal coin.* A and B are to choose "heads" or "tails" without communicating. If both choose "heads," A gets $3 and B gets $2; if both choose "tails," A gets $2 and B gets $3. If they choose differently, neither gets anything. You are A (or B); which do you choose?

4'. *Unequal money.* You and your partner are to be given $100 if you can agree on how to divide it without communicating. Each of you is to write the amount of his claim on a sheet of paper; and if the two claims add to no more than $100, each gets exactly what he claimed. If the two claims exceed $100, neither of you gets anything. How much do you claim?

For the unequal coin game, the two partners should still converge on "heads," since otherwise they both lose money. They did: 73 percent of the A's and 68 percent of the B's chose "heads" (compared to 86 percent in the original game). For the unequal money game, the goals shouldn't change either, and 90 percent of the players split the money fifty-fifty (compared to 88 percent in the original game). All it takes to be a coordination problem, as Lewis (p. 24) put it, is that "coincidence of interest predominates."

Everyday coordination problems are more varied than these examples suggest. They vary in number of possible solutions (from two to infinity), number of participants (from two to entire communities), what is at stake (from minor incivilities to nuclear war), and coincidence of interest (from partial to complete). They may be discrete, like the one-shot Schelling games, but more often they are continuous, like playing duets, paddling a canoe, or conversing, and that complicates matters immensely. Despite their differences, all these problems share certain characteristics. One of these is the coordination of expectations.

COORDINATION DEVICES

What does it take to solve coordination problems? It isn't enough, as Schelling noted, simply to predict what one's partner will do, since the partner will do what he or she predicts the first will do, which is whatever the first predicts that the partner predicts the first to do, and so on *ad infinitum*. Schelling argued:

> What is necessary is to coordinate predictions, to read the same message in the common situation, to identify the one course of action that their expectations of each other can converge on. They must "mutually recognize" some unique signal that coordinates their expectations of each other. (Schelling, p. 54)

Schelling went on:

> Most situations – perhaps every situation for people who are practiced at this kind of game – provide some clue for coordinating behavior, some focal point for each person's expectation of what the other expects him to expect to be expected to do. Finding *the* key, or rather finding a key – any key that is mutually recognized as the key becomes *the* key – may depend on imagination more than on logic; it may depend on analogy, precedent, accidental arrangement, symmetry, aesthetic or geometric configuration, casuistic reasoning, and who the parties are and what they know about each other. (p. 57)

With Lewis, I shall call such a focal point, or key, a *coordination device*.

The six Schelling games illustrate several devices. Of heads and tails, heads seems more prominent because one says "heads or tails" or perhaps because fronts are more salient than backs. In the number problem, 7 has a certain prominence (the only single digit, the smallest number), and so do 100 (a standard round number) and 13 (a common unlucky number), but the other numbers don't. In New York, Grand Central Station is a place many people outside New York pass through and even use as a meeting place; of the two most conspicuous times of the day, noon is more sensible for meeting. And of various money splits, fifty-fifty is an obviously unique solution, since it is symmetrical for A and B.

Coordination devices range even more widely. When you and I want to meet, we can meet in Jordan Hall at eight on the basis of an *explicit agreement*, or on the basis of *precedent* – that's when and where we met last week. We can meet for a seminar in Room 100 at noon on the basis of a *convention* – that's when and where the seminar conventionally meets. If we lose each other wandering through the Tate Gallery, we could meet at van Gogh's *Self-portrait* on the basis of a prior conversation about your coming especially to see it, or at the entrance on the basis of its uniqueness as a location in the gallery. I can meet you getting off a plane, without knowing what you look like, by having you wear a carnation in your lapel. Or, as has happened to me, we could meet on the basis of signs of personal uncertainty: You and I look for a passenger and a reception party who are obviously looking for a reception party and passenger they don't know.

What does all this have to do with joint actions? When Ann and Ben pick "heads" in the coin game, they are performing a joint action. They are each performing individual actions as parts of an action by the pair of them, denoted as follows:

Joint [Ann picks "heads," Ben picks "heads"]

The coordination device – the prominence of "heads" – is what enables them to choose the right participatory actions to perform.

JOINT SALIENCE

What coordination devices do is give the participants a rationale, a *basis*, for believing they and their partners will converge on the same joint action. These rationales can, in principle, come from any source so long as they lead to a unique solution. What they must do, as Schelling put it, is enable the participants to form a "mutual expectation" about the individual actions each participant will take.[2]

What is a mutual expectation? Intuitively, it is a type of shared belief. To describe it, we need the technical notion of common ground I take up in Chapter 4. For now, I will define it this way:

---

[2] Kraus and Rosenschein (1992; Fenster, Kraus, and Rosenschein, 1995) have studied automated procedures for identifying focal points in a limited set of domains.

For two people *A* and *B*, it is common ground that *p* if and only if:

1. A and B have information that some basis *b* holds;
2. *b* indicates to A and B that A and B have information that *b* holds;
3. *b* indicates to A and B that *p*.

Suppose you and I agree to meet in Jordan Hall at eight. That agreement is a basis *b* for a certain piece of common ground. You and I each have information that the agreement holds. The agreement indicates to each of us that we both have information that it holds. Finally, it indicates to you and me that we each expect to go to Jordan Hall at eight. We can conclude: It is common ground for you and me that we each expect to go to Jordan Hall at eight. A mutual expectation is a mutual belief or supposition (a part of common ground) about what the participants will do.

It is mutual expectations like this that enable an ensemble of people to perform a joint action. Take meeting in Jordan Hall at eight. I won't believe I am taking part in that joint action unless I believe you are intending to go to Jordan Hall at eight too, and the same logic holds for you. But once we are armed with the mutual expectation, I can do my part (going to Jordan Hall at eight) in the belief that you are doing yours (going to Jordan Hall at eight), and you can do your part in the belief that I am doing mine. It is only with that mutual belief that we both believe we are taking part in the same joint action – meeting in Jordan Hall at eight.

Common ground, then, is a prerequisite for coordination – for joint actions.[3] The point is easy to demonstrate. Suppose I am asked, in a Schelling game, to choose one of these three balls:

basketball   baseball   squash ball

Which should I choose? That depends on my assumptions about my partner.

Case 1. I don't know who my partner is. I therefore choose the basketball, reasoning: "My partner and I can take for granted that the basketball is perceptually the most salient one for any two humans.

---

[3] As Schelling noted, an effective coordination device will have "some kind of prominence or conspicuousness." "But," he went on, "it is a prominence that depends on time and place and who the people are."

Since I know nothing else about my partner, and I suppose he or she knows that, we must rely on perceptual salience alone."

Case 2. My partner and I are old friends; indeed, we arrived together to play the Schelling game. Further, she and I play squash three times a week (and not basketball or baseball). I therefore choose the squash ball. I reason: "We mutually know we play squash, making the squash ball especially salient for the two of us. The basketball may be the most salient perceptually, but that salience isn't unique to the two of us. That makes the squash ball the solution of choice."

Case 3. My partner is the same as in 2, and I have been told that she is my partner, but that she doesn't know I am her partner. I therefore choose the basketball, reasoning: "Even though she and I mutually know we play squash, that cannot guide her choice since she has no idea I am her partner. The game reduces to case 1, hence the choice of the basketball."

It is easy to show that, with other configurations of common ground, I should always make my choice against what I take to be my partner's and my current common ground, and this is just what people do (Clark, Schreuder, and Buttrick, 1983; see also Clark and Marshall, 1981).

The ideal solution to a coordination problem, then, isn't the solution that is most salient *simpliciter.* It is the solution that is the most salient with respect to the participants' current common ground. The principle is this:

Principle of joint salience. The ideal solution to a coordination problem among two or more agents is the solution that is most salient, prominent, or conspicuous with respect to their current common ground.

(For short, I will use *joint salience* to mean "salience with respect to the participants' current common ground.") Not that two people will always agree on what is jointly the most salient. They may have discrepant conceptions of their current common ground, or of the most salient solution in it. But people are sensitive to potential discrepancies (Clark, Schreuder, and Buttrick, 1983) and adept at managing those that arise (Chapter 8). Still, they should strive for the ideal – within limits – for they can take for granted that their partners are striving for the ideal too. This way they reduce the possibility of miscoordination.

Participant coordination problems

The standard Schelling game ("Name heads or tails") is a *third-party* coordination problem. Two partners, say Ann and Ben, are given a problem by a third party or by nature. It is never specified who the third party is, or what his or her motives are, but these can be critical. The third party may know Ann and Ben well and have given them a problem they would find easy. But for all they know, the third party may be diabolical and have given them an unsolvable problem ("Choose 59 or 83 or 71").

Participant coordination problems are fundamentally different, as when Ann poses a coordination problem for Ben and herself. For such a problem, Ben can reason: "Ann, being rational, must want to win and expect me to want to win too. Since she had leeway in her choice of problem, I assume she has chosen one she believes has a unique solution that we can converge on. Furthermore, she should think I will reason this way." And she should. If so, Ann and Ben have four additional premises they can use in solving the problem:

The solvability premises. In a coordination problem set by one of its participants, all of the participants can assume that the first party:

1. chose the problem,
2. designed its form,
3. has a particular solution in mind, and
4. believes the participants can converge on that solution.

These are premises Ann and Ben couldn't take for granted for third-party coordination problems.

Riddles and puzzles, for example, differ in solvability. Modern riddles have solutions that their creators don't expect solvers to discover, as here (from Augarde, 1986):

Ann: When is a thought like the sea?
Ben: (after thinking a bit) I don't know. When?
Ann: When it's a notion.

Riddles aren't participant coordination problems precisely because they violate the solvability premises. Puzzles, in contrast, have solutions their creators *do* expect solvers to discover, as here (from Smullyan, 1978):

Ann: Twenty-four red socks and twenty-four blue socks are lying in a drawer in a dark room. What is the minimum number of socks I must take out of the drawer that will guarantee that I have at least two socks of the same color?
Ben: (after working out the answer) Three.

So puzzles fulfill the solvability premises. And whereas riddles take three steps (Ann, Ben, Ann), puzzles take only two (Ann, Ben).

The solvability premises have an important corollary. When Ann presents her puzzle to Ben, she specifies twenty-four red socks, twenty-four blue socks, a dark room, and other information. The two of them assume this is all Ben needs to solve it. If they didn't, the puzzle wouldn't be solvable. Ben cannot add convenient assumptions: "Let me assume I can turn on the light. So the answer is two." Or: "Let me assume there is also a pair of Argyle socks in the drawer. So the answer is four." Nor should Ann assume Ben will do this. If he were allowed to, the puzzle would no longer have a unique solution. The only information Ann and Ben can add is information from their common ground that is consistent with the principle of joint salience.[4] The assumption they make is this:

The sufficiency premise. In a coordination problem set by one of its participants, the participants can assume that the first party has provided all the information they need (along with the rest of their common ground) for solving it.

The solvability and sufficiency premises are merely corollaries of the principle of joint salience as applied to participant coordination problems.

Some participant coordination problems have an added constraint: They come in sequences so that the participants have to coordinate not only on the solution, but also on *when* to present the solution. In such a situation, Ann won't give the socks puzzle, because she cannot know how long Ben will take – an hour, two minutes, thirty seconds. The completion time, to be predictable, must itself satisfy joint salience, solvability, and sufficiency. It cannot be twenty seconds, ten seconds, or five seconds, for these aren't unique solutions. It must be effectively zero, or immediate. If it weren't, there would be unpredictable delays that would get compounded on the next problem:

The immediacy premise. In a coordination problem set by one of its participants in a time-constrained sequence of problems, the participants can assume that they can solve it immediately – with effectively no delay.

So for a time-limited problem posed by Ann, Ben can assume she designed it so he would solve it immediately, readily, in no time at all.

It is crucial, therefore, who the coordination problem is set by and why. Joint salience applies whatever the problem. Solvability and sufficiency can be assumed for problems set by a participant. And immediacy can be assumed for problems that must be solved in a predictable

---

[4] See McCarthy's (1980, 1986) characterization of circumscription in so-called non-monotonic reasoning.

interval of time. By now, it should be clear why participant coordination problems are of such interest: They are the form most coordination takes in language use.

Conventions

Of all the coordination devices I have noted, two are uniquely suited for solving coordination problems. One is explicit agreement. When you and I agree to meet at Jordan Hall at eight, we do so to solve the problem of when and where to meet. Indeed, explicit agreements generally pre-empt other potential coordination devices. If you and I agree to choose tails on the next coin problem, our agreement takes precedence over the usual rationale for choosing heads. The other coordination device *par excellence* is convention.

Tom, Dick, and Harriet have a recurrent coordination problem: They want to meet for lunch every Tuesday – a joint action. Week after week, they agree to meet at the faculty club at 12:15. After a while, they no longer have to say when and where they are to meet. They each simply go to the faculty club at 12:15 – their participatory actions – because that is what they mutually expect each other to do based on the regularity in their recent behavior. What they have evolved is a convention, and that is now the device by which they coordinate their meeting – by which they carry out their joint action.

A convention, according to Lewis (1969), is a community's solution to a recurrent coordination problem. In some societies, bowing is a solution to the recurrent problem of how to greet one other; in others, it is shaking hands. In America and Europe, placing knives, forks, and spoons on the table is a solution to the recurrent problem of what utensils to use in eating. In China and Japan, it is to place chopsticks. In North America, leaving a tip at the table in a restaurant is a solution to the recurrent problem of how to help pay the waiter or waitress. In Europe, it is to include the tip in the bill. Conventions come in many forms – for large and small communities, for simple and complex problems.

What makes something a convention? According to Lewis, it has these five properties:[5]

---

[5] I have updated Lewis' (1969) account slightly to deal with minor problems noted by Burge (1975), Gilbert (1981, 1983), and others. For consistency, I have also changed Lewis' "population P" to "community C" and "common knowledge" to "common ground" and simplified his formulation in other ways. See Lewis for the full story.

A convention is:
1. a regularity *r* in behavior
2. partly arbitrary
3. that is common ground in a given community C
4. as a coordination device
5. for a recurrent coordination problem *s*.

Take greeting. When any two old friends meet, they have a recurrent coordination problem of how to greet. In some American communities, the solution is for two men to shake hands and for a man and woman, or two women, to kiss each other once on the cheek. These actions constitute a regularity *r* in behavior. They are a coordination device that solves the recurrent coordination problem of how to greet. The regularity is common ground for the members of those communities. And it is partly arbitrary, for it could have been different; in other communities, two men hug; in still others, two people kiss two, or three, times.[6] I say "partly" because the options available may be constrained. In greetings, the available options may exclude slapping or kicking, actions that hurt or injure.

Most conventions don't evolve as Tom, Dick, and Harriet's did. Shaking hands with the right hand, for example, didn't evolve for just me and the people I met. It was already in use in my culture when I learned it. Most conventions are arbitrary in being accidents of history: It is an accident of history that we shake hands with the right hand. If history had been different, we could be using the left.[7] Becoming a member of a community means in part acquiring the conventions in that community that were already in place.

Most conventions belong to systems. In every culture, for example, the problem of greeting people face to face has evolved a system of solutions. Here is a fragment of one system:

---

[6] Still, as Tyler Burge (1975) argued, it needn't be common ground in a community that a convention has alternatives. If people thought *cockadoodledoo* was the only way one could express a rooster's crow, the word would be no less conventional for that.

[7] It is really an empirical question for each regularity in behavior whether it could have been different. Right-handedness, for example, may be so strong that it dominates all other interests in coordinating on shaking hands, making the choice of the right hand not a true convention. Most conventions vary across cultures, thereby demonstrating their historical arbitrariness.

Situation *s*	Joint action *r*
gender: man and woman; two women *relationship*: intimates	A and B hug
gender: man and woman; two women *relationship*: acquainted equals	A and B kiss each other once on the right cheek
gender: two men *relationship*: unacquainted equals *introduction*: by oneself or third party	A and B shake hands
gender: man and woman; two women *relationship*: unacquainted *introduction*: formal, by third party	A and B exchange "How do you do?"
gender: man and woman; two women *relationship*: unacquainted *introduction*: informal, by third party	A and B exchange "Hello"

In this example, the recurrent coordination problem – the situation s – is partitioned into five mutually exclusive classes, each with a different solution – a different joint action r. The system is so tightly constrained that it may be impossible to change one convention without changing others. If hugging were broadened to new situations, kissing, shaking hands, and the rest would have to be narrowed. And there are probably links between related conventions. Is it accidental that we shake the right hand and kiss the right cheek? A change in one might induce a change in the other.

Conventions, Lewis argued, aren't habits or practices. All the same, they seem to be maintained in part by habits and practices. Shaking hands with the right hand remains intact partly because it has become habitual for people to extend their right hand when shaking hands. And when the practice of men wearing hats disappeared, so did the convention of men greeting women by tipping their hats. How are conventions maintained? This is surely related to the processes by which people coordinate with each other, an issue we will return to.

Coordination in language use

In discourses, as in other joint activities, the participants advance their interests by creating joint actions as solutions to coordination problems. They create entire joint activities when faced with such coordination problems as how to plan a party, complete a business transaction, get a story told, or exchange gossip. At each step in these activities, they create smaller joint actions as solutions to smaller coordination problems, such as how to make and accept offers, how to speak and be understood, and who is to speak when. These problems in turn divide into smaller coordination problems, leading to more local joint actions. Discourses emerge as solutions to hierarchies of coordination problems. If this is right, people should exploit the same coordination devices inside discourses as outside them, and they do.

In language use, a central problem is coordinating what speakers mean and what their addressees understand them to mean. These are really participant coordination problems – Schelling games set by speakers for their addressees and themselves to solve. Their solutions should therefore reflect joint salience, solvability, and sufficiency: Speakers and addressees should take for granted, within limits, that speakers have in mind unique solutions they believe their addressees will converge on. To see this, let us examine an analysis of signaling systems by David Lewis (1969).

SIGNALING SYSTEMS

As a model situation, Lewis drew from a legend of the American Revolutionary War about Paul Revere riding through the Massachusetts countryside to warn everyone that the redcoats – the British – were coming.[8] The scene Lewis chose has two participants, the sexton of the Old North Church and Paul Revere – a speaker and an addressee. The sexton acts according to one contingency plan:

If the redcoats are observed staying home, hang no lantern in the belfry.
If the redcoats are observed setting out by land, hang one lantern in the belfry.
If the redcoats are observed setting out by sea, hang two lanterns in the belfry.

And Revere acts according to another:

If no lantern is observed hanging in the belfry, go home.
If one lantern is observed hanging in the belfry, warn the countryside that the redcoats are coming by land.
If two lanterns are observed hanging in the belfry, warn the countryside that the redcoats are coming by sea.

---

[8] The legend is best known from Henry Wadsworth Longfellow's poem "Paul Revere's Ride" (1861), which every American schoolchild used to know by heart.

The sexton's contingency plan is a function Fs from states of affairs to signals – observable actions – and Revere's is a function Fr from observable signals to responses he could take. For Revere and the sexton to succeed, they need to coordinate contingency plans, and they do just that with their choice of plans.

Revere and the sexton have created a *signaling system.* They begin with a coincidence of goals: Both want Revere's response to be appropriate to the state of the British army as the sexton sees it. As Lewis put it, "Each agent will be acting according to the contingency plan that is best given the other's contingency plans and any state of affairs." A signaling system is a combination $<Fs, Fr>$ that achieves "the preferred dependence of the audience's response upon the state of affairs."

Signaling systems are ideal for coordinating what speakers mean with what their addressees understand them to mean. By hanging one lantern in the belfry, the sexton *meant* that Revere was to warn the countryside about the redcoats coming by land. Since he believed the signaling system to be common ground for the two of them, he could use one lantern and count on Revere to recognize what he meant. As Lewis pointed out, all this can be said without any mention of the meaning of the signals themselves – for example, that one lantern meant that the redcoats were coming by land. "But nothing important seems to have been left unsaid, so what has been said must somehow imply that the signals have their meanings." What one lantern means is a consequence of the pairing of the sexton's and Revere's contingency plans. This anticipates a point I will return to in Chapter 5: Speaker's meaning is primary, and signal meanings derivative.

When the sexton hangs out a single lantern, he is posing a *participant* coordination problem. Revere can assume the sexton (1) chose the problem, (2) designed its form of presentation, (3) had a particular solution in mind, and (4) believed he and Revere would converge on that solution. He didn't design it to be solvable by just anyone. He might even have devised it to confound British spies. Coordination in language use is like this. When Ann tells Ben "Bob went out with Monique last night," she expects to be understood by Ben, but not by just any overhearer. Most overhearers wouldn't know who Bob and Monique were. If Ann said "You-know-who did you-know-what with you-know-who last night," she would be posing a coordination problem unsolvable by anyone not privy to the special common ground she shares with Ben (Clark and Carlson, 1982a; Clark and Schaefer, 1987b, 1992).

Signaling systems are therefore bases for joint actions. Revere's and the sexton's contingency plan gives them a rationale for this joint action:

Joint [the sexton hangs one lantern in belfry, Revere takes the sexton to mean that the redcoats are coming by land]

As in any joint action, Revere and the sexton each take individual actions in the belief that each of them is doing so as part of a joint action by the pair of them. So what for Lewis is an account of coordination in language use is for us also an account of joint actions in language use. One is the basis for the other.

"It is not at all necessary," Lewis noted, "to confine ourselves to conventional signaling systems in defining meaning for signals." It didn't matter that Revere and the sexton came to their signaling system by explicit agreement. One lantern in the belfry still meant that the redcoats were coming by land. Signaling systems can be based on explicit agreement, precedent, salience, convention – on any coordination device that works. Naturally occurring signaling systems exploit all types of coordination devices.

CONVENTIONS AND LANGUAGE

Languages like English are conventional signaling systems *par excellence*. Most English speakers, for example, have contingency plans that include this pairing of conditionals, which I will call a *signaling doublet*:

Speaker: If you intend to denote the cipher naught, you can utter the word *zero*.
Addressee: If a speaker utters the word *zero*, he or she can be denoting the cipher naught.

This doublet happens to be conventional. It is a regularity in behavior – when people want to denote naught, they can use *zero*, and others can understand them to be denoting naught. It is a coordination device for a recurrent coordination problem – speakers wanting to denote naught and their addressees wanting to recognize this. As a coordination device, it is common ground in the community of English speakers (not Japanese or Navaho speakers). And it is arbitrary – another doublet (like *null* for "naught") might have evolved instead if the history of English had been different. In de Saussure's classic *Cours de linguistique générale* (1916), he called such a doublet a *linguistic sign* and argued that "the linguistic sign is arbitrary."[9] So just as the Old North Church signaling system has doublets, so does English. It is just that English has many more, organized in a complex system (Lewis, 1969).

Conventional doublets in language use come in many guises. Here are four broad categories:

Lexical entries. Many doublets are treated as lexical entries linking forms and meanings.[10] There is a lexical entry in English, for example, that pairs the signal type *zero* – its phonetic shape – with the signal meaning "naught." Construction types that have lexical entries include:

1. elementary words (e.g., *dog, zero, from*)
2. inflectional morphemes (e.g., *-s, -ed, -est*)
3. productive derivational morphemes (e.g., *-able, -er, un-*)
4. lexicalized complex words (e.g., *business*, whose meaning is not entirely derivable from the meanings of *busy* and *-ness*)
5. idioms (e.g., *by and large*, whose meaning is also not entirely derivable from the meanings of its parts)

Together these entries make up a complex signaling system. Not only is *zero* paired with "naught," but *one* is paired with "one," *two* with "two," etc., in a set of contrasting doublets for numbers. These, in turn, contrast with other quantifiers, such as *none, some,* and *all,* and eventually with all other lexical entries. How this is to be represented is one of the basic questions in linguistics.

Grammatical rules. Other doublets are expressed as grammatical rules that describe the composition of these basic forms. These include:

1. phonological rules (e.g., for what is a possible phonetic sequence in English)
2. morphological rules (e.g., for deriving adjectives like *shippable* from *to ship* and *-able*)
3. syntactic rules (e.g., for how a noun phrase may consist of an article plus a noun)
4. semantic rules (e.g., for how the meaning of a noun phrase is a composition of the meanings of its parts).

---

[9] "Le lien unissant le signifiant au signifié est arbitraire, ou encore, puisque nous entendons par signe le total résultant de l'association d'un signifiant à un signifié, nous pouvons dire plus simplement: *le signe linguistique est arbitraire*" (1916/1968, p. 100).
[10] For a related idea, see the notion of *lemma* (Levelt, 1989).

Conventions of use. Other doublets have been studied as conventions of use. In many cultures, you greet people by asking about their health, e.g., "How are you?" and in others, by asking where they are going. In some cultures, when a person sneezes, you say "Bless you," and to wish someone luck on stage, you say "Break a leg" (Morgan, 1978).

Conventions of perspective. Other doublets are really conventions about how one is to view certain entities. In Britain, a street is conceived of as an area that includes the roadway and the adjacent land on which the houses sit. So the British say, "My house is *in* Maiden Lane." In North America, a street is conceived of as a one-dimensional roadway that the adjacent land and houses touch. So North Americans say, "My house is *on* Maiden Lane." In Britain (and the rest of Europe), the "first" floor of a building is one story above the ground floor, but in North America, it *is* the ground floor. It isn't that the two communities have different meanings for *in, on,* and *first.* What differs are their conventional perspectives on streets and floors (Clark, 1996). Differences in conventional perspective are easy to confuse with differences in word or construction meaning.

As Lewis argued, the phonological, lexical, morphological, syntactic, and semantic rules of a language – its grammar – constitute a conventional signaling system. They describe regularities of behavior – what English speakers regularly do, and expect others to do, to achieve part of what they intend to do in using sounds, words, constructions, and sentences for communication.

NONCONVENTIONAL COORDINATION

The conventions of English are hardly enough to make communication work. They specify only the *potential* uses of a word or construction – and only some of these. They never specify the *actual* uses. The doublet for *zero* says how the word *can* be used. It doesn't say how it actually *is* used on some particular occasion. Every use of language raises non-conventional coordination problems, which depend for their solution on joint salience, solvability, and sufficiency. Here are four classes of problems that require non-conventional solutions.

Ambiguity. Almost every expression has more than one conventional meaning. Suppose *zero* has four conventional senses – "cipher naught," "nil," "freezing temperature," and "nonentity." The traditional idea is that when we are told, "I met a zero," or "It's zero outside," or "Write down zero," we select the lexical entry that "best fits" the utterance in context. But what "best fit" comes down to really is joint salience – which sense is the most salient solution given our current common ground. We tend to underestimate the coordination problems created by ambiguity, which arise not only for ambiguous words like *zero*, but for ambiguous constructions like *criminal lawyer* and *I discovered the guy with my binoculars*.

Contextuality. In San Francisco in 1980, a woman telephoned directory assistance to ask about toll charges, and the operator told her, "I don't know – you'll have to ask a zero."[11] If the caller had selected one of the conventional senses for *zero*, she might have chosen "nonentity" ("I don't know – you'll have to ask a nonentity"). Yet she reportedly interpreted the operator as meaning "person one can reach on a telephone by dialing the cipher naught." The operator used *zero* with a novel, non-conventional interpretation, and the caller interpreted it on the spot. How did they manage? The operator created a participant coordination problem that they solved on the basis of solvability, sufficiency, immediacy, and joint salience.

The operator's use of *zero* is a type of *contextual construction* (Clark and Clark, 1979; Clark, 1983). Contextual constructions aren't merely ambiguous, having a small fixed set of conventional meanings. They have in principle an infinity of potential non-conventional interpretations, each built around a conventional meaning of the word or words it is derived from. The operator's use of *zero* was built around "naught." In other circumstances, *zero* could have been used with an infinity of other interpretations. Contextual constructions rely on an appeal to context – to the participants' current common ground. They always require non-conventional coordination for their interpretation.

Contextual constructions are ubiquitous. In English, they include such types as these (Clark, 1983):[12]

---

[11] *San Francisco Chronicle*, November 24, 1980
[12] For discussions of these constructions, see Clark and Clark (1979), Clark (1978, 1983), Clark and Gerrig (1984), Downing (1977), Gleitman and Gleitman (1970), Kay and Zimmer (1976), Levi (1978), Nunberg (1979), and Sag (1981), though Levi assumes, contrary to the conclusion here, that nonpredicating adjectives have entirely conventional interpretations (see Clark, 1983).

Contextual construction	Examples
indirect description	You'll have to call a *zero*. I bought a *Henry Moore*.
compound noun	Sit on the *apple-juice chair*. I want a *finger cup*.
denominal noun	He's a *waller*. She's a *cupper*.
denominal verb	She *Houdini'd* her way out of the closet. My friend *teapotted* a policeman.
denominal adjective	She's very *San Francisco*. He's *Churchillian*.
nonpredicating adjective	That's an *atomic* clock, not a *manual* one.
possessive	That's *Calvin's* side of the room. Let's take *my* route.
main verb *do*	He *did* the street. He *did* a Nixon.
pronoun *one*	He has *one*.
pro-adjective *such*	He has just *such* a car.

This list also includes the main verb *do*, the indefinite pronoun *one*, and the pro-adjective *such*, which work like contextual constructions. When a friend tells you, "George *did* all three roofs," you understand what George did by assuming solvability and sufficiency and by appealing to joint salience.

The common ground needed for contextual constructions often lies far outside language. For Ann to tell Ben "I Houdini'd my way out of the closet," she must suppose they share salient biographical facts about Harry Houdini, the great escape artist (Clark and Gerrig, 1984). For her to say "Max went too far this time and teapotted a policeman" and by "teapot" mean "rub the back of with a teapot," she must suppose she and Ben share knowledge of Max's peculiar penchant for sneaking up behind people and rubbing them with a teapot (Clark and Clark, 1979). And for satirist Erma Bombeck to write "Stereos are a dime a dozen" and by "stereos" to mean "potential roommates who own a stereo," she must suppose she and her readers understand she is writing about difficulties in finding a roommate (Clark, 1983). Contextual constructions offer a convincing demonstration of the cumulative view of discourse: They can only be understood against the current state of the discourse.

Indexicality. Most references to particular objects, events, states, and processes are indexical: The referents cannot generally be identified without knowledge of the participants' current common ground. When I tell you, "That man is my cousin," I rely on conventions about the meanings of *that*, *man*, and noun phrases, but there is no convention linking the expression *that man* to my actual cousin. That link we have to coordinate by non-conventional means. Perhaps you have just mentioned an infamous criminal, or we have just seen a man fall on an icy sidewalk, or I have pointed at a book about cars. We hit on the same referent by appealing to solvability, sufficiency, and joint salience (Clark, Schreuder, and Buttrick, 1983; Nunberg, 1979; see Chapter 6). Similar principles apply to definite descriptions (like *the man in the poster*), definite pronouns (*I, she, here*), and even proper names (*George, Connie*).

Indexicality poses even more of a problem in *indirect reference*. When Jack tells Connie, "Our house celebrates birthdays with strawberries and champagne," he is using *our house* to refer directly to his house, but only as a means for referring indirectly to its inhabitants. The link from Jack's house to its inhabitants is not conventional and has to be coordinated by Jack and Connie. The principle is, once again, joint salience.

Layering. Suppose Jack utters "Frankly, I don't give a damn." In talking to Connie, he could be speaking seriously and mean what he says. In other circumstances, he could be speaking nonseriously at another layer of action. He might be practicing the line for a play, demonstrating someone's tone of voice, offering a linguistic example, or citing Rhett Butler's line from the movie *Gone with the Wind*. Whether he is speaking seriously or nonseriously isn't a matter of convention, but of nonconventional coordination (Chapter 12).

NONCONVENTIONAL COORDINATION DEVICES

If convention isn't the only coordination device we exploit in language use, what are the others? The answer is, almost any device we can appeal to successfully. The ultimate criterion is, as before, joint salience. Three such devices are explicit agreement, precedent, and perceptual salience.

Take explicit agreement. In scholarly writing, the meaning of a term is often stipulated. When Peter Strawson (1974, p. 75) says: "I begin by introducing the notion of a perspicuous grammar. A perspicuous grammar is...," he is making an explicit agreement with his readers about what he will mean by *perspicuous grammar* for the rest of that article. Its very purpose is to preempt conventions that would otherwise apply. Stipulations can be made on the spot with locutions like *what I shall call, let us call this, hereafter, for short, termed, named,* and *abbreviated*, but they can also be established through more elaborate codes. In principle, any convention of language can be preempted by stipulation.[13]

Explicit agreement is also found in baptismal dubbing and its secular counterparts. When a child is born, the parents explicitly agree on its name and then call it by that name or a derivative. The name then ordinarily becomes conventional, though it is assumed to have originated in an explicit agreement. All types of proper nouns and technical terms have similar origins, though the origins are generally much less formal (Ziff, 1977).

Precedent is another important coordination device in using language. Picture Helen and Sam each looking at the diagram of a maze and talking about it on the telephone. The horizontal passages in this maze can be described as rows, lines, columns, or paths, and so can the vertical passages. But once Helen has described the horizontal passages as *rows*, that sets a precedent. From then on, Sam must use *rows* for the horizontal passages and some other term – say, *columns* or *lines* – for the vertical ones. The reason: Helen's precedent becomes the jointly most salient solution to Sam's next reference to the passages, and Sam must conform or risk misunderstanding (Garrod and Anderson, 1987). Entrainment of terms like this is ubiquitous in conversation – powerful evidence for precedent as a major source of coordination in language use.

Perceptual salience is all too often ignored as an essential coordination device in language use. When I tell you, "Please stand by that tree," I may be pointing at a clump of ten trees. Still, you take the one I am referring to to be the biggest, nearest, or most unusual tree, the one that is jointly the most salient perceptually. Or I can say, "What was that?" and refer to a sudden explosion, flash of light, or eerie creak based on the jointly most salient perceptual event at the moment. Perceptual salience can be brought about by gestures, by third parties, by acts of nature, by almost anything. The sources of perceptual salience are limitless (Clark, Schreuder, and Buttrick, 1983).

---

[13] This is the basis for private codes among spies, and even between husbands and wives, or lovers. In Noel Coward's *Private Lives*, Amanda proposes to Elyot that the moment either one notices the two of them bickering, he or she should utter *Solomon Isaacs* (later shortened to *Solomon*) as a signal to stop all talk for five minutes (later shortened to two). Elyot agrees, and the signal works, for a bit. Similarly, Mad Margaret and Sir Despard Murgatroyd, in Gilbert and Sullivan's *Yeomen of the Guard*, agree that when he says *Basingstoke*, she will try to pull herself together, and that works too.

Processes in coordinating

In Schelling's and Lewis' schemes, coordination problems are treated as discrete events. The tacit assumption is that all coordination is achieved via such events. Nature serves people with one-shot Schelling games in which they make distinct choices, and that is that. The processes inside the event – setting the problem, understanding it, deciding on solutions, specifying the solutions – are irrelevant. It doesn't matter whether the players ruminate over their choices, as in diplomacy, bargaining, and chess, or make split-second decisions, as in canoeing, dancing, and shaking hands.

Most everyday coordination, however, is continuous, demanding adaptive moment-by-moment decisions that don't readily divide into discrete coordination problems. The difference is between a joint *act* and a joint *action*. When we view shaking hands as a joint act, we are treating it as a one-shot coordination problem, an event occurring at a single moment in time. But when we view it as a joint action, we are treating it as a process that unfolds in time. We might see it as a sequence of joint acts that are coordinated in time, or as a process of another kind. For continuous coordination, we must think of actions not acts. The added element is timing.

CONTINUOUS COORDINATION

All coordination, even in one-shot problems, is at least quasi-continuous. In the coin game, players A and B are asked to name "heads" or "tails." Whether they are allowed two seconds or two years to respond is left unspecified. When there are twenty Schelling games in a row, timing cannot be left unspecified. A's choice in game 6 must be paired with B's choice in game 6, not in game 5 or 7. A and B really need to coordinate on three things: (1) the current coordination problem; (2) their solution to it; and (3) the moment of response. In truly continuous problems, A and B coordinate (1), (2), and (3) moment by moment. In the general case, joint activities are continuous.

Continuous coordination is *periodic* whenever the actions are synchronized mainly by a cadence or rhythm – waltzing, playing a duet, paddling a canoe, marching in step. More often, it is *aperiodic* – two people shaking hands, eating dinner together, helping each other on with their coats, waving good-bye, negotiating a doorway without bumping. Joint actions can also be mixtures of the two. Conversation is aperiodic.

Coordination can also be *balanced* or *unbalanced*. In some joint actions, the participants take similar actions with no one in the lead. Hand shaking, duet playing, and team juggling may be initiated by one person, but are otherwise balanced. Most joint actions, however, are unbalanced. At any moment, they are led, or directed, by one of the participants, and the rest follow. In waltzing it is the man who leads, in orchestras the conductor, in canoeing the fore paddler, and in conversation the speaker. Not, of course, that these leaders have *carte blanche* to go any direction they want. But their actions are the main basis for synchrony and for the actions taken by the other participants. Most aperiodic unbalanced activities alternate in who takes the lead. In playing catch, it is largely the thrower, not the catcher, who leads, but who is thrower and who is catcher alternates. Conversation is unbalanced.

PHASES AND SYNCHRONY

Joint actions can be coordinated, I suggest, because they divide into *phases*. By phase, I mean a stretch of joint action with a unified function and identifiable entry and exit times. Playing a Mozart string quartet has four obvious phases – the first, second, third and fourth movements. Shaking hands has three – extending the hands, shaking hands proper, and withdrawing the hands. Most phases are hierarchical, dividing into subphases, which divide into further subphases, and so on. In music, phase hierarchies are represented directly in the notation: Entire pieces divide into sections, which divide into phrases, which divide into measures, which divide into beats. And in shaking hands, the second phase seems to divide into three subphases – grasping, pumping, and releasing – as diagrammed here:

extend hands	shake hands			withdraw hands
1	2			3
	grasp hands	pump hands	release hands	
	2.1	2.2	2.3	

With time running from left to right, the overall handshake divides into phases 1, 2, and 3, and phase 2 divides into subphases 2.1, 2.2, and 2.3.

Phases are what actually get coordinated. A phase is really a joint

Phases are what actually get coordinated. A phase is really a joint action with an entry, a body, and an exit (see Chapter 2). It can be diagrammed this way:

The entry is the moment the participants believe they have entered the action – the tail of the arrow – and the exit is the moment they believe they have left it – the head of the arrow. The body is what they do between the entry and the exit – the shaft of the arrow. The participants have to coordinate on all three features.

Synchrony of action requires coordination on the entry and exit times to each phase. To achieve synchrony, the participants must be able to project both times from what went before. They should be helped whenever the times are: (1) good reference points – jointly salient moments in time; and (2) easy to project from the previous phases. The participants achieve continuous synchrony, I suggest, by means of three main *coordination strategies*.

The *cadence strategy* is limited to periodic activities. In these, entry times are highly salient, and the duration of a phase is entirely predictable from the cadence. So the participants can coordinate by reaching agreement on three features:

1. an entry time t
2. a duration d
3. for all participants i, the participatory action $p(i)$ that i is to perform in d

In music, entry times are marked by heavy beats for phases and by lighter beats for subphases; it is significant that in musical notation the salient beats mark entry times to a measure, not exit times. In marching, entry times are marked by footfalls, and in canoe paddling, by the starts of paddle pulls, which also occur in rhythm. In rhythmic activities, the duration of a phase is a fixed number of beats long and depends little on what the participants do during each phase.

The *entry strategy* is more general than the first strategy. In continuous actions, the exit from one phase coincides with the entry into the next. In shaking hands, you know you have left the "extending hands" phase the moment you have entered the "grasping hands" subphase. When this holds, the participants only have to coordinate on two features:

1. an entry time t
2. for all participants i, the participatory action $p(i)$ that i is to perform in the phase

For this strategy to work, the entry times must be salient and projectable from the participatory actions of the previous phase. These conditions hold for many unbalanced aperiodic activities.

Most aperiodic activities have jointly salient entry times. Playing catch – tossing a ball back and forth – might have three main phases:

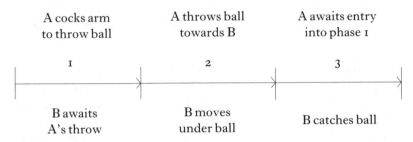

These phases define a cycle – a superphase in playing catch – and each time it is repeated, A's and B's roles are reversed. And these three phases themselves have subphases. The entry times into phases 1, 2, and 3 are as follows: the moment A begins to cock his or her arm; the moment of A's release of the ball; and the moment of B's contact with the ball. As the boundary strategy requires, these are major landmarks visible to both players.

The problem in aperiodic actions is projecting the entry times. Without a cadence, the participants need other devices, and the main device is the leader's actions. In playing catch, the entry time to phase 2 (the ball's leaving A's hand) can be projected by estimating how long A will take in throwing the ball. That can be projected more precisely from the subphases of 1 – say, bringing the arm back and thrusting it forward. The entry time to phase 3 (B's catching the ball) can be projected from the subphases of 2 – say, the ball rising to its apex, and the ball falling from its apex. So, to synchronize their actions, the participants track the subphases, and the easier they are to track, the more accurate the synchrony.

Aperiodic phases are usually *extendible*. Suppose that B in phase 3 goes to catch the ball, drops it, and has to pick it up again. The extra time he takes is added to phase 3 – or rather only one subphase of phase 3 – and doesn't affect phases 1 or 2 or any other subphases of 3. To keep in synchrony, all A and B have to do is extend the one subphase by the right amount and continue. Extendibility is useful because it allows for local repairs, for inserting other joint actions – like time-outs – and for accommodation to temporary lapses from synchrony.

The third strategy is the *boundary strategy*. In continuous actions, the exit from one phase sometimes doesn't coincide with the entry into the next, and there is no cadence to help out. In these, the participants must coordinate on three features:

1. an entry time t
2. an exit time u
3. for all participants i, the participatory action $p(i)$ that i is to perform in the phase

In the final phase of shaking hands, the entry time is projected from the participatory actions of the previous phase. But the exit time must be projected from the actions of the current phase since there is no following phase to mark it. In a handshake, the two people withdraw their hands together to end at the same time. It would be unseemly for one person to withdraw the hand too quickly.

People trying to coordinate need to estimate time accurately. When I throw a ball, I need to throw it to where my partner can catch it, and he needs to go to where I have thrown it. On my part, that takes estimates of how far and how fast he can run, and these will depend on the situation – the terrain, the type of ball, my partner's skill. If I overestimate, he won't catch the ball, and if I underestimate, the catch will be too easy, and he will get bored. The same goes for my partners. They must estimate how hard, how high, and in which direction I have thrown the ball, or they will miss it. Making moment-by-moment estimates like this is one of the great feats of joint actions.

In all three strategies, synchrony is achieved by the participants projecting entry times and participatory actions for each phase. The principle I suggest is this:

The synchrony principle. In joint actions, the participants synchronize their processes mainly by coordinating on the entry times and participatory actions for each new phase.

Put simply, joint actions are largely organized around entries and expected participatory actions.

Language processes

Conversation is an example *par excellence* of a joint activity in which the joint actions are aperiodic, unbalanced, and alternating. It is aperiodic because it has no cadence, unbalanced because it is led largely by the speaker, and alternating because who speaks alternates turn by turn. Not that language use is always this way. It can be balanced, as when parishioners recite prayers in unison, and periodic, as when football fans, picketers, and opera choruses chant or sing in rhythm. Yet its primary form is aperiodic and alternating.

PHASES IN CONVERSATION

If conversation does consist of joint actions, it should divide into phases that have jointly salient entry times, and it does. Conversations divide into a well-known hierarchy of phases – from broad sections to phonetic segments. Some of these phases are illustrated here (1.3.986):

Cal: well what was the óUTcome of all this, what . transPÍRED,

Viv: -- NÓTHing, I haven't heard a wÓRD,-

Each line denotes a turn, and turns divide into intonation units, the ends marked here by commas (Chapter 9). Intonation units, which are themselves phrases, divide into smaller phrases (e.g., "what | was | the outcome | of all this"), which divide into words, syllables, then segments.

The entries and exits of these phases are marked in the syntax, morphology, and intonation. Intonation units, for example, tend to begin on a high pitch, drop gradually in pitch over the unit, and end with a distinctive fall or rise. They also tend to have a focal accented syllable at or near the end that allows listeners to project the exit time with great accuracy. Moreover, they are thought to be found in all languages.

They are precisely what speakers and listeners need for synchronizing their processing.

For the entry and boundary strategies to work, the participants must be able to project the entry times for the next phase with accuracy. And to do that, they must coordinate on the time the current phase consumes. Enter the immediacy premise. With the intonation unit "What . transpired?" Cal is posing a participant coordination problem – he is asking Viv a question. Viv cannot initiate the next phase – her answer – until she has solved that problem, until she has understood his question. By the immediacy premise, she can assume that Cal expected her to be able to grasp what he meant on completion of that phase.

In conversation, then, addressees are expected to have completed their processing of a phase roughly by the time speakers finish that phase. The immediacy premise should hold for phases of all sizes. At the level of single words, addressees should have completed hearing, identifying, and grasping a word by the time speakers go on to the next word. At the level of intonation units, they should have understood what was meant in the current unit before speakers initiate the next one. If processing weren't roughly immediate, delays in one phase would accumulate with delays in the next, making synchrony even more difficult down the line.

PRECISION OF TIMING

People are able to project entry and exit times in conversation with surprising precision (Jefferson, 1972, 1973; Sacks, Schegloff, and Jefferson, 1974; Chapter 9). For a preview of the issue, consider the coordination problem of how to enter the next turn as illustrated in this actual bit of conversation (1.3.215):

Kate: how did you get on at your interview, . do tell us,
Nancy: . oh - - god, what an experience, - - I don't know where to start, you
        know, it was just such a nightmare - - I mean this whole system, of
        being invited somewhere for lunch, and then for dinner, - and
        overnight, . *and breakfast*
Nigel: *oh you st-* you you did stay

Speakers often try to initiate a new turn precisely as the previous turn ends. When they cannot, they create problems that have to be resolved. There are two such problems in this example – Nancy's and Nigel's.

Nancy's problem is that she doesn't immediately know what she wants to say. She has been selected to start speaking precisely at the end of "your interview." Because she doesn't, Kate prompts her after a brief pause with, "Do tell us." Nancy knows that, if she doesn't start soon, she may be taken as not having heard or understood, or as opting out. So she commits herself with "oh - - god" and then hesitates to plan her answer in earnest. What Nancy and Kate do, then, is shaped by their mutual expectation that Nancy should initiate her turn immediately. Nigel's problem is different. He incorrectly projects the end of Nancy's turn after "and overnight," so his speech overlaps with Nancy's. He repairs the problem by stopping, making a new projection, and beginning again after "and breakfast." So Nigel's overlap and restart are also a result of a mutual expectation of immediate entry into the next turn.[14]

Entry times, as a result, carry evidence about the participants' mental states – their understanding, readiness, plans. Nancy's delayed entry showed her uncertainty about what to say next. Nigel's premature entry revealed his belief about when Nancy had completed her turn. Mistiming can also be used as a deliberate tactic, as when speakers time their turns to overlap with the end of a previous turn to show that they already recognize what is being said (Chapter 8). Entry times are useful both as evidence and as instruments of communication.

What sort of information do entry times provide? The principle that applies is quite straightforward:

Principle of processing time. People take it as common ground that mental processes take time, and that extra processes may delay entry into the next phase.

The principle is useful because we have surprisingly accurate heuristics for estimating processing difficulty. Here are a few. In speaking, processing should take longer, all else being equal, (a) the rarer the expression; (b) the longer the expression; (c) the more complex the syntax or morphology; (d) the more precise the message; and (e) the more uncertain a speaker is about what he or she wants to say. And in understanding, processing should take longer, all else being equal, (a) the rarer the expression; (b) the longer the expression; (c) the more complex the syntax or morphology; (d) the more precise the message; (e) the more extensive the implications; and (f) the less salient the referents. These are only some of the heuristics we use.

---

[14] That is, the current speaker provides evidence about when the next speaker can or should begin, and potential next speakers are expected to use this evidence to enter their turns at precisely those moments. This goes for all entry times. See Chapter 8.

So content and process are interdependent: The more complicated the content, generally, the longer the process. This helps us discover what our interlocutors are thinking, and reveal to them what we are thinking. Processing time is a resource we make exquisite use of (Chapters 7, 8, and 9).

ASYNCHRONOUS JOINT ACTIONS

Synchrony is required in conversation because speech is evanescent. If addressees are ever to recover an utterance, they must attend to the speech while it is being produced, and that requires speakers and addressees to synchronize their processes. Written language, however, is not evanescent, and writers' and readers' processes are asynchronous. When I write my sister a letter, I may take half an hour, pausing halfway through for coffee and revising it several times. She may read it in thirty seconds and reread it. Not only are her actions and mine not synchronized. There may be no point-by-point correspondence between them at all.

Writing and reading are no less joint actions for the lack of synchrony. My actions depend on what I expect my sister to do, and her actions depend on what she thinks I would expect her to do. We still coordinate on content. I use English, refer to people we mutually know, and allude to family matters all on the assumption she will recognize the coordination devices I am using – conventions, joint salience, precedent, and all the rest. But I will also design – and redesign, edit, and reedit – my sentences to match the processes I judge she will read them by. I expect her to scan the sentences in order at a certain pace and to do so optimally when I pack information at the right density. Even though our processes are not synchronous, she and I coordinate on them.

Joint actions are required in language use regardless of setting. The coordination of content required is much the same across settings, but the coordination of processes is not. In conversation, speakers and addressees synchronize the phases of their actions. In asynchronous settings, speakers try to make processing optimal for their addressees.

Summary

When two people talk, they coordinate on both content and process. They have to do this in performing any joint action – playing a duet, paddling a canoe together, or shaking hands. Many properties of language use are common to all joint actions.

Joint actions require the participants to coordinate on their individual actions. In each joint act, the participants face a coordination problem: What participatory actions do they expect each other to take? To solve this problem, they need a coordination device – something to tell them which actions are expected. Now, according to the principle of joint salience, the ideal coordination device for any such problem is the solution that is most salient, prominent, or conspicuous with respect to the common ground of the participants. The device may be a convention, a precedent, an explicit agreement, a jointly salient perceptual event – any device, really, that satisfies the principle. In language use, coordination problems have additional properties because they are devised by one of the participants. Two of these are solvability and sufficiency: The participants can assume that each coordination problem has a unique solution they can figure out with the available information. Joint salience, solvability, and sufficiency already allow us to account for many properties of language use. Later, we will see how they account for even more.

But language use requires continuous coordination. The participants have to coordinate not only on *what* they do but on *when* they do what they do. They accomplish that, I have suggested, by coordinating on the entry times, content, and exit times of each phase of their actions on the assumption that the addressees' processing of the current phase is expected to be complete roughly by the initiation of the next phase. Yet they also realize that additional mental processes may delay entry into the next phase. Later, we will see how these properties are put to good use.

4 | Common ground

If a lion could talk, we could not understand him.
Ludwig Wittgenstein, *Philosophical Investigations*

Everything we do is rooted in information we have about our surroundings, activities, perceptions, emotions, plans, interests. Everything we do jointly with others is also rooted in this information, but only in that part we think they share with us. The notion needed here is common ground.

Common ground is a *sine qua non* for everything we do with others – from the broadest joint activities (Chapter 2) to the smallest joint actions that comprise them (Chapter 3). For my son and me to act jointly, he and I have to coordinate what we do and when we do it. And to coordinate, we have to appeal, ultimately, to our current common ground. At the same time, with every joint action he and I perform, we add to our common ground. This is how joint activities, from chess games to business transactions, progress (Chapter 2). When my son and I enter a conversation, we presuppose certain common ground, and with each joint action – each utterance, for example – we try to add to it. To do that, we need to keep track of our common ground as it accumulates increment by increment.

Common ground is important to any account of language use that appeals to "context." Most accounts don't say what context is, but rely on our intuitions about the circumstances of each utterance. These appeals are no better than a psychic's visions of next year's stock prices – and less predictive. With an undefined notion of context, as with an indefinite future, anything is possible. What these approaches need is a proper theory of common ground.

What, then, is common ground? What forms does it take? What information does it represent? How is it created, maintained, and incremented?

What is common ground?

The technical notion of common ground was introduced by Robert Stalnaker (1978; cf. Karttunen and Peters, 1975) based on an older family of notions that included *common knowledge* (Lewis, 1969), *mutual knowledge* or *belief* (Schiffer, 1972), and *joint knowledge* (McCarthy, 1990). Two people's common ground is, in effect, the sum of their mutual, common, or joint knowledge, beliefs, and suppositions. There has been considerable confusion about these notions. At issue is how they are to be represented. Three main representations have been proposed, and although they may seem equivalent, they aren't (Barwise, 1989; Clark and Marshall, 1981). Paradoxically, the best-known one is impossible psychologically, whereas the other two are not. I will argue that it is the second and third representations we need for language use.

THREE REPRESENTATIONS

I am at the beach examining a rare conch shell I just found. Although my attention is focused on the shell, I am vaguely aware of the entire situation – the beautiful day, the beach, the sea, the shell, and, of course, myself. It is as if ten meters down the beach there is a gigantic mirror in which I can see all these things reflected. In it I see myself, not as another inanimate object, but as a sentient being looking at the entire situation. I see myself thinking about what I am seeing – including me thinking about all this. If I am agent A thinking about the current situation *s*, we might represent the circumstances as follows:

s includes the beautiful day, the beach, the sea, A, and a conch shell near A.
s includes A's awareness of *s*.

What is represented by the second statement along with the first is a piece of my *self-awareness*.

Now my son walks up, and the two of us examine the conch shell together. How does my representation change? If all I did was add his name to the list in the first statement, that wouldn't do him justice. After all, I am sure he too is vaguely aware of the entire situation – that what he sees in the mirror is analogous to what I see. What I add instead is his version of the second statement, where he is B:

s includes the beautiful day, the beach, the sea, A, B, and a conch shell between A and B.
s includes A's awareness of *s*.
s includes B's awareness of *s*.

Note that this representation doesn't change when my son and I switch places. So long as I assume he is like me in his awareness of the situation, his and my self-awarenesses are exact analogs. If my wife comes along and the three of us look at the shell together, I will add: s includes C's awareness of s.

What I have just described is a shared basis representation of common ground. It is common ground for my son and me that, among other things, there is a conch shell between us. It is part of our common ground because it is included in a situation that also includes his and my awareness of that very situation. The situation s is the *shared basis* for our common ground. In this view, common ground is a form of self-awareness – self-knowledge, self-belief, self-assumption – in which there is at least one other person with the analogous self-awareness.

Common ground for a proposition p in a community C of people can therefore be represented this way (Lewis, 1969):

Common ground (shared basis)

p is common ground for members of community C if and only if:

1. every member of C has information that basis b holds;
2. b indicates to every member of C that every member of C has information that b holds;
3. b indicates to members of C that p.

In this form, b is the basis for the piece of common ground that some proposition p holds. C is a community of two or more members. And *has information* is intended to allow "believe," "know," "is aware that," "supposes," and verbs like "see," as in "I see my son looking at the conch shell." On the beach, my son and I form a minimum community. (1) He and I have information that a certain basis b holds – the beach scene in front of us exists. (2) It indicates to each of us that he and I have information that this very beach scene exists, and (3) it indicates to each of us that there is a conch shell between us. Conclusion: It is common ground for him and me that there is a conch shell between us. If in place of *have information* we substitute *believe, know, assume,* or *is aware,* we get the technical notions of *mutual belief, mutual knowledge, mutual assumption,* and *mutual awareness.* These notions are all subtypes of common ground. Let me denote this representation of common ground *CG-shared.*

In CG-shared, the basis for each piece of common ground is explicit. The conch shell is common ground for my son and me on the basis of the beach scene as we perceive it. But once he and I have established this piece of common ground, we can derive a second representation that eliminates any mention of the shared basis:

Common ground (reflexive)

p is common ground for members of C if and only if:
(i) the members of C have information that p and that i.

What this represents, instead, is my son's and my information – say, our belief – that there is a conch shell between us (the proposition p) and that he and I have that very information (the entire proposition labeled i). The proposition i is reflexive because it contains a reference to itself – just as the following statement does: "This sentence contains five words." Let me denote this representation $CG\text{-}reflexive$.[1]

A third representation can be derived from CG-reflexive, but only by adding certain assumptions. Suppose my son and I each start drawing the inferences that follow from i. He infers he has information that I have information that p, that I have information that he has information that p, that he has information that I have information that he has information that p, and so on ad infinitum. If I infer the analogous propositions, the result is this:

Common ground (iterated propositions)

p is common ground for members of C if and only if:

1. members of C have information that p,
2. members of C have information that members of C have information that p,
3. members of C have information that members of C have information that members of C have information that p,
   and so on ad infinitum.

For my son and me, proposition 1 really expands into two propositions: "A has information that p," and "B has information that p." Likewise, 2 expands into four propositions, 3 into eight, and so on. Let me denote this representation as $CG\text{-}iterated$.

MENTAL REPRESENTATIONS

CG-iterated obviously cannot represent people's mental states because it requires an infinitely large mental capacity. Also, it is unrealistic to

[1] CG-shared also contains a reflexive statement, namely "b indicates to every member of C that every member of C has information that b holds." Both of these represent the fundamental idea, expressed in the conch shell example, that common ground is a type of self-awareness: I am aware of myself, including that very awareness.

think my son or I represent such mind-boggling statements as "I think he thinks I think he thinks there is a conch shell between us," which is only level 4. And the moment my wife joins us, my son and I each increase the number of propositions at level (1) from 2 to 3, at level (2) from 4 to 9, at level (3) from 8 to 27, and at level (4) from 16 to 81. When we are joined by a fourth, the numbers go up to 4, 16, 64, and 244. My son and I wouldn't welcome any company at all if they put us to that much work. Plainly, CG-iterated is inconceivable as a mental representation (Clark and Marshall, 1981).

The basic representation, I suggest, is CG-shared. First, for my son and me to have a mutual belief, we have to assume it has a basis. Ordinarily, we are vaguely aware of that basis – e.g., the beach scene with the conch shell between us. Second, the basis for that mutual belief must be the same for the two of us. Suppose, under CG-reflexive, that my son and I mutually believe I will be home at six. If I hold this belief because of a note I left him but he didn't read, and he holds it because of a note he left me but I didn't get, we hold our mutual beliefs on different bases, and neither of us is justified in our beliefs. Put another way, we can infer CG-reflexive from CG-shared, but not vice versa.

The suggestion is that people are ordinarily able to justify their common ground. They believe or assume each piece has a basis that meets the requirements for CG-shared:

The principle of justification. In practice, people take a proposition to be common ground in a community only when they believe they have a proper shared basis for the proposition in that community.

If this principle is correct, people should work hard to find shared bases for their common ground, and that should affect how they proceed in language use.

INDIVIDUAL REPRESENTATIONS

Common ground isn't information that I have by myself, or that my son has by himself. Only an omniscient being can say: "It is common ground for the two of them that there is a conch shell between them." All my son and I can do, as individuals, is make claims like: "I believe that it is common ground for us that there is a conch shell between us." When he and I act "on the basis of our common ground," we are in fact acting on our individual beliefs or assumptions about what is in our common ground.

Individual beliefs about common ground are directly represented in CG-shared but not in CG-reflexive. In CG-shared, here is how an omniscient being would represent my son's and my mutual belief that there is a conch shell between us:

1. A and B each believe that the situation s holds
2. s indicates to A and to B that A and B each believe that s holds
3. s indicates to A and to B that there is a conch shell between them

By the first statement, I believe that the situation s holds. That situation is also the shared basis on which my son and I mutually believe there is a conch shell between us. So the first statement, paired with the second and third, also represents my belief that he and I mutually believe there is a conch shell between us. For CG-reflexive, I would have to add to the omniscient being's representation in this way:

A believes that (i) A and B believe that a conch shell is between them and that i.

With the addition of *A believes that*, we get a more complex form, suggesting, again, that CG-shared is more basic.

Two people may have conflicting information about what is common ground between them, and they recognize this. On the beach I might assume my son and I mutually believe that the shell I'm holding is a snail shell, but he assumes we mutually believe it is a conch shell. An omniscient being would realize we didn't have a mutual belief about this, but he and I would believe we did. In the end, it is our individual beliefs that count. Later, I might ask my son, "What did you think of the snail shell?" believing we mutually believed the shell was a snail shell. Only when he asked "What snail shell?" would I discover the error.

People are also deceivable. To get my son to a surprise party, I might tell him an outright lie: "Our neighbors have a new dog they want to show you." In CG-reflexive, he (B) represents the resulting mutual belief this way:

B believes that (i) A and B believe that the neighbors have a new dog and that i.

For me (A), the representation is more complicated:

A believes that B believes that (i) A and B believe that the neighbors have a new dog and that i.
A believes that the neighbors do not have a new dog.

Lies ought to require a more complicated representation, and in CG-reflexive and CG-shared they do. In CG-iterated, they don't, another reason for rejecting it as a mental representation of common ground.

QUALITY OF EVIDENCE

Shared bases vary a great deal in how much they justify each piece of common ground. They vary in what I will call *quality of evidence*. For my son and me, our joint gaze on the conch shell is *excellent* evidence that we each have information that there is a conch shell between us. Yet it is *poor* evidence that we each have information that the shell is six years old. I would judge it highly likely that the conch shell is part of our common ground, but unlikely that its age is. People tacitly evaluate shared bases for quality, recognizing that pieces of common ground range in likelihood from 0 to nearly 1.

Shared bases also vary in the type of information they give rise to. With the evidence at hand, my son and I might infer (1) that we mutually *know* there is a conch shell between us, (2) that we mutually *believe*, and strongly so, that it washed up on the beach that morning, (3) that we mutually *assume* that we want to take it home, and (4) that we mutually *see* that it is so long. People also evaluate the *type* and *strength* of information indicated by a shared basis.

People are fallible in these judgments, and they know it. I might take the beach scene as a strong indication of some common ground, whereas my son may take it as a weak indication. I might take the beach scene as justifying mutual knowledge, whereas he might take it as justifying only a weak mutual belief. Fortunately, we have practical strategies in using language for preventing such discrepancies and repairing them when they arise (Chapter 8).

COORDINATION AND COMMON GROUND

Common ground is essential to coordination with joint actions, and I suggest that the shared basis for common ground plays a crucial role in that coordination. When you and I make an explicit agreement to meet at Jordan Hall at eight, we are creating an entity b with three properties:

1. you and I both believe that we reached agreement b
2. b indicates to you and me that we reached agreement b
3. b indicates to you and me that we each expect to go to Jordan Hall at eight

But this is just CG-shared for our mutual belief that we each expect to go to Jordan Hall at eight. An explicit agreement is nothing more than a shared basis b for a mutual belief, and it is that shared basis that enables you and me to coordinate in performing a joint action.

The point holds for any coordination device – not only explicit agreements but conventions, precedents, perceptual salience, and all the rest. The principle is this:

Principle of shared bases. For something to be a coordination device, it must be a shared basis for a piece of common ground.

When it comes to coordinating on a joint action, people cannot rely on just any information they have about each other. They must establish just the right piece of common ground, and that depends on them finding a shared basis for that piece. The shared basis is what Schelling called the key to the coordination problem and what Lewis called the coordination device (Chapter 3).

HISTORICAL ASIDE

Common ground and its relatives mutual knowledge, mutual beliefs, and mutual expectations have had a rough history – and all because of the issue of representation. One of the first formal representations of common ground was proposed by Lewis (1969, p. 56), and it was CG-shared. Lewis showed, among other things, how it led to the higher order beliefs of CG-iterated, but he warned, "Note that this is a chain of implications, not of steps in anyone's actual reasoning. Therefore there is nothing improper about its infinite length" (p. 53). CG-reflexive was proposed not long afterwards by Gilbert Harman (1977) and Philip Cohen (1978).

Despite Lewis' well-known proposal, most investigators assumed that the only proper representation for common ground and its relatives was CG-iterated (e.g., Green, 1989; Radford, 1966; Schiffer, 1972; Sperber and Wilson, 1986). They focused on infinite sequences such as "I know that p; I know that you know that p; I know that you know that I know that p..." and noted that all these statements had to be satisfied simultaneously. But once they pointed out its fatal defects, they dismissed the notion of common ground in general (e.g., Cargile, 1969/70; Green, 1989; Sperber and Wilson, 1986).[2] Some investigators who saw these defects tried to make CG-iterated work by cutting off all

---

[2] For example, when Radford (1966), describing a case of mutual knowledge, claimed, "Any adequate account of what is learned and known in the most simple of conversations requires a complex description involving many iterated 'know(s) that's'" (p. 336), Cargile (1969/70) replied that there could be "no such structure" (p. 155) because people cannot reason this way.

statements beyond level 3 or 4.[3] But this solution had its own problems and only sidestepped the problem posed by the infinite regress (Clark and Marshall, 1981).

CG-shared and CG-reflexive, which have none of these problems, were apparently shunned for another reason: They contain self-reference, as in "I am aware that I am looking at a conch shell and that I have this very awareness." The problem is that self-reference isn't permitted in traditional logics, where it leads to such paradoxes as the liar's paradox and Russell's paradox. But to dismiss CG-shared and CG-reflexive for this reason is like dismissing Einstein's relativity theory because it cannot be accommodated within Newtonian physics. Self-reference is now a legitimate part of certain logics and is no longer an issue (Barwise, 1989; Barwise and Etchemendy, 1986).[4]

Let us now turn to the problem for language users: How to find or create shared bases for common ground in coordinating on joint actions. I suggest people make use of two broad types of shared bases. The first type is evidence about the cultural communities people belong to. Shared bases of this type lead to *communal common ground*. The second type is evidence from people's direct personal experiences with each other, which leads to *personal common ground*.

Communal common ground

We often categorize people by nationality, profession, hobbies, language, religion, or politics as a basis for inferring what they know, believe, or assume. When I meet Ann at a party and discover she's a classical music enthusiast, my picture of her suddenly expands. I assume she knows everything any such enthusiast would know – and that is a great deal. Once she and I establish we are both enthusiasts, we have a shared

[3] Bach and Harnish (1979) limited mutual beliefs to level 3, arguing "Higher beliefs are in principle possible, and indeed among spies or deceptive intimates there could be divergence at the first three levels, but we think such higher-level beliefs are not possible for a whole community or large group" (p. 309). In a similar move, Harder and Kock (1976) remarked, "There is no logical limit to the number of levels that may be necessary to account for a given speech event. But there are psychological limits...Probably not even the most subtle mind ever makes replicative assumptions in speech events involving more levels than, say, six" (p. 62). And Kaspar (1976), in reply to Keller (1975), said he doubted the need to go beyond "the first four or five orders" (p. 24). See Clark and Marshall (1981).

[4] For discussions of mutual knowledge in artificial intelligence, see Halpern and Moses (1990); in game theory, see Aumann (1976) and Brandenburger (1992); and in double binds, see Dreckendorff (1977).

basis for taking all this information to be common ground. That, in turn, opens the door to a plethora of new topics – from *Aïda* to *Die Zauberflöte*. How does this work?

CULTURAL COMMUNITIES

The main categories we exploit identify people as members of certain cultural groups, systems, or networks that I will call *cultural communities*. When I discover that Ann is (1) an English speaker, (2) a New Zealander, and (3) an ophthalmologist, I am identifying her as a member of three communities: (1) English speakers, (2) New Zealanders, and (3) ophthalmologists. From that point on, what I infer depends on whether or not I am also a member of these communities. (1) I assume Ann tacitly knows basic English vocabulary, syntax, phonology, and usage. Since I too am an English speaker, I assume I tacitly know the particular features of English I expect her to know. (2) I also assume Ann knows basic New Zealand history, geography, and customs. But not being a New Zealander, I assume I know only the types of information she knows and only scattered pieces of the information itself. Likewise, (3) because I know what an ophthalmologist is, I assume Ann knows all about eyes – their anatomy, diseases, and treatment. I assume I know some of the *types* of information she has but few of the particulars.

The information people have about a community depends on whether they are insiders or outsiders. Let me contrast two types of information:

Inside information of a community is particular information that members of the community mutually assume is possessed by members of the community.

Outside information of a community is types of information that outsiders assume is inside information for that community.

I have inside information about English speakers and classical music enthusiasts, but only outside information about New Zealanders and ophthalmologists. That leads to shared bases for two different types for common ground.

Case 1. Suppose Ann and I establish the mutual belief that she is a New Zealander and I am not. We can use the mutual belief as a shared basis b for common ground. What propositions does b justify – what can she and I now take to be common ground? Only outside information about New Zealand. We can mutually assume that Ann knows such things as the population, the name of the prime minister, the appearance of the coins, and the current price of gasoline. We cannot mutually assume that we both have this information. That is inside information I wouldn't be expected to know.

Case 2. Suppose Ann and I establish the mutual belief that we are both classical music enthusiasts. Again, that gives us a shared basis b, but this time for taking all inside information to be common ground. She and I can now mutually assume such information as who the Bachs were, what Mozart sounds like, what a minor key is, what bassoons look like.

Inside information goes beyond outside information in two ways. Outside information covers only a fraction of the types of information insiders actually have. And inside information surpasses outside information in sheer volume. Ann and I, realizing this, look especially hard for communities in which we are both insiders.

SHARED EXPERTISE

A cultural community is really a set of people with a shared expertise that other communities lack. Ophthalmologists don't all live in one place or know each other. What makes them a community is a shared system of beliefs, practices, nomenclature, conventions, values, skills, and know-how about eyes, their diseases, and their treatment. New Zealanders are experts on New Zealand, English speakers on the English language, philatelists on stamps, and Presbyterians on the Presbyterian church. Each type of expertise consists of facts, beliefs, procedures, norms, and assumptions that members of the community assume they can take for granted in other members. This expertise is graded. Some information is assumed to be central – highly likely to be part of every member's repertoire – and other information is only peripheral.

Cultural communities are therefore identifiable by their expertise. Here are some common types of expertise and the communities they define:

Basis for expertise	Examples of community	Examples of expertise
Nationality	American, Canadian, Dutch	nation's cultural practices, civil institutions
Residence	New Zealanders, Californians, Glaswegians	local geography, civil institutions, practices, argot
Education	university students, law students, high school graduates	book knowledge, educational practices
Occupation	ophthalmologists, plumbers, used car dealers	occupational practices, jargon, conventions, values, skills, know-how
Employment	Ford auto workers, Stanford faculty, *Newsweek* reporters	facts about employer, other employees, company practices
Hobby	pianists, baseball fans, philatelists	special skills, know-how, training, jargon
Language	English speakers, Japanese speakers, Gaelic speakers	phonology, morphology, syntax, semantics, lexicon
Religion	Protestants, Baptists, Muslims	religious doctrines, rituals, icons, historical figures
Politics	Democrats, libertarians, Fabians	political stands, values, prominent politicians
Ethnicity	Blacks, Hispanics, Japanese Americans	facts of heritage, ethnic experiences, ethnic practices
Subculture	rock musicians, drug addicts, teenage gangs	underground resources, subculture slang, know-how
Cohort	teenagers, senior citizens, thirty-year-olds	historical events of cohort, life concerns of cohort
Gender	men, women	bodily functions, gender-specific social mores

Once Ann becomes an ophthalmologist, she believes she has done more than become expert in ophthalmology. She has joined a select group of people – those who share certain beliefs, practices, conventions, values, know-how. She has become an insider and expects to be viewed as an insider by those who know about her membership.

Cultural communities like these generally form nested sets. San Franciscans, for example, are a subset of Californians, who are a subset of Western Americans, and so on. Here are several illustrative nestings:

Residence	North Americans ⊃ Americans ⊃ Westerners ⊃ Californians ⊃ Northern Californians ⊃ San Franciscans ⊃ Nob Hill residents
Education	high school graduates ⊃ university graduates ⊃ medical school graduates
Occupation	middle class ⊃ professionals ⊃ physicians ⊃ ophthalmologists ⊃ ophthalmic surgeons
Employer	Stanford University employees ⊃ Stanford faculty members ⊃ Stanford psychology faculty members ⊃ Stanford professors of psychology
Language	English speakers ⊃ speakers of New Zealand English ⊃ speakers of Auckland English dialect
Religion	Christians ⊃ Protestants ⊃ Baptists ⊃ Missouri Synod Baptists

Nestings like these allow graded inferences about what people are likely to know. When a San Franciscan and a Los Angeleno identify themselves to each other, they establish as common ground the inside information for Californians but not for smaller categories. These judgments can be quite subtle. When I meet a psychologist named Kay, I infer more and more specialized common ground as I discover she is an experimental psychologist, a cognitive psychologist, a psycholinguist, a psycholinguist working on speech production, a student of Charles Osgood's, and a recent visitor to the Max Planck Institute for Psycholinguistics.

We all belong to many communities at once. We each have a nationality, residence, level of education, occupation, employment, set of hobbies, set of languages, religion, political affiliation, ethnic affiliation, cohort, and gender. Many of these communities are correlated. A San Franciscan is likely to speak a California dialect of English. A professor of psychology is likely to be a psychologist, have a Ph.D. in psychology, and be over thirty. The organization of these communities is complex, and these few observations hardly do it justice. For deeper theories, we must consult sociologists, anthropologists, economists, and geographers.

A cultural community, I stress, isn't just any collectivity of people. Its very definition depends on the members' possession of a common ground. Football fans comprise a cultural community, not because they know one another or have a sure-fire way of identifying each other, but because they take certain information about football to be universal, indeed common ground, for members of the community. What defines such a community, Thomas Scheff (1967) argued, is consensus, which he based on Schelling's notion of mutual expectation: "Complete consensus on an issue exists in a group when there is an infinite series of reciprocating understandings between the members of the group concerning the issue. I know that you know that I know, and so on" (p. 37). Although Scheff's consensus is CG-iterated, his arguments go through for CG-shared and CG-reflexive too. The point is, consensus is fundamental to defining cultural communities. According to Scheff, it is essential to the sociological and anthropological notions of norms, roles, institutions, group goals, tradition, and culture itself (see also Klapp, 1956/7).

Do we identify people by their cultural communities? English – like most languages – has a wealth of nouns for classifying people by community. Here are examples for the categories just listed:

Nationality	Scot, Frenchman, Spaniard, Finn
Residence	American, Westerner, Californian, San Franciscan
Education	college graduate, psychology major, Yalie, Oxonian
Occupation	physician, lawyer, plumber, ophthalmologist, bricklayer, cowboy
Employment	Stanford employee, Stanford psychologist
Hobby	birder, philatelist, baseball fan
Language	English speaker, Japanese speaker
Religion	Christian, Protestant, Mormon, Baptist, Southern Baptist
Politics	Republican, Democrat, liberal
Ethnicity	Black, white, Chicano, gypsy
Subculture	drug addict, Hell's angel, thief
Cohort	teenager, senior, baby boomer
Gender	man, woman, boy, girl, he, she

Although terms like *Stanford employee* and *English speaker* are compound, most are simple and common in everyday use. These terms have evolved, I suggest, because they denote people by their membership in cultural communities, which are especially informative about what they know, believe, take for granted.

According to many psychologists, we habitually classify people by personality traits – for example, "Julia is reliable, kind, and imaginative."

The study of traits over the last sixty years has led to the "big five" dimensions of traits (Goldberg, 1993; Krahé, 1992): extroverted vs. introverted; kind vs. selfish; reliable vs. unreliable; emotionally stable vs. neurotic; and creative vs. unimaginative. But classifying by traits is very different from classifying by community – and it is no substitute. In using language, we classify people so that we can identify the conventions and other information we share with them. Traits are no good for this purpose. They are dispositions that people have more or less of, which don't lead to categories. There is also no evidence that we seek to establish mutual beliefs about our personality traits. We would have to if we were to use them as a basis for common ground. Personality traits have little to do with background expertise in actions that require coordination. For establishing common ground, we must classify by communities.

Contents of communal common ground

What information do we infer from community membership? It is useful to think of it organized as a large mental encyclopedia (Clark and Marshall, 1981). The encyclopedia is divided into chapters by cultural communities, properly nested and correlated, and when we want inside information or outside information about a community, we consult the right entry. There has been little research on what this information consists of and how it is organized, yet there is a good deal we can say about it.

HUMAN NATURE

Whenever I meet other humans – adults from anywhere in the world – I assume as common ground that they and I think in the same way about many things. I may be wrong, but I would still draw the inferences, and these would inform my actions as we tried to coordinate with each other. I possess a folk psychology about people in general – about human nature – and, right or wrong, it allows me to get started.

All of us take as common ground, I assume, that people normally have the same senses, sense organs, and types of sensations. If a sound is audible to me, it would normally be audible to others in the same circumstances. People also perceive motion, perceptual depth, pitches, and rhythms, and assume these ways of perceiving to be common ground. Less obviously, people are limited in what they can attend to at once, and the raw perceptual experiences that grab my attention – loud noises or sudden movements – will grab yours too. Certain varieties of perceptual salience are common ground to us all.

We all take it as common ground, also, that everyone knows the basic facts and laws of nature. People universally assume that they live in a world populated by animate and inanimate objects that are subject to gravity, Newton-like laws of motion, and laws of cause and effect. They take certain facts of biology for granted – for example, that animate things are born, take in food and water to live, then cease to function. They suppose that everyone assumes certain social facts – that people generally possess and use language, live together in groups, exchange goods and services, have names, play roles in various institutions, and so on. It is hard to exaggerate the number and variety of basic concepts we take as common ground to everyone.

COMMUNAL LEXICONS

Many inferences are based more narrowly on the language communities we know someone belongs to. If Soonja is a Korean speaker, I assume she takes as common ground to Korean speakers all the conventional features of Korean – its phonology, morphology, syntax, semantics, and pragmatics. This follows from Lewis' characterization of conventions as common knowledge within a community of speakers (Chapter 3). Precisely how these conventions are represented is a fundamental question for students of language, and there are diverse proposals on the table. I also assume Soonja takes for granted certain facts about how Korean speakers speak and understand – that they need more time and effort to deal with some aspects of Korean than others. All this is outside information that I take as common ground about using any language.

In Lewis' account, conventional word meanings hold not for a word *simpliciter*, but for a word *in a particular community*. You can't talk about conventional word meaning without saying what community it is conventional in. Word knowledge, properly viewed, divides into what I will call communal lexicons, by which I mean sets of word conventions in individual communities. When I meet Ann, she and I must establish as common ground which communities we both belong to simply in order to know what English words we can use with what meaning. Can I use *fermata*? Not without establishing that we are both music enthusiasts. Can I use *rbi*? Not without establishing that we are both baseball fans.

Every community has a specialized lexicon. We recognize these lexicons in the terms we have for them in English:

Residence	regional or local dialects, patois, provincialisms, localisms, regionalisms, colloquialisms, idiom, Americanisms, etc.
Occupation	jargon, shoptalk, parlance, nomenclature, technical terminology, academese, legalese, medicalese, Wall Streetese, etc.
Subculture	slang, argot, lingo, cant, vernacular, code, etc.

Most regions have their own dialect, patois, idiom, or regionalisms, with distinctive terms for everything from food to geographical features. Most occupations and hobbies, from physics to philately, have a technical jargon or terminology. So do most subcultures, from drug addicts to high school cliques.

When we think of jargon, slang, and regionalisms, we tend to focus on the words unique to a communal lexicon. *Meson*, *pion*, and *quark* are terms only a physicist could love. But most common word forms belong to many communal lexicons – though with different conventional meanings. In Britain, *biscuits* can be sweet or savory, but in America, they are always savory. In common parlance, *fruit* denotes a class of edible, sweet, fleshy agricultural products; among botanists, it denotes the ripened ovary or ovaries of seed-bearing plants, whether or not they are edible, sweet, and fleshy. Two botanists in conversation would have to establish which lexicon they were drawing on. You and I would be forced to stay with common parlance. It is essential to identify the cultural communities our interlocutors do and don't belong to just to know what vocabulary we can use.

CULTURAL FACTS, NORMS, PROCEDURES

If Sam is an American, I can suppose he takes lots of things as common ground for Americans. Virtually all adult Americans assume a certain background of *facts*: the basics of history, geography, mathematics, science, and literature learned in school; certain current events – including names of prominent politicians, movie stars, television personalities; and certain cultural artifacts – professional football teams, the major television networks, newspapers, and magazines, and the major religious and political groups and their characteristics.

Americans also take for granted among Americans certain *conventions* and *norms* – driving on the right, eating three meals a day, not waiting in queues at bus stops, paying one's taxes, and wearing dark clothes to funerals. If Jack is a middle-class Californian, I suppose he takes it as common ground that most of his group will follow norms about when to arrive at a party, what to wear where, and what are acceptable topics of conversation when, and will have certain social skills, such as how to argue, how to meet new people, and how to behave toward shopkeepers. They will take for granted certain social roles, such as those of husband, wife, child, neighbor, and how these roles fit into larger institutions, such as the family, the neighborhood, the tennis club.

Much of what people take as common ground may be represented in the form of *procedures* for joint activities. There are the routine actions, such as shaking hands and offering thanks – when, with whom, and how (Galambos and Rips, 1982). There are also the larger "scripts," specifying the expected course of the joint activities that take place in restaurants, doctors' offices, supermarkets (Minsky, 1975; Schank and Abelson, 1975). The script for patronizing a restaurant, for example, specifies certain props, roles, entry conditions, results, and actions, as here:[5]

Script name	Restaurant
Props	Tables, menu, food, bill, money, tip
Roles	Customer, waiter or waitress, cook, cashier, owner
Entry conditions	Customer is hungry
	Customer has money
Results	Customer has less money
	Owner has more money
	Customer is not hungry
Actions	Customer enters restaurant
	Customer looks for table
	Customer decides where to sit
	Etc.

The script proper represents the expected joint activities as a customer goes to a restaurant. Scripts such as this have been shown to influence people's understanding and memory of stories about going to restaurants, attending lectures, shopping for groceries, and visiting a doctor (Bower, Black, and Turner, 1979). To have this influence, they must be assumed to be common ground. When I meet Soonja, I take it as common ground that we have outside information about the scripts for restaurants in America and Korea, but not that we both have inside information. Restaurant scripts may be very different in the two countries. Other scripts vary by local region and social class as well.

---

[5] Adapted from Bower, Black, and Turner (1979), who adapted it from Schank and Abelson (1975).

INEFFABLE BACKGROUND

If Nancy is a San Franciscan, I assume she takes as common ground to San Franciscans not merely a large range of facts about San Francisco – about people, places, buildings, history, cultural life – but also certain information about *appearance* and *perspective*. She takes for granted what the Golden Gate Bridge, Coit Tower, and Chinatown look like, what happens when the fog comes in, how gaudy it is on Broadway near Columbus, and what you can see from Fisherman's Wharf. She assumes adult San Franciscans have some mental map of the city and know roughly what they would see traveling from one point to another.

As an accomplished pianist, Michael can take for granted among accomplished pianists not just knowledge of musical conventions, but also a repertoire of performance skills. They have not only knowledge-that but *know-how*. He might assume, for example, that they can all play certain scales and arpeggios, produce certain varieties of staccato and legato, play certain rhythms at many speeds, and play at a range of volumes. They know what actions are and aren't possible. They know how it feels to play well and assume other accomplished pianists take this for granted too.

As a skillful skier, Julia can take for granted among skiers what it is to have experiences that all skiers must have – the feel of cold wind on your face, the pressure of deep versus hard pack snow on your skis, the smell of pine forests in winter, the sensation of warming up cold hands and feet. Many of these experiences are ineffable. Others cannot understand them unless they have had them themselves. For other cultural communities, we might include such experiences as how a woman feels in a male society (and vice versa), how a member of a minority group feels, and how it feels to be a born-again Christian. These experiences are the ultimate inside information.

GRADING OF INFORMATION

The information we infer from membership in a community isn't all or none but *graded*, and what is remarkable is how accurate we are in this grading. Consider a series of studies by Susan Fussell and Robert Krauss (1991, 1992; Krauss and Fussell, 1991). In one of them, Columbia University students were shown pictures of fifteen public figures and asked to rate how identifiable they were to other Columbia students. Their judgments were graded. The actors Woody Allen and Clint

Eastwood were judged to be highly identifiable; the financiers Carl Icahn and T. Boone Pickens – who are they anyway? – were not. These judgments were also accurate. Columbia students could name Allen and Eastwood 93 and 80 percent of the time, but Icahn and Pickens only 7 and 0 percent of the time. The correlation between judgments and actual identifiability was .95. There was a similar pattern for New Yorkers' ability to name New York landmarks, and for men's and women's ability to name kitchen implements, tools, and musical instruments.

As individuals, we have an intuitive feeling for what we do and don't know, even when we cannot recall a piece of information at the moment. This has been called one's *feeling of knowing*, and its accuracy is well documented (e.g., Hart, 1965, 1967; Nelson, Leonesio, Landwehr, and Narens, 1986). As Fussell and Krauss' findings show, we also have an intuitive feeling about what others know, which we might call *feeling of others' knowing*, and it too is often very accurate (Brennan and Williams, 1995; Jameson, Nelson, Leonesio, and Narens, 1993; Nickerson, Baddeley, Freeman, 1987). Where does this feeling come from? Partly from our own feeling of knowing. It makes good sense to judge what others are likely to know based on what we know (Dawes, 1990). Do you know the number of US senators? As an American, I know the number, and if I generalize from my sample of one, if you are an American, you might well know too.

Our feeling of others' knowing does, in fact, have a strong egocentric bias: If I know something, I am more likely to expect others to know it too. This has come to be known as the *false consensus effect* (Ross, Greene, and House, 1977), and it is ubiquitous in judgments of factual information, political opinions, personal problems, and other types of information (Hoch, 1987; Marks and Miller, 1987; Mullen et al., 1985). In Fussell and Krauss' study, about half of the Columbia students tested were able to name a picture of General Alexander Haig. These same students thought that Haig would be much more identifiable than did the other students who were not able to name Haig's picture.

In judging what others know, we take into account the communities we and others belong to. It is because I am an American that I know the number of US senators. For Ann, a New Zealander, this is not inside information, and she may not know it. After all, I don't know the size of New Zealand's parliament. I would judge Ann less likely than another American to know the size of the Senate. In Fussell and Krauss' study, male and female students were quite accurate in judging which kitchen implements, tools, and musical instruments males would know better than females and vice versa. Here again, people identify inside and outside information based on community membership.

Common ground based on membership in cultural communities includes facts, beliefs, and assumptions about objects, norms of behavior, conventions, procedures, skills, and even ineffable experiences. These may be represented in many ways – as verbalized statements, as mental images and maps, as ways of perceiving and behaving we cannot or ordinarily do not describe. All this information is graded. There is little question that we exploit some such notion of common ground in language use and other joint actions.

Personal common ground

Much of our common ground is based on joint personal experiences. When my son and I look at a conch shell together or talk about the Isle of Lewis, we can later use these personal experiences, events, or episodes as shared bases for inferring that what we saw or talked about is common ground. Most of these experiences fall into two categories – *joint perceptual experiences* and *joint actions*. Perceptual experiences rely on the perception of natural signs of things, whereas joint actions depend on the interpretation of intentional signals.[6]

PERCEPTUAL BASES

One prototypical basis for personal common ground is an event in which two people share a perceptual experience. When my son and I look at the conch shell together, I take it that we are perceiving an event e with three properties:

1. he and I are aware of e
2. e indicates to him and me that we are both aware of e
3. e indicates to him and me that there is a conch shell between us

The event as perceived doesn't indicate to either of us, for example, that there is a snail shell between us, or that I or my son are merely feigning attention to the shell. He, I, and the object *qua* conch shell can be said to be "openly present together," a case of *perceptual copresence* (Clark and Marshall, 1981). This is precisely the sort of event that serves as the shared basis for our mutual belief that there is a conch shell between us.

---

[6] The contrast here is between Grice's notions of natural meaning and nonnatural meaning (see Chapter 5).

Each of us lives in a world of perceptible things, entities we can look at, feel, hear, smell, taste. At any moment, we have perceptual access, with more or less effort, to only part of that world, our *perceptual shell*. You and I have distinct perceptual shells, but when we are together, they overlap. But having overlapping perceptual shells isn't sufficient for perceptual copresence. You and I must manage to attend to the same things and to become confident that we have done so in the right way.

How do two people manage to attend to the same things and establish cases of perceptual copresence? Generally, it takes some salient event that leads each of them to assume they are jointly experiencing the same thing. Jointly salient events get established in three main ways (see Chapter 6).

1. *Gestural indications.* As speaker, I can gesture toward a chair, saying "that chair," and get you, as addressee, to turn and look at the chair. Executed properly, this becomes an instance of perceptual copresence, and I can infer that the chair's presence is common ground. With gestures, I can locate objects, places, events, and even states.

2. *Partner's activities.* You can look at people, pick up objects, and attend to things without the intention of letting me know you are doing so. But if I am also part of such an event, it can become an instance of perceptual copresence. If I notice you looking at a painting in a gallery, I could say "That is by Picasso," by which you could assume I noticed you looking at the painting and, now that you knew this, its presence was common ground.

3. *Salient perceptual events.* If I hear a loud scream from the next room, and you are with me, I can assume that it caught your attention as much as it did mine and so it is perceptually copresent. I can then ask "Who was that?" Our attention may be captured by a horse in a parade that fell, the distinctive smell of a sugar factory we are passing, or the oaky flavor of a bad wine we are drinking – any perceptually distinctive event.

Perceptual events are never dealt with in the raw. They are always perceived *qua d*, where *d* is a description that depends on communal common ground. In the gallery, it must be common ground that I am using *Picasso* to refer to the painter, not to a color, the name of the person portrayed, or the style of painting. Otherwise, the object "*qua* painting by Picasso" won't be common ground. With perceptual events, discrepancies of interpretation will lead to discrepancies in two people's beliefs about their common ground.

ACTIONAL BASES

Another basis for personal common ground is joint action, and the prototype is talk. If I say to you "She's going outside" in the right circumstances, from then on I can take it as common ground to the two of us that I had asserted that Elizabeth was just then leaving her house. How? As with joint perceptual experiences, I need an event *e* with three properties:

1. you and I are aware of *e*
2. *e* indicates to you and me that we are both aware of *e*
3. *e* indicates to each of us that I asserted to you that Elizabeth was just then leaving her house

At first, these conditions seem easy to satisfy. As long as I assume you know English, all I have to do is say to you "She's going outside." But the more closely we look at it, the more complicated it is for you and me to engineer an event that satisfies these three conditions – a proper basis for my assertion. This is a fundamental issue for theories of language use, and one I will take up in detail in the next several chapters.

Using joint actions as a basis for common ground rests on communal common ground – just as using joint perceptual experiences does. For you to understand "She's going outside," we must each take as common ground the linguistic conventions on which this utterance is based – the meanings of *she, go,* and *outside,* the syntax of intransitive verbs, the semantics of progressive aspect. We must also go into our common ground about Elizabeth, her house, our purposes in the discourse at the moment, who else is in the conversation, and even who might be over-hearing us. These are issues I will return to as well.

PERSONAL DIARIES

What sort of memory representations do we need for inferring personal common ground? We need more than an encyclopedia, with its facts, beliefs, and assumptions about entire communities, since it won't represent your or my personal experiences. We need a personal diary, a log of those events we have personally experienced or taken part in with others (Clark and Marshall, 1978).

Why? All of the shared bases for personal common ground are auto-biographical events of a special type – joint perceptual experiences or joint actions. If I keep a mental diary of the events I experience, it will contain, along with other entries, records of just these events. Suppose I search through the entries in my diary and find a record of the actional copresence of you, me, and my assertion that Elizabeth was leaving her house an hour ago. That entry is all I need for thinking that you and I mutually believe I asserted that. We can think of the shared bases for personal common ground as derived from entries in our personal diaries.

How are personal diaries organized? For an entry to be used as the shared basis for common ground, it must represent the diarist, another person, and the entity that they jointly experienced. These should also be organized so they can be searched quickly and without effort. Entries organized chronologically wouldn't seem very useful, so we might anticipate other modes of organization.

FRIENDS AND STRANGERS

If communal common ground defines cultural communities, then personal common ground defines friends versus strangers. Ann and Ben may jointly belong to many cultural communities and still be strangers. They won't be friends or acquaintances until they have a history of joint personal experiences – things done, talked about, or experienced together. A third party, Connie, may be a clever spy and learn as much about Ann as Ben knows, but that doesn't make her Ann's friend or acquaintance. The information she gathers must be in their common ground – part of their personal common ground. Whereas ophthalmologists are experts in ophthalmology, friends are experts about each other (Planalp, 1993; Planalp and Benson, 1992: Planalp and Garvin-Doxas, 1994).

Acquaintedness comes in degrees defined largely by the type and amount of personal common ground two people have. Here, for illustration, are four degrees:

1. *Strangers*: no personal common ground
2. *Acquaintances*: limited personal common ground
3. *Friends*: extensive personal common ground
4. *Intimates*: extensive personal common ground, including private information

If Ann and Ben have had no contact with each other, they have no personal common ground. They are strangers. If they have had limited contact, they have limited personal common ground, and they are acquaintances. As they expand their joint experiences, they are more likely to consider themselves friends. Friendship normally implies liking and trust. That is what it takes to experience and do things together over a long time. If Ann and Ben are intimates, they will also share private information about each other – about their most personal feelings, attitudes, and behavior – and that normally takes even deeper liking and trust.

Just as cultural communities develop communal lexicons, acquaintances, friends, and intimates develop *personal lexicons*. Families often develop special words for private matters and personal problems, and so do small circles of friends. The best-studied personal lexicons are among intimates.

Married partners and other couples often develop what have been called *personal idioms*, which are not conventional in the community at large (Hopper, Knapp, and Scott, 1981). Here are the major categories of these idioms (from Hopper et al.):

Category	Examples
Nicknames for partner	"Boo," "Toots," "Honski"
Names for others	"motz" for a slow disorganized person
Expressions of affection	"Hunch nickle" for "I love you"
Expressions of confrontation	"Jelly beans" for "You're talking over my head"
Requests and routines	"Let's go for a bike ride" as invitation to smoke marijuana
References to sexual parts	"Bozo" for the male partner's genitals
Invitations to sex	"Too-hoot"
Teasing insults	"Futtbutt" for a wife with large buttocks

Some of these terms – like pet names – may be used in public, but others are used strictly in private. In general, the larger the lexicon, the greater the solidity of the couple (Bell and Healey, 1992).

Personal lexicons are as much a part of language use as communal lexicons. It is just that they originate and get maintained in joint personal experiences, and are used for local, often private, purposes.

Building up common ground

Common ground isn't just there, ready to be exploited. We have to establish it with each person we interact with. Communal common ground, as we have seen, is based on two people's mutual belief that one or both are members of a particular community – women, English speakers, New Zealanders, ophthalmologists – and personal common ground, on joint perceptual experiences and joint actions. The first step in establishing either type of common ground is finding the right shared bases – the right evidence.

EVIDENCE OF COMMUNITY MEMBERSHIP

If Susan is trying to infer what cultural communities Bill is a member of, she might use *circumstantial evidence* – that is, enduring features of the circumstances she finds Bill in. Or she might use *episodic evidence* – actions that Bill performs or events he is part of.

Circumstantial evidence is surprisingly useful. Susan can infer a great deal from *natural evidence* about Bill. His physical appearance types him as human, adult, male, middle-aged. On the telephone, his voice types him as human, adult, and male. His language and accent may identify where he is from, how educated he is, and what language communities he belongs to. And Susan realizes that Bill can draw the corresponding inferences about her. For any of these types to become common ground, Susan must assume that the evidence itself is manifestly part of their common ground. Sherlock Holmes may identify a man as a shoemaker from the calluses on his thumb, but unless the shoemaker realized this, neither of them would take his occupation to be common ground.

People *deliberately display* certain community affiliations in their dress, manner, and possessions. If Bill wears a Macy's badge in Macy's Department Store, a Texaco uniform at a Texaco gasoline station, or a white coat and stethoscope in a hospital, he makes it public – he provides mutually recognizable evidence for him and those he meets – that he claims to be a member of these organizations and available to serve. By wearing a conservative suit and tie, he claims to be a middle-class businessman or professional. Dress is reflected in the very terms *blue-collar* and *white-collar worker*. Bill would type himself as a Giants' baseball fan by wearing a Giants' cap, as a Jew by wearing a yarmulke, as a rural Western American by wearing a bolo tie, and as a man by wearing male clothing. By driving a new Mercedes-Benz or living in a mansion, he is manifestly displaying a claim to high socio-economic status. Susan can assume he intended such evidence to be mutually obvious and to justify the mutual belief that he is a member of these communities.

People also display community membership by their location in the *current situation*. In drugstores, supermarkets, restaurants, hospitals, and offices, people stand behind desks, service counters, and checkout stands in order to display themselves as employees and servers. The people who take part in church, synagogue, or mosque rites are displaying their membership in that religion. Baseball aficionados sit in the rooting section of a Giants' game to show themselves to be Giants' fans. Taken together, these types of circumstantial evidence are highly effective bases for community membership:

Community	Type of circumstantial evidence
Nationality	dress, language, dialect, current situation
Residence	dress, language, dialect, current situation
Education	dress, dialect, current situation
Occupation	dress, current situation, jargon
Employment	dress, current situation
Hobby	dress, current situation, jargon
Language	language, dialect, vocabulary
Religion	dress, current situation, vocabulary
Ethnicity	bodily appearance, dress, dialect, accent
Subculture	dress, jargon
Cohort	bodily appearance, dress, voice quality
Gender	bodily appearance, dress, voice quality

Episodic evidence may be just as useful as circumstantial evidence. Susan and Bill can establish community membership, for example, by what they *assert*. In introducing himself, Bill may tell Susan, "I am a computer scientist. I was raised in Manhattan, but I have lived in San Francisco now for ten years." Once these assertions become part of a conversational record, Susan can take it as common ground that he is a computer scientist, native of Manhattan, and resident of San Francisco.

People also disclose communal affiliations in what they *presuppose*. In a study by Ellen Isaacs and myself (1987), a person we called the director was asked to tell another person we called the matcher how to arrange sixteen post cards of New York landmarks in a particular order. One or both or neither of the two people – there were thirty-two pairs in all – were New Yorkers. Although the two of them didn't know ahead of time who were New Yorkers and who weren't, they found out immediately, as in this exchange about a postcard of the Citicorp Center:

Director: Number ten is just one huge building pointed at the top, Citicorp Center.
Matcher: And you're looking, are you looking at it from the base?
Director: Yes, there's there's just two buildings that are visible.
Matcher: Okay.

Here the director revealed her expertise on New York (1) by naming the building and (2) by describing the building itself, not the picture of the building. The matcher revealed his *lack* of expertise (1) by not recognizing the building from its name and (2) by focusing on the picture of the building, not seeing through the picture to the building itself. Using this information (and not accent), people in this study were able to distinguish New Yorkers from non-New Yorkers 85 percent of the time after just two postcards.

Disclosure of expertise can be subtler. In a gambling casino, when Bill sprinkles his speech with gambling jargon, he gives Susan evidence for the mutual belief that he is an experienced gambler. Such a disclosure is to be seen as adventitious. Bill doesn't use the jargon just to get Susan to think he is an expert gambler. Their mutual belief is merely a consequence of his doing that. At least, it is ostensibly so. Bill may use the jargon to deceive Susan into thinking he was an expert gambler. It would defeat his purpose if she suspected the deception.

It is easy to demonstrate that people use both circumstantial and episodic evidence. When a Harvard student named Kingsbury approached pedestrians in Boston and asked in a local accent "Can you tell me how to get to Jordan Marsh?" (a nearby department store), the directions he got were brief and practical for someone from the Boston area (Krauss and Glucksberg, 1977; Krauss and Fussell, 1991). When he added "I'm from out of town," the directions became more elaborate, mentioning more landmarks and describing how to identify the destination. They were just as elaborate when he adopted a rural Missouri accent.[7] Presumably, they would have been equally elaborate if he had revealed his lack of local expertise, say, by misnaming the store "Jordan March" (Schegloff, 1972). Bostonians designed their directions to suit the relevant communities they and Kingsbury could mutually believe he was a member of – locals, out-of-towners, or southerners.

STRATA IN COMMON GROUND

Every new piece of common ground is built on an old piece. Ann and I, for example, took it as common ground that she had inside information about New Zealand. That was based on our mutual belief that she was a New Zealander. But that mutual belief was based on another old piece of common ground, her assertion that she was from New Zealand. That in turn was based on the mutual beliefs that she uttered "I'm from New

---

[7] This is the source of a complaint I have heard from many people with non-local accents or dialects. No matter how long they have lived in an area, the locals treat them as out-of-towners or foreigners when giving them directions.

Zealand" and that I construed it as intended. These mutual beliefs in turn were based on the mutual belief that I was attending to what she was saying and that she accepted my acknowledgment that I understood what she meant. These were based in turn on, among other things, our mutual belief that I understood English and knew what New Zealand referred to. And on it went.

Common ground gets built up in strata. For Ann and me, not all the strata were laid down the instant she told me she was from New Zealand. We had already established as common ground that we were attending to each other, that we were both English speakers, that she was addressing me, that she and I were adhering to the same practices of reaching a joint construal of her utterances, that she was speaking seriously and not just practicing a line from a play, and more. Our common ground got built up stratum by stratum.

We are left with an apparent paradox: If every new piece of common ground is built on an old one, where does it start? Is there a first piece of common ground, and if so, what is it based on? The paradox is more apparent than real. Each of us has built up information about others from infancy. Originally, we may have taken much of this information as common ground – as children often do – without a proper basis. Children first appear to think that their interlocutors are omniscient, and it is only with age that they set higher standards. By that time, the lower strata are in place, and the rest can follow. And we have systematic methods for correcting incorrect pieces of common ground. It isn't necessary – or even usual – to get things right the first time around.

Conclusions

People cannot take joint actions without assuming certain pieces of common ground. But what is common ground, and how does it get established?

Common ground is a form of self-awareness. Two people, Susan and Bill, are aware of certain information they each have. To be common ground, their awareness must be reflexive – it must include that very awareness itself. Ordinarily, people can justify a piece of their common ground by pointing to a shared basis for it – a joint perceptual experience or a joint action. These shared bases range in quality, which leads to a grading of judgments. Some shared bases are excellent evidence that a piece of information is part of common ground, and others are poor evidence. If I identify Susan as an American adult, I can be certain she knows the name of the current US President, but not that she knows the Thirteenth Amendment to the Constitution.

The common ground between two people divides into two broad types. Communal common ground is information based on the cultural communities a person is believed to belong to – from nationality and occupation to ethnic group and gender. Personal common ground is information based on personal acquaintance: It is lacking in strangers and greatest for intimates. The information people take to be common ground ranges from broad inferences about human nature through languages and dialects and jargons, cultural standards and procedures, to ineffable sights and sounds and feelings.

What is important for us is how common ground gets staked out and exploited. So far we have looked at some circumstantial and episodic bases for common ground. But the topic is vast – and really the topic of the rest of the book.

PART III

Communicative acts

5 | Meaning and understanding

All speech, written or spoken, is a dead language,
until it finds a willing and prepared hearer.
Robert Louis Stevenson,
Reflections and Remarks on Human Life

When people take part in joint activities – business transactions, chess games, piano duets – they perform a variety of joint actions. They say things to each other, hand things to each other, nod at each other, gaze at each other, and through these advance their joint activities. Many of these joint actions, or their parts, are *communicative acts* through which they get others to understand what they mean. What sort of acts are these, and how do they work?

The traditional view is that communicative acts are performed by a speaker autonomously. In the drugstore, when Stone said "I'll be right there," she was making a promise on her own. Although she directed it at me, I had no real part in it. A promise expresses a commitment to do something in the future, and speakers express such commitments on their own. In that tradition, the focus is on speakers. There is no mention, no hint, that addressees have any role.

Paradoxically, the traditional view carries the seeds of its own destruction. The very notion of meaning – speaker's meaning – requires addressees to join speakers in a special way, and so do other notions of speech acts. We will discover, on closer examination, that communicative acts are inherently joint acts, and that they are just one level of an entire ladder of joint actions. To begin, let us turn to what is at the heart of all communicative acts: meaning.

Meaning
In 1957, in a ten-page paper entitled "Meaning," Herbert Paul Grice[1] presented a theory of meaning that revolutionized the study of language

---

[1] Grice, for some reason, went by Paul rather than Herbert.

use. He began by distinguishing the meaning of certain natural events, which I will call *natural signs* or *symptoms*, from the meaning of certain deliberate human acts, which I am calling *signals*. Compare these two statements:

1. Those spots mean that Margaret has the measles.
2. The doctor's hand wave means that Margaret has the measles.

The spots described in 1 are a natural sign – a symptom or direct evidence – that Margaret has the measles. If I tell a friend, "Those spots mean that Margaret has the measles," I am committed to the belief that Margaret has the measles. But the hand wave in 2 (say, through a glass barrier in a hospital) means what it does in part because of the doctor's intentions toward me, which are to tell me that Margaret has the measles. Unlike the spots, the gesture bears no natural connection to measles. And if I tell a friend, "The doctor's hand wave means that Margaret has the measles," I am not committed to the belief that Margaret has the measles – the doctor could be wrong. Grice called these two kinds of meaning *natural meaning* and *non-natural meaning*. In my terminology, symptoms have natural meaning, and signals have non-natural meaning.

Language use depends on both natural signs and signals. Take natural signs. The sounds I hear mean that the radio is on. The shape of the object my friend is holding means that it is a book. The pitch of a caller's voice means that he is a man. A speaker's involuntary hesitation in uttering a word means that he probably had difficulty thinking of, choosing, or pronouncing it in time. Most things have a natural meaning, and these can be important for language use because they are all natural signs that this or that is true. What distinguishes language use is that it always involves non-natural meaning as well.

SPEAKER'S MEANING AND SIGNAL MEANING

Non-natural meaning itself, according to Grice, divides into two types: *speaker's* (or utterer's) *meaning*, and what I will call *signal meaning*. Consider these descriptions:

3. By uttering "I surrender," Sam meant that he was surrendering.
4. By waving a white flag, Sam meant that he was surrendering.
5. By uttering "I am hungry," Elizabeth meant that she was in need of food at that moment.
6. By pointing at her mouth and an empty plate, Elizabeth meant that she was in need of food at that moment.

All four examples describe what a speaker meant. They each fit a standard frame for speaker's meaning:

Speaker's meaning. By presenting *s* to A, S meant for A that *p*.

In this frame, S denotes the agent of the action, like a speaker or letter writer; A denotes a certain audience; and *s* denotes a deliberate human action, a signal, like waving a flag or uttering a sentence. The following descriptions, in contrast, describe what a signal means or meant:

7.   The sentence *I am hungry* can mean that the speaker, whoever that is, is in need of food at the moment he or she utters the sentence.
8.   The word *hungry* can mean "in need of food."
9.   Elizabeth's utterance, "I am hungry," meant that she was in need of food at the moment she produced the utterance.
10. Elizabeth's gesture at her mouth and empty plate meant that she was in need of food at that moment.

All these examples fit a standard frame for signal meaning:

Signal meaning. s means or meant "*y*," or that *p*.

As before, *s* denotes a deliberate human action, a signal; in addition, *p* denotes a proposition, and *y* a paraphrase.

It is odd to have to explain the difference between speaker's meaning and signal meaning. In German, they are called *Gemeintes* and *Bedeutung*, in Dutch, *bedoeling* and *betekenis*, and in French, *intention* and *signification*. For theorists working in German, Dutch, and French, they are as different as apples and oranges. Yet for theorists working in English, they are a chronic source of confusion because they have the same name – *meaning*.[2] In language use, it is essential to keep them straight.

Signal meaning comes in several varieties. Example 7 describes an instance of sentence meaning, one way in which the sentence *I am hungry* can be used on a particular occasion. (The same sentence can be used in other ways too.) Example 8 describes an instance of word meaning, or one way in which the word *hungry* can be used on a particular occasion. And example 9 describes an instance of utterance meaning, what Elizabeth's act of uttering the sentence meant on that particular occasion. In 9, one of the conventional meanings of the

---

[2] It is almost enough to make one believe in Benjamin Lee Whorf's linguistic determinism.

sentence Elizabeth uttered bears a relation to the meaning of her utterance, but that relation could have been very indirect, even absent. The doctor's hand wave in 2, for example, may have been a signal she and I decided on for that occasion alone. Other times it might mean nothing or something entirely different.

These distinctions are important. Words and sentences are *types* of signals, linguistic units abstracted away from any occasion on which they might be used, stripped of all relation to particular speakers, listeners, times, and places. To describe them is to describe the conventions for their use within speech communities (see Chapters 3 and 4). But utterances are the actions of producing words, sentences, and other things on particular occasions by particular speakers for particular purposes. The study of language structure is primarily about the conventions that govern words, sentences, and their meanings. But in conversations, books, and newspapers, we deal with *utterances* of words, sentences, and other things, and that requires a different approach.

Non-natural meaning isn't confined to uses of conventional languages like English, Japanese, or Dakota, nor did Grice ever intend it to be. Signals can be both "linguistic" (belonging to a conventional language), as in 3, 5, 7, 8, and 9, and "non-linguistic," as in 2, 4, 6, and 10. In the frame for speaker's meaning, the speaker is "presenting *s*" and not merely "uttering *s*." Ordinary language use depends on both. In conversation, people not only issue words, but also pause, gesture with their hands, head, eyes, and shoulders, and present other non-linguistic signals (Chapter 6). They use these in combination to say what they mean. So when I use the terms *utterances*, *speakers*, and *speaker's meaning*, I normally intend *signals*, *signalers*, and *signaler's meaning*.

Speaker's meaning and signal meaning, though different, are obviously connected. Speakers mean something only by using signals, and signals mean something only because they are used by speakers to mean something. Still, speaker's meaning is logically prior in several respects. Many signals have no *conventional* meaning. What these mean gets fixed only by what speakers meant in using them on particular occasions. One noon at a lunch with friends, I reminded my wife of an impending dentist appointment by taking an obvious look at my watch. But looking at one's watch doesn't conventionally or usually mean "you are due at the dentist's soon." Here what the speaker is inferred to mean helps us determine what the signal means, and not just vice versa.

The principle is general. We cannot talk about a signal having meaning without assuming an agent or speaker behind it. The doctor's hand wave from the other side of the glass meant that Margaret had the measles only because I assumed the doctor waved with those intentions in mind. If I discovered that the doctor was waving at someone behind me, or that her gesture wasn't intended to be the one we had agreed on, I wouldn't take her to mean that Margaret had the measles. The same is true of a word like *hungry*. It can mean "in need of food" only because of a convention that it can mean that – there is a community of people who can mean "in need of food" by uttering it in the right situations (Chapter 3). So to say "*s* meant (or means) something" is tantamount to saying "somebody meant (or can mean) something by *s*": the agent, the somebody, must be included. In this sense, speaker's meaning is primary, and signal meaning secondary.

WHAT IS SPEAKER'S MEANING?

It was Grice's insight that speaker's meaning has to do with getting other people to do things, but only by certain means.[3] Suppose Sam took you to the window to let you see the rain outside. He got you to believe that it was raining out, and you recognized his intention to get you to believe that. Still, you wouldn't say, "By presenting this scene to me, Sam meant that it was raining out." For speaker's meaning, Grice argued, your recognition of Sam's intention must serve as part of your reason for thinking that it's raining out. If, instead, Sam had said simply, "It's raining out," his intentions would have been essential. If you had thought he was practicing a line from a play, or reading from a novel, or offering an example of a present progressive verb, you wouldn't have taken him as meaning it was raining out. You thought that was what he meant in part because you recognized his intention that you think that.

Precisely how to formulate speaker's meaning has been debated ever since Grice's first proposal. Here is a formulation that is faithful to Grice's original idea, but has been amended in several ways:[4]

---

[3] See Grice (1957, 1968), Schiffer (1972), Strawson (1964), and Searle (1969), among others.

[4] This formulation is based on some but not all arguments in Strawson (1964), Grice (1968, 1982), Searle (1969), Bach and Harnish (1979), Harman (1977), Sperber and Wilson (1986), Récanati (1986), and Thomason (1990).

Speaker's meaning (reflexive)
In presenting *s* to audience A, a speaker S means for A that *p* if and only if:
(*i*) S intends in presenting *s* to A that A recognize that *p* in part by recognizing that *i*.

Speaker's meaning is a type of intention. When I say to you "Please sit down," my intention is for you to recognize that I want you to sit down. But as part of your reason for thinking this, you must recognize my very intention in presenting what I did. So speaker's meaning is a *reflexive* intention: intention *i* contains a reference to *i* itself. Grice called it an *m-intention* (for "meaning intention"), which he took to be essential to all non-natural meaning.

SIGNALING AND RECOGNIZING

Grice's m-intention – the heart of speaker's meaning – is a curious type of intention: It is one the speaker cannot discharge without the audience's participation. When I say "Please sit down" and mean you are to sit down, I rely on you doing your part by recognizing what I mean. In Grice's formulation, my intention depends directly on your recognition of that intention. I can discharge my intention to shake a stick, an autonomous action, without anyone else's actions. But I cannot discharge my intention to do my part of our hand shake, a joint action, without you doing your part. Here my individual act is a participatory act, which I perform as part of a joint act that requires you to do your part too (Chapters 1 and 3). The same is true of signaling and recognizing. The principle I wish to defend is this:

Signal recognition principle. Signaling and recognizing in communicative acts are participatory acts.

The joint act of one person signaling another and the second recognizing what the first meant I will call a *communicative act*.

To see how signaling and recognizing work, let us examine them from the inside, as actions in progress. Recall that when Ann and Ben play a flute-piano duet, we have a joint action *r* and their individual participatory actions:

Ensemble A-and-B are playing a flute–piano duet *r* in situation *w* if and only if:
0. the duet *r* includes 1 and 2;
1. A is playing the flute part as part of *r*;
2. B is playing the piano part as part of *r*.

So for Ann to be playing her flute part as part of the duet, she must be playing it believing Ben to be playing his piano part as part of the same duet. If half way through the duet she thinks Ben is no longer doing his part – he has stopped playing because his music blew away – she will no longer consider them to be playing the duet – to be performing participatory actions as parts of that duet. If she does play on, she will consider herself to be playing alone. The point is crucial. Ann's and Ben's participatory actions are interlinked: Ann cannot consider herself to be playing her part as part of the duet without assuming Ben is playing his part as part of the same duet, and vice versa.

So it goes with the participatory acts of signaling and recognizing. Suppose Ann presents signal s to Ben (e.g., she utters "Please sit down") meaning that p (e.g., that he is to sit down). Again we have a joint act r and participatory acts (1) and (2):

Speaker's meaning (joint)
In presenting s to A, speaker S means for A that p if and only if:
  0. the communicative act r includes 1 and 2;
  1. S presents s to A intending that p as part of r;
  2. A recognizes that p as part of r.

When Ann utters "Please sit down" as part of r, she expects Ben to do his part. Ben must recognize what she means in part by seeing that she is uttering "Please sit down" with the intention in 1. As in the duet, Ann's and Ben's actions are linked: Ann cannot consider herself to be asking Ben to sit down without assuming that Ben is intending to recognize these intentions, and vice versa.

Consider Ann's and Ben's actions half way through her utterance. If she thinks Ben is no longer doing his part, she will no longer consider them to be communicating; she will no longer consider herself to be asking Ben to sit down. Suppose Ann assumes Ben knows Dutch and says "Ga je even..." when Ben interrupts with "What?" before she can finish "zitten alsjeblieft." Although she begins her utterance intending Ben to recognize that she wants him to sit down, she is forced to abort that intention undischarged when she realizes Ben isn't doing his part. And although Ben may realize she has been trying to signal him, he realizes that she isn't succeeding (see Chapters 8 and 9).

The two-part representation just given brings out several basic properties of speaker's meaning. It divides communicative acts into their two natural parts – signaling and recognizing. Part 1 specifies the speaker's actions and responsibilities, and part 2, the hearer's actions and responsibilities. It also shows how the two actions are linked – how A's intentions depend on B's recognition, and vice versa. Finally, instead of putting all the onus on speakers, it treats speakers and addressees as partners. The idea, in short, is to treat signaling and recognizing for what they are – two parts of a joint act.

SIGNALING AS A COORDINATION DEVICE

Signals aren't important merely because they mean things. They are important because they are used in discourse to accomplish the participants' goals. When the server in the drugstore said "I'll be right there," she meant that she would be ready to serve me soon. But she was using the signal to coordinate her and my actions at that point in our transaction. Viewed in isolation, a signal is an act by which a speaker means something. Viewed within joint activities, it is an act by which the participants coordinate the next step in their ongoing activity. Signals are coordination devices.

Viewing signals as coordination devices gives us yet another perspective on speaker's meaning and audience's understanding. In the cumulative model of joint activities, participants use utterances and other signals to increment their current common ground. A signal is then the speaker's way of introducing into the discourse a shared basis for the piece of common ground to be added. Recall that a shared basis b for common ground has three properties (Chapter 4):

p is common ground for members of community C if and only if:
1. every member of C has information that b holds;
2. b indicates to every member of C that every member of C has information that b holds;
3. b indicates to members of C that p.

A signal that is recognized satisfies the same three properties:

1. S and A have information that S presented s to A;
2. s indicates to S and A that S and A have information that S presented s to A;
3. s indicates to S and A that S means for A that p.

So when the server uttered "I'll be right there," she was providing a shared basis for the next step in our transaction, a shared basis for incrementing our common ground.

Signaling is the prototypical coordination device in joint activities.

If the drugstore server wants to coordinate her actions with mine, her usual strategy is to present a signal and get me to recognize what she meant by it. Her signal serves as a shared basis for a mutual belief that we can then add to our common ground. In that way it carries the discourse forward to the next step.

Speech acts

Speakers get their addressees to recognize what they mean, in Grice's scheme, by taking actions toward them – by signaling them. What sorts of actions are these? One of the first to take this question seriously was John Austin. His 1957 William James Lectures were called "How to do things with words" (Austin, 1962), but they were really about how to do things with utterances. In them he proposed a general theory of speech acts – acts that people perform in speaking – in which he distinguished among many things people do with utterances. Some details of his argument have been eclipsed by work since then, but many of his basic insights remain.

Certain actions we take, Austin argued, are designed to get our audience to do things on the basis of their understanding of what we mean. Suppose I speak to my son, and he responds, as follows:

I request of him "Please pass the horseradish." He says "Okay," and passes it.
I ask him "What are you doing?" He answers "Getting ready to leave."
I tell him "That book is terrific." He believes me and starts reading it.
I warn him "Bruno is coming." He believes me and gets frightened.

My son complies with my request, answers my question, comes to believe what I assert, follows my advice, and gets scared, all based on his understanding of what I meant. In Austin's terminology, these are *perlocutionary effects*, or *perlocutions*, of my actions, and my acts in getting him to do them are *perlocutionary acts* (see Davis, 1979). Some perlocutionary effects are intended, and others aren't. If I unintentionally make my son laugh by asking him for the horseradish, his laugh is still a perlocution.

Perlocutions aren't part of understanding itself. My son could have understood my request for the horseradish, but refused to comply. He could have understood my assertion about the book, but not believed me. All he needed for understanding was to recognize my meaning. The act of getting the audience to recognize the speaker's meaning Austin called an *illocutionary act* and the recognition itself came to be called an *illocutionary effect* (Searle, 1969). My request, question, assertion, and warning are illocutionary acts, and my son's understanding of them are illocutionary effects.

TYPES OF ILLOCUTIONARY ACTS

Illocutionary acts come in many types. They include telling, asserting, requesting, ordering, asking, promising, apologizing, thanking, firing, and baptizing – there are over 150 such illocutionary verbs in English (Verschueren, 1980). Is there any order behind these acts? John Searle (1975c) argued there is. The primary way they differ is in what he called their *illocutionary point* – their publicly intended perlocutionary effect. For some illocutionary acts, the point is to get listeners to do things; for others, it is to commit the speaker to doing things; and so on. Searle used this notion to divide illocutionary acts into five main categories, the last of which I have divided into two:[5]

1. *Assertives*. The point of an assertive is to get the audience to form, or to attend to, the belief that the speaker is committed to a certain belief. When Sam told you, "It's raining out," he was trying to get you to think he believed it was raining out. The prototypical assertive is the assertion, but the category also includes diagnoses, predictions, notifications, confessions, denials, disputations, retorts, conjectures, suppositions, and many others.

2. *Directives*. The point of a directive is to get the audience to do things. When I asked my son, "Please pass the horseradish," I was trying to get him to pass me the horseradish. Directives fall into two major classes: requests for action (as with most commands and suggestions), and requests for information (as with most questions). With my question, "What are you doing?" I was asking my son for information. Directives vary in how forceful they are – from mild hints to stern commands – and in other ways too.

3. *Commissives*. The point of a commissive is to commit the speaker to a future action. The prototype is the promise, as when George says to Jane, "I'll get some coffee," committing himself to Jane to getting some coffee. One subtype is the conditional promise, or offer, as when George says to Jane, "Can I get you some coffee?" committing himself to getting her coffee if she wants it.

4. *Expressives*. The point of expressives like thanking, apologizing, congratulating, and greeting is to express certain feelings toward the

---

[5] The emendations come from Bach and Harnish (1979) and Hancher (1979).

audience. When Verona says to Wilfred, "Sorry I'm late," she takes for granted that she came late and tries to get Wilfred to believe she regrets it.

Next come illocutionary acts Searle called *declarations*. These rely on codified conventions of institutions such as the law, the church, and organized games. Within these institutions, speakers can do certain things by virtue of a privilege the institution grants them because of their role as judge, priest, referee, or whatever. Declarations divide into two main subcategories.

5a. *Effectives.* The point of an effective is to change an institutional state of affairs. In industry, a boss may fire, promote, or appoint someone. In court, a judge may indict, pardon, or sentence someone. A policeman may arrest someone. In football, a referee may start the game and call time outs. In church, a minister may baptize, marry, or bless someone. In each case, the speaker has the institutional power to change things merely by saying, "You're fired," "You are hereby sentenced to three years in jail," or "Time out" in the appropriate circumstances.

5b. *Verdictives.* With verdictives, the point is to determine what is to be the case within the institution. In baseball, umpires have to judge whether a ball that has been pitched has passed through the strike zone – whether it has crossed the plate between the batter's shoulder and knees. The umpire may try to be accurate, but when he says "Strike," his verdict is law from then on regardless of whether the ball actually passed through the strike zone. As far as the game is concerned, the ball did pass through the strike zone, and the pitch was a strike. Verdictives also occur when a jury finds a prisoner innocent or guilty, when the presiding officer in a meeting rules a motion out of order, and when a journal editor accepts or rejects a paper for publication.

Illocutionary act	Illocutionary point
assertives	to get the addressee to form or attend to a belief
directives	to get the addressee to do something
commissives	to commit the speaker to doing something
expressives	to express a feeling toward the addressee
effectives	to change an institutional state of affairs
verdictives	to determine what is the case in an institution

Searle's scheme, as summarized here, has many problems. One is that it doesn't generate all potential illocutionary acts. We can invent new rituals, new games, new social customs, each with its own special illocutionary acts, *ad infinitum*, but the scheme has no principles to say what is allowed, and what isn't. Another problem is that every illocutionary act is assumed to belong to one and only one category. But consider a general's order to a sergeant. Under military regulations, that order changes an institutional state of affairs just as surely as a judge's sentencing does – the sergeant could be court-martialed for not obeying – and that makes it an effective. Yet it is also surely a directive. The same goes for other illocutionary acts (see Hancher, 1979; Wunderlich, 1977). Despite its problems, the scheme is useful as a gross classification and for its widely accepted nomenclature. I shall use it for both.

ILLOCUTIONARY ACTS AND THEIR RECOGNITION

How do speakers get their addressees to recognize the illocutionary act they are performing? The classical answer is that they do so by their choice of sentence modality (e.g., Vanderveken, 1990). In English, there are five modalities:

Modality	Examples
Declarative	That book is awful. It is raining out.
Yes/no interrogative	Is it raining out?
WH- interrogative	What are you doing?
Imperative	Pass the horseradish.
Exclamatory	What a beautiful day! Is it ever hot out!

To assert something, you choose a declarative; to ask a question, an interrogative; to make a request or command, an imperative; and for an exclamation, an exclamatory. Your partners, by noting your choice of modality, can immediately recognize the illocutionary act you are performing.

This view is inadequate from the very start (Levinson, 1983). With only five modalities, we should be able to distinguish only five types of illocutionary acts, but we easily distinguish scores. The imperative, for example, can be used for at least these illocutions (Sadock and Zwicky, 1985; Sperber and Wilson, 1986, p. 250):

Illocutionary act	Example
Commands	To the rear, march
Requests	Please pass the horseradish
Promises	Mow the lawn and I'll pay you a dollar
Threats	Stop or I'll shoot
Warnings	Watch out!
Offers	Have some cake
Well wishing	Have a good trip
Advice	For a dry martini, mix six parts gin with one part vermouth
Curses	Go to hell
Exclamations	Well, look at you!
Exhortations	Fly American Airlines

Worse, these illocutionary acts range over four of Searle's five main categories. There is much the same variation for declarative and interrogative modalities.

A more sophisticated view makes use of what Levinson (1983) has called *illocutionary force identifying devices*, or *ifids*. The idea is that speakers use conventional devices in addition to sentence modality for specifying the illocutionary act they are performing. They might mark an utterance as a request with *please*, *Why not?*, or *I'd appreciate it very much if*; as a promise or offer with *I'll* or *Let me*; and so on. But it is easy to see that ifids, while informative, cannot do the job alone. Many utterances do not have enough ifids to pin down the illocutionary act the speaker is performing. The bare *Sit here* can be used as a request, command, advisory, threat, promise, exhortation, or offer, and it has no ifids to tell us which.

RECOGNITION AND UPTAKE

There is something missing in this picture of speech acts. At the center are speakers and what they do, but if there are any listeners, they are nowhere to be seen. It is as if the official portrait of a wedding included a groom but no bride. The terms *speech acts*, *illocutionary acts*, and *perlocutionary acts* describe what speakers do, but there are no comparable terms for what listeners do – as if their actions were irrelevant. Searle (1969) even argued: "The unit of linguistic communication is not ... the symbol, word, or sentence, but rather the production or issuance of the symbol, word, or sentence, in the performance of a speech act" (p. 16). For him, linguistic communication is like writing a letter and dropping it in the mail. It doesn't matter whether anybody receives, reads, or understands it. This view is, of course, absurd.[6] There can be no communication without listeners taking actions too – without them understanding what speakers mean.

Austin recognized the problem, but his suggestions were ignored by most who followed (e.g., Bach and Harnish, 1979; Searle, 1969, 1975). Suppose, Austin said, that he has promised a friend to return some money by uttering "I'll pay you back tomorrow."

It is obviously necessary that to have promised I must normally (A) have been *heard* by someone, perhaps the promisee; (B) have been understood by him as promising. If one or another of these conditions isn't satisfied, doubts arise as to whether I have really promised, and it might be held that my act was only attempted or was void.[7] (Austin, 1962, p. 22)

That is, promises require recognition by the addressees, who hear and understand what is being promised. This is nothing less than a coordinated action by the addressees. In my terminology, that makes a promise and its recognition – two participatory actions. They are the two parts of a joint action or communicative act.[8]

Austin noted a similar problem for perlocutionary acts. To complete certain illocutionary acts, he argued, the speaker has to secure their acceptance. His examples included betting, marrying, giving, and appointing:

My attempt to make a bet by saying "I bet you sixpence" is abortive unless you say "I take you on" or words to that effect; my attempt to marry by saying "I will" is abortive if the woman says "I will not." (p. 36)

Likewise, a person cannot give or bequeath something to others, or appoint them to some position, without their acceptance, either "expressed or implied." Illocutionary acts like these are cooperative or bilateral instead of unilateral (Hancher, 1979). Without your acceptance, I may have tried to give you something, or appoint you to some position, but I will have failed.

Diehard unilateralists might deny that betting, giving, bequeathing, appointing, and their kind are illocutionary acts at all – even though they are on everyone's list of illocutions. These acts, they could argue, are

---

[6] See also Streeck (1980).

[7] Later, Austin asked, rhetorically: "One of the things that cause particular difficulty is the question whether when two parties are involved '*consensus ad idem*' is necessary. Is it essential for me to secure *correct understanding* as well as everything else?" (p. 36).

[8] Later I will adopt the term *uptake* but with a more restricted meaning than Austin's.

really *pairs* of illocutionary acts. A bet consists of (1) a proposal by the bettor ("I bet you sixpence"), and (2) its uptake by the bettee ("I take you on"). What these examples show, they might continue, is that the pair of illocutionary acts is achieved jointly. They show nothing about the proposal and uptake as separate acts. What is needed to complete an illocutionary act, however, is not its uptake, but its recognition. For Austin to make a promise to his friend, he "must normally have been heard [and] have been understood by him as promising." This requirement isn't hard to satisfy, but it takes the friend's coordinated actions. He and his friend have to work jointly to establish, to a reasonable criterion, that his friend has understood him as intended (see Chapter 8).

These paths lead to a new outlook on speaker's meaning, illocutionary acts, and perlocutionary acts. Speaker's meaning is a type of intention that can be discharged only through joint actions. Illocutionary acts, as Austin himself realized, can be accomplished only as parts of joint actions, and the same is true of perlocutionary acts. The issue is how to bring the long neglected addressee back into the picture.

SOCIAL PRACTICES

Whatever its status, Searle's classification of illocutionary acts illustrates one point over and over again: Illocutionary acts have their origins in social practices. Acts such as arresting, overruling, and calling time out – the effectives and verdictives – belong to highly codified social activities and wouldn't exist without the social institutions in which they are formalized. All the other acts belong to well-developed social activities as well. It is just that these activities are informal and not codified. Directives arise when one person wants another person to do something and has some authority to oblige the other to do it. The authority may not come from a formal institution, but it does come from accepted social practices – as in ordering food in a restaurant, asking a librarian for a book, or asking a bank customer for identification. Assertives, commissives, and expressives work in similar ways. Illocutionary acts arise in joint activities (see also Cohen and Levesque, 1990).

The stronger assumption, which Austin seems to have held, is that illocutionary acts cannot be defined without reference to the joint activities of which they are parts. We cannot specify what constitutes a marriage vow, christening, bequest, or bet – Austin's primary examples – without saying how they are performed within the appropriate ceremonies. Although Austin was later faulted for stressing these institutional and conventional features, his assumption still seems fundamentally correct. The problem lies in our understanding of joint activities. It is easy to specify how sentencing, indicting, and dismissing are created within well-codified court procedures. It is more difficult to specify how offers, greetings, and questions are created within uncodified social practices.

Cooperation

If Austin is right, to understand what speakers mean, we must look at the joint activity or social practice they are engaged in. Grice argued much the same point in his own 1967 William James Lectures ten years after Austin's. He put it this way (Grice, 1975, p. 45):

Our talk exchanges do not normally consist of a succession of disconnected remarks, and would not be rational if they did. They are characteristically, to some degree at least, cooperative efforts; and each participant recognizes in them, to some extent, a common purpose or set of purposes, or at least a mutually accepted direction. The purpose or direction may be fixed from the start (e.g., by an initial proposal of a question for discussion), or it may evolve during the exchange; it may be fairly definite, or it may be so indefinite as to leave very considerable latitude to the participants (as in a casual conversation). But at each stage, some possible conversational moves would be excluded as conversationally unsuitable.

The participants of a conversation, Grice argued, therefore expect each other to adhere to the *cooperative principle*, which he expressed as an exhortation to speakers:

Cooperative principle. Make your conversational contribution such as is required, at the stage at which it occurs, by the accepted purpose or direction of the talk exchange in which you are engaged.

In Grice's view, people take it for granted that "contributions" to conversations are to be interpreted against the "accepted purpose or direction of the talk exchange." One might pursue Grice's insight in many ways. He chose to apply it to the problem of what people mean by their utterances.

SAYING AND IMPLICATING

To see what speakers mean, Grice argued, we generally go beyond what they actually say. He asked us to imagine A standing next to an obviously immobilized car and striking up a conversation with passerby B:

A: I am out of petrol.
B: There is a garage round the corner.

All B has said is that there is a garage, a gas station, around the corner. Yet that isn't all A takes him as doing. A can suppose B was trying to offer information relevant to the situation at hand – that A is stranded and has just remarked that he is out of gasoline. So B must also mean, in Grice's words, "that the garage is, or at least may be open, etc."[9] This he called an *implicatum* but is more often called an *implicature*. So in Grice's scheme, speaker's meaning divides into two parts: *saying* and *implicating*.

What is the difference? What is said (in Grice's special sense) is what speakers mean mostly through the conventional content of the sentences they utter – indeed, through only that part that affects the truth of their utterances. In uttering "There is a garage round the corner," B is saying only that there is a garage around the corner. The rest of what B meant is implicated. Some implicatures are conventional and, therefore, part of the sentence meaning. The ones I shall be concerned with Grice called *conversational implicatures*. One example is B's implicature that the garage may be open and selling petrol. A recognizes it not because of any conventional link with what B said. Rather, as Grice put it, A "works it out."

For Grice, conversational implicatures have three main properties (but see Nunberg, 1981; Sadock, 1978). (1) They are *non-conventional*. They are not conventionally associated with the words or sentence uttered. "There is a garage round the corner" doesn't conventionally mean that the garage is open. Yet (2) they are *calculable*. Speakers intend addressees to be able to work them out. A is to work out that B means that he believes the garage may be open. Conversational implicatures are those parts of what speakers mean that addressees recognize only by "working them out." Finally, (3) they are *defeasible* – the speaker can cancel them, rendering them null and void. B could have said "There's a garage round the corner, but I doubt if it's open," canceling the implicature A would otherwise work out.

FOUR MAXIMS

How are implicatures to be worked out? Since Grice argued that every utterance "contributes" to the "accepted purpose or direction of the talk exchange," we might have expected him to develop the notions of

---

[9] Grice's "etc." is usually ignored, but it is important. He seems to be suggesting that we may not be able to enumerate A's implicatures explicitly – that unlike what it said what is implicated may be vague or lacking in clear limits.

"contribution" and "accepted purpose" and show how implicatures follow, but he didn't. Instead, he offered four rules of thumb, four *maxims*, that he argued enable listeners to work out implicatures. Paradoxically, he expressed the maxims as exhortations to speakers (Grice, 1975, pp. 45-46):

Maxim of quantity	1.	Make your contribution as informative as is required (for the current purposes of the exchange).
	2.	Do not make your contribution more informative than is required.
Maxim of quality	1.	Do not say what you believe to be false.
	2.	Do not say that for which you lack evidence.
Maxim of relation		Be relevant.
Maxim of manner	1.	Avoid obscurity of expression.
	2.	Avoid ambiguity.
	3.	Be brief (avoid unnecessary prolixity).
	4.	Be orderly.

Once listeners take for granted that speakers adhere to these maxims and to the cooperative principle itself, they can work out what the speakers are implicating.

Speakers create implicatures in two main ways. The first is by direct appeal to the maxims. Take this invented exchange:

Burton: How many children do you have?
Connie: I have two children.

All Connie has said is that she has two children, which would be literally true even if she had three or four or twelve. Yet, by the maxim of quantity, Burton can assume she has been as informative as she needs to be for the current purposes of this exchange. And because he was asking for the *total* number of children, she must be giving him the total. Contrast that exchange with this one:

Burton: Do you have two quarters I could borrow for the pay phone?
Connie: Yes, I have two quarters.

Here, Burton is trying to find out not how many quarters Connie has in total, but merely whether she has two quarters he could borrow. She may have three, four, or twelve quarters, but she is being "as informative as is required for the current purposes of the exchange" by saying that she has two quarters. In these contrasting circumstances "I have two children" implicates "and no more than two children," whereas "I have two quarters" does *not* implicate "and no more than two quarters." These are meanings Connie expects Burton to work out. The other maxims apply directly in similar ways.

The second method of creating implicatures is by blatantly violating, or *flouting*, a maxim. In the following example, Kate is describing a visit to a women's college (1.3.560):

Kate: and . um then, . a bell rang, - - and - millions of feet, . ran, . along corridors, you know, and then they . it all died away, it was like like sound effects from the Goon Show

When Kate claimed "millions" of feet ran along the corridors, she was blatantly violating the maxim of quality, "Do not say what you believe to be false." The violation was so blatant that she could expect her audience to reason: "Kate flouted the maxim, yet was otherwise cooperative. She must therefore not have meant 'millions' literally, but as hyperbole. It only *seemed* as if there were millions of feet." Flouting maxims also leads to understatement, metaphor, irony, sarcasm, and other tropes.

Both methods of implicating have serious difficulties. Flouting maxims, for example, is really a type of joint pretense in which speakers and addressees create a new layer of joint activity. Kate and her audience jointly pretend that she heard "millions" of feet run along the corridors. Pretending to say something is not the same type of action as actually saying something, so hyperbole and other such tropes require a different explanation (see Chapter 12). Another difficulty for both methods lies in the notion of saying itself.

PROBLEMS WITH SAYING

In Grice's scheme, implicatures are based on what is said. But what is saying? According to Grice – though he was vague on this point – it is the literal meaning of the sentence uttered with its ambiguities resolved and its referents specified. Take B's "There is a garage round the corner." In British English, *garage* is ambiguous between "parking structure" and "service station," so to know what B said we must choose between them. We must also identify the time referred to in *is* and the object referred to with *the corner*. Behind Grice's scheme are three assumptions:

Assumption 1   What is said is logically prior to what is implicated.
Assumption 2   The way listeners determine what is said is different in principle from the way they "work out" what is implicated.
Assumption 3   What is said is well defined for every type of utterance.

There are major problems with all three assumptions.

According to assumption 1, listeners have to know what is said in order to work out what is implicated. Even Grice's own example shows the problem with this assumption. To determine what B said, A had to decide whether *garage* meant "parking structure" or "service station." But he could only determine that it meant "service station" by first working out what B was implicating, namely, that B's remark was relevant to A's being out of petrol. Suppose the exchange had gone this way:

A: I think I am parked in an illegal parking zone.
B: There is a garage round the corner.

This time A would work out a different implicature and choose "parking structure" instead. That is, the only way A could determine what B was *saying* was by working out what B must be *implicating*, and this violates assumption 1. The very notion of literal meaning is problematic, which also undermines assumption 1 (Gibbs, 1989, 1994; Searle, 1978, 1980).

According to assumption 2, listeners determine what is said according to one set of principles or procedures, and they "work out" (or *calculate*) what is implicated according to another. But listeners often have to calculate parts of what is said. Consider the novel word meanings in these remarks from a friend:

The photographer asked me to do a **Napoleon** for the camera.
Diane's approach to life is very **San Francisco**.
Never ask two **China trips** to the same party.

I cannot determine what my friend has said (in Grice's sense) because the literal meanings of *Napoleon, San Francisco*, and *China trip* don't fit these sentences (see Chapter 3). When I decide that "do a Napoleon" means "tuck my right hand under my coat flap," I apply the same principles or procedures that I apply in working out implicatures (Clark and Clark, 1979; Clark, 1983; Clark and Gerrig, 1983; Nunberg, 1979; Sag, 1981). But if I have to "work out" what is said for *Napoleon, San Francisco*, and *China trip*, that violates assumption 2.

Indirect reference is another problem, and is illustrated in Grice's own example. When A tells B "I am out of petrol," he uses *I* to refer to himself and, thereby, indirectly to his car. After all, it isn't A but A's car that is out of petrol.[10] How does B determine that? Knowing the conventional mean-

[10] For similar examples, consider "I am parked up the street," or "I am the blue Volvo over there," or "Could you please fill me up with gasoline."

ing of *I* isn't enough, because in other situations A could have meant "my lawn mower" or "my service station" or "the can for my Molotov cocktails." What A is saying with *I* is something B must "work out" as he would any implicature, and the same goes for all indirect references (see Chapter 4). Indirect references are another violation of assumption 2.

Finally, according to assumption 3, what is said must be well defined for every type of utterance. If it weren't, we would have no basis for working out implicatures. But counter-examples are plentiful. The first type are *phrasal utterances*. When you tell a bartender, "Two pints of Guinness," are you saying (in Grice's sense) "I'd like" or "I'll have" or "Get me" or "Would you get me" or "I'd like you to get me two pints of Guinness"? There is no way in principle of selecting among these candidates. Whatever you are doing, you don't appear to be *saying* that you are ordering beer, and yet you cannot be implicating it either because you cannot cancel the order – it makes no sense to say "Two pints of Guinness, but I'm not ordering two pints of Guinness." Saying simply isn't well defined for phrasal utterances.[11]

Another type of counter-example are utterances like "hello," "well," and "ah" (see Chapter 6). Traditionally, these are said to have not literal meanings but conventional uses. The dictionary defines *hello* as "an informal expression used to greet another," *well* as "used to express surprise," and *ah* as "used to express various emotions, such as surprise, delight, pain, satisfaction, or dislike." So when a friend tells you, "Helen is coming today," and you utter a delighted "Ah," what are you saying? Because literal meaning isn't defined for "ah," it is impossible to specify either what is said or what is implicated.

The same goes for nonlinguistic signals (Chapter 6). In conversation,

---

[11] Wittgenstein (1958), in *Philosophical Investigations*, describes a communication system between builder A and his assistant B (see also Chapter 10).

> A is building with building-stones: there are blocks, pillars, slabs and beams. B has to pass the stones, and that in the order in which A needs them. For this purpose they use a language consisting of the words "block," "pillar," "slab," "beam." A calls them out; – B brings the stone which he has learnt to bring at such-and-such a call. (p. 3)

About these phrasal utterances, Wittgenstein remarks:

> But what about this: is the call "Slab!" in example (2) a sentence or a word? – If a word, surely it has not the same meaning as the like-sounding word of our ordinary language, for in (2) it is a call. But if a sentence, it is surely not the elliptical sentence: "Slab!" of our language...But why should I not on the contrary have called the sentence "Bring me a slab" a lengthening of the sentence "Slab!"?...And why should I translate the call "Slab!" into a different expression in order to say what someone means by it? (p. 9)

speakers use their hands, body, face, eyes, and voice to make a wide range of both indicative, or deictic, gestures (e.g., pointing) and iconic gestures (e.g., smirking). These signals are essential to what speakers mean, and yet Grice's notion of what is said doesn't apply to them at all.

To sum up, the cooperative principle has offered an influential account of many phenomena, and Grice's insights have been widely adopted. Most attention has been focused on the maxims – how they should be formulated and applied. Some investigators have offered their own versions of the maxims (e.g., Horn, 1984; Kasher, 1977; Leech, 1983; Levinson, 1987); Dan Sperber and Deirdre Wilson (1986) have even reduced them all to the maxim of relevance. This effort seems misdirected, because Grice's rules of thumb can never be more than just that – rules of thumb. Although Grice recognized that speakers and addressees must cooperate, the maxims were exhortations to speakers, not addressees, and coordination became a sequence of two autonomous actions, the first by speakers and the second by addressees. For a proper understanding of speaker's meaning, we must return to three notions the maxims are based on: (1) "the accepted purpose or direction of the talk exchange," and (2) how people "contribute" to that accepted purpose or direction by means of (3) signals, both linguistic and nonlinguistic. These are just the topics I will consider in the next three chapters.[12]

LEVELS OF COMMUNICATIVE ACTS

There are many speech acts besides illocutionary and perlocutionary acts. According to Austin (1962), when I say to you "Please sit down," I am performing these acts among others:

Phonetic act	I am producing the noises that constitute "Please sit down."
Phatic act	I am uttering the words *please*, *sit*, and *down*.
Rhetic act	I am using the words *please*, *sit*, and *down* with a certain sense and reference.
Locutionary act	I am saying to you "Please sit down."
Illocutionary act	I am asking you to sit down.
Perlocutionary act	I am trying to get you to sit down.

Some of these acts differ in level of action – producing noises is at a lower level than asking you to sit down – and others differ in function. There is no

---

[12] In this book, however, I will not take up many of the particular linguistic phenomena that have been accounted for by direct appeal to the maxims, though I will take up many phenomena that have been accounted for as flouting of the maxims (Chapter 12).

mention of acts by addressees. So from our perspective, the list is incomplete and lacking in organization. The ideal scheme would have levels and include both speakers and addressees. I will propose just such a scheme.

ACTION LADDERS

Many actions come in hierarchies that I will call *action ladders*. Consider Alan calling an elevator to take him up:

Level	Action in progress from t_0 to t_1
5	A is getting an "up" elevator to come
4	A is calling an "up" elevator
3	A is activating the "up" button
2	A is depressing the "up" button
1	A is pressing the right index finger against the "up" button

Alan is taking five distinct actions, but they are cotemporal – they begin and end together. The act of pressing the finger against the "up" button, for example, is in progress over the same time interval (t_0 to t_1) that the act of activating the "up" button is in progress.

It is tempting to say that Alan is really doing only one thing. It is just that I have described it in five different ways. It is easy to show, however, that Alan *is* doing five things and they are in a causal relation going up the ladder. As we move up the ladder, Alan presses his finger against the "up" button *in order to* depress "up" button, which he does *in order to* activate the "up" button, which he does *in order to* call an "up" elevator, and so on. Or as we go down the ladder, Alan is getting an "up" elevator to come *by means of* calling an "up" elevator, which he is doing *by means of* activating the "up" button, and so on. I will call this property *upward causality*. With upward causality, the relation between any two actions in a ladder is asymmetric, irreflexive, and transitive.[13]

Upward causality leads directly to a property I will call upward completion:

Upward completion. In a ladder of actions, it is only possible to complete actions from the bottom level up through any level in the ladder.

Alan, for example, might press his finger against the "up" button without depressing it because it was stuck. If so, he would complete level 1 while failing to complete level 2. Or he might depress the button (level 2)

---

[13] See Goldman (1970) for a discussion of what he calls "level-generational" acts.

without activating it (level 3) because it was defective. Or he might activate the button (level 3) without calling an "up" elevator (level 4) because the elevators were turned off that day. Or he might call an "up" elevator (level 4) without getting it to come (level 5) because some idiot had propped the doors open. Actions in such a ladder are completed from the bottom up.

Upward completion entails another property I will call downward evidence:

Downward evidence. In a ladder of actions, evidence that one level is complete is also evidence that all levels below it are complete.

When Alan sees the "up" light go on, he has good evidence that he has activated the "up" button (level 3). Because of upward completion, that same evidence is also evidence that he has succeeded in pressing his finger against the "up" button (level 1) and in depressing it (level 2). On the other hand, when Alan feels the "up" button depress under his finger (level 2), that isn't necessarily evidence that he has activated the "up" button (level 3). That is what makes "up" buttons without lights so frustrating. Impatient button pushers have no idea when they have succeeded, so they jab at the buttons over and over and over again.

Austin referred to action ladders in his discussion of speech acts,[14] but only two of his speech acts fit such a ladder, illocutionary and perlocutionary acts: I am trying to get you to sit down *by* asking you to sit down. Locutionary and illocutionary acts do *not* fit this scheme, as Austin was careful to point out: I am asking you to sit down not *by* saying "Please sit down," but *in* saying that. This is why Austin used the Latin prefix *in-* in coining the term *illocutionary act*. According to Austin, phonetic, phatic, and rhetic acts are all aspects of locutionary acts. To form such a ladder, we will have to knead Austin's scheme into a new shape.

JOINT ACTIONS

Any ladder of actions for language use must satisfy several requirements. It must represent the *joint* actions of speakers and addressees as they coordinate what they do. It must capture their actions in progress, not just at the end of a signal. Its levels must conform to upward causality, upward completion, and downward evidence. And, as Grice's analysis

---

[14] Austin's example: A man shoots a donkey, which he does by firing a gun, which he does by pulling the trigger, which he does by tensing his trigger finger (Austin, 1962, p. 107).

demands, it must accommodate signals of all types – flag waving, belfry lanterns, and gestures as well as words, phrases, and sentences. The proposal here is that in ordinary conversation we have at each moment an action ladder of at least four levels, each level consisting of a joint action. I will take up these levels in the order 3, 2, 1, and 4.

Level 3. We have already met one level of joint action: signaling and recognizing. When I say to you "Please sit down" or gesture to a chair, I mean you are to sit down, and you in coordination recognize my intention. The joint action, expressed in the notation of Chapter 3, is this:

Joint[A signals to B that *p*, B recognizes that A means that *p*]

In the terminology I will use, the speaker is *signaling that p*. Signaling subsumes Austin's locutionary acts (saying that you should sit down) and his illocutionary acts (asking you to sit down) – and it isn't confined to linguistic signals. And I will describe addressees as *recognizing*, or *understanding*, what speakers mean by their signals, though later I will revise this notion radically (Chapter 7).

Level 2. I signal something to you, in turn, by getting you to identify my behavior as a particular signal – as an act by which I mean a specific thing for you. I do this by presenting the signal (an instance of the sentence *Please sit down*, or a gesture toward the chair) for you to identify. I cannot get you to identify the signal without your help. You and I must coordinate what I present with what you identify, and that too is a joint action:

Joint[A presents signal *s* to B, B identifies signal *s* from A]

In my terminology, the speaker *presents* a signal to the addressees, and they, in turn, *identify* the signal.

Level 1. I present a signal for you to identify, in turn, by executing a bit of behavior specifically for you to perceive – by articulating "Please sit down" in your hearing or by moving my arm within your vision. I cannot get you to perceive my behavior without your coordination. In conversation, you must be attending to and perceiving it precisely as I am executing it.[15] This too results in a joint action:

[15] In asynchronous settings, like writing and reading a letter, writers intend readers to attend to their marks, not simultaneously, but at a later time, and readers attend to the marks on that assumption. The delay between executing the marks and attending to them is only one of the reasons why coordination takes a different form in asynchronous settings – and has different consequences (Clark and Brennan, 1991).

Joint[A executes behavior *t* for B to perceive; B attends perceptually to behavior *t* from A]

In my terminology, speakers *execute* a behavior for addressees, who in their turn *attend* to that behavior.

Level 4. What am I doing by asking you to sit down – by performing an illocutionary act? I am proposing, suggesting, posing, or putting forward a project for us to carry out jointly – namely, that I get you to sit down. Now, getting you to sit down is another thing I can't do by myself. It is a joint action that I am projecting for the two of us to do, and that requires us to coordinate our actions. I will call this joint action a *joint project* .

Joint projects have two parts. In my terminology, the speaker *proposes* a joint project, and the addressees *take* it *up*. I propose that you sit down, and you take up my proposal by sitting down or by agreeing to sit down. A *proposal* is expected to be followed by its *uptake*. Recall that Austin argued that "My attempt to make a bet by saying 'I bet you sixpence' is abortive unless you say 'I take you on' or words to that effect," and that marrying, bequeathing, and appointing also require uptake.[16] That makes betting, marrying, bequeathing, and appointing joint projects. Getting you to do something and getting you to accept my beliefs are also joint projects; they are initiated by the illocutionary acts of asking and telling.

Joint projects are usually achieved by two actions in sequence. "Please sit down" is followed by your sitting down, and "I bet you sixpence" is followed by your "I take you on." But for a ladder of actions, the paired actions by the speaker and addressee must be cotemporal – they must be in progress simultaneously. The joint action I will argue for is this: By asking you to sit down, I am *proposing* a joint project; and by understanding my request, you are *considering* taking up that proposal. The joint action is this:

Joint[A proposes joint project *w* for A and B; B considers joint project *w* for A and B]

In this scheme, proposing is different from signaling, and considering is different from recognizing. The differences are easy to see in conversations with more than two participants. In the following exchange, two British academics, Arthur and Charles, are interviewing a prospective student, Beth (3.1.174):

---

[16] So what I am calling uptake is only one part of what Austin called uptake. It is the "taking on" part of the bet, once it has been heard and understood.

Arthur: u:m - well you are . proposing . taking on . quite something Mrs.
              Finney aren't you,
Beth: yes, I am,

In the course of Arthur's utterance, Arthur is asking Beth a question, and she is trying to recognize what he means. Charles, the third participant in the conversation, is also trying to recognize what Arthur means. These actions are all at level 3. At level 4, Arthur is proposing that Beth answer his question, and she is considering taking up that proposal. But Arthur is *not* proposing a joint project for *Charles* to consider. Speakers propose joint projects for addressees and *not* for all participants. That is precisely what distinguishes addressees from participants (Clark & Carlson, 1982a, b).[17] In short, Arthur means what he means for both Beth and Charles to recognize, but proposes what he proposes for only Beth to consider. Once Charles has understood Arthur's question, he is done. The point is subtle, but essential for distinguishing level 4 from level 3.

THREE ACTION LADDERS

Individual action ladders, like the one for calling an "up" elevator, describe the several actions that are in progress during a single slice of time. Remarkably, the four joint actions just described also form such a ladder. To see this, let us consider an utterance by a university instructor (Adam) to a student (Bart) (3.5b.552):

Adam: sit down **here [pointing at a chair]** would you[18]

And let us focus on the actions in progress over the time interval in which Adam is producing the word *here* and gesturing at a chair (in boldface). We can identify three distinct action ladders over this interval, one for Adam's actions, one for Bart's actions, and one for their joint actions.

The ladder of Adam's individual actions is really a reformulation of Austin's speech acts, and it looks like this:

---

[17] Clark and Carlson (1982a, b) provide a broad range of evidence that distinguishes "participant-directed informatives" from "addressee-directed illocutionary acts." That is equivalent to the distinction here between signaling something to all participants and proposing joint projects only for addressees.

[18] Gestures weren't marked in the transcripts, but it is reasonable to assume that a gesture like this accompanied the word *here*.

Level	A's actions in progress
4	A is proposing to B that B sit here for A.
3	A is asking B to sit here.
2	A is presenting to B a signal composed of "here" plus pointing at the chair.
1	A is executing for B's perception the articulation of "here" and the movement of his arm.

Within this interval, Adam is *in the process of*, or *in the middle of*, proposing, asking, presenting, and executing things. These actions *in progress* form a genuine action ladder with upward causality, upward completion, and downward evidence. The same time interval yields a ladder for Bart's actions:

Level	B's actions in progress
4	B is considering A's proposal that B sit here for A.
3	B is recognizing A's request for B to sit here.
2	B is identifying A's signal as composed of "here" plus pointing at the chair.
1	B is attending to A's articulation of "here" and the movement of A's arm.

During this interval, Bart is in the process of, or in the middle of, considering, recognizing, identifying, and attending to things, and may not have completed any of them. Bart's ladder is also an action ladder complete with upward causality, upward completion, and downward evidence.

These two ladders are linked. Adam's actions at each level are participatory actions – parts of joint actions – each linked to a participatory action by Bart. The result is a ladder of *joint* actions, which, in general, looks like this:

Level	Speaker A's actions	Addressee B's actions
4	A is *proposing* joint project *w* to B	B is *considering* A's proposal of *w*
3	A is *signaling* that *p* for B	B is *recognizing* that *p* from A
2	A is *presenting* signal *s* to B	B is *identifying* signal *s* from A
1	A is *executing* behavior *t* for B	B is *attending* to behavior *t* from A

At each level we find a joint action by Adam and Bart. And like the single ladder, the joint ladder has upward causality, upward completion, and downward evidence. Adam must get Bart to attend to his voice or movement (level 1) in order to get him to identify the word and gesture he is presenting (level 2). Adam must succeed at that in order to get Bart to recognize what he means (level 3), and he must succeed at that in order to get Bart to consider the joint project he is proposing (level 4). Likewise, evidence that Adam got Bart to understand what he means (level 3) is also good evidence that he got Bart to attend to his voice and arm movement (level 1) and to identify the word and gesture (level 2). Again, causation goes upward, and evidence downward. Because there is no natural terminology for the joint actions in this ladder, I will make do with these cumbersome names:

Level 4   Proposal and consideration
Level 3   Signaling and recognition, or meaning and understanding
Level 2   Presentation and identification
Level 1   Execution and attention

With this analysis, we move from Austin's mixed collection of speech acts to a ladder of joint actions performed in the use of language. Its advantage is that it satisfies upward causality, includes what addressees do, and specifies the link between speakers' and addressees' actions. Yet this is so far only a blueprint. It will take the next several chapters to fill in the details.

Conclusions

To communicate is, according to its Latin roots, "to make common," to make known within a group of people. As we saw in Chapters 2, 3, and 4, people have to coordinate closely to make a piece of information common for them – to add it to their common ground. The same argument applies to what is traditionally called communication, and it leads to the conclusion: Communicative acts are joint acts.

Surprisingly, this conclusion is entailed by Grice's very characterization of speaker's meaning. Suppose Ann says "Please sit down" to Ben, meaning that he is to sit down. Her meaning is a type of intention that she cannot discharge without Ben doing his part in recognizing that intention. For speakers to mean something, they must act jointly with their addressees. The same holds for the various types of speech acts – locutionary acts, illocutionary acts, perlocutionary acts, and the rest – as Austin himself seemed to recognize. It is time to take the jointness of these actions seriously.

Communication with language takes actions at many levels, as Austin also recognized. I have argued that these levels form a ladder of joint actions. An action ladder is a set of cotemporal actions ordered with upward causality, upward completion, and downward evidence. In language use, these levels are joint actions. At the bottom, Ann executes behaviors and, in coordination with her, Ben attends to them; by these joint actions, Ann presents a signal and, in coordination, Ben identifies it; by these joint actions in turn, Ann signals something to Ben and, in coordination, Ben recognizes what she means; and by these joint actions, Ann proposes a joint project and, in coordination, Ben considers her proposal. These may not be the only levels, but they are the main ones.

6 | Signaling

The right word may be effective,
but no word was ever as effective as a rightly timed pause.
Mark Twain

Language use could not proceed without signals – the acts by which one
person means something for another – but what exactly are they? The
question is crucial because signals help define what is and what isn't
language use – and language – and determine how communication is
actually achieved. This chapter is addressed to what signals are and how
they work.

The traditional assumption is that signals are "linguistic" objects –
utterances of speech sounds, words, sentences – that work via their conventional meanings. That assumption is reflected in Austin's and
Searle's terms *locutionary*, *illocutionary*, *perlocutionary*, and *speech acts*
(Chapter 5). It is also reflected in the term *pragmatics*, the study
of language use, which is treated as parallel to phonology, morphology,
syntax, and semantics in the study of language. And it is reflected in
the term *language use*, which I have felt obliged to use for this domain.
More to the point, it is the working assumption of most students of
language use.

That assumption, of course, isn't right. Many signals aren't "linguistic"
at all (Chapters 3 and 5). The doctor waved his hand to signal Margaret
that she had the measles. Sam waved a white flag to surrender.
Elizabeth pointed at her mouth and an empty plate to ask for food. The
sexton put one lamp in the belfry to signal Paul Revere that the
Redcoats were coming by land. And as Grice (1957) noted, British bus
conductors used to ring a bell twice to signal the bus driver to drive on.
Everyday examples are also easy to come by. When I am offered a cup of
coffee, I can assert I would like a cup – an "illocutionary" act – just as
surely by nodding yes as by uttering "yes."

From these examples, some might conclude that signals are *either* linguistic *or* nonlinguistic. Saying "yes" is linguistic, and nodding yes is nonlinguistic. This wouldn't be right either. It isn't *signals* that are linguistic or nonlinguistic, but *methods of signaling*. Most signals are *composite signals*, the artful fusion of two or more methods of signaling. From these examples, some might also conclude that the nonlinguistic methods are crude, unsystematic, ad hoc, and marginal, and deserve to be relegated to the periphery of language use. This also wouldn't be right. On the contrary, the nonlinguistic methods are subtle, highly systematic, and not at all ad hoc. And they are part and parcel of most signals that are usually classified as "linguistic." Ignoring nonlinguistic methods has distorted people's picture of language use, and it is important to put that picture right.

This chapter, then, is really about *methods* of signaling. It is tempting to start with linguistic methods and treat the others as mere additions. Instead, I will start with a general account of signs and signals, because that is the surest way to put all the methods in perspective.

Signs

Signals are built on signs that speakers deliberately create for their addressees – words, gestures, noises, and more. But what is a sign? For an answer, let us turn to a theory of signs, or semiotics, developed by the American philosopher Charles Sanders Peirce (1839-1914). Peirce applied his theory to a wide range of philosophical issues, including logic, inference, belief, perception, and metaphysics, but oddly enough, ₙot directly to communication or language use. Still, his theory is useful in the analysis of signals.

ICONS, INDICES, AND SYMBOLS

Signs, for Peirce, are part of a relation among an *object*, a *sign*, and an *interpretant*. Holbein's portrait of King Henry VIII, for example, is a sign. "The sign stands for something, its *object*" (p. 99).[1] In this case, the object is the historical figure Henry VIII. Something is a sign, however, only if it "addresses somebody," creating in the mind of that person an idea, which Peirce called the interpretant of the sign. When I look at Holbein's painting, I take it to be a likeness of Henry VIII. I am assumed to be acquainted with the object, Henry VIII, and the sign

[1] All citations to Peirce are from Buchler (1940).

simply conveys further information about it.[2] In this example, the three parts of Peirce's relation are these:

object	sign	interpretant
King Henry VIII	Holbein's portrait of King Henry VIII	the idea of King Henry VIII

Not all signs are alike. "A sign is either an icon, an index, or a symbol."

An *icon* resembles its object perceptually. Holbein's portrait of Henry VIII is an icon because it resembles Henry VIII in appearance. The prototypical icons are paintings and drawings – "such as a lead-pencil streak as representing a geometrical line." Philosophers have sometimes argued that the notion of similarity, resemblance, or likeness is empty because any arbitrary thing is similar to any other arbitrary thing in at least some respect (Goodman, 1968). But Peirce intended resemblance only in perceptual respects. The icon's "qualities resemble those of [its] object, and excite analogous sensations in the mind for which it is a likeness." When I look at Holbein's portrait, I perceive Henry VIII – his heavy face, regal clothes, and imposing presence – in many ways as if I were looking at Henry VIII himself (see Walton, 1973, 1990).

Icons vary in the qualities of the object they represent (p. 105). *Images* represent the "simple qualities" of the object. *Diagrams* represent "the relations, mainly dyadic, or so regarded, of the parts of one thing by analogous relations in their own parts." Peirce's notion of diagram was very broad. He considered an algebraic equation, for example, to be an icon "in so far as it exhibits, by means of the algebraical signs (which are not themselves icons), the relations of the quantities concerned." *Metaphors* signify their objects by "representing a parallelism in something else."

An *index*, in contrast, is a sign that designates its object "because it is in dynamical (including spatial) connection both with the individual object, on the one hand, and with the senses or memory of the person for whom it serves as a sign, on the other hand." Take a weathercock:

A weathercock is an index of the direction of the wind; because in the first place it really takes the self-same direction as the wind, so that there is a real connection between them, and in the second place we are so constituted that when we see a weathercock pointing in a certain direction it draws our attention to that direction,

---

[2] "The Sign can only represent the Object and tell about it. It cannot furnish acquaintance with or recognition of that Object; for that is what is meant in this volume by the Object of a Sign; namely, that with which it presupposes an acquaintance in order to convey some further information concerning it" (p. 100).

and when we see a weathercock veering with the wind, we are forced by the law of mind to think that direction is connected with the wind. (p. 109)

Many signs are indices because of a *spatial* connection between the sign and object. A weathercock indexes the wind direction, the pole star indexes north, and a plumbob indexes vertical. For these indices there is also a *causal* connection between sign and object. For other indices there is *only* a causal connection. A sundial, or clock, indexes the time of day, and the calluses on a man's thumb index his occupation as shoemaker. Many indices have what Grice called natural meaning (Chapter 5). When we say "Those spots mean measles" or "Those clouds mean rain," the spots and clouds are indices of the measles and the rain.

Indices work in part by capturing our attention. "A rap at the door is an index. Anything which focuses the attention is an index. Anything which startles us is an index, in so far as it marks the junction between two portions of experience" (p. 108-109). As Peirce put it, indices "direct the attention to their objects by blind compulsion" (p. 108). And again: "Psychologically, the action of indices depends upon association by contiguity" (p. 108).

A *symbol*, finally, is a sign "whose representative character consists precisely in its being a rule that will determine its interpretant. All words, sentences, books, and other conventional signs are symbols" (p. 112). Peirce noted:

Any ordinary word, as "give," "bird," "marriage," is an example of a symbol. It is *applicable to whatever may be found to realize the idea connected with the word*; it does not, in itself, identify those things. It does not show us a bird, nor enact before our eyes a giving or a marriage, but supposes that we are able to imagine those things, and have associated the word with them. (p. 114, Peirce's emphases)

"A symbol is a law, or regularity of the indefinite future." And like Lewis (1969), Peirce believed that symbols evolve (Chapter 3). "Symbols grow. They come into being by development out of other signs, particularly from icons, or from mixed signs partaking of the nature of icons and symbols" (p. 115).

Icons, indices, and symbols, then, differ in the connection they represent between sign and object, as summarized here:

Type of sign	Relation of sign *S* to its object *O*
Icon	*S* resembles *O* perceptually
Index	*S* is physically connected with *O*
Symbol	*S* is associated with *O* by rule

Symbols differ from icons and indices in another way too. An icon such as Holbein's portrait is an individual thing, not a type or a general class, and so is its object, Henry VIII. An index, like the weathercock, and its object, the direction of the wind, are also individual things. "A genuine index and its object must be existent individuals (whether things or facts)" (p. 108). Symbols and their objects, on the other hand, are *types* of things:

A symbol, as we have seen, cannot indicate any particular thing; it denotes a kind of thing. Not only that, but it is itself a kind and not a single thing. You can write down the word "star," but that does not make you creator of the word, nor if you erase it have you destroyed the word. The word lives in the minds of those who use it. (p. 114)

One final point. Many signs, according to Peirce, are "mixed signs" – mixtures of icons, indices, and symbols. One example he offered was this:

A man walking with a child points his arm up into the air and says, "There is a balloon." The pointing arm [an index] is an essential part of the symbol without which the latter would convey no information. But if the child asks, "What is a balloon," and the man replies, "It is something like a great big soap bubble," he makes the image [an icon] a part of the symbol. (p. 112)

That is, a single sign may have iconic, indexical, *and* symbolic properties. And for Peirce, most signs are parts of chains. The interpretant of one sign is the object of the next sign, and so on, so an interpretant of one sign may depend on a series of objects, signs, and interpretants.

DEMONSTRATING, INDICATING, AND DESCRIBING-AS

Signs can be either signals or symptoms, although Peirce didn't make this distinction. Icons include both drawings deliberately produced by one person for others, and markings, such as bullet holes, left by nature or accident. And indices include both gestures deliberately produced by one person for others, and natural signs such as weathercocks and plumbobs that require no human intervention. Peirce also didn't distinguish between the type of thing a symbol (like "give" or "bird") could potentially signify and the type of thing a person actually uses it to signify on a particular occasion. Peirce was missing several distinctions that were made only fifty years later.

A signal is really *the presentation of a sign by one person to mean something for another*. If Peirce is right, people must have three quite different methods of signaling – with icons, with indices, and with symbols.[3] And they do. To distinguish among these methods, I will adopt the following terms:

Method of signaling	Sign created
demonstrating a thing	icon
indicating a thing	index
describing as a type of thing	symbol

The everyday meanings of these terms are roughly what we want. When I gesture to show you how Queen Elizabeth holds a teacup, I am creating an icon by which I mean something: I am *demonstrating* how Queen Elizabeth holds a teacup.[4] When I point at a bicycle for you, I am producing an index by which I mean something. I am *indicating* the bicycle.[5] And when I use *dog* in telling you "I see a dog," I am producing a symbol by which I mean something. I am *describing* the type of thing I am seeing *as* a dog. At one point, Peirce argued for much the same functions (p. 111):

Icons and indices assert nothing. If an icon could be interpreted by a sentence, that sentence must be in a "potential mood," that is, it would merely say, "Suppose a figure has three sides," etc. Were an index so interpreted, the mood must be imperative, or exclamatory, as "See there!" or "Look out!" [Symbols] are, by nature, in the "indicative," or, as it should be called, the declarative mood.

In conversation, most signals are discrete events that leave no physical trace. Words and gestures are audible and visible only while they are being produced. This is unlike many of Peirce's signs, such as the painting or weathercock, which are static and open to repeated viewing. Not that all signals in conversation are evanescent events. Putting on a uniform or badge, drawing a diagram, and putting up a sign all leave static traces. And, of course, printed words and diagrams are

---

[3] For an earlier analysis of demonstrating, indicating, and describing-as, see Clark and Gerrig (1990).

[4] I intend *demonstrate* in its everyday sense of showing how, not its technical sense as in demonstrative references.

[5] I intend *indicate* in the sense of "I indicated the man in the blue shirt," not as "indicate that" as in "I indicated that I was happy."

permanent. It is the discrete evanescent signals that pose the greatest challenge, for they are pervasive in conversation.

Demonstrating, indicating, and describing-as rarely occur in pure form. Just as most of Peirce's signs are "mixed signs" – mixtures of icons, indices, and symbols – most signals are *composite signals*. They rely on more than one method of signaling. That is why we must think of demonstrating, indicating, and describing-as, not as types of signals, but as *methods of signaling* that combine in various ways.

Describing-as

Describing-as – using symbols – is the most familiar method of signaling and has long dominated the study of language. The reason is clear. Established languages like English, Finnish, and Dakota are systems of symbols, in Peirce's sense,[6] and characterizing these systems is the bread and butter of most students of language. Yet language use depends only partly on describing-as, and it cannot work without indicating or demonstrating as well.

SENTENCES AND UTTERANCES

Conventional words like *give, bird,* and *marriage,* as Peirce observed, are symbols par excellence, and so are the sentences they are constituents of. To use a word or sentence is, therefore, to describe-as. Linguists and philosophers have long investigated complex linguistic symbols such as these. They would note, for example, that the sentence *I like that one in the corner* consists of several noun phrases (*I, the corner, that one in the corner*), a verb phrase (*like that one in the corner*), a prepositional phrase (*in the corner*), and, ultimately, certain words and morphemes, all arranged in a tidy syntactic structure. They would also note that the meaning of the sentence is a composition of the meaning of its parts. So much is known about sentences and their constituents that I will say little more about them.

Utterances, however, are not sentences. Recall that signs are types, and they signify types of things, not individual things. Whereas sentences are entirely symbolic, utterances of sentences can never be,

---

[6] *Symbol* is sometimes used in the sense of Peirce's sign, or human-created sign, which would include icons and indices as well (see, e.g., McNeill, 1992, p. 105, "Gestures Are Symbols"). The precision of Peirce's terminology, however, has much to recommend it, especially once we add the contrast between signs and signals, so I will continue to use *symbol* in his sense.

because they are particular occurrences and are used to refer to particular objects, states, and events. The word *I* in the sentence *I like that one in the corner*, for example, means "whoever is uttering a token of this symbol," which is a type of thing. It doesn't designate any actual speaker, which is a particular thing. As it happens, this sentence was used in 1969 by Alva in talking to Brenda about paintings hanging in the room they were in (1.8.90), so when Alva used *I*, she was referring to herself, a particular thing. Her use of *I* on that occasion, in short, had both symbolic and indexical features: She used it both to describe-as and to indicate. And to understand Alva's use of *I*, Brenda combined what Alva was describing something as (in using "I" Alva was describing something as "the person uttering this item") with what she was indicating (in emitting "I" Alva was indicating herself).

Every word and construction in Alva's utterance depended on both symbolic and indexical elements and couldn't have been understood without both:

Symbol	Object of symbol	Object of index
I	"oneself"	the self indicated by origin of voice
like	"enjoy" "now"	the time indicated by moment of speaking
that	"the one singled out there"	the location indicated by nodding
one	"single element of a kind"	the kind indicated by what we have just talked about
in	"within the area of"	the area indicated by the corner referred to
the	"particular, specified within the participants' common ground"	the participants indicated by the current conversation
corner	"area enclosed by meeting of two walls"	the two walls indicated by participants' orientation

If Brenda had heard "in the corner" without its index, she would have imagined very different locations depending on what she thought the corner was of – a room, a wall, a sheet of paper, Connecticut, a billiards table. Even if she knew it was a room, she could have imagined different locations depending on what she thought was in the corner – a mouse, spider, shelf, group of ten people, broom, or Persian rug. To complete her interpretation, Brenda had to register Alva's indication of both the room and the picture and, even then, infer that the picture was on the wall some distance from the corner proper. Alva's sentence, as a complex symbol, signified only types of things. Her concurrent indications were needed to complete the picture.

Not all symbols have meanings in the sense that *give*, *bird*, and *marriage* do. The words *yes*, *well*, and *oh*, for example, don't belong to any of the major or minor syntactic categories (like noun or preposition), hence cannot take part in syntactic constructions. They have to be used solo. I will call these words *atomic words* or *symbols*. The dictionary defines *yes* as "used to express affirmation, agreement, positive confirmation, or consent," *well* as "used to express surprise," and *oh* as "used to indicate understanding or acknowledgment of a statement" (see also Heritage, 1984). They have conventional uses but no literal meanings (Chapter 5). As we will see, their use depends crucially on concurrent indications: All utterances of atomic symbols are composites of describing-as and indicating (Wilkins, 1992).

GESTURES

Many gestures are signals, but only some are symbolic, and they have been called *emblems* (Ekman and Friesen, 1969). Here are ten common North American examples:

Gesture	Meaning	Gesture	Meaning
head nod	"yes"	head shake	"no"
thumb up	"I approve"	thumb down	"I reject"
greeting wave	"hello"	farewell wave	"good-bye"
shoulder shrug	"I don't know"	wink	"I'm kidding"
thumb and index finger in circle	"that's excellent"	index finger to protruding lips	"be quiet"

This is only a small sample. According to Adam Kendon (1981), emblems tend to be used for interpersonal control (e.g., "Hello" and "Be quiet"), personal states (e.g., "I approve" and "I don't know"), and evaluations of others (e.g., "He's crazy"), but rarely for objects or actions.

Emblems are really atomic symbols – gestural equivalents of atomic words such as *yes*, *no*, and *hello*. Emblems don't divide into component symbols, and they are regularly used as complete utterances. Waving good-bye is atomic in the same way that saying "Good-bye" is. Many atomic words have emblem counterparts – nodding for "yes," shaking the head for "no," waving for "hello" and "good-bye" – and the emblems can often be used in place of the words.

Emblems are symbols because they are associated with their objects by rule. For most emblems, the rule is a convention, making them interpretable only against the common ground of particular cultural communities. As Desmond Morris and his colleagues (1979) showed, for example, crossing the fingers – putting the middle finger over the index finger – means "May I be protected" in England, Scandinavia, parts of Sicily, and Yugoslavia, but "I am breaking a friendship" in Turkey and Corfu. It appears to mean "May I have good luck" in North America. What it is a symbol for is common ground within these communities, and to use it, people must establish that common ground first. The same goes for the nineteen other common emblems Morris and colleagues studied – from the cheek screw to the chin flick. Many of these emblems can be traced to icons – crossing the fingers derives from the Christian cross – but are now used and interpreted by convention.

When we think of emblems, we think of gestures, but there are *auditory emblems* too (these are North American):

Gesture	Gloss	Gesture	Gloss
clap	"I approve"	hiss	"I disapprove"
wolf whistle	"How beautiful!"	rise-fall whistle	"How surprising!"
raspberry	"I dishonor you"	tongue-click	"Shame on you!"

Many of these may have iconic origins, but are now conventional and used the way any other emblem would be used.

Another class of symbolic gestures are what I will call *junctions* – certain joint physical actions by pairs of people. These include shaking hands, hugging, and kissing used for expressing affection in greetings and farewells. The details of shaking hands, hugging, and kissing vary enormously from one cultural community to the next, and so does what they mean. Junctions have been ignored as signals probably because they are joint actions – generally symmetrical – that require behavior from two participants at once. They are no less symbolic for that. Every signal requires the coordination of actions between speaker and addressees. With junctions it is just that both participants express their feelings simultaneously.

Indication

Every signal, every actual bit of language use, occurs at a particular place and time. They need to be *anchored* to that place and time, and that is done by their indexical elements. Indicating is the method of signaling by which people create indices for the objects they want to refer to. When we think of indicating, we usually think of pointing, but there are many other methods as well.

When speakers want to indicate an object, event, or state for other people, they must present an index, a sign that is "physically connected" to the thing they want to refer to. The index must satisfy these requirements:

1. Attention   The index is in the participants' *joint focus of attention*.
2. Location   The index *locates* the object in space and in time.
3. Physical connection The index locates by means of a *physical connection* with the object.
4. Description   The object is specified under a particular description.
5. Computability   The speaker presupposes that the addressees can work out 1 through 4 based on their current common ground.

The first four requirements embody Peirce's notion of index; the fifth holds for all signals.

Suppose George points at a book for Helen and says "That is mine." His act of pointing is the index (*index* is Latin for "forefinger") and the book is the object. His intention is to get Helen to recognize that he is using that index to locate the book for her. To that end, he must point while she is attending. He must locate the book for her by the direction of his forefinger – a physical connection. And he must get her to see that he is pointing at the object *qua* "book" and not *qua* "example of blue," "piece of junk," or whatever.

George's index isn't a static sign, but an event. In the course of conversation, his forefinger is aligned with many things – but not

Index   ☞ ——— locates ———→   📖   Object

deliberately. It is only when he is manifestly pointing that Helen is to construe him as indicating the book. And his act locates a region not only in space but in time. The object is the book at the moment of indicating. Some indications locate things primarily in space and others primarily in time.

CREATING INDICES

Most indices can be divided into two components – the *instrument* used, and the *locative action* performed with it. George's instrument was his forefinger, and his locative action was pointing it at the book. People exploit a variety of instruments and locative actions depending on how available and useful they are. I will mention only a few.

The most obvious instruments are body parts that people can orient. In the following examples, I stands for instrument, and O for object:

Instrument	Locative Action	Example
finger	pointing at O with I	"**That** [on shelf] is the book I want."
finger	touching O with I	In photograph: "**This** is my sister."
hand	displaying O in I	"**This** cup of coffee is for you."
arm	sweeping at O with I	Of books on table: "**All of these** books are mine."
eyes	gazing at O with I	"I want **you** [person A] and **you** [person B] to come with me."
head	nodding at O with I	"Connie was standing **right over there**."
torso	turning toward O with I	"Let **us** talk."
body	occupying O with I	In chair: "I am going to sit **here**"

George can direct Helen's attention to the object with his finger, hand, arm, eyes, head, torso, or entire body. All of these are exploited in face-to-face conversations.

A less obvious instrument is the voice. When George speaks, he realizes that his voice reveals his identity ("I"), the moment of speaking ("now"), his location ("here"), and even, by its loudness, who he is talking to ("you"). That makes the voice an effective instrument for indicating "I," "now," "here," and "you," as in these examples:

Instrument	Locative action	Example
voice	identifying O with I	To roomful of people: "Who wants to come along?" "**I** do."
voice	identifying O with I	On telephone: "Who's there?" "It's **me**."
voice	locating O with I	In dark room: "Where are you, Helen?" "**Here** I am."
voice	timing O with I	At start of race: "Ready, set, **go**!"
whisper	identifying O with I	To the nearest of several people: "Do **you** want to come along?"

| loud voice | drawing attention to O with I | Shout at a distance: "**Hey, Helen!**" Or by drowning person: "**Help!**" |

The voice indexes "I" in the first two examples, "here" in the third, "now" in the fourth, and "you" in the fifth. It seems to index all four ("I," "here," "now," and "you") in the sixth.

People also exploit artificial instruments such as door bells, telephone rings, pager beeps, alarm clocks, starting pistols, church bells, school bells, ambulance sirens, and turn signals on a car. When George causes Helen's telephone or doorbell to ring, he is indicating, pointing to, a person who at that moment is on the telephone or at the door waiting for an answer. A school bell indicates the opening of class, and a siren the location of an ambulance or police car in a hurry. The waving of a checkered flag indicates the start of a car race. These instruments are like prosthetic extensions of the speakers' arms and voices.

People are opportunistic in their choice of indices and may even exploit fortuitous events. When George hears a loud crash, he can ask Helen, "What was that?" He assumes the crash was in their joint attention and locates the source of the crash by a physical connection – the source caused the crash – and he appropriates the fortuitous index for the demonstrative reference "that." Almost any event will do – sudden sounds, conspicuous sights, salient smells, another person's silly actions – as long as it can be brought to the joint attention of speaker and addressees (Clark, Schreuder, and Buttrick, 1983).

People can also indicate by performing an action in a manifestly conspicuous manner. When a clerk in a drugstore says "Can I help you?" I can respond by conspicuously placing the items I wish to buy on the counter. That is, I don't simply place the items on the counter. I place them in such a conspicuous or stylized manner that I intend the clerk to recognize that I am indicating the placement for her (so she will recognize those as the items I wish to buy). My action isn't coincidental, but a response to her offer.[7]

I will call the added features of my action a *manifesting* action, which is distinct from the action it manifests. Such an action tends to look like this:

Index. Manifesting an action has all the properties of an index to that action.
Stylization. Manifesting an action makes use of stylized, exaggerated, or

---

[7] I am indebted to Janet Bavelas for the notion of stylization in gestures.

conspicuous movements that distinguish the manifested action from the same action not being manifested.

Timing. Manifesting an action often depends on its timing.

The idea here, though subtle, is essential. Placing items on a drugstore counter isn't itself a signal. Yet when I take the action in a stylized manner at just the right moment, I am using the extra features of my behavior to manifest that action, and manifesting the action *is* a signal – an indication.

COMPOSITE SIGNALS

In language use, indicating is usually combined with describing or demonstrating. The most obvious example is the demonstrative pronoun *this* or *that* (Clark, Schreuder, Buttrick, 1983; Nunberg, 1979). Suppose George points at two women in a photograph and says "This is a woman from San Francisco, and that is my neighbor." His pointings are indices, and the perceptual images are the objects of those indices – their referents. Note that the women themselves aren't the referents, for George cannot say "This now lives in San Francisco, and that lives next door to me."[8] The descriptive content of *this* and *that* signify that the perceptual images are near and far from him, not that the women themselves are near and far – which would contradict what he says.

References with demonstrative adjectives, in contrast, embody *two* indices and *two* referents. Suppose George points at a copy of Wallace Stegner's novel *Angle of Repose* and says:

1. *That man* was a friend of mine.
2. I find *that period of American history* fascinating.
3. *That publisher* has brought out some great books.
4. *That book* is mine.

In 1, the gesture indexes the perceptual object, but it is that object, under its description "copy of a novel by Wallace Stegner," that indexes its author Wallace Stegner. The gestures index the same perceptual object in 2, 3, and 4, but that object indexes a "period in American history" in 2, a "publisher" in 3, and a "book" in 4. What emerges is a chaining of indices, a pattern that Peirce himself argued for. We might picture the system of references this way:

---

[8] He could have said "She [pointing] now lives in San Francisco, and she [pointing] lives next door to me." *She* can refer to people, but *this* and *that* cannot.

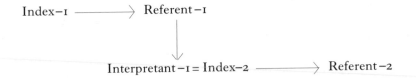

The descriptive content of the expression *that man* also divides into two parts. The content of *that* helps identify referent-1, the perceptual object George is locating for Helen, as an inanimate object relatively far from him. The content of *man*, in contrast, helps identify referent-2 as the man who wrote the book – namely Stegner. The same division of labor applies to *that period of American history*, *that publisher*, and *that book*, the descriptions in 2, 3, and 4. Even when George makes the demonstrative reference with a pronoun, "He [pointing at the book] was a friend of mine," he is using the gesture to index the perceptual image of the book (referent-1), and the masculine pronoun to describe Stegner (referent-2). In a demonstrative reference, the *primary index* (often a gesture) locates the immediate perceptual object, which serves as a *secondary index* that locates the ultimate referent.

I, *here*, and *now* are what John Perry (1979) called the *essential indexicals*, and their uses also depend on indicating. As I noted earlier, when George utters a word, he is necessarily indexing who is speaking ("I"), where he is ("here"), and when this is happening ("now"), and he expects Helen to recognize this.[9] *I, here,* and *now* are really demonstrative references for which the accompanying "gestures" are performed with the voice. Indicating "I," "here," and "now" is essential to other parts of language use as well. "I" is needed for specifying the agent of all locutionary, illocutionary, and perlocutionary acts. "Here" is needed for interpreting such deictic expressions as *in front of*, *behind*, *beyond*, *to the right of*, *straight ahead*, *next*, and *the other side* – not to mention *here*, *there*, *this*, and *that*. "Now" is needed for interpreting such temporal expressions as *now*, *then*, *today*, *yesterday*, *once*, *already*, and *soon*, and for specifying the time referred to in the various tenses – as in "I will have left" and "I had left."

---

[9] Since the invention of audio recording, the place and time Helen hears George's utterance may be different from the time and place he produced it, so George has to reckon with the disparities. He may even identify now and here as the time and place of Helen's reception: "As you listen to this, I am lying on a beach in the Riviera" (Fillmore, 1975).

Most definite references are composites of descriptions and indications. Suppose George tells Helen, "I just met the principal," using "the principal" to refer to Gretel. To make this reference, he must presuppose that Gretel's identity is inferable from what is jointly salient in Helen's and his common ground at that moment,[10] and for that he must indicate whose common ground at what time ("the salient principal in *your* and *my* common ground *now*"). He uses his voice and eye gaze to index himself as speaker, Helen as addressee, and the time of utterance as "now." The same utterance in different circumstances would have indexed a different referent. At the same time, George uses the description "principal" to help specify the referent qua principal. Definite descriptions, then, are also like demonstrative references: They are composites of indications and descriptions, and embody a chain of indications.

What holds for definite reference holds for every feature that is based on speakers' presuppositions – what is in "*your* and *my* common ground *now*." That includes, for example, all appeals to conventions, from choice of language – English vs. Dutch vs. Japanese – down to choice of jargon and technical terms. When George says "The difference is significant," he presupposes mutual knowledge of the statistical jargon *significant*. For Helen to realize this, he must indicate their mutual knowledge of its specialized meaning (Chapter 3). The paradox is that George cannot use the word *significant*, a symbol, without indicating, via an index, the rule it is to be interpreted by. There can be no symbol use without indices, though there can be index use without symbols.

TEMPORAL PLACEMENT

The placement of a signal in time – its *temporal placement* – is often used to indicate things, as we have seen with "now." Time can be viewed at three levels of measurement:

Ordinal scale: events are merely ordered in time
Interval scale: events are ordered with measurable intervals between them
Ratio scale: events lie on an interval scale that has a zero or origin

Temporal order, or *order*, is the mere sequence of two signals – say, word 1 comes before word 2. Yet two signals can be also measured on an interval scale – say, word 2 begins 1.262 seconds after word 1 ends – or on a ratio scale – say, word 3 is delayed 1.53 times as long as word 2 from the

[10] Notice that George couldn't say "I just met the person someone saw" and make any sense, precisely because the referent of "the person someone saw" cannot be indexed to anything in George and Helen's current common ground.

end of word 1. I will call temporal placement on interval or ratio scales *timing*. Order in language use has been studied for a long time, but timing has not. One reason is that order is represented in written language, but timing is apparent only in spoken language. In conversation, timing is as important as order.

Temporal order has been studied as word order, clause order, and sentence order. Word order is essential in indicating syntactic function – compare "Man bites dog" and "Dog bites man." Clause order is used in indicating emphasis and topics – compare "Lou Ann ate dinner before she left" and "Before she left, Lou Ann ate dinner." Sentence order lies behind certain implicatures – compare "Jack took a pill; he got sick to his stomach" and "Jack got sick to his stomach; he took a pill." It is also important for ellipsis (Hankamer and Sag, 1976; Sag and Hankamer, 1984), as in the second of this pair (1.8.233):

| Brenda: | but they're too big you know |
| Alva: | yes, of course **they are** |

Alva indicates what "they are" is elliptical for – namely "they're too big" – by placing it immediately after Brenda's utterance "but they're too big you know."

Speakers are expected to deliver words not just in the right order, but with the right timing. People can achieve and perceive timing with such precision that they can exploit it for many purposes (Chapter 9), as in this example (1.1.1191):

Sam:	but you daren't set synthesis again you see, . you set analysis, and you can put the answers down, and your assistant *examiners will work them,*
Reynard:	*yes quite, yes, yes*
Sam:	but if you give them a give them a free hand on synthesis, and they'd be marking all sorts of stuff, . because they don't do the stuff *them-selves, .*
Reynard:	*quite, m*

Reynard deliberately initiates his acknowledgment "yes quite, yes, yes" to overlap with the last few words of Sam's clause. Why? To indicate which clause he is acknowledging and, at the same time, to signal that he isn't taking a turn. The timing was essential to what he did (Chapters 8, 9).

Timing is also essential for atomic utterances such as "yes," "well," and "oh." Since these are in the present tense (Wilkins, 1992), speakers must indicate the precise "now" they are referring to. Consider Alva's *oh* in her discussion with Brenda about paintings along the wall of the room (1.8.65):

Brenda: that green is is not bad, is it, that landscape
Alva: what the bright one, -
Brenda: yes,
Alva: *it's*
Brenda: *well it's* not very bright, no I meant the *second one along*
Alva: *oh that one over* there

When Brenda refers to "that landscape," Alva isn't sure which painting Brenda meant and guesses "what the bright one." Once Brenda discovers the mistake, she corrects her, "no I meant the second one along." Alva places "oh" in the middle of that correction to indicate precisely *when* she has grasped it. If she had waited until the end, she wouldn't have displayed how quickly she had understood (see Jefferson, 1973). Alva's "oh" indexes four things: "I" (Alva), "you" (Brenda), "now precisely," and what her "oh" is about (the painting). She needs all four to establish what she meant: "I have just now discovered which painting you were referring to." One could tell similar stories for Brenda's "yes," "well," and "no."

Emblems – the gestural counterparts of atomic utterances – have many of the same indexical elements. When there is a good-bye wave, it is always one person ("I") waving good-bye to one or more others ("you") at a precise moment ("now"). The gesturer indicates all three in the timing and direction of the gesture. So it goes for all emblems.

Another type of spontaneous gesture is the *beat*, or baton (Efron, 1941; Ekman and Friesen, 1969; McNeill, 1992), in which "the hand moves along with the rhythmical pulsation of speech" (McNeill, p. 15). The typical beat is a quick flick of the hand or fingers up and down, or in and out. In its purest form, its function is to indicate moments in time. The beat "indexes the word or phrase it accompanies as being significant, not for its own semantic content, but for its discourse-pragmatic content" (ibid., p. 15). It is used to emphasize events being mentioned, points being introduced, and other types of information. Think of the orator pounding a fist on the podium to emphasize a point. Beats, then, are indexical signals *par excellence*.

Demonstrations

The final method of signaling is demonstrating. Suppose George tells Helen, "Elizabeth drinks tea like this." He holds an imaginary saucer in his left hand. Then, with his right hand, pinkie up, he picks an imaginary cup off the saucer, lifts it to his lips, tips it, purses his lips with eyes half closed, and pretends to drink. Then he returns his hands, relaxed, to his lap. With these actions, George demonstrates to Helen how Elizabeth drinks tea. He *means* that Elizabeth drinks tea in such and such a way, and that makes his action a signal. What distinguishes demonstrating from describing and indicating is the use of icons. To demonstrate is to signal with icons. At first glance, demonstrating seems to play little role in language use. But on a closer look, it is ubiquitous and essential.

WHAT ARE DEMONSTRATIONS?

Demonstrations, Richard Gerrig and I have argued (Clark and Gerrig, 1990), are *selective depictions*. Each demonstration divides into four types of aspects:

1. *Depictive aspects.* These are the aspects of a demonstration that are intended to depict aspects of the referent. George depicts the way Elizabeth holds her hands, sticks out her pinkie, purses her lips, holds her head, and closes her eyes; he also depicts the trajectory of her hand from the saucer to her mouth. Yet he doesn't even try to depict a great many other things – the way she sits, holds her shoulders, or licks her lips. The depictive aspects define the *demonstration proper*, the actions essential to the demonstration.

2. *Supportive aspects.* These are the aspects of a demonstration that aren't intended to depict, but to support or enable the performance of the depictive aspects. George doesn't use a real cup and saucer, or sip actual liquid, or swallow, or become small and female. And Helen, for her part, doesn't assume that Elizabeth drinks tea without a real cup and saucer, without sipping or swallowing, or by becoming a large man. She merely takes these as the aspects George has to include to perform the depictive aspects.

3. *Annotative aspects.* These are the aspects of a demonstration that are included as simultaneous commentary on what is being demonstrated. When George exaggerates the daintiness of Elizabeth's gestures, the pursing of her lips, the closing of her eyes, Helen isn't to take these as depictive. The exaggerations are merely commentary on what he *is* depicting. The annotative aspects are sometimes as important as the depictive ones.

4. *Incidental aspects.* These are the aspects of a demonstration that are incidental to the demonstrator's purpose, what is left over once he or she has chosen the depictive, supportive, and annotative aspects.

Effective demonstrating is an art, for speakers must enable their addressees to decouple the depictive, supportive, and annotative aspects. George had to make it clear to Helen that his lack of cup, saucer, tea, swallowing, and gender change were supportive aspects, and his daintiness was an exaggeration. If Helen had construed these as depictive, he would have failed. There has been little investigation of how people engineer all this, even though they do it all the time.

HOW TO DEMONSTRATE

The point of demonstrating a thing is to enable addressees to experience selective parts of what it would be like to perceive the thing directly. When Helen sees George demonstrate, she has a partial experience of what it would be like to see Elizabeth herself drinking tea. The demonstrator's problem is how to arrange for this experience.

The act of demonstrating, like the act of indicating, generally encompasses an *instrument* and *depictive actions* performed with it. George used his arms, hands, mouth, and eyes to mime Elizabeth's tea drinking. People exploit a variety of instruments and depictive actions. The list I offer is hardly exhaustive.

People use their bodies as instruments, choosing parts for what they can readily depict. Here are examples (in which I stands for instrument and O for object):

Instrument	Depictive action	Example
forefinger	drawing O in air with I	"Utah is shaped like this [demo]."
two hands	measuring O with I	"I caught a fish this long [demo of length]."
hand	forming I into O's shape	"He held out a gun [demo of gun]."
arm	swinging I like O	"The drawbridge swings up like this [demo of movement]."
legs	moving I like O	"George limps like this [demo]."
entire body	miming O with I	"You serve a volleyball like this [demo]."

When George traces the outline of Utah in the air, the shape of the tracing is a depictive aspect, and its size, orientation, and tracing direction are supportive aspects. People also depict things with their face, as in these examples:

Instrument	Depictive action	Example
mouth	mimicking O with I	"He smiled like this [demo of smile]."
face	mimicking O with I	"I caught my thumb in a door [demo of wince]."

| head, eyes | mimicking O with I | "He looked me up and down [demo]." |

People are surprisingly creative in how they use their body to depict things.

The perceptual experiences induced by demonstrations may be auditory or tactual as well as visual. People are skillful, for example, at demonstrating with their voices:

Instrument	Depictive Action	Example
voice	mimicking O with I	"She sang Yankee Doodle like this [demo of singing]."
voice	mimicking O with I	"Paris ambulance sirens go [demo of siren sound]."
voice	mimicking O with I	"Garbo was famous for the line, 'I want to be alone' [demo of Swedish accent]."

People can selectively depict all manner of speech characteristics – speed, gender, age, dialect, accent, drunkenness, lisping, anger, surprise, fear, stupidity, hesitancy, power. Many demonstrations combine sights and sounds, as when George demonstrates Greta Garbo's "I want to be alone" in a Swedish accent while clutching his arms to his chest in a Garboesque pose.

One of the commonest forms of demonstrations is direct quotation (Clark and Gerrig, 1990). Take these examples:

- So my mom said, "[Whiny voice] You can't go out until you make your bed."
- "Nothingth changed!" he yelled. "By God, Thally, you're the meaneth, thtubborneth, bitchieth, mule-headedeth, vengefulleth cold-blooded therpent in the Thtate of Vermont." [John Gardner, October Light]
- The car engine went [brmbrm], and we were off.
- The boy went [rude gesture] and ran away.

What speakers do in quotations is demonstrate selected aspects of what someone or something did or could have done. In the first example, a child is depicting not only the content of her mother's utterance but her whiny tone. In the second, the narrator is demonstrating the original speaker's lisp as well as his scornful assertion. In the third and fourth, we find nonlinguistic quotations depicting a car sound and a gesture. What is depicted in quotations isn't necessarily linguistic or even auditory, but any perceptible thing, state, or event.

In conversation, people often don't have access to tennis rackets, volley balls, teacups, or pencils. They make do with the instruments at hand – their limbs, body, faces, and voices – so most demonstrations are manual, facial, vocal, or some combination.

ICONIC GESTURES

People gesture in telling stories, giving directions, explaining how things work, and many of these gestures depict what is being talked about (Goodwin, 1981; Kendon, 1980; McNeill, 1992; Schegloff, 1984). These have been called *iconic gestures*.[11] Most iconic gestures are by speakers, although addressees may gesture in response to speakers, as with smiles, looks of surprise, or grimaces. In an example analyzed by Kendon (1980), Fran tells a joke based on the movie *Some Like it Hot*. Her speech is on the left, her gestures in the middle, and the aspects they depict on the right:

	Speech	Gestures	Depicted Aspects
1	they wheel a big *table* in	F sweeps her left arm inward in a horizontal motion.	height and forward movement of table
2	with a big with a big [1.08 sec] *cake* on it	During pause F makes series of circular motions with forearm pointing downward and index finger extended.	shape and orientation of horizontal dimension of cake
3	and the *girl*	F raises her arm until it is fully extended vertically above her.	vertical movement of girl jumping out of cake
4	jumps *up*		

While describing the scene in words, Fran uses her hands and arms to portray selective pieces of it. The example illustrates several features of iconic gestures.

Iconic gestures generally have three main stages: (1) *preparation*; (2) *stroke*, the peaking of effort within the gesture; and (3) *recovery* (Kendon, 1980; McNeill, 1992). Within these stages, one can identify other points

---

[11] They have also been called *illustrators* (Ekman and Friesen, 1969). What I am calling iconic gestures are divided by McNeill (1992, p. 145) into two types: *iconic gestures*, which "exhibit images of events and objects in a concrete world (real or fictive)," and *metaphoric gestures*, which "create images of abstractions." Since both are iconic in Peirce's sense, I will keep *iconic gestures* as the cover term for both.

in time: the onset of movement; the moment of peak thrust or energy; the acme or point of maximum extension; the beginning of retraction; and the moment the limb reaches the position from which it originally started, its rest or home position (Schegloff, 1984).

Iconic gestures are tightly synchronized with speech (Goodwin, 1981; Kendon, 1980; McNeill, 1992; Schegloff, 1984). Fran's speech divides into four units Kendon called *tone units* (see Chapter 9). Each is a short clause or phrase under a single intonation contour, usually with a single prominently accented word or syllable (marked with italics in the example). Gestures tend to be associated with tone units, one gesture per unit, or one spanning two units (Kendon, 1980; McNeill, 1992). The stroke, or peak thrust, of a gesture ordinarily falls on the accented syllable. In tone unit 3, the stroke of Fran's gesture falls on *girl*. In tone unit 2, when Fran's speech is disfluent, delaying the word *cake*, the stroke of her gesture falls in the pause before *cake* – perhaps where she projected *cake* would occur.

Iconic gestures tend to anticipate the words they go with (Butterworth and Beattie, 1978; Kendon 1980; McNeill, 1992; Morrel-Samuels & Krauss, 1992; Schegloff, 1984). Fran portrayed the girl jumping out of the cake in tone unit 3, but described it in tone unit 4. It is sometimes possible to single out a word or phrase – a *lexical affiliate* – that corresponds to the content of the gesture. In tone unit 2 the lexical affiliate of Fran's gesture might be *cake*, and in tone unit 3, *jump up*. In one study of sixty iconic gestures (Morrel-Samuels and Krauss, 1992), all were initiated before their lexical affiliates – by an average of 1.0 seconds. In no instance was the gesture initiated *after* its lexical affiliate.[12] The same gestures were terminated an average of 1.5 seconds after their lexical affiliates. Iconic gestures are timed to peak on the stressed words they are affiliated with.

FUNCTIONS OF ICONIC GESTURES

Most iconic gestures are genuine signals by which speakers mean things. This point isn't trivial, for it has led to heated debate (Kendon, 1980, 1983; Krauss, Morrel-Samuels, and Colasante, 1991). The main alternative is that speakers produce iconic gestures merely to help them formulate utterances – a facilitative function. Although iconic gestures may be facilitative,

---

[12] The sample didn't include *component* demonstrations, which have quite different properties, as we will see.

I will argue that they are primarily communicative.

Iconic gestures, like other demonstrations, divide into two kinds (Clark and Gerrig, 1990), *component* and *concurrent* gestures. Component gestures are embedded as parts of other utterances, just as the word *table* is embedded as part of the utterance "they wheel a big table in." Now, Fran means something by "table" because she means something by "they wheel a big table in," of which it is a component. The same holds for component gestures.

One class of component gestures are those in quotations, as in this example (Polanyi, 1989, p. 92):

Kate: I went out of my mind and I just screamed and I said "Take that out! That's not for me!"...And I shook this I-V and I said "I'm on an I-V, and I can't eat. Take it out of here!"

In delivering her quotation Kate "shakes her arm as if shaking the I-V and shouts in the conversational setting as she shouts in the story." Her gestures are as much a part of her quotation as her words. In some quotations, all there is is the iconic gesture, as in "The boy went [rude gesture] and ran away." Another class of component gestures are those that complete utterances, as in this example (Clark and Gerrig, 1990):

Damon: I got out of the car, and I just [demonstration of turning around and bumping his head on an invisible telephone pole].

A third class are those indicated by *this*, as in "Lilian caught a fish this [extending hands apart] long" and "He walked like this [tracing a crooked path with hand]." All of these gestures are components of complex signals, so they are themselves signals.

Concurrent iconic gestures are produced at the same time as other utterances. When Fran utters "they wheel a big *table* in," she also gestures, depicting the height and forward movement of the table. She clearly intends the gesture as a signal. It expresses information that is not found in her words, but is necessary to her narrative. Her audience wouldn't fully understand what she meant without identifying it. Her gesture, as I will put it, is *informative*. In fact, she produces the speech and gesture as part of a *single* composite signal, timing its stroke to fall on *table*, the main accent in the phrase. It seems wrong to say she is making *two* assertions at the same time, one with her words and another with her gesture. She is making a *single* assertion, but with a composite of words and gesture. Schematically: composite signal = spoken utterance + iconic gesture. Although the gesture isn't a component of the utterance, it *is* a component of the composite signal, which makes it a signal too. The gesture is *integral* to the composite signal.

There is good evidence that most concurrent iconic gestures are informative. When people are asked to tell others how a lock works, they rely heavily on iconic gestures, almost all expressing at least some information not found in the accompanying words (Engle and Clark, 1995). When people are asked to describe cartoons for others, they too use a plethora of iconic gestures, most of which are patently informative (McNeill, 1992). Many iconic gestures, indeed, are uninterpretable by outside viewers without the accompanying speech (Krauss, Morrel-Samuels, and Colasante, 1991), and that would follow if they were designed to be informative, to be interpreted as part of the ongoing discourse and adding to it.[13] And, finally, speakers gesture less when their addressees cannot see them. In one study (Cohen and Harrison, 1973), speakers produced twice as many iconic gestures in face-to-face conversation as over an intercom.

There is also good evidence that concurrent iconic gestures are integral to composite signals. If they are truly integral, it should be difficult to produce the speech without the gestures, and vice versa. For one thing, speakers should find it difficult to speak when they are prevented from gesturing – especially when they would be most likely to gesture. Imagine sitting on your hands while telling someone how to tie a double bowline. Indeed, when gestures are prevented, speakers become less fluent, slower, and less vivid (Rimé, Schiaratura, Hupet, and Ghysselinckx, 1984), especially in spatial descriptions (Bilous, 1992; Krauss, 1991).

On the same grounds, speakers should find it difficult to eliminate gestures even when they don't need to use them. As an analogy, imagine trying to eliminate intonation when dictating a letter that won't be heard by your addressee. Indeed, on the intercom speakers still use some gestures (Cohen and Harrison, 1973). Similarly, in Japan, people sometimes bow at the end of a telephone conversation, and in America, they sometimes nod on the telephone. Now, bows and nods, as emblems, are quintessentially communicative, and if anything should be eliminated on the telephone, they should be. But if, like intonation, they are integral

---

[13] Krauss et al. (1991) used the data instead to argue that, if the gestures aren't interpretable, they couldn't have been intended to be communicative. But this argument isn't decisive. Most words aren't fully interpretable when isolated from their spoken contexts, yet words are patently communicative. Gestural utterances are no different.

to composite signals, it should take special effort to eliminate them.[14] So people should be more fluent on the linguistic half of a composite signal if they don't have to suppress the gestural half.

Most iconic gestures are easier to formulate and execute than the words they are to be integrated with. Recall that iconic gestures invariably anticipate their lexical affiliates. And the rarer the lexical affiliate (the longer it takes to retrieve the word), the longer it lags behind the gesture (Morrel-Samuels and Krauss, 1992). Because of this asymmetry, iconic gestures might help speakers formulate utterances – especially in retrieving words (DeLaguna, 1927; Ekman and Friesen, 1972; Krauss, Morrel-Samuels, and Colasante, 1991). Fran, for example, appears to have trouble finding the word *cake*: "with a big with a big [1.08 sec] *cake* on it." When she gestures during the pause, she may be trying to help herself retrieve *cake* from memory. Hence the idea that iconic gestures are facilitative.

But iconic gestures may be facilitative only as a side effect of their communicative function. Suppose George is gesturing something integral with a word he is about to use, but has trouble retrieving the word. He might proceed with the gesture anyway for one of three reasons. First, he may find it easier to continue a gesture than to restart or delay it. Second, he may use the gesture to let Helen know he is searching for a word; speakers ordinarily account for delays in speaking, and gestures provide an ideal account (see Chapter 9). Or third, George may be inviting Helen to help find the word, and he intends the gesture to help her do that.

FACIAL GESTURES

People also produce facial gestures, many of which are clearly demonstrations (Bavelas, 1992, 1994; Bavelas, Black, Lemery, MacInnis, and Mullett, 1986; Bavelas, Black, Lemery, and Mullett, 1986). Janet Bavelas illustrated one such gesture in a lecture:

I walked into a sports store and asked whether they had Merco squash balls. The clerk said, "No, we have Dunlops." I responded with [Bavelas does a facial gesture for her audience]; that is, I wrinkled my nose, laughed, and said, "No thanks," and he laughed and said "OK." The nose-wrinkle in this context meant (and was understood to mean) "It is AS IF Dunlop squash balls are disgusting to me." It used the *metaphor* of physical disgust to convey dislike for something not at all rotten or smelly. (Bavelas, 1992, p. 2)

[14] I'm indebted to Scott Mainwaring for this point.

The nose-wrinkle *depicted* a person in a state of disgust, by which Bavelas meant that she disliked Dunlop squash balls. So it is communicative, a type of demonstration. When Bavelas wrinkled her nose in the lecture itself, she depicted what she did in the sports store, as she would in any quotation. Her second nose-wrinkle was a demonstration of a demonstration. Other examples are winces and grimaces (meaning "That's scary" or "That's awful"), raised eye-brows (meaning "I'm surprised" or "I'm skeptical"), and looks of dejection or sadness (meaning "How sad!") (Chovil, 1991, 1991/2; Chovil and Fridlund, 1991; Ekman, 1979).

Although many facial gestures depict pain, disgust, surprise, happiness, they don't depend on speakers' being in those emotional states. When Bavelas wrinkled her nose at the store clerk, she wasn't actually in a state of disgust. The point is illustrated in an experiment by Bavelas and her colleagues (1986). A student watched an experimenter carry a large television set into the room and, in a carefully staged accident, drop it on his finger. Then the experimenter, showing pain, either made eye contact with the student, or hunched over the television set. The scene was videotaped. Most students began to form a grimace within a fraction of a second of the accident. If the experimenter looked up, they continued to develop the grimace, displaying it to the experimenter. But if he didn't look up, most of them dropped it. So the students prepared and displayed grimaces to communicate sympathy to the injured experimenter (see also Chovil, 1991). The grimaces weren't automatic expressions of their emotional states.

In conversation, most facial gestures don't express emotional states, so must have other origins anyway. Consider Nicole Chovil's (1991/2) study of more than 1,000 facial displays in conversation (excluding smiles). Although 25 percent of the displays were judged incidental to the conversation, the rest were tightly organized with the talk. Some were associated with the illocutionary acts being performed; one speaker raised his eyebrows while asking "Are we supposed to eat this meal too?" and another did a "facial shrug." Others depicted what the speakers were talking about; one speaker wrinkled her nose while saying "I think liver is disgusting." Most of the displays were performed by speakers, but a few were performed by addressees in reaction to them. Some of the facial gestures (e.g., nodding, rolling the eyes) were emblems; others were like beats. But many of the rest were depictive, serving much the same purpose as iconic hand gestures.

What, finally, about smiles? They are used the world over to express happiness (Ekman et al., 1987), so in conversation they might be thought to be purely expressive: I smile when I'm happy, and not when I'm not. In fact, most smiles are *not* merely expressive. They are demonstrations. In one study (Kraut and Johnston, 1979), bowlers were observed to smile nine times as often when facing their friends as when facing the pins. They almost never smiled when bowling alone, nor did they smile more often after a strike or spare – which should have made them happy – than after other scores. That is, they used smiling to communicate with their friends. And in conversation, smiles by both speakers and addressees are tightly organized with the talk and mostly disappear when the participants cannot see each other (Fridlund, 1991, 1994). They are often used by interlocutors at the ends of clauses, like nods and "uh huh," to signal understanding (Brunner, 1979). So many facial gestures are demonstrations – signals that work by selective depiction.

VOCAL GESTURES

In spoken language, people have to deliver an utterance with intonation or prosody. Intonation is very different from words and syntax. Although some aspects may be conventional and therefore symbolic (see Pierrehumbert and Hirschberg, 1990), many aspects appear to be indexical or iconic. This point has been argued by Dwight Bolinger (1985). As he put it, "intonation is part of a gestural complex whose primitive and still surviving function is – however elaborated and refined – the signaling of emotions and their degrees of intensity" (p. 98). He went on, "It assists grammar – in some instances may be indispensable to it – but is not ultimately grammatical" (p. 106).

Bolinger's idea was that intonation is iconic. Pitch is a central element in intonation. "Suppose," he said, "we take the obvious emotive correlation as basic: high pitch symptomizes a condition of high tension in the organism, low pitch the opposite…When we come to elements in an utterance that interest or excite us, we mark the spot with a rise in pitch – the more interesting and exciting they are, the greater the rise" (pp. 99-100). Although Bolinger illustrated the idea with many intonation patterns, the point is especially clear with atomic utterances – "hi," "oh," "ah," "okay," "yes," etc. – because they get so much of their interpretation from intonation. When you greet someone with "hi" or "hello," the more you raise your pitch, the more pleasure you signal. And when you say "oh," the greater the rise in pitch, the more surprise you signal. When you produce a heightened "hi" or "oh," you are depicting a person evincing pleasure or surprise and, in that way, mean "I am *very* delighted" or "I am *very* surprised." As with facial gestures, you don't have to feel what you are demonstrating. You can merely pretend pleasure or surprise. Still, people may be mostly truthful with their intonation, just as they are with their words.

Tone of voice is a vague term for other vocal gestures that are used to communicate emotion and attitude. People can communicate anger, mystery, boredom, disdain, or sadness by selecting a tone of voice that mimics someone in that state. In reading "Little Red Riding Hood" to a five-year-old, you might speak in a low, whispery voice when the wolf enters the scene. You communicate mystery by depicting how a person would speak in sharing a secret.

Demonstrations, in summary, take many forms. They can be performed by means of any available part of the body – arms, legs, face, eyes, voice – or by extensions of the body – pencil and paper, computers, musical instruments. All demonstrations depict selected aspects of an object, property, or event. They are icons created to mean something for addressees.

Signaling processes

How do people select and interpret signals? According to the standard picture, speakers begin with communicative intentions, and they encode these in linguistic symbols – in words and constructions. Their addressees in turn decode these symbols and infer their intentions. The process is complicated because words and constructions are complex, and so are the inferences required (Chapter 5). Still, in the standard picture, selecting and interpreting signals deals primarily with symbols – their choice and interpretation. Indices play a secondary role that is largely unspecified, and icons play no role at all.

The standard picture is radically incomplete. In conversation, most utterances are composites of the three methods – describing-as, indicating, and demonstrating – not just one or two. What is more, the three methods depend on fundamentally different processes, and these have to be integrated. For a realistic picture of language use, we must characterize the three processes and their integration.

THREE PROCESSES

The processes people recruit in describing-as, indicating, and demonstrating are different every step of the way. Recall that symbols, indices, and icons are associated with their objects in different ways – by rule, by physical connection, and by perceptual resemblance. When people talk, they have to coordinate in establishing these associations, and the processes they need change with the connection they have to establish. Here are the main contrasts:

Method	Sign created	Memory resource	Basic process
describing-as	symbols	mental lexicon, grammatical rules	activating rules
indicating	indices	representation of spatial, temporal surroundings	locating entities
demonstrating	icons	memory for appearances	imagining appearances

In describing-as, speakers and addressees coordinate on *activating* the same rule for each symbol (Chapter 3). Suppose George uses the word *hold* in talking to Helen. To select the word, he must consult his *mental lexicon* – a vast memory store of information about the conventional meanings of all the symbols he knows – and activate a representation of the word shape, /hold/, corresponding to the type of thing he wants to denote. Helen, in turn, must consult her own mental lexicon and, working in reverse, activate a representation of the type of thing that is conventionally denoted by the word shape /hold/. None of this is simple. *Hold* has many conventional meanings both as a noun and as a verb, so it takes subtle coordination for George and Helen to activate one in common.

In indicating, speakers and addressees coordinate instead on *locating* entities in their immediate surroundings. When George points at a dog, he must be confident his gesture will lead Helen to locate and attend to the dog *qua* dog, and in interpreting George's gesture, Helen must do just that. Coordinating on spatial and temporal locations is just as delicate a process as coordinating on conventional symbols, but in a fundamentally different modality.

In demonstrating, speakers and their addressees coordinate on something different again: imagining the way things appear. By appearance, I mean the way something looks, sounds, feels, tastes, or smells, and by imagining, I mean creating a mental representation of those appearances. When George gestures that he caught a fish "this long," he must be confident that his gesture depicts the fish's length, and that Helen will be able to perceive that information in imagining the fish's length.

So describing-as, indicating, and demonstrating rely on very different cognitive resources for both speaker and addressee. Describing depends on a vast memory store of conventional symbols – the mental lexicon – and the grammatical rules for their combination. Indicating depends on a representation of the surrounding space and time. And demonstrating depends on a knowledge of perceptual appearances.

COMPOSITE SIGNALS

Most signals, as we have seen, are composites that are knitted together from the three methods. George sees Helen and says "Hello." He uses the conventional meaning of *hello* to *describe* his action as a greeting. He uses his voice and eye gaze to *indicate* himself as speaker, Helen as addressee, and now as the time of greeting. He uses his smile, open eyes, and magnified intonation to *demonstrate* his enthusiasm. Helen, in turn, not only interprets each of these methods, but integrates them to understand him as meaning, roughly, "I, George, now greet you, Helen, enthusiastically." The point is this: "Hello" is treated not as three *parallel* signals with separate interpretations, but as a *single* signal with a unified interpretation (see Bavelas, 1994).

The composition of signals, however, is usually more complex, as illustrated by a spontaneous example recorded by Nicole Chovil (1991/2, p. 180). Jane is telling Ken about her son's incessant questions and how they irritate her at times:

Jane: Sometimes I find them amusing, other times I find them *exasperating*.

As Jane said *exasperating*, she "raised her eyebrows, and widened and rolled her eyes." Here Jane used words and morphemes – elementary symbols – to compose a sentence – a complex symbol – whose meaning is a composition of the meanings of its parts. She also created indices to establish who she was referring to with *I*, *them*, and other elements. Already, this poses an issue of integration. Jane's index to her son's questions went with *them* and not other expressions, and this she had to coordinate with Ken.

The same goes for her demonstrations. When Jane raised her eyebrows and widened and rolled her eyes – and may have spoken in a weary voice – she was demonstrating an especially exasperated person. Her demonstration elaborated on what she meant by *exasperating*, and not what she meant by *amusing*, or *find*, or *other times*. She indicated this in part by the timing of her demonstration. Ken was to integrate what she meant by the gesture – roughly "what is a person to do!" – with the conventional meaning of *exasperating* just as he was to integrate the interpretation of each index with the right expression.

Many demonstrations have no lexical affiliates. Some elaborate on an entire clause (McNeill, 1992). Some are constituents of a clause, as when Damon said "I got out of the car, and I just [demonstration of turning around and bumping his head on an invisible telephone pole]." Some are performed alone, as when Bavelas wrinkled her nose at the sporting store clerk. It won't be easy to specify how speakers and addressees integrate descriptions, indications, and demonstrations.

CHOICE OF COMPOSITE

The final issue is how to choose the right composite. Jane, for example, chose a description *exasperating* plus a demonstration of an exasperated person. She *could* have chosen a description alone ("really exasperating"), or a demonstration alone ("other times I find them [demonstration of an exasperated person]"). And Kate, in telling her story, chose a direct quotation – a demonstration:

I went out of my mind and I just screamed and I said "Take that out! That's not for me!"

She *could* have chosen an indirect quotation – a description plus indication:

I went out of my mind and I just screamed and I said that they should take it out, that that was not for me.

How speakers make their choices is part of their broader decisions about what they are doing and why.[15] Here I will merely point to three dimensions of their decision – purpose, availability, and effort.

The choice of composite always depends on people's *purposes*. Some choices are obligatory. If George wants to refer to an individual – himself, his house, his son's fall off a bicycle – he cannot do it by description alone. He must anchor the reference, which requires an indication. Other choices are optional. Kate's story was more vivid with direct quotation ("'Take that out! That's not for me!'") than it would have been with indirect quotation ("that they should take it out, that that was not for me")

[15] For choices in direct vs. indirect vs. so-called free indirect quotation, which is one area in which speakers choose type of composite signal, see Clark and Gerrig (1990), Cohn (1978), Macaulay (1987), Sternberg (1982), Tannen (1989).

(Clark and Gerrig, 1990; Tannen, 1989). In so far as describing-as, indicating, and demonstrating serve different purposes, speakers' choices of composite must conform to their purposes.

Yet people's choice of composite is constrained by the *availability* of the method. When George and Helen are face to face, he can point at objects and make iconic manual and facial gestures. When they are on the telephone, he cannot. If George wants to buy paté from a Parisian charcutier and his French is shaky, he must resort to indication and demonstration. Written language is particularly constraining. Print cannot represent voice pitch or identity, manual or facial gestures, or pointing, and it has only crude ways of representing intonation, tone of voice, timing, and vocal demonstrations.[16] Writers are forced to rely on description and a few types of indication.

The final factor is *effort*. It is far easier to demonstrate than describe how to tie a double bowline, or how large a fish you caught. On the other hand, it is far easier to indicate than describe the taste of a fine burgundy, and it may be impossible to demonstrate it. Effort is related to availability. The more fluent George is in French, the more easily he can pick out the paté by describing than by indicating or demonstrating. What is the metric for effort? At the moment there is no obvious answer.

A proper theory of signal composition faces at least two challenges. The first is to say how speakers design descriptions, indications, and demonstrations to make clear how they are to be knitted together. The second is to account for speakers' choice of composite – what is the most effective available mix of description, indication, and demonstration for current purposes.

Conclusions

Signaling is often viewed as a homogeneous process. Speakers represent what they mean in symbols, which they intend their addressees to interpret. In this view, signaling is largely or solely the use of symbols. In reality, signaling is a mixture of three methods – describing-as, indicating, and demonstrating. Describing-as is the only method that uses symbols, and it never works alone. In conversation, indicating is always

---

[16] Two examples of vocal demonstrations represented in print are: "The pounding of the cylinders increased: ta-pocketa-pocketa-pocketa-pocketa-pocketa" (James Thurber, "The Secret Life of Walter Mitty"), and "The room reeked of camphor. 'Ugf, ahfg,' choked Briggs, like a drowning man" (James Thurber, "The Night the Bed Fell"). See Clark and Gerrig (1990).

required too. Of the three methods, demonstrating is the most neglected, yet is essential to everything from quotations to intonation to iconic gestures. What is more, these methods rely on different processes: Describing-as works by activating rules in memory, indicating by locating individuals in the spatial and temporal surroundings, and demonstrating by imagining appearances. Signaling can never be understood without accounting for all three methods.

Signaling is also often viewed as a solely linguistic process – the use of words and phrases from a language like English. In reality, it has both linguistic and nonlinguistic features. Indeed, it is better characterized by the methods and instruments used, as summarized here:

Method of Signaling

Instrument	Describing-as	Indicating	Demonstrating
Voice	words, sentences, vocal emblems	vocal locating of "I" "here" "now"	intonation, tone of voice, onomatopoeia
Hands, arms	emblems, junctions	pointing, beats	iconic hand gestures
Face	facial emblems	directing face	facial gestures, smiles
Eyes	winks, rolling eyes	eye contact, eye gaze	widened eyes
Body	junctions	directing body	iconic body gestures

"Linguistic" methods comprise only the upper left-hand corner of this classification.

The view of signaling that emerges here challenges the traditional notion of "language." It is fine to speak of "a language" such as English, Urdu, or Tzeltal as a system of signals that are conventional within a speech community – what Lewis (1969) called a conventional signaling system (Chapter 3). It is this system that supplies what is traditionally called the "linguistic" methods of signaling. But these linguistic methods work only in combination with nonlinguistic methods, and even many parts of "linguistic" signals – aspects of intonation, tone of voice, the vocal location of the speaker, here, and now – are not properly part of "a language." If so, "language" must be taken to be broader than "a language." At least in the notion of "language use," it must include every method by which one person means something for another – describing-as, indicating, and demonstration – regardless of the instrument used – voice, hands, arms, face, eyes, or body. To assume anything less would beg the question of what language use is.

PART IV

Levels of action

7 | Joint projects

Signaling is of interest only because it is used in advancing the joint activities people are engaged in. Take this exchange from an interview by a British academic of a prospective student (3.1.174):

Arthur:　　u:h what modern poets have you been reading -
Beth:　　　well I'm . I like Robert Graves very much -

When Arthur says "u:h what modern poets have you been reading -" he doesn't want Beth merely to understand what he means – that he wants to know what modern poets she has been reading. He wants her to *take up* his question, to answer it, to *tell* him what modern poets she has been reading. She could refuse even though she has understood. To mean something, you don't have to achieve uptake, and to understand something, you don't have to take it up. Still, Beth's uptake is needed if she and Arthur are to achieve what Arthur has publicly set out for them to do at this point in their interview.

Arthur and Beth's exchange is used to carry out a *joint project*. The joint project begins with Arthur *projecting* a joint task for Beth and him to carry out – she is to tell him what modern poets she has been reading. It continues with Beth agreeing to that project, and it becomes complete, though slightly altered, with her answer. *A joint project is a joint action projected by one of its participants and taken up by the others.* Recall levels 3 and 4 of the joint action ladder for communicative acts (see Chapter 5):

4　A is proposing joint project *w* to B　　B is considering A's proposal of *w*
3　A is signaling that *p* for B　　　　　　　B is recognizing that *p* from A

Arthur and Beth go beyond the meaning and understanding of their signals at level 3 to the proposing and uptake of joint projects at level 4.

With it, they advance their official business, the interview, by one step.

Uptake, however, presupposes understanding. If Beth is to take up Arthur's proposal, she must settle on what he means. What does he really intend by "modern poets" and "reading"? How many names will he be satisfied with? Does he want more than just names? Although Beth reaches a construal of Arthur's utterance, is it the one he intended – is it one he will accept? I will call this the *joint construal problem*. Note that Beth gives Arthur evidence of her construal in her answer, "well, I'm . I like Robert Graves very much -." If her construal had been unacceptable, Arthur would have corrected it, and he didn't. There is a tight link between the way two people settle on a joint construal of a signal (level 3) and the way they propose and take up joint projects (level 4). Once we realize this, we are led to two surprising conclusions. First, the joint construal of an utterance, a signal, gets established in an interactive, sequential process that depends on the joint projects they contribute to, and vice versa. And second, exchanges like Arthur's and Beth's are the joint actions from which larger joint actions in discourse emerge. The goal of this chapter is to substantiate these conclusions.

Public displays

Reaching a joint construal of a signal isn't easy. When Arthur says "u:h what modern poets have you been reading," Beth must settle on a construal acceptable to Arthur – one they can take as a joint construal. How do they do that? One source of information is the form of Arthur's utterance, and another is their mutual beliefs about the current situation. But a third source of information, ignored in most accounts, is Beth's public display of her construal and Arthur's evaluation of that display. To see how this works, let us look at public displays of construals in general.

EVENTS AND REACTIONS

People try to make sense of the world around them. When they see things happen, they try to interpret them, to construe them as one thing and not another. Many things are easy to construe. I see a fish, and I construe it as a fish, as a trout, or as food for a grizzly bear. Social events aren't always so easy. I see a strange man walking toward me. Is he approaching me by accident, or by design? Does he want to ask me directions, rob me, or what? My construal will determine what I do next.

It is often useful to signal a construal – to display it publicly. Suppose Jack and Kate are watching a tennis match when one of the players makes a double fault and Jack goes "Uh oh!" With this signal, he makes public to Kate his construal of selected aspects of what he has just seen: The double fault is not to his liking. He signals Kate about his construal to show his solidarity with her on the course of the match. Kate might have suspected his disappointment with the double fault, but his signal gives her public evidence. Or suppose Kate wins a race, and Jack is proud of her accomplishment. To make his construal public, he needs to display it, which he can do by congratulating her: "Congratulations." Or suppose Jack steps on Kate's toe, an accident he regrets. Since he isn't certain that she thinks he construes it that way, he needs to make his construal public, which he can do with an apology: "Sorry." People display construals of many types of public events, as in these examples:

Instigating event	B's Reaction to event
A and B see tennis player double fault	"Uh oh," or B frowns
A and B notice a beautiful sunset	"What a beautiful sunset!"
B notices A wearing new earrings	"What beautiful earrings!"
A holds out cup of coffee for B	"Thank you" as B takes cup
A plays piano for B	B applauds
A holds money out for B	B takes money

Displaying an attitude toward an event is apparently so important that languages have evolved a special type of illocutionary act for the purpose, namely expressives (see Chapter 5). Here are illustrations:

Type of event	Expressive	Example
B is offended by A	A apologizes to B	"Sorry!"
B achieves something positive	A congratulates B	"Congratulations!"
B does a favor for A	A thanks B	"Thanks!"
B approaches A	A greets B	"Hi!"

In each case there is an instigating event followed by A's construal of it. An apology shows that an event is being construed as an offense, and a congratulations is for a positive achievement, a thanks is for a favor, and a greetings is for a desirable meeting. It is precisely these displays that give expressives their uses.

More often, people display their construals by the next step they take in the social process they are engaged in. When Kate trips, Jack helps her stand back up. Not only does he keep her from falling down, but he shows her that he has construed the trip as accidental and unwanted. And when Kate holds money out for Jack, he takes it, displaying that he has construed her action as one of transferring the money to him.

Certain social events come in what I will call *event–reaction pairs*. They have five main properties:

1. Event–reaction pairs consist of two ordered events – an *instigating event* and a *reaction*.
2. The two events have different origins.
3. The instigating event is any event mutually recognized by A and B.
4. The reaction is an action by B that is or includes a signal to A.
5. B's reaction is intended, among other things, to display B's construal of the target event.

Example: A car accident is an instigating event, and B's "How awful!" is a reaction. When the instigating event is an action by A toward B, we have an *action–response pair*, e.g., A's offering B a cup of coffee, and B's accepting it.

VALIDATING AND CORRECTING CONSTRUALS

Almost every event is open to differing construals – and this is especially true of social actions. When Kate places a glass of wine in front of Jack, he may construe the action in one of several ways:

K's action	J's construal of K's action	J's response
K places wine on table	K is doing a favor for J	"Thanks."
K places wine on table	K is doing a duty for J	"Right."
K places wine on table	K is showing J a new skill	"Nicely done."

When he says "Thanks," that is public evidence that he is treating Kate's action as a favor, and he expects her to see that. His response is a shared basis for the mutual belief that he has taken her action to be a favor.

What if Jack doesn't construe Kate's action as intended? If Kate has brought the wine for Helen and not for Jack, and Jack says "Thanks," she has two main choices. She can consider his construal to be incorrect and correct it, "Oh, this is for Helen – what would *you* like?" This way she provides a shared basis for the mutual belief that her action was intended as a favor to Helen and not him. Or she can accept Jack's construal unchanged. She might reason: "Aha, Jack wanted wine too. I can just as well leave this glass for him and bring another for Helen." She would then answer "You're welcome," laying down a shared basis for the mutual belief that her action was indeed to be taken as a favor to Jack. As far as Jack is concerned, that may be all Kate ever intended, and Kate knows that.

Kate's second option is an instance of revised intentions – a *revised construal*. Suppose I start driving from Palo Alto to shop in San Francisco. But halfway there, in San Mateo, a violent storm breaks out and I decide to shop in San Mateo instead. All I have done is change my mind, revise my intentions. In San Mateo I reason: "Well, I was originally intending my drive to San Mateo to be the first half of a drive to San Francisco, but I can just as easily treat it as the completion of a full drive to San Mateo. So what I originally construed as 'a half-trip to San Francisco to go shopping,' I now construe as 'a full-trip to San Mateo to go shopping.'" People regularly change their minds, revising their intentions to accommodate to the circumstances.

Suppose, instead, that Kate brought the wine for *either* Jack *or* Helen: She is indifferent to whether Jack construes her action as a favor for him or for Helen. So when Jack says "Thanks," she can accept his construal, reasoning this way: "Although I brought the wine for either Jack or Helen, he has construed it as a favor for him alone. That is consistent with my intention, so even though it is more specific, I can accept it." She could then answer "You're welcome." She would thereby lay down a shared basis for the mutual belief that her action was intended as a favor to Jack alone. As far as Jack is concerned, that may be all Kate ever intended, and Kate knows that. This we might call a *narrowed construal*.

A final possibility is that Jack misconstrues Kate without either of them noticing it. Suppose Kate has brought the wine for Helen and not for Jack, and Jack says "How nice!" thinking the favor was for him, but Kate thinks he is referring to the favor for Helen and accepts his apparent construal with a smile. They may or may not catch their error later. Here is an *undetected misconstrual*. In all, Jack's construal of Kate's actions may take one of five forms:

J's initial construal	K's intervening action	J's final construal
full construal	accept	verified construal
misconstrual	detect and correct	corrected misconstrual
misconstrual	detect yet accept	revised construal
narrowed construal	accept	narrowed construal
misconstrual	not detect yet accept	undetected misconstrual

In social processes, the argument goes, people often need to agree on what is taking place. One way of reaching consensus is by displaying construals of what is taking place for the others to accept or correct, and that often leads people to revise their intentions in greater or smaller ways. The process is sequential and interactive. We should expect the same in the understanding and uptake of utterances.

Local projects

In conversation, utterances tend to come in pairs. The point is illustrated in this brief telephone conversation (8.11.851):

Jane:	⌈ (rings C's telephone)
Kate:	⌊ Miss Pink's office -
	⌈ hello
Jane:	⌊ hello,
	⌈ is Miss Pink in .
Kate:	⌊ well, she's in, but she's engaged at the moment,
	⌈ who is it?
Jane:	⌊ ⌈ oh it's Professor Worth's secretary, from Pan-American College
Kate:	⌊ m,
Jane:	⌈ could you give her a message *for me*
Kate:	⌊ *certainly*
Jane:	⌈ u:m Professor Worth said that, if . Miss Pink runs into difficulties, .
	on Monday afternoon, . with the standing subcommittee, .
	over the item on Miss Panoff, - - -
Kate:	⌈ Miss Panoff?
Jane:	⌊ yes,
	that Professor Worth would be with Mr Miles all afternoon, - so she
	only had to go round and collect him if she needed him, - - -
Kate:	⌊ ah, - - -
	⌈ thank you very much indeed,
Jane:	⌊ right
Kate:	⌈ Panoff, right *you* are
Jane:	⌊ *right,*
Kate:	⌈ I'll tell her, *(2 to 3 syllables)*
Jane:	⌊ *thank you*
Kate:	⌈ bye bye
Jane:	⌊ bye

As the bracketing suggests, Jane and Kate don't merely take turns. Rather, Jane says something and Kate responds, or vice versa. Pairings like this are characteristic of everyday talk: Conversations are not so much sequences of *individual* actions as they are sequences of *paired* actions.

The paired utterances in Jane and Kate's conversation are what Schegloff and Sacks (1973) have called *adjacency pairs*. The prototype is the question and answer, as in this exchange:

Kate: who is it?
Jane: oh it's Professor Worth's secretary, from Pan-American College

According to Schegloff and Sacks, adjacency pairs have five essential properties:

1. Adjacency pairs consist of two ordered utterances – the *first pair part* and the *second pair part*.
2. The two parts are uttered by different speakers.
3. The two parts come in types that specify which part is to come first and which second.
4. The form and content of the second part depends on the type of the first part.
5. Given a first pair part, the second pair part is *conditionally relevant* – that is, relevant and expectable – as the next utterance.

Jane's question is the first pair part, and Kate's answer, the second. And given Jane's question, Kate's answer is conditionally relevant as the next utterance.

Adjacency pairs come in many types. Jane and Kate's brief conversation illustrates many of them, but there are others as well:

Adjacency pair		Example	
1.	Summons	Jane:	(rings)
2.	Response	Kate:	Miss Pink's office
1.	Greetings	Kate:	hello
2.	Greetings	Jane:	hello
1.	Question	Kate:	who is it?
2.	Answer	Jane:	oh it's Professor Worth's secretary, from Pan-American College
1.	Assertion	Jane:	oh it's Professor Worth's secretary, from Pan-American College
2.	Assent	Kate:	m
1.	Request	Jane:	could you give her a message *for me*
2.	Promise	Kate:	*certainly*
1.	Promise	Kate:	I'll tell her
2.	Acknowledgment	Jane:	thank you

1.	Thanks	Kate:	thank you very much indeed
2.	Acknowledgment	Jane:	right

1.	Good-bye	Kate:	bye bye
2.	Good-bye	Jane:	bye

Why do adjacency pairs take the form they do? The answer, I suggest, is that they solve two problems at once. At level 3, speakers and addressees face joint construal problems, and they solve them in two-part exchanges. In the first part, speakers present a signal, and in the second, addressees display their construal of it for speakers to accept or correct. At level 4, speakers and addressees try to complete joint tasks, and that also requires two-part exchanges. In the first part, speakers propose a joint project, and in the second, addressees take up their proposal. In the ordinary case, these two two-part structures coincide, and the result is adjacency pairs.

UPTAKE AND UNDERSTANDING

When Jane asks Kate "Who is it?" she is trying to get Kate to tell her who she is. She is proposing a joint project – a transfer of information. If Kate is willing and able, she will complete it and tell Jane who she is. Let me stress that Kate's answer ("oh it's Professor Worth's secretary, from Pan-American College") is not just any perlocutionary effect of Jane's utterance. She might have been surprised, outraged, or pleased by Jane's question. Rather, it is the perlocutionary effect projected by Jane's illocutionary point. It is an uptake of the particular joint project Jane proposed. Such joint projects become complete only through uptake, so completion at level 4 requires not only Jane's question but Kate's answer.

Proposals and their uptake provide a rationale for the first four properties of adjacency pairs. In particular, there are these correspondences:

First pair part A proposes a joint project for A and B.
Second pair part B takes up the proposed joint project.

In this scheme, there are two utterances (property 1) from different speakers (property 2). The two parts come in types – a proposal and an uptake – that specify which part comes first and which second (property 3). And the form and content of the second part, Kate's uptake, depends on the type of the first part, Jane's proposal (property 4). In short, proposals and their uptake often map directly onto the first and second parts of adjacency pairs.

What about conditional relevance (condition 5)? It has been characterized by Schegloff (1968, p. 1083) this way:

By conditional relevance of one item on another we mean: given the first, the second is expectable; upon its occurrence it can be seen to be a second item to the first; upon its non-occurrence it can be seen to be officially absent – all this provided by the occurrence of the first item.

The second part must be expectable from the first – a property I will call *expectability* – and as the very next utterance – a property I will call *adjacency*. The rationale for expectability is already clear. For Jane and Kate to complete the joint project, Kate's uptake (the second part) must be contingent on, and therefore follow, Jane's proposal (the first part).

To understand why Kate's uptake is adjacent, let us return to level 3 – meaning and understanding. At that level, Jane uses "Who is it?" to signal Kate that she is to say who she is. But how can they reach the mutual belief that Kate has understood Jane as intended? What better way than for Kate to *display* her construal of Jane's utterance in her next move, because that way Jane can accept or correct it. And Kate does just that. With "Oh it's Professor Worth's secretary, from Pan-American College," she displays her construal in two ways. Identifying herself as Professor Worth's secretary is an appropriate uptake for a question about who she is. And the form of her answer "it's ..." matches the syntax of the question "Who is it?"

The two parts of an adjacency pair, then, also give an optimal fit to the two-part structure of meaning and displayed understanding. That leads to these correspondences:

First pair part	A signals to B that p
Second pair part	B displays B's construal of A's signal

Because A's signal must come before B's display of its construal, this provides a rationale for the adjacency property of conditional relevance. The second pair part is expectable as the next utterance because it displays B's construal of the first part for A to accept or correct.

All this is in line with the property of *downward evidence* introduced in Chapter 5. "In a ladder of actions," according to the property, "evidence that one level is complete is also evidence that all levels below it are complete." When Jane produces "Who is it?" she means (at level 3) that Kate is to say who she is and, thereby, proposes (at level 4) that Kate tell her who she is. So when Kate takes up the proposed joint project (at level 4), she is also giving evidence that she has understood what Jane means (at level 3). The generalization is this: *Uptake is evidence of understanding.* That is why second parts of adjacency pairs serve both functions – uptake and evidence of understanding – and why they are expected to be adjacent.

Although the second part of an adjacency pair is *expected* to be adjacent, it often isn't, and the argument just offered explains why. Take this example (4.2.193, simplified):

A: that wasn't the guy I met, was it - when we saw the building? -
B: saw it where -
A: when I went over to Chetwynd Road
B: yes

Here the answer "yes" is separated from the question by two turns, a *side sequence* (Jefferson, 1972; Schegloff, 1972). B realizes that he cannot take up A's question until he has cleared up a point about what she meant, so he initiates a query about that point, and only when it is cleared up does he answer. B must come to some construal of A's question before he can use his uptake to display that construal. Side sequences between first and second pair parts are designed to complete that process.

Adjacency pairs, therefore, are emergent structures. Two people, A and B, face the problem of how to complete what they are doing. They must both establish a joint construal and effect the uptake. The most efficient solution is to do both at once, and that results in adjacency pairs.

ACTION AND RESPONSE

Adjacency pairs are clearly a type of action–response pair. A's action toward B is followed by B's reaction toward A that, among other things, displays B's construal of A's action. It is just that adjacency pairs accomplish something else too – the proposal and uptake of a joint project.

With this comparison, it is easy to see several problems in the original definition of adjacency pairs. First, neither first nor second part need be an utterance. The first part may be any type of signal, and the second, any action that takes up the proposal of the first part, as here:

Adjacency pair		Example	
1.	Summons	Jane:	(ring's Kate's telephone)
2.	Response	Kate:	Miss Pink's office
1.	Question	Burton:	Are you coming with us?
2.	Answer	Connie:	[nods]

Questions like "Which finger did you cut?" and commands like "At ease, soldier" and requests like "Two tickets please" often yield non-linguistic responses, yet they are surely best classified as adjacency pairs too.

According to properties 3 and 4, the two pair parts of adjacency pairs also come in types. But just as there is no principled typology for illocutionary acts, there is also no principled typology for the first and second pair parts. They get labeled question, request, offer, acceptance, and thanks, but these are merely types of illocutionary acts and inherit all the problems of classifying illocutionary acts. Even if adjacency pairs had their own typology, there is no reason to think that they can be typed any more clearly.

Adjacency pairs, we must conclude, are a special type of action–response pair. Properties 1, 2, and 3 are inherited from action–response pairs, but they have an additional property 4:

1. Adjacency pairs consist of two ordered actions – a first part and a second part.
2. The two parts are performed by different agents A and B.
3. The form and content of the second part is intended, among other things, to display B's construal of the first part for A.
4. The first part projects uptake of a joint task by the second part.

What makes adjacency pairs special is that the first part projects the uptake of a joint task, and the second part effects that uptake.

Minimal joint projects

When Jane and Kate talk on the telephone, they have official business to complete. In the view I have been taking, they do that through joint projects. Joint projects can be of any size. The entire conversation is one type of joint project, and so are many of its sections. I will argue that the *minimal* joint project is the adjacency pair – a proposal plus its uptake.

COORDINATING ON JOINT PROJECTS

In any joint action – from shaking hands to planning a party – the participants must go from the state of not being engaged in the joint action to being engaged in it and back out again (see Chapter 2). Every joint action has three parts:

1. *Entry* into the joint action
2. *Body* of the joint action, i.e., the joint action proper
3. *Exit* from the joint action

When Dan and Melissa play a piano–flute duet, there is, ideally, an instant at which they mutually believe they have begun playing the duet. That marks the entry. That is followed by a stretch of activity they mutually believe to be the duet proper, and that is the body. Finally, there is an instant at which they mutually believe they are no longer playing the duet, and that marks the exit. Playing the duet depends on establishing these mutual beliefs well enough for current purposes.

How do people coordinate on the entry, body, and exit of a joint action? For many joint actions, they need to coordinate on only three features (see Chapter 3):

1. *participants*: who is participating in the joint action in what roles
2. *entry time*: the entry time t into the joint action
3. *content*: the individual action $x(i)$ that participant i is to take in the joint action

To play measure 5 of their duet, Dan and Melissa need to identify themselves as the participants, synchronize their entry, coordinate who plays what notes and how. There is no need to synchronize the exit because it coincides with the entry into the next measure. (Recall the synchrony principle: In joint actions, the participants synchronize their processes mainly by coordinating on the entry times and participatory actions for each new phase.) Measure 5 is a sequence of smaller phases, or joint actions, each of which works the same way.

Joint actions in conversation are more complicated. Conversations, unlike duets, have no written score, so the participants must create their joint actions as they go. And when there are more than two parties, the participant roles change from one moment to the next. Dan may address Melissa, then Susan; next, Susan may address Melissa, then both Dan and Melissa; and so on. For each joint project, the three parties must coordinate on the participants, entry time, and content.

Adjacency pairs – in our revised definition – are ideal as minimal joint projects. The reason: They establish the participants, entry times, and contents of the joint projects with a minimum of joint effort. Let us return to Jane and Kate's joint project:

Jane: who is it?
Kate: oh it's Professor Worth's secretary, from Pan-American College

The participants are established by who addresses whom in the first pair part – Jane addresses Kate. The entry time is marked by Jane's initiation of the first pair part, "Who is it?" while she has Kate's attention. The content is also established jointly. The process begins with Jane's proposal "Who is it?" and it is completed with Kate's answer, "Oh it's Professor Worth's secretary, from Pan-American College," which not only establishes a joint construal of the project but completes it. Adjacency pairs are the perfect vehicle for coordinating the participants, entry times, and contents of joint projects.

JOINT PURPOSE

Joint projects serve joint purposes, and any joint purpose must fulfill these four requirements:

For A and B to commit themselves to joint purpose r
1.	*Identification*	A and B must identify r
2.	*Ability*	It must be possible for A and B to do their parts in fulfilling r
3.	*Willingness*	A and B must be willing to do their parts in fulfilling r
4.	*Mutual belief*	A and B must each believe that 1, 2, 3, and 4 are part of their common ground

People ordinarily establish joint purposes through negotiation. In their adjacency pair, Jane's proposal sets forth a possible joint purpose – the joint project – for their exchange (property 1) and shows that she is willing and able to do her part (properties 2 and 3). Kate's response, in turn, displays that she has identified Jane's purpose (property 1) and that she too is willing and able to do her part (properties 2 and 3). Together, these public displays help establish the mutual belief that both Jane and Kate have identified Jane's purpose and that both are willing and able to do their parts (property 4).

Joint purposes aren't always so easy to establish. When I ask you to sit down – when I propose that you sit down for me – you may understand me perfectly and yet be unable or unwilling to take up my proposal. You may respond in several ways. Here are the four main ways, which are illustrated with responses to questions (see Goffman, 1976; Stenström, 1984).

1. *Full compliance.* Respondents may comply fully with the project as proposed:

Jane: who is it?
Kate: oh it's Professor Worth's secretary, from Pan-American College

Jane wants to know who Kate is, and she tells her, completing the joint project as originally proposed in its entirety.

2. *Alteration of project.* Respondents may *alter* the proposed project to something they are able and willing to comply with (1.2.349):

Reynard: Oscar is going to the States?
Charles: well, this is what I heard just before I came away - - -

Charles isn't in a position to give a certain "yes" or "no" about Oscar's going to the States, so he alters the project to one of telling Reynard about what he heard just before he went away. He signals the change in stance with a tell-tale "well." Charles chose his altered project presumably because it would give Reynard information relevant to Oscar's going to the States. He was trying to be cooperative, though alterations may also be uncooperative.

3. *Declination of project.* When respondents are unable or unwilling to comply with the project as proposed, they can *decline* to take it up, usually by offering a reason or justification for why they are declining (1.8.40):

Betty: what happens if anybody breaks in and steals it, - are are is are we covered or .
Cathy: um - I don't know quite honestly .

Betty presupposes that Cathy knows whether they are covered by insurance, but Cathy doesn't and declines with her reason "I don't know." A declination leaves the joint project incomplete. It also displays an unwillingness or inability to find an altered project that might serve some broader purpose.

4. *Withdrawal from project.* Respondents can also *withdraw* entirely, for example, by deliberately ignoring the question and changing the topic. Here is an example from the beginning of a telephone conversation (8.2e.1042):

Susan: who's calling .
Jane: well, could you give her a message -

Here Jane withdraws from Susan's proposed joint project, not telling Susan who's calling, and makes a request instead. The four options can be summarized as follows:

	Category	A's proposal	B's response
1.	Compliance	A proposes *w*	B takes up *w* as proposed
2.	Alteration	A proposes *w*	B takes up an altered form of *w*
3.	Declination	A proposes *w*	B declines to take up *w*
4.	Withdrawal	A proposes *w*	B withdraws from considering *w*

With these four options – and there are further subtypes – people create not just adjacency pairs strictly defined (option 1, full compliance), but other pairings. The pairings result from two people trying to coordinate on a joint project and finding success (option 1), partial success (option 2), failure (option 3), or a termination of the attempt (option 4). Their form comes from what the participants are trying jointly to do and how well they succeed, not vice versa.

To speakers proposing joint projects, the four types of responses aren't equivalent. Publicly at least, they would prefer completion to alteration, alteration to declination, and declination to withdrawal. This ordering accounts for what are called preferred and dispreferred second pair parts of adjacency pairs (see Davidson, 1984, 1990; Drew, 1984; Houtkoop, 1987; Levinson, 1983; Pomerantz, 1978, 1984; Sacks, 1987). For each first pair part (e.g., "What time is it?"), the second pair part is expected to be conditionally relevant. A direct answer (e.g., "Five after three") is more relevant, hence more preferable, than an indirect answer ("Well, Susan left quite a while ago"), declination ("I don't know"), or withdrawal ("Gosh, what a beautiful sunset!"). Other adjacency pairs have similar preference orderings. In terms of joint projects, a second pair part is preferred the more fully it completes the joint project proposed in the first pair part.

Treating adjacency pairs as minimal joint projects also accounts for why dispreferred responses tend to be linguistically marked, or more complex. For "What time is it?" the most preferred response is highly elliptical ("Five after three"), determined by the syntax of the question, and the dispreferred responses are not. Dispreferred responses are also often marked by expressions such as "well" or "sorry" and produced with hesitations and self-repairs. In joint projects, it should be simpler to continue the first speaker's project than to alter it. Altering it requires rejection of the first speaker's perspective ("It is such and such a time") and establishment of a new perspective with new syntax ("Susan left quite a while ago") and marking that alteration, as with "well." Alterations should take time to choose and formulate.

Minimal joint projects, then, are shaped by both of the participants. Jane may propose one project, and although Kate can complete it as proposed, she can also alter it to something else, decline to complete it, or withdraw from it altogether.

Extended joint projects

Conversations pose a paradox. On the one hand, people engage in conversation – as in any joint activity – to do things with each other. On the other hand, they cannot know in advance what things they will actually do. Jane and Kate's conversation is a good illustration. Jane rang up to tell Miss Pink where Professor Worth would be that afternoon. When she discovered Miss Pink was busy, she recruited Kate to pass on the information. Kate had her own aims in answering the telephone. Her job was to take messages and keep callers from interrupting Miss Pink, but she had no idea who was calling or what they would say. Even though Jane and Kate began with their own aims, they couldn't know what they would end up doing. As Sacks et al. (1974) argued, they had to manage their conversation turn by turn. They had to adapt their actions to deal with the exigencies of each moment. In conversation, the participants' actions are *local* and *opportunistic*.

The paradox leaves us with a puzzle: How do people in conversation ever achieve their broader goals or interests? Part of the answer is that they engineer *extended joint projects* of more than one adjacency pair. These projects don't come prefabricated, but emerge through the opportunistic deployment of minimal joint projects. Here I will describe three basic ways in which extended projects emerge, deferring a fuller account to Chapters 10 and 11.

EMBEDDED JOINT PROJECTS

Respondents aren't always prepared to take part in the joint actions that others have contemplated for them. Indeed, they can alter, decline, or withdraw from joint projects that speakers have proposed. And speakers can't always anticipate the obstacles that respondents face in taking up their proposals. Often it is simpler for speakers to forge ahead, propose a joint project, and let the respondents deal with the obstacles that arise. The result is often an *embedded joint project*.

Take this hypothetical exchange in a restaurant between a waitress and customer:

| Waitress: | What'll ya have? | [1. request for order] |
| Customer: | I'll have a bowl of clam chowder and a salad with Russian dressing. | [2. uptake of request] |

The waitress asks for an order, and the customer gives it, creating a minimal joint project. But if the customer isn't prepared, she can interrupt the exchange, as in this actual example (Merritt, 1976, p. 333):

| Waitress: | What'll ya have girls? | [1. request for order] |
| Customer: | What's the soup of the day? | [1'. request for information] |

| Waitress: | Clam chowder | [2'. uptake of request] |
| Customer: | I'll have a bowl of clam chowder and a salad with Russian dressing. | [2. uptake of request] |

This time the waitress asks for the order, but to take her up, the customer needs to know the soup of the day and initiates a side sequence to find out. Once she has what she needs, she returns to take up the joint project originally proposed. The result is one joint project (the side sequence about the soup of the day) embedded within another (an exchange of the order). The embedded project is introduced to satisfy a *preparatory condition* of the customer's uptake – here the ability condition.

The issue is, as Schegloff (1972, p. 114) put it, "how do people see when a question follows a question that it is not any other question, not an evasion?" The side sequence, he suggested, "is specifically done and heard as prefatory to the activity made conditionally relevant by the question" (p. 114), and so "attention both to that activity and to the question is thereby exhibited." When the customer places her question where the waitress has projected an answer, she makes it clear she is initiating a joint project in preparation for such an answer. The side sequence needn't start with a question, as we see in this interchange in a British shop (Levinson, 1983, p. 305, simplified):

Customer:	U:hm . what's the price now eh with V A T do you know eh	[1. request for information]
Server:	Er I'll just work that out for you	[1'. promise of information]
Customer:	thanks	[2'. uptake of promise]
	(10 second pause)	
Server:	Three pounds nineteen a tube sir	[2. uptake of request]

The server initiates the side sequence to work out the tax in preparation for taking up the customer's proposal. Side sequences are used to establish preparatory conditions of all kinds – ability, willingness, or identification – and can be initiated in many ways.

CHAINING

When people take up one minimal joint project, they are usually initiating another one too. The second part of one adjacency pair is almost invariably the first part of a second one. Questions, for example, project answers, but because those answers are assertions, they in turn project assents, as here (8.1n.921):

Jane: do you know when when he'll be back in
Rod: he's around now, u:m I don't know where he is, . at the moment
Jane: oh.

Rod's response completes a question – answer pair, but initiates an asser-
tion-assent pair, which Jane completes with "oh." Here we have a *chain*
of two joint projects – question–answer, and assertion–assent – that are
linked by the part they share, the assertion. If a1 and a2 are the two parts
of one minimal joint project, and b1 and b2 are those of another, chaining
might be represented this way: $^{[}a1 +\ _{[}a2 = b1^{]} + b2_{]}$.

Chaining is remarkably useful for creating extended joint projects.
When Jane asks Rod her question, she is projecting not just his answer,
but her uptake of his answer. She is projecting not just an exchange of
information, but an *evaluated* exchange of information – question +
answer + evaluation. Such evaluated exchanges are common in
conversation (Heritage, 1984; Mehan, 1979; Stenström, 1984). Here are
several three- part chains illustrated with schematic exchanges:

Chain	Part 1	Part 2	Part 3
Real question–answer–evaluation	Where's Duncan?	At school.	Oh.
Test question–answer–verdict	What's pi?	3.14159.	Correct.
Offer–agreement–compliance	Want some cake?	Yes, please.	Here.
Request–compliance–thanks	I'll have cake.	Here.	Thanks.
Favor–thanks–acknowledgment	Here's your bag.	Thanks.	No problem.

Speakers can also project chains of more than three parts. Because
offers project agreements, which project compliances, which project
thanks, a speaker making an offer may project the entire sequence, as
here (8.1f.655):

B: do you want the telephone number? [offer]
A: u:m . might as well have it I *suppose* [agreement to offer]
B: *yeah* . one? -
A: yes? .
B: one two one? .
A: yes?
B: five one seven eight - [completion of compliance with offer]
A: thanks very much [gratitude for compliance]

B's offer is taken up by A's agreement to it, which is taken up by B's assertion of the information offered, which is taken up with A's thanks. With
chaining, speakers project extended joint actions, even though each
move through the chain depends on local actions, on minimal joint

projects. Of course, it is one thing to project an extended joint action and quite another thing for it to go through as projected.

PRE-SEQUENCES

If speakers anticipate that their respondents aren't prepared to take up a joint project, they can often do something about it ahead of time. One way is by using what Schegloff (1980) and others have called *pre-sequences*, and the result, once again, is an extended joint project. A good example is the *pre-question*, as illustrated in this sequence (7.1d.1320):

Ann: **oh there's one thing I wanted to ask you**
Betty: **mhm -**
Ann: in the village, they've got some of those . i- you're going to get to know, . what it is, but it doesn't matter really
Betty: mhm
Ann: u:m . those rings, that are buckles - -
Betty: that are buckles
Ann: yes, tha- they they're flat,
Betty: mhm
Ann: and you wrap them round,
Betty: oh yes I know
Ann: and, . you know, . *they're* a little belt .
Betty: *m* m
Ann: **would you like one .**
Betty: oh I'd love one Ann -

When Ann says "Oh there's one thing I wanted to ask you," she is performing a pre-question. On the surface, she is asking Betty to let her ask a question, and Betty consents with "Mhm." But why didn't she ask the question she really wanted to ask? Apparently, she realized Betty wasn't prepared for it. She needed to establish that she and Betty both understood the type of buckle she wanted to offer. It is only once that is accomplished that she goes on to ask "Would you like one?"

Pre-questions request space not just for questions, but for preliminaries – preparatory conditions – to those questions. Pre-questions are, as Schegloff (1980) put it, preliminaries to preliminaries. The result is a structure like this:

Joint project	Speaker A	Speaker B
I.	Pre-question	Consent
II.	Preliminaries to III	Acknowledgment
III.	Question	Answer

Locally, the pre-question and its response (I) form a minimal joint project: Ann seeks permission to ask a question and Betty grants it. But with that pre-question, Ann also projects a larger enterprise consisting of I, II, and III, and when Betty consents, she is committing herself to the larger enterprise too. Ann and Betty use the minimal joint project (I) to initiate the larger joint project (I + II + III). So when Ann says "Oh there's one thing I wanted to ask you," Betty construes her as proposing not one, but *two* joint projects: (1) that Betty let her ask a question; and (2) that Betty give her space to provide the preliminaries to that question. When Betty gives consent with "Mhm," she is simultaneously taking up both joint projects.

Pre-questions and their responses are only one type of pre-sequence. Just as pre-questions gain consent to ask a question, pre-announcements gain consent to make an announcement, pre-invitations to make an invitation, pre-requests to make a request, and pre-narratives to tell a story. Here are some examples:

Pre-sequence		Example
Pre-question	A:	Oh there's one thing I wanted to ask you.
Response	B:	Mhm.
Pre-announcement	A:	tell you who I met yesterday -
Response	B:	who
Pre-invitation	A:	What are you doin'?
Response	B:	Nothin' what's up.
Pre-request	A:	Do you have hot chocolate?
Response	B:	Yes, we do.
Summons	A:	Hey, Molly
Response	B:	Yes?
Telephone summons	A:	(rings telephone)
Response	B:	Miss Pink's office
Pre-closing statement	A:	Well okay
Response	B:	Okay
Pre-narrative	A:	I acquired an absolutely magnificent sewing-machine, by foul means, did I tell you about that?
Response	B:	no

With each pre-sequence, the initiators seek to satisfy a preparatory condition, and once they have accomplished that, they proceed to the projected question, announcement, invitation, request, conversation, closing, or narrative.

Pre-sequences vary in how extended a joint project they initiate. The pre-request "Do you have hot chocolate?" was followed immediately by the request "I'll have hot chocolate and a Danish." In contrast, the pre-narrative "I acquired an absolutely magnificent sewing-machine, by foul means, did I tell you about that?" opened a five-minute narrative. The summons on Miss Pink's telephone – the telephone ring – opened a minute-long conversation. The length of the larger project depends not only on what is projected – a request, narrative, or conversation – but on whether the participants carry it through as projected.

Because pre-sequences check on preparatory conditions, they should fail precisely when that check fails. On the telephone, Ben might expect "Is Susan there?" to work out this way:

Ben: Is Susan there?
Charlotte: Yes, she is.
Ben: Can I speak to her please?
Charlotte: Sure.
            Hold on.

If the preparatory condition holds, Ben's pre-request will be affirmed ("Yes, she is"), and he can ask to talk to Susan. If it doesn't hold, the course will be different, as here (9.1j.700):

Jane: is Mrs Davy there please.
Margaret: sorry, she's interviewing this morning

Another course is illustrated in Jane and Kate's telephone conversation:

Jane: is Miss Pink in.
Kate: well, she's in, but she's engaged at the moment

The speaker may have made the wrong presupposition altogether, as here (Hopper, 1992; p. 69):

Gordon: is Dawn there (0.2)
Dawn: this is Dawn

In all three examples, the respondents take up altered, but helpful joint projects. So there are good reasons for checking on preparatory conditions. Pre-sequences are engineered to make optimal use of the current opportunities (see Chapters 10 and 11).

Embedding, pre-sequencing, and chaining are the three basic ways of creating extended projects on the fly. With embedding, the initial minimal project emerges with another minimal project embedded within it: [a1 [b1 b2] a2]. With chaining, the initial project is linked to the next to form a more encompassing joint project, $^{[}$a1 $_{[}$a2 = b1$^{]}$b2$_{]}$. And with pre-sequencing, the initial minimal project becomes embedded in a more encompassing one: [[a1 a2] b1 b2]. All three methods are achieved locally and opportunistically. Most extended joint projects in conversation – no matter how large – are created by a combination of these methods.

JOINT CONSTRUALS

We are now in a position to return to the joint construal problem – how speakers and addressees settle on what speakers mean. The classical view is this. When Jack says to Kate "Sit here," he has a particular meaning in mind, and it is Kate's job to recognize it. "What the speaker means" is a specific, objective intention of the speaker, and addressees are to identify that intention. Addressees are said to have misunderstood when they don't identify it. Although there is a lot wrong with the classical view, the underlying problem is that it treats the speaker's and addressee's actions as autonomous: Speakers fix their intentions unilaterally, never changing their minds, and addressees try independently to identify those intentions. If communicative acts are joint acts, that just won't work. But if the classical view is wrong, what are we to replace it with?

In the view I will argue for, the notion "what the speaker means" is replaced by "what the speaker is to be taken to mean." The change is small, but radical. The idea is that speakers and addressees try to create a joint construal of what the speaker is to be taken to mean. Such a construal represents not what the speaker means per se – which can change in the very process of communicating – but what the participants *mutually take* the speaker as meaning, what they *deem* the speaker to mean (see Grice, 1982). The idea is captured in this principle:

Principle of joint construal. For each signal, the speaker and addressees try to create a joint construal of what the speaker is to be taken to mean by it.

By this principle, Kate isn't trying simply to identify what Jack means by "Sit down." She is trying to create a construction that the two of them are willing to accept as what he meant by it. She will usually try to infer his initial intentions, but the joint construal they arrive at will often be different from those intentions. Indeed, for many signals, the classical idea of "what the speaker means" doesn't even make sense, whereas "what the speaker is to be taken to mean" does.

CONSTRUALS IN UPTAKE

Recall the problem with imperatives. When Jack says "Sit here" to Kate, he may be performing a command, request, offer, advisory, threat, exhortation, or other illocutionary act, and the form doesn't say which. Now Kate may have a good idea of what he is doing, but that isn't enough either. Jack and Kate must reach the mutual belief that her construal of his action matches his intentions – or at least is all right with him. To do that, Kate needs to provide Jack with evidence of her construal that he can validate or correct. And what better way than by using her uptake as she completes the joint project she believes he is proposing.

If uptake is used this way, it should regularly distinguish among alternative construals of first pair parts, and it does. Take these four choices for Kate's response to "Sit here":

A's utterance	B's construal	B's uptake
Sit here	an order	Yes, sir.
Sit here	a request	Okay.
Sit here	an offer	No thanks.
Sit here	an advisory	What a good idea!

When Kate responds "What a good idea!" she shows Jack that she is construing his utterance as an advisory. That is equivalent to saying that she shows him she is construing the joint project he is proposing as an exchange of advice. And she expects him to see that her uptake is a proper shared basis for the mutual belief that she considers his illocution to be an advisory. It is also evidence that she doesn't consider it to be an order, request, offer, or warning. And once he accepts her construal, it becomes their *joint* construal.

Kate's uptake is also important because it makes clear what joint project she is willing and able to commit to. She may be happy to take up "Sit here" if it is an advisory, but not if it is an order. "I think Jack intends 'Sit here' as an advisory," she might reason. "But if I take it up without signaling that, he may think I am committing myself to an order, which I am not willing to do. I had better display what I am committing myself to." Hence she says, "What a good idea!"

People have at their disposal an array of expressions for displaying construals of what they are taking up. Many are idioms that seem to have evolved for just this purpose. Here are a few, classified by the illocutionary act they take up:

Type of illocution	Example	Idioms of uptake
Assertive	The movie was great.	Uh huh. Yes. Right. Of course. Quite. Indeed. Oh?
Order	Sit down.	Yes sir. Yes ma'am.
Request	Please sit down.	Okay. Right. All right.
Yes/no question	Was the trip dangerous?	Yes. Yes it was. Indeed. No. No it wasn't. Not a bit. Not at all.
WH- question	Who brought the gift?	Mildred did. [Ellipsis]
Promise	I'll get you a beer.	Thanks. Thank you. Thank you very much. Thanks a lot. Much obliged. Many thanks.
Offer	Want a beer?	Please. Yes please. No thanks. No thank you.
Thanks	Thank you.	You're welcome. Don't mention it.
Compliment	What a nice sweater.	Thanks.
Greeting	Hello.	Hello. Hi.
Farewell	Good-bye.	Good-bye. Bye. Bye bye. See you. So long.

Although these categories overlap a bit, the overlap is benign. Much of it is between categories that are unlikely to be confused. Speakers can make their uptake as precise as they want.

An uptake often displays more than the construal of a joint project. It may express one's *commitment* to that project. When Jack promises "I'll get you a beer," Kate can choose among "Okay," "Thanks," "Thanks a lot," and "Thanks very much indeed," which differ in their enthusiasm. Much of this attitude is carried by intonation. For Jack's "Sit down," Kate can deliver "Okay" or "Right" with an enthusiastic, business-like, disappointed, or subdued intonation, each expressing a different commitment. Or for Jack's assertion "The movie was awful," Kate can display agreement with "Uh huh," "Yes it was," or "Quite," or lack of prior knowledge or skepticism with "It was?" or "Oh?" each with many different melodies.

VALIDATION AND CORRECTION OF CONSTRUALS

One reason for displaying construals is to give partners the opportunity to validate or correct them. Much of the time, the displayed construal matches the speaker's original intentions, and the partner validates it by initiating the next contribution at that level. If it doesn't match, as we saw for Kate serving wine, the partner has several options.

Suppose Jack utters "Sit here" intending it to be a request, but Kate replies "What a good idea!" Jack has two choices. He can consider Kate's construal to be incorrect and correct it: "I'm not just advising you to sit here – I'm asking you to." Or he could leave her construal unchanged and revise his own intentions – change his mind about what he is to be taken as doing. He might reason: "So what if Kate doesn't interpret my utterance as a request. She is still going to sit down, and that is my goal." He might then answer "Good," laying down a shared basis for the mutual belief that his action is to be taken as an advisory. As far as Kate is concerned, that may be all he ever intended, and he knows that.

Another possibility is that Jack intended his utterance to be a vague directive, and he is indifferent to how it is construed within broad limits. He simply wanted Kate to sit down. So when Kate says "What a good idea!" he accepts her construal even though it is narrower than intended. He might then answer "Good," laying down a shared basis for the mutual belief that "Sit down" is to be taken as an advisory. As far as Kate is concerned, the narrower construal may be all Jack ever intended, and Jack knows that.

The final possibility, again, is that Kate misconstrues Jack without either of them noticing. Suppose she replies "Uh huh," interpreting Jack's utterance as an advisory, whereas Jack thinks she is taking it up as a request. Jack may accept her apparent construal (e.g., with "Good") in such a way that she doesn't realize he was making a request. They may or may not catch their error later. Here we have an undetected misconstrual.

With minimal joint projects, there are six main patterns of A's proposal, B's uptake, and A's validation:

Pattern	Display in B's uptake	A's response
Verified construal	full construal A intended	Acceptance
Revised construal	a construal A didn't intend but finds acceptable	Acceptance
Narrowed construal	one of several intended construals	Acceptance

Corrected misconstrual	a construal A finds unacceptable	Correction
Undetected misconstrual	a construal A would find unacceptable if it were known	Acceptance
Elective construal	one of an inclusive disjunction of acceptable construals	Acceptance

Each pattern starts with A's proposal of a joint project. What happens next depends on B's uptake. It may show B's construal to be complete, acceptable though unintended, acceptable but narrowed, or incorrect. Or it may be inadequate to show whether B's construal is correct or not. (I will take up elective construals shortly.) A then has to choose whether to accept or to follow up on B's construal.

A and B, then, have a procedure for establishing a joint construal of A's utterance. Although it begins with A's utterance, it depends on B display-ing a construal for A to inspect – and to correct if necessary. Even when the procedure is successful, the joint construal arrived at may differ from A's original intentions. It may be a revision or a narrowing of it. What counts in the end is not A's original intentions, but what A accepts as a construal of his or her public intentions ("what A is to be taken as meaning"). Just as people can change their minds about other things, speakers can change their minds about what they are to be taken as meaning, and they often do.

ELECTIVE CONSTRUALS

The final type of construal, *elective construals*, emerges from what have traditionally been called *indirect speech acts*. When Jack asks Kate, "Can you reach the mustard?" he appears to be asking whether or not she can reach the mustard, a yes/no question. Yet if the situation is right, he appears also to be asking her to pass the mustard, a request. The question is a *direct* or *literal speech act*, and the request is an *indirect speech act*. In this view, Jack is performing two illocutions:

| Direct speech act (a question): | "Do you have the ability to reach the mustard?" |
| Indirect speech act (a request): | "Please pass the mustard." |

Indirect speech acts come in a great variety. Almost any illocutionary act, it seems, can be performed indirectly.

Indirect speech acts have usually been viewed as Gricean implica-tures (e.g., Searle, 1975a; see Chapter 5). Jack expects Kate to see that he realizes she can reach the mustard, so he cannot be asking whether or not she is able to. He is flouting the maxim of quality, "Be truthful," and from that, she is to work out that he is asking her to pass the mustard. The traditional treatment has many problems, but the main one is that it assumes: (1) speakers have a particular interpretation in mind ("what the speaker means"); (2) addressees are to recognize that interpretation; and (3) they are to do so autonomously. All three assumptions are suspect.

Utterances like "Can you reach the mustard?" can be viewed, instead, to have elective construals. In one study (Clark, 1979), a woman named Susan telephoned fifty restaurants in and around Palo Alto, California, and asked "Do you accept credit cards?" Here were three forms of uptake:

Case 1	Susan:	Do you accept credit cards?
	Manager:	Yes, we do.
Case 2	Susan:	Do you accept credit cards?
	Manager:	Yes, we accept Mastercard and Visa.
Case 3	Susan:	Do you accept credit cards?
	Manager:	We accept Mastercard and Visa.

In case 1, the manager's uptake displayed a construal of Susan's utterance as a question ("Yes, we do"). Nothing suggests he also construed it as a request for the credit cards. In case 2, the manager displayed a construal of her utterance *both* as a yes/no question ("Yes") *and* as a request for credit cards ("We accept Mastercard and Visa"). In case 3, he displayed a construal of her utterance as a request for the credit cards ("We accept Mastercard and Visa"), and that was all. If he thought she was seriously asking whether he accepted credit cards, he displayed no evidence of it. The three cases are summarized here:

Case	Manager's response	Manager's construal
1	"Yes, we do."	question
2	"Yes, we accept Mastercard and Visa."	question + request
3	"We accept Mastercard and Visa."	request

In each case, the manager's construal was validated by Susan and became their joint construal.

So what illocutionary act did Susan perform here? It wasn't a question alone, or a request alone, or even a question plus a request. She accepted all three construals – indeed, she had to. In 1, if she had corrected the manager with "No, I meant what credit cards do you accept," he could rightly have complained that she had been unclear. In 2 and 3, if she had corrected him with "No, I was only asking whether you accept credit cards," that would have been obtuse because he had already told her. The remarkable thing is that by using this utterance Susan left it up to the *manager* to determine which of these options she was to be taken to mean. She put herself in a position where it was impossible to correct whichever option he chose.

The two construals of "Do you accept credit cards?" are elective construals: Susan designed her utterance so the manager could *elect* what she was to be taken as doing – asking a question, making a request, or both. She performed not simply an illocutionary act, but an inclusive disjunction of illocutionary acts: a question, or a request, or both. She intended the manager to see it was up to him to choose, and he chose.

One reason for offering elective construals is to allow short cuts. When Susan used "Do you accept credit cards?" as a pre-request, she was checking on a preparatory condition just as if she were saying, "If you accept any credit cards, please tell me which ones you accept." That condition may fail, as in case 4, which was yet another way managers responded:

Case 4   Caller: Do you accept credit cards?
          Manager: No, we don't.

The preparatory condition didn't hold, so the request interpretation became moot, and the manager had to elect the question construal alone. I will return to elective construals in Chapters 10 and 12.

ILLOCUTIONARY ACTS REVISITED

What, then, is an illocutionary act? The traditional view is that it is an act entirely determined by the speaker who performed it. The addressees may be right or wrong in interpreting it, but it is the speaker's intentions that count. The traditional view, however, cannot be correct.[1] When Susan asked the restaurant managers "Do you accept credit cards?" it didn't matter whether she had intended a question, a request, or both. She left it up to the manager to decide which she would be taken as meaning.

Elective construals sound paradoxical only because we are used to thinking of illocutionary acts as autonomous. But speakers can only perform illocutionary acts by reaching joint construals with their respondents, and that takes actions from them both. Sometimes speakers

[1] See also Streeck (1980).

are led to revise or narrow their original intentions. Other times they leave the construal of their actions open to several interpretations, as with elective construals. Yet as far as both speakers and respondents go, it is their *joint* construal that counts – what the speaker is to be taken to mean. They have a shared basis for that mutual belief and for no other.

With these steps we return to a view of illocutionary acts that is surprisingly close to Austin's. He argued (1962, pp. 115-116):

I cannot be said to have warned an audience unless it hears what I say and takes what I say in a certain sense. An effect must be achieved on the audience if the illocutionary act is to be carried out...Generally the effect amounts to bringing about the understanding of the meaning and of the force of the locution.

If illocutionary acts require actions from both speakers and addressees, as Austin argued, that makes them participatory acts. Most investigators dropped Austin's requirement that illocutionary acts include "bringing about the understanding of the meaning and of the force of the locution" simply because they refused to treat illocutionary acts within a framework of joint actions. The view championed here might have suited Austin very well.

Conclusions

In conversation people accomplish business one piece at a time. They do that, I have argued, largely via joint projects: One participant projects a joint action for all the participants to complete, and the others take it up and complete it. The canonical joint project is accomplished with adjacency pairs, as illustrated in this question–answer pair:

1. Proposal   Ann: when is it
2. Uptake   Ben: four thirty tomorrow - - -

With "When is it?" (part 1) Ann *proposes* a transfer of information from Ben to Ann, and with "four thirty tomorrow" (part 2), Ben *takes up* her proposal and completes it. The two parts of adjacency pairs are ideal for joint actions for many reasons. They identify the two participants. They require individual actions from both. And these actions are the required participatory actions for a larger unit of work – here, the transfer of information. In conversation, people create extended joint projects out of minimal joint projects by embedding, chaining, and pre-sequencing. Global joint projects are created out of local joint projects that take advantage of the opportunities that arise.

Minimal joint projects are essential to reaching joint construals of

8 | Grounding

Joint projects aren't easy to complete. Success on even a minimal joint project requires success on all lower levels of action as well. Take this exchange (8.2a.335):

Roger: now, - um do you and your husband have a j- car
Nina: - have a car?
Roger: yeah
Nina: no -

When Roger tries to ask Nina whether she and her husband have a car, she isn't sure she has heard his last phrase and queries it, "Have a car?" Only when that is cleared up does she take up his question with "No." For success on their joint project, Roger and Nina need success in attending to, hearing, and understanding each other. How do they reach that success? In Chapter 7, we saw how two people, in pursuing a joint project, arrive at a joint construal of what the speaker is to be taken to mean. In this chapter, we look more closely at what else it takes to assure success.

The hypothesis is that people try to *ground* what they do together. *To ground a thing*, in my terminology, *is to establish it as part of common ground well enough for current purposes* (Clark and Brennan, 1991; Clark and Schaefer, 1989; Clark and Wilkes-Gibbs, 1986). On this hypothesis, grounding should occur at all levels of communication. Recall the ladder of joint actions from Chapter 5:

	Speaker A's actions	Addressee B's actions
4	A is proposing joint project *w* to B	B is considering A's proposal of *w*
3	A is signaling that *p* for B	B is recognizing that *p* from A
2	A is presenting signal *s* to B	B is identifying signal *s* from A
1	A is executing behavior *t* for B	B is attending to behavior *t* from A

To succeed in their joint projects (level 4), A and B need to ground what A is to be taken to mean for B (level 3), and to do that, they need to ground what A is presenting to B (level 2), and to do that, they need to ground what behavior A is executing for B (level 1). Dealing with all these levels is simplified by two properties of action ladders – upward completion and downward evidence.

To see how grounding works, we must look beyond language use. There are general principles about how people discharge intentions in performing any action, both autonomous and joint actions. If so, they should also apply to signaling and recognizing, presenting and identifying, executing behaviors and attending to them.

Closure on actions

It is a fundamental principle of intentional action that people look for evidence that they have done what they intended to do. If I want to call an "up" elevator, I press the "up" button. I get immediate evidence that I have pressed the "up" button when I feel and see the button depress under my finger, and if I don't, I try again. But I get evidence that I have *called* the elevator only if the "up" light goes on. If it doesn't, or if there is no "up" light, I can't be certain I have called the elevator, so I may press the button again and again and again. People tend to do just that when there is no "up" light. Why? Because they cannot verify that they have in fact called the elevator.

People need *closure* on their actions. The general principle, due to Donald Norman (1988), might be expressed this way:

Principle of closure. Agents performing an action require evidence, sufficient for current purposes, that they have succeeded in performing it.

To get closure on the action of calling an elevator, I look for evidence that I have succeeded. The principle applies to intentional actions of all types. As Norman has shown, it is crucial in the design of personal computers, television sets, cars, telephones, common appliances, and to disregard it is to foster misuse, frustration, failure. Telephone buttons that don't beep when pressed, computer commands that don't change the display, and car turn signals that don't click – these invite failure because they don't allow users to get closure on their actions.

EVIDENCE OF CLOSURE

At the heart of the principle of closure is the idea that evidence of success must be "sufficient for current purposes." What makes evidence sufficient?

Validity. Evidence of success must be valid to be useful. In practice this means it must be reliable and interpretable. For calling an "up" elevator, an "up" light wouldn't be reliable evidence of success if it went on only sporadically or regardless of the button I pushed. And it wouldn't be readily interpretable, even if reliable, if it went on only when I pressed the "down" button, or only on odd-numbered days. Most evidence is reliable only to some degree, and interpretable only to some level of confidence. An "up" light is strong evidence that an "up" elevator has been called, but an audible click somewhere in the elevator shaft only weak evidence. No perceptible change is ordinarily no evidence at all.

Economy of effort. Evidence must also be easy to get, economical in effort. What if the "up" light flashed on for only a tenth of a second, or only if I pressed the button for ten seconds? The evidence might be too costly. The one takes too much attention at the right moment, and the other too much work. Other things being equal, the less effort evidence takes to acquire, the better.

Timeliness. Evidence must also be timely. I want the "up" light on the elevator to go on when I press the "up" button and not five, ten, or twenty seconds later. Why? Because calling the elevator is part of a sequence of actions, each contingent on the completion of the last one. I must get closure on the current action before I can start the next. We might learn to live with "up" lights that had five-second delays, but we wouldn't be happy about it.

The optimal evidence for completion isn't usually the strongest, most economical, and most timely evidence possible, for that may be too costly. All we need is evidence "sufficient for current purposes." Even that varies with our purposes. In manufacturing a toxic chemical, I may be willing to put a lot of effort in getting highly valid evidence of completion, even if it takes time to get. In calling an "up" elevator, I may be unwilling to work for evidence that isn't immediately accessible. Each action has its own mix of evidence that is deemed sufficient.

LEAST EFFORT

The very notion of sufficiency rests on the idea that people prefer to conserve effort. They appear to adhere to this principle:

Principle of least effort. All things being equal, agents try to minimize their effort in doing what they intend to do.

In moving a box from one part of the kitchen to another, I wouldn't carry it to the dining room and then back to the kitchen. This principle has been used to account for a range of everyday phenomena. With closure, minimizing effort has an added twist. Ordinarily we think of effort as what it takes to carry out an action proper – e.g., to press the "up" button. But it takes additional effort to confirm that I have completed my action. In counting effort, we must include both the action proper *and* verification of its completion.

Many actions become complete only once some criterion is reached. Eating all the spaghetti on my plate means eating the spaghetti until it is all gone; further eating isn't part of the act. Filling a bottle with water means pouring water into the bottle until the bottle is full; pouring more water in isn't part of the act. We might call these *criterial actions*: They aren't complete until a criterion is met. Agents cannot perform them without adhering to the principle of closure. An inherent part of doing them is deciding when they are complete.

We treat many actions as criterial even when we don't have to. In waiting for an "up" elevator at a bank of elevators, I'm not forced to get on the first "up" elevator to come along. I could choose to wait for the second or fifth or fiftieth, or for the first one at the door I am standing next to. But if I am trying to minimize effort, I will treat "waiting for an 'up' elevator" as a criterial action, as if it were "waiting for the *first* 'up' elevator." A corollary of the principle of least effort is this:

Principle of opportunistic closure. Agents consider an action complete *just as soon as* they have evidence sufficient for current purposes that it is complete.

If agents can treat an action as a criterial action, they will.

DOWNWARD EVIDENCE AND HOLISTIC EVIDENCE

With action ladders, agents can exploit especially powerful forms of evidence. Let us return to the action ladder for getting an elevator (from Chapter 5):

Level	Action in progress from t_0 to t_i
5	A is getting an "up" elevator to come
4	A is calling an "up" elevator
3	A is activating the "up" button
2	A is depressing the "up" button
1	A is pressing the right index finger against the "up" button

By the principle of closure, Alan needs evidence that he has completed each of the five actions, and that seems like a tall order. Yet it isn't, because he can exploit the property of downward evidence: "In a ladder of actions, evidence that one level is complete is also evidence that all levels below it are complete." He needn't check separately for evidence at each level. If the "up" light goes on, he has evidence that he has succeeded not only at level 4, but also at levels 1, 2, and 3. He need only check on the highest level evidence available.

Agents can exploit a related principle for part–whole relations. Suppose I type "p" "r" "i" "n" and "t" into my computer as a command to print out a file. Did I really type the letter "i"? I have evidence that I did if the computer begins printing. The property is this:

Holistic evidence. Evidence that an agent has succeeded on a whole action is also evidence that the agent has succeeded on each of its parts.

These two properties – downward evidence and holistic evidence – give agents powerful ways of reaching closure. If they are trying to minimize effort, they should look for the most powerful evidence that is valid, cheap, and timely enough for current purposes. They should look for evidence at the highest level available and for the largest action attempted.

JOINT CLOSURE

The principle of closure applies as much to joint actions as to autonomous ones. You and I need evidence that we have succeeded in shaking hands or playing the first measure of our duet, or that I have succeeded in helping you on with your coat. Without such evidence, we may try the action again, or try to repair what went wrong, or stop before taking the next step – each disrupting our ongoing activity. What evidence do we need?

Recall that joint acts are performed by means of participatory acts by the participants. When Ann and Ben are rowing a canoe, there are three acts involved:

0. Ann-and-Ben's paddling a canoe includes 1 and 2;
1. Ann is paddling at the bow as part of 0;
2. Ben is paddling at the stern as part of 0.

Let's take Ann's point of view. She can get closure on "paddling at the bow" by seeing and feeling her paddle dip into the water with the right motion and pressure. But for closure on "paddling *as part of* 0" she needs evidence that Ben is doing his part as well. She hears him behind her paddling and feels the canoe surge forward with each stroke. She also realizes that Ben needs evidence that she is doing her part, which she assumes he gets from seeing her paddle and feeling the canoe surge with her strokes. Ultimately, the two of them try to reach joint closure (see Clark and Schaefer, 1989):

Principle of joint closure. The participants in a joint action try to establish the mutual belief that they have succeeded well enough for current purposes.

Ann and Ben try to get closure not only on their individual paddling, but on their joint rowing of the canoe. And that requires evidence that can serve as a shared basis for the mutual belief that they are succeeding. And by the principle of least effort, they will try to succeed with the least *joint effort.*[1]

What I have argued so far is this. When we act intentionally, we seek evidence that we have completed what we set out to do. In that process, we try to minimize the total effort of both doing the act proper and confirming its completion. When our actions belong to action ladders or action wholes, we can use evidence in especially efficient ways. Because of the principle of least effort, we are opportunistic in carrying out our actions. We reach closure on them and go on to the next action just as soon as we have sufficient evidence they are complete. Joint actions are no different, for they too require closure. The question is how to reach closure.

Contributions
People in conversation ordinarily go to some effort to reach joint closure on their actions. As illustration, let us return to the exchange between Roger and Nina:

---

[1] For more discussion of least joint effort, see Clark and Wilkes-Gibbs (1986) and Schober (1995).

Roger:	now, - um do you and your husband have a j- car
Nina:	- have a car?
Roger:	yeah
Nina:	no -

When Roger finishes his first turn, he apparently thinks he has presented all Nina needs for recognizing what he means. Has he succeeded? No, as he learns immediately from Nina's "Have a car?" Apparently, she believes she has identified his utterance except for the last phrase, which she thinks is "have a car." Roger concludes that once he clears up her question "Did you say 'have a car'?" with "Yeah," she will have identified what he presented and understand what he meant. He gets evidence of her understanding when she answers "No." With that, the two of them reach the mutual belief that she has understood him well enough for current purposes. They reach closure on the joint act of signaling and recognizing.

What I have just illustrated is a *contribution* to discourse – a signal successfully understood. I will sometimes use contribution for the joint act of Roger and Nina completing the signal and its joint construal. Other times I will use it for Roger's participatory act, his *part* of that joint act, as when we speak of Roger's contribution to the discourse. When necessary, I will make clear which sense I mean. In either case, contributions require actions from both parties.

PRESENTATION AND ACCEPTANCE

Contributions are ordinarily achieved in two main phases. In the first phase of Roger's contribution, he presents Nina with an utterance. In the second, Nina provides evidence of what she does and doesn't perceive, identify, or understand until the two of them accept that she has understood him well enough for current purposes. It is natural to call these two phases the *presentation phase* and the *acceptance phase* (Clark and Schaefer, 1987a, 1989). They are characteristic of contributions to conversation.

It is through these two phases that participants reach closure for each signal and its recognition. The two phases work like this (assume A is male and B is female):

Presentation phase. A presents a signal s for B to understand. He assumes that, if B gives evidence e or stronger, he can believe that B understands what he means by it.

Acceptance phase. B accepts A's signal s by giving evidence e' that she believes she understands what A means by it. She assumes that, once A registers e', he too will believe she understands.

In this terminology, A presents an action, a signal, for B to understand, and B, in turn, eventually validates that action, that signal, as having been recognized or understood. When these two phases are done properly, they constitute the shared basis for the mutual belief that B understands what A means by signal *s*. And with that A completes his contribution to the discourse.[2]

What distinguishes this model is the requirement of positive evidence. In traditional accounts, Roger could assume that Nina understood him unless there was evidence to the contrary – *negative evidence* (see Grosz and Sidner, 1986; Litman and Allen, 1987; Stalnaker, 1978). But by the principle of joint closure, contributors require *positive evidence* that their partners have understood what they meant. Roger can assume Nina has understood him only when he sees positive evidence of understanding. If so, contributors should look for positive evidence, and their partners should try to provide it. And they do.

Positive evidence most often comes from signals by the respondent – utterances, gestures, manifesting actions (see Chapter 6). These signals divide into four main classes:[3]

1. *Assertions of understanding.* When Roger presents an utterance, Nina can respond "uh huh" or "I see" or "m" or nod or smile. With these signals, she *asserts* that she understands Roger and expects him to accept her claim.

2. *Presuppositions of understanding.* When Nina takes up Roger's proposed joint project, she *presupposes* that she has understood him well enough to go on. So uptake, or initiating the relevant next turn, is a signal of understanding (Chapter 7).

3. *Displays of understanding.* When Nina takes up Roger's proposed joint project, she is also ordinarily *displaying* parts of what she has construed him to mean (Chapter 7). An answer, for example, displays in part how she construed his question.

4. *Exemplifications of understanding.* In the right circumstances, Nina can also *exemplify* what she has construed Roger to have meant. She

[2] For computational formalizations of collaborating on contributions, see Edmonds (1993), Heeman (1991), Heeman and Hirst (1992), and Hirst, McRoy, Heeman, Edmonds, and Horton (1994), and for a computational theory of grounding, see Traum (1994).

[3] In aviation, the Federal Aviation Administration has mandated that pilots and air traffic controllers use certain of these signals (e.g., "readbacks") in all conversations (Morrow, Lee, and Rodvold, 1993; Morrow, Rodvold, and Lee, 1994)

might offer a paraphrase or verbatim repetition, grimace, look disappointed, or perform some other iconic gesture. In each case Roger is able to check her exemplification for an acceptable construal.

Displays and exemplifications tend to be more valid evidence than assertions and presuppositions. When I give instructions to a ten-year-old boy, and he merely asserts or presupposes understanding, I may doubt whether his criterion is up to mine. He is more convincing when he displays what he has understood. It is like a school examination. I am better off asking him "What is the capital of Alaska?" than "Do you know the capital of Alaska?" If he answers yes to the second question, can I really be sure he knows?

Positive evidence may also come in the form of symptoms – spontaneous reactions. Roger may say something to cause Nina to blush, look startled, or get angry, revealing her construal of what he is saying. If she is startled by a comment she shouldn't have been startled by, Roger can suspect a misconstrual, identify it, and repair it.

In this model, all contributions eventually get completed with positive evidence judged sufficient for current purposes. The two most common types of contributions are accomplished solely with positive evidence – they are trouble-free, without hitches, without explicit problems to repair. I will call them *concluded* and *continuing contributions*.

CONCLUDED CONTRIBUTIONS

In concluded contributions, A presents a signal that B accepts by presupposing understanding – by initiating the next contribution at the same level as A's contribution. Take Alan asking Burton a question (1.2b.1433):

Alan: and what are you then
Burton: I'm on the academic council
Alan: ah very nice position

Alan initiates his contribution by presenting the utterance "and what are you then." Burton immediately gives evidence of understanding by construing the utterance as a question, taking it up, and answering it, "I'm on the academic council." The evidence is of three types:

1. Burton passes up the opportunity to ask for clarification. He thereby implies he believes he understands what Alan meant.
2. Burton initiates an answer as the next contribution. He thereby displays that he has construed Alan as having asked a question.
3. Burton provides an appropriate answer. He thereby displays his construal of the content of Alan's question.

With 2 and 3 Burton gives Alan the opportunity to check on his construal of Alan's utterance. If Alan doesn't accept that construal, he can repair it – "No, I meant..." In fact, he accepts it by taking up Alan's assertion with "ah very nice position."

Alan and Burton reach joint closure on Alan's contribution entirely by means of downward evidence. When Burton takes up Alan's question, he provides Alan with evidence that he has agreed to take up his question (at level 4). In a ladder of joint actions, evidence of success at level 4 is also evidence of success at levels 1, 2, and 3. The two of them can conclude that Burton has succeeded in attending to, identifying, and understanding Alan's utterance as well.

CONTINUING CONTRIBUTIONS

In continuing contributions, A presents a signal that B accepts by asserting understanding with a backgrounded acknowledgment like "m" or "uh huh" or a nod or a smile. Take this example (1.1.90):

Sam:	I wouldn't want it before the end of June anyhow Reynard, because I'm going to Madrid, . on the tenth and coming back on the twenty-ninth, - *u:h*.
Reynard:	***I see***
Sam:	I *shall*
Reynard:	***yes***
Sam:	not be away from home then until at any rate the end of -
Reynard:	**m**
Sam:	about the end of August - - so any time in July and August but u:h
Reynard:	**yes**
Sam:	not too far into August if *possible*
Reynard:	***no***

Although Sam is talking throughout, in the background Reynard is adding acknowledgments – "I see," "yes," "m," and "no." The first two lines have the following structure:

Presentation phase
Sam: I wouldn't want it before the end of June anyhow Reynard, because I'm going to Madrid, . on the tenth and coming back on the twenty-ninth, - *u:h*.

Acceptance phase
Reynard: *I see* - yes

With "I see - yes" Reynard asserts that he has understood Sam's last utterance, and once Sam accepts that acknowledgment, Sam's contribution is complete.

Continuing contributions are useful precisely because they allow A to keep talking, contributing to the conversation, with minimal disruption from B. They achieve this through these five features (again, assume that A is male and B is female):

1. *Acknowledgments.* B's simplest acknowledgments comment explicitly on her understanding of A's utterance. Reynard's "I see" means "I understand what you are saying," and "m" means "Yes, I understand what you are saying." Others, called assessments, are really uptakes to A's assertions, as with "gosh," "really?" "oh," and "good God" (Goodwin, 1986a), and by downward evidence, they imply understanding as well.

2. *Scope.* B generally marks the part of the total utterance she is accepting by placing her acknowledgment at or near the end of that part. Reynard accepts "so any time in July and August" by uttering "yes" after it and before the proper start of the next clause.

3. *No turns.* B generally accepts what A says without taking a turn. Reynard acknowledged Sam's utterances without taking the floor.

4. *Overlapping speech.* B often shows she doesn't intend to take a turn by overlapping her acknowledgments with A's speech.

5. *Backgrounding.* Acknowledgments are marked as backgrounded, as less prominent than the speech around them. When spoken, they are brief – *m* and *uh huh* are the commonest ones in British and North American English – and are delivered with reduced volume. When gestured, they are also simple and brief, as with nods and smiles.

These five features enable acknowledgers to do their work while letting the contributors get on with theirs.

A variant of the backgrounded acknowledgment is the *unison completion*, as in the last line of this example (Tannen, 1989, p. 60):

Deborah: Like he says that he says that American*s...*
Chad: *Yeah*
Deborah: or Westerners tend to be u:h ... think of the body and the soul as two different th*ings,*
Chad: *Right.*
Deborah: because there's no word that expresses **bo*dy and soul together.***
Chad: ***Body and soul together.*** Right.

When Deborah finishes her utterance "body and soul together," Chad finishes it in unison with her. He gives positive evidence of understanding by showing that he is following her closely enough to complete her utterance with her. Like Chad's "yeah" and "right," the unison completion is backgrounded and designed not to take the floor.

So contributions are joint actions that require individual actions from both contributors and their partners. A presents a signal for his partner B to recognize, and then the two of them work jointly to accept that she has understood what he meant well enough for current purposes.

Patterns of contributions

Contributions become more complicated when there are problems of joint closure. The acceptance phase often gets expanded when B has trouble understanding A's presentation, and that leads to a hierarchical form. The presentation phase often gets expanded when A anticipates B will have trouble understanding it. A may divide it up, making that hierarchical too. Both phases get expanded because of the principle of joint closure along with the properties of upward completion and downward evidence.

UPWARD COMPLETION

When Roger says to Nina "now, - um do you and your husband have a j- car" the two of them are performing a ladder of joint actions:

Level 4 Roger is proposing to Nina that she tell him whether she and her husband have a car.
Level 3 Roger is asking Nina whether she and her husband have a car.
Level 2 Roger is presenting the signal "now do you and your husband have a car?" for Nina to identify.
Level 1 Roger is articulating the sequence of sounds "now, - um do you and your husband have a j- car" for Nina to attend to.

By the property of upward completion, Roger and Nina may complete level 1 without completing level 2, level 2 without level 3, and level 3 without level 4. For any piece of A's attempted contribution, partner B may be in any one of these states:

State 4 B is considering taking up A's proposed joint project.
State 3 B has understood what A meant by his utterance (but isn't in state 4).
State 2 B has identified A's presentation correctly (but isn't in state 3).
State 1 B has noticed that A has executed a presentation (but isn't in state 2).
State 0 B hasn't noticed that A has executed some communicative behavior.

In reality, B is often in a mixed state. Immediately after Roger's presentation, Nina was in state 3 for most of the utterance but in state 1 for the last phrase. By the joint closure principle, they need evidence that she is in at least state 3 for the entire utterance.

When B isn't in state 3 for the full presentation, according to the joint closure principle, she should initiate a process that will bring her to state 3. She should initiate a repair. When she is in state 1, she can do that with "pardon" or "what?" or "m?" as here (7.2.481):

A: ((where are you))
B: **m?**
A: **where are you** .
B: well I'm still at college .

B's "m?" leads A to believe B has noticed A's presentation but hasn't identified it, so A repeats it in its entirety. When B is in state 2, she can pinpoint what she doesn't understand and ask about it, as here (9.1.1133):

A: can I speak to Jim Johnstone please?
B: **senior?**
A: **yes** .
B: yes - - -

With "Senior?" B presupposes she has identified the entire presentation and has understood everything except which Jim Johnstone A was referring to. Most such signals, then, have two parts: (1) a presupposition of what was understood; and (2) a query about what was not understood. They are designed to resolve the misunderstanding as efficiently as possible.

Repairs initiated by partner B lead to acceptance phases with embedded contributions. In the last example, A's main contribution, his request to speak to Jim Johnstone, looks like this:

Presentation phase
A: can I speak to Jim Johnstone please?

Acceptance phase
B: senior?
A: yes .

But the acceptance phase itself contains a question and answer, a minimal joint project, and both of these parts have their own presentation and acceptance phases. B's "Senior?" is the presentation phase of a question, for if A didn't hear it, he could say "Pardon?" to get B to repeat it. A does hear and understand it and makes it a concluded contribution by initiating the answer "Yes." Even that is a presentation, for if B didn't hear it, she could ask "Pardon?" to get A to repeat it. The embedded question and answer is a side sequence (Jefferson, 1972) – the commonest and most powerful device two partners have for clearing up troubles in acceptance phases.

Repairs can also be initiated by the original contributor after seeing a misunderstanding in the partner's uptake. Here is an example of a *third-turn repair* (4.2.298):

B: k- who evaluates the property - - -
A: u:h whoever you asked, . the surveyor for the building society
B: **no, I meant who decides what price it'll go on the market -**
A: (- snorts) . whatever people will pay - -

B asks A a question, and A takes it up, displaying his understanding of the question. But A's display reveals a misconstrual, which B proceeds to correct, "No, I meant..." A then takes up the same question, but now with a revised construal.

Every signal is part of a presentation phase of a projected contribution. Even the briefest utterances, like "Pardon?" and "Yes" and "Uh huh," are open to misunderstanding and need to be accepted. But speakers don't present brief utterances like these unless they are confident there won't be trouble. If they had expected trouble, they would have formulated something more elaborate. Almost all minor utterances like this emerge in concluded or continuing contributions. In the contribution model, all acceptance phases must end with positive evidence, with concluded or continuing contributions. If they didn't, they would go on forever.

COMMUNICATIVE PROBES

Some actions are *probes* carried out with the expectation that they may not succeed. I enter a public building on a Sunday and wonder if the elevators are working. So I press the "up" button, and when the "up" light doesn't go on, I conclude the elevators aren't working. I reason: "I have evidence of completing the ladder of actions to the level of pressing the 'up' button but not beyond. And since pressing the button doesn't call an elevator, the elevators must not be working." I apply the same logic to failures as I do to successes.

Communicative probes can fail in the analogous way at any of the four levels of action.

1. *Hearing.* When I enter my house, I call out "Is anyone home?" and get no answer. My probe is an attempt to get anyone hearing me to arrive at level 4, but it has failed to get anyone even to state 1. My son may actually be home, but unable to hear me because he is listening to music on earphones. Think of yelling "Help" in the woods, ringing a doorbell, or telephoning a friend.[4]

2. *Identification.* In Tokyo, I get lost and say to a passerby "Do you speak English?" She looks blank, and we turn away in frustration. My probe is an attempt to ask her a question, but it fails to get her beyond state 1.

3. *Reference.* At a party, I ask a friend "Which of those women is Nina Searles?" and he replies "Sorry, I don't know who Nina Searles is." I have tried to refer to Nina Searles, but have failed to get him beyond state 2 for that reference.

4. *Joint project.* At the same party, I ask my friend "Who is that?" and he replies, "I don't know." I have tried to get him to tell me who that person is, but have failed to get him beyond state 3 to take up the proposed joint project.

With each probe, I presented an utterance realizing it might not succeed. And each time I was as informed by the failures as I would have been by the successes. Probes like these cannot be accounted for without the logic of upward completion and downward evidence.

PACKAGING

Packaging is always an issue in contributing to discourse: How large a contribution should the two participants try to complete if they are to minimize their joint effort? If there were a presentation and acceptance phase for each word separately, conversation could double in length. On the other hand, if each contribution were a paragraph long, a minor misunderstanding at the beginning might snowball into a major misunderstanding by the end. With limited working memory for what the speaker said, the two people would have great trouble repairing it. The optimal size of a contribution ought to be somewhere in between.

Participants, in fact, vary the size of these packets depending on their skills and purposes. When the going is easy, they make their packets large, but when the going gets tough, they make them smaller, sometimes no more than a word long. When contributors have complicated

---

[4] One day, I called out "Is anyone home?" and my son replied "What?" The probe elicited the information I wanted without getting him past state 1.

information to present, they can present it in *installments*. Here Darryl is giving June his London address (9.2a.979):

June:	ah, what ((are you)) now, *where*
Darryl:	*yes* forty-nine Skipton Place
June:	forty-one
Darryl:	nine . nine
June:	forty-nine, Skipton Place,
Darryl:	W one .
June:	Skipton Place, . W one, ((so)) Mr D Challam
Darryl:	yes
June:	forty-nine Skipton Place, W one,
Darryl:	yes
June:	right oh .

Darryl has packaged his address in two installments, then June reconfirms his name and address in two more installments.

Each installment is a separate contribution. It begins with the contributor presenting a chunk of information and pausing to invite the partner to respond, and it ends with the two of them accepting that the chunk has been understood. Darryl's first installment looks like this:

Presentation phase
Darryl: forty-nine Skipton Place

Acceptance phase
June: forty-one
Darryl: nine . nine
June: forty-nine, Skipton Place,

Darryl presents a number and street name and stops. June then displays "forty-one," giving Darryl a chance to check it. He does and corrects the second digit. June then repeats the whole street address, which Darryl accepts by going on to his second installment. June's two installments work the same way.

Darryl's two installments "forty-nine Skipton Place" and "W one" together form the presentation phase of a more inclusive contribution. June helps create it by reconfirming the information of the two installments together – even though she does that in installments. The presentation and acceptance of Darryl's name and address form an even more inclusive contribution, for June's "right oh" claims an understanding not just of Darryl's last installment, or even of his last two installments, but of the entire name and address.

Speakers divide presentations into brief repeatable installments because they tacitly recognize that people have limited immediate memory spans. Speakers often use installments, for example, to help addressees register addresses, telephone numbers, and recipes verbatim, and perhaps write them down (Clark and Schaefer, 1987a; Goldberg, 1975). The telephone company recognizes this when it divides telephone numbers into conventional packets of three or four digits.

Speakers also use installments in giving instructions – to make sure their partners understand each step before going on. In this example, Jane is giving Wendy directions to a professor's office (8.1j.782):

Wendy:	and where do I go to, .
Jane:	t's I s u:h do you know Pan-American College,
Wendy:	**yes.**
Jane:	u:m it's Lester Court, - which if you come in the Salad Street side, .
Wendy:	**yeah, .**
Jane:	and through the gate, .
Wendy:	**mhm,**
Jane:	and, about a hundred yards ahead, there's an archway on the right,
Wendy:	**yeah, .**
Jane:	[continues]

Jane gets Wendy to confirm that she understands the first leg, then the second leg, and so on through her directions.[5] Installment presentations are useful in quite ordinary descriptions, as in Anna's answer to Burton's "How was the wedding?" (7.3l.1441):

Burton:	how how was the wedding -
Anna:	oh it was it was really good, it was uh it was a lovely day
Burton:	yes
Anna:	and . it was a super place, . to have it . of course
Burton:	yes -
Anna:	and we went and sat on sat in an orchard, at Grantchester, and had a huge tea *afterwards (laughs -)*
Burton:	*(laughs - -)* .
Anna:	**uh**
Burton:	**it does** sound, very nice indeed

By presenting her description in installments, Anna gets Burton to help her complete her extended answer without interruption (see Schegloff, 1982).

[5] For related examples see Geluykens (1987, 1988, 1992) and Ono and Thompson (1994).

Installment contributions are like continuing contributions, but with a difference in who is in control. In both, contributors present utterances that are accepted with responses like "yes" and "uh huh." In continuing contributions, the partners are largely in control. The contributors may expect and look for acknowledgments as they go along, but it is the partners who decide where to place them and complete a contribution. In installment utterances, it is the contributors who are most in control. They fix the size of each installment by choosing when to invite their partners to respond. Responses to continuing presentations tend to overlap with the end of the contributor's presentation, but responses to installments don't.

ACTIONS MIDUTTERANCE

Packaging in presentations can take other forms as well. I will illustrate with collaborative completions, truncations, fade-outs, and constituent queries.

Although speakers usually try to present entire utterances for their partners to accept, they don't always succeed. Sometimes they get part way when their partners offer a completion, as in this example from a conversation about tape recorders (Lerner, 1987):

Marty: Now most machines don't record that slow. So I'd wanna- when I make a tape,
Josh: **be able tuh speed it up.**
Marty: Yeah.

Marty presents "So I'd wanna - when I make a tape," and then stops, perhaps looking for a way to express what he wants to say next. Josh then offers a plausible completion "be able tuh speed it up." Apparently it is what Marty intended, because he agrees to it with "yeah." Josh's contribution is a *collaborative completion* (Goodwin and Goodwin, 1986; Grimshaw, 1987; Lerner, 1987; Wilkes-Gibbs, 1986).

Collaborative completions, like other contributions, have presentation and acceptance phases. When Josh initiated his completion "be able tuh speed it up," he was accepting Marty's presentation so far. He was passing up the opportunity to ask for clarification. More than that, he was showing just how well he understood what Marty meant: He was offering an appropriate way to complete Marty's thought, his assertion. But Josh's utterance "be able tuh speed it up" is itself a presentation, and Marty explicitly accepts it with "Yeah." Completions are often accepted or rejected explicitly.

What is the status of an accepted completion like Josh's? There are two contributions here. Josh contributed the proposition of "being able to speed the tape recorder up": That proposition was presented and accepted. Still, it was Marty who asserted that he'd want to be able to speed it up. That was *his* contribution. The one contribution contains the other as its part.

Truncations and *fade-outs* are the opposite of completions. With truncations, partners interrupt contributors part way through their presentations – truncating the presentations – because they think they understand already and don't need any more. Eve and Herb are in a car on a rainy Dutch day, waiting at a stop light, when they see a woman with an umbrella cross the street in front of them. Fifteen minutes earlier, they had talked about bringing a second umbrella for Herb:

Herb: Where's the other -
Eve: **On the back shelf.**
Herb: Good.

Herb presents part of what he intended, but Eve initiates her uptake before he is done. In doing so, she shows she believes she understands what Herb is asking. Herb completes the process by accepting her answer.

In other truncations, contributors invite their partners to interrupt as soon as they understand (see also Clark and Schaefer, 1987b; Goodwin, 1987; Goodwin and Goodwin, 1986; Jefferson, 1973), as here (1.4.887):

Justin: this Polly, . you know that girl, whom I've- I m- I m m presented . a rather
          absurd report in a way, that genuinely represented what I felt, I said she
          might
Ken: *who's that*
Justin: fail? or get a two A, do you remember? at the end? I thought she'd
          get further than two B, do you know her?
Ken: **oh yes, . yes, well ((3 to 4 syllables))***
Justin: she's a very funny girl

Justin presents one description of Polly after another until Ken interrupts with a recognition of who he is referring to. With that Justin truncates his presentation and goes on to his next contribution "she's a very funny girl."

With fade-outs, contributors truncate presentations on their own – they fade out – and their partners accept the presentations as understood anyway. Here is an example (Lerner, 1987):

Barbara:	and uh but then she says she gets to thinking, oh well she's just not gonna worry about it.
Alan:	Mm hm.
Barbara:	you know, **she's just gonna - -**
Alan:	yeah

With "you know, she's just gonna - -" Barbara deliberately leaves her presentation incomplete. Alan accepts Barbara's presentation as having been understood anyway. Fade-outs are especially useful when the rest of the presentation is too embarrassing or touchy to make public.

Another way of grounding mid-utterance is with *trial constituents*. Sometimes speakers find themselves about to present a name or description they aren't sure is correct or comprehensible. They can present that constituent – often a noun or noun phrase – with what Sacks and Schegloff (1979) have called a *try marker*, a rising intonation followed by a slight pause, to get their partners to confirm or correct it before completing the presentation, as here (3.2a.59):

Morris:	so I wrote off to . Bill, . uh who ((had)) presumably disappeared by this time, certainly, a man called **Annegra?** -
June:	**yeah, Allegra**
Morris:	Allegra, uh replied, . uh and I . put . two other people, who'd been in for . the BBST job . with me [continues]

In the middle of his presentation, Morris apparently becomes uncertain about the name *Annegra*, so he presents it with rising intonation and a slight pause. June responds "yeah" to confirm she knows who he is referring to, then corrects the name to "Allegra." Morris accepts the correction by re-presenting "Allegra" and continuing on. The entire check and correction is deft and brief. The local contribution looks like this:

Presentation Phase
Morris:	Annegra? -

Acceptance Phase
June:	yeah, Allegra

But this contribution is embedded within A's larger presentation of "a man called Allegra replied."

Mid-utterance queries can also be initiated by the partner, as in the telephone conversation between Jane and Kate (Chapter 7):

Jane:	u:m Professor Worth said that, if . Miss Pink runs into difficulties, . on Monday afternoon, . with the standing subcommittee, . over the item on Miss Panoff, - - -

Kate:	**Miss Panoff?**
Jane:	**yes,**
Jane:	that Professor Worth would be with Mr Miles all afternoon, - so she only had to go round and collect him if she needed him, - - -

Kate and Jane confirm a name ("Miss Panoff?" "yes") while Jane goes on hardly missing a beat.

Contributions are therefore hierarchical. Both the presentation and acceptance phases may themselves contain contributions, each with its own briefer presentation and acceptance phases. What is remarkable is the many different forms these embedded contributions come in – side sequences, installment utterances, collaborative completions, fade-outs, truncations, trial constituents. Each is shaped by the purpose it serves.

Collateral communication

By the grounding hypothesis, talk consists of two parallel tracks of actions. Officially, Roger is trying to get Nina to tell him whether she and her husband have a car. At the same time, the two of them are trying jointly to construct a successful communicative act. They talk to accomplish both. I will refer to these as *track 1* and *track 2*, and I will speak of track 2 as *collateral* to track 1. The difference between the two tracks is subject matter. Track 1 represents attempts to carry out official business, and track 2, attempts to create a successful communication. Put differently, track 1 contains the basic communicative acts, and track 2 contains *meta-communicative acts* – acts about the basic communicative acts. We might picture the tracks this way:

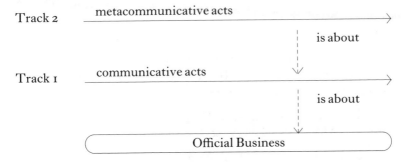

Although it is helpful to think of the two tracks as talk and meta-talk, these terms aren't precise enough for the work they have to do.

The contrast between the two tracks isn't a mere abstraction: There are concrete signals in both tracks. Compare these two exchanges:

Speaker	Track 1	Track 2
Waitress:	What'll ya have girls?	
Customer:	What's the soup of the day?	
Waitress:	Clam chowder	
Customer:	I'll have a bowl of clam chowder and a salad with Russian dressing.	
Roger:	now, - um do you and your husband have a j- car	
Nina:		- have a car?
Roger:		yeah
Nina:	no -	

Although both exchanges consist of a question and answer with a side sequence in between, the two side sequences serve different functions. The first ("What's the soup of the day?" "Clam chowder") deals with the waitress's and customer's public business – ordering food. The second ("Have a car?" "Yeah") deals with Roger's and Nina's communicative act – getting Roger's utterance correctly identified and understood. The first has to do with official business, and the second, with the signals by which the business is done.[6]

When we think of language use, we tend to think of track 1 – of talk about the business at hand, the topic of conversation. But talk about talk is still talk. Take the side sequence in Roger and Nina's exchange:

Nina:	- have a car?
Roger:	yeah

Although it is in track 2, it is still an adjacency pair – a minimal joint project with a proposal and uptake. It is just that its subject matter is Roger's utterance. What we really have is this:

Proposal:	Did you utter "have a car"?
Uptake:	Yeah, I uttered "have a car."

These two contributions are built on quotations, or demonstrations, of the talk being referred to.

Talk in track 2 isn't a homogeneous category. Its subject matter can

---

[6] Roger's "um" is not official business, a point I take up in Chapter 9.

be any level of communicative acts in track 1. With "Have a car?" "Yeah," Nina and Roger addressed Roger's presentation (level 2), but they could instead have addressed his execution (level 1), meaning (level 3), or proposal (level 4). In Chapter 9, I will take up collateral signals about levels 1 and 2. Here I consider collateral signals directed at meaning and understanding (level 3).

COLLATERAL PROJECTS

Whenever contributors present a signal in track 1, according to the principle of joint closure, they are tacitly asking, "Do you understand what I mean by this?" and their respondents are expected to take them up. They are carrying out these actions in track 2. Consider a continuing contribution from an earlier example:

	Utterance	Track 1	Track 2
A:	it was uh it was a lovely day	1. [I assert] it was a lovely day	1. [Do you understand this?]
B:	yes	2. [I ratify your assertion]	2. yes [I understand that].

(The interpretations in square brackets are those not directly expressed in the speaker's words.) In track 1, A is asserting to B that it was a lovely day, and B doesn't demur. But what does B mean by "yes"? It isn't "Yes, it was a lovely day," but "Yes, I understand what you mean by that." "Yes" is B's uptake of the implied question, "Do you understand what I mean by this?" Here is a minimal joint project (question plus uptake) in track 2.

The claim is this: Every presentation enacts the collateral question "Do you understand what I mean by this?" The very act of directing an utterance to a respondent is a signal that means "Are you hearing, identifying, and understanding this now?" This is one goal of the presentation phase, and one goal of the acceptance phase is to take up that question. Respondents complete the joint project immediately when they answer or imply "yes"; they alter it when they initiate a repair sequence that implies "no." Although the claim may seem radical, it is just a concrete form of the grounding hypothesis – that the participants in a conversation try to ground what they say. And it provides a rationale for the presentation and acceptance phases of contributions.

Many joint projects in track 2 are initiated by the contributor in track 1, as in these extracts from earlier examples:

Type	Example	Joint project in track 2
Continuing contribution	A: it was uh it was a lovely day	1. [Do you understand this?]
	B: yes	2. yes [I understand that]
Concluded contribution	A: and what are you then	1. [Do you understand this?]
	B: I'm on the academic council	2. [I understand you as displayed in my answer]
Installment	A: if you come in the Salad Street side, .	1. [Do you understand the directions so far?]
	B: yeah	2. yeah
Third-turn repair	A: no, I meant who decides what price it'll go on the market -	1. no, I meant who decides what price it'll go on the market -
	B: (- snorts) . whatever people will pay - -	2. [I understand as displayed here]
Fade-out	A: you know, she's just gonna - -	1. [I am sure you understand without my completing this]
	B: yeah	2. yeah [I understand]
Constituent query	A: Annegra?	1. [Confirm that you understand] Annegra
	B: yeah, Allegra	2. yeah, [I understand, but the name is] Allegra

Other collateral projects are initiated by the respondent in track 1, as in these extracts:

Type	Example		Joint project in track 2
Second-turn repair	A:	senior?	1. [Do you mean Jim Johnstone senior?]
	B:	**yes**	2. yes, [I mean that]
Collaborative completion	A:	be able tuh speed it up	1. [Do you mean], be able to speed it up
	B:	**yeah**	2. yeah, [I mean that]
Truncation	A:	on the back shelf	1. [I understand you as displayed in this answer]
	B:	**good**	2. [I accept your construal]

In every case A and B create a joint project in track 2 that deals with what A meant and B construed A as meaning.

Tracks are recursive. Every collateral track can have its own collateral track. Here is an illustration from an earlier example:

Utterance		Track 1	Track 2	Track 3
D:	forty-nine Skipton Place	1. [The address is] forty-nine Skipton Place	1. [Confirm that you heard] "forty-nine" Skipton Place"	
J:	forty-one	2. [I ratify the address as] forty-one	2. [I heard] "forty-one"	1. **[Did you present] "forty-one"?**
D:	nine . nine			2. **[No, the "one" is] "nine"**
J:	forty-nine	2'. [I ratify the address as] forty-nine	2'. [I heard] "forty-nine"	

When June says "forty-one" she is displaying in track 2 what she thought Darryl said. But because she is wrong, Darryl corrects her with "nine . nine" in track 3. If she hadn't heard and said "what?" she would have started track 4. Participants add collateral tracks as needed, but rarely go beyond track 2.

In the study of language, much attention has been paid to signals in track 1 – words, sentences, iconic and pointing gestures – and almost none to signals in track 2. One reason is clear. Collateral signals, which are hard enough to identify in spontaneous talk, do not occur in citation forms, the favorite medium for studying language. Yet they are real.

The collateral signals just surveyed all have to do with meaning and understanding. All of them fit these frames or their variants:

Speaker	About contributor's meaning	About respondent's understanding
Contributor:	By x, I mean y.	By x, do you understand y?
	By x, what do you understand?	
Respondent:	By x, do you mean y?	I understand x.
	By x, what do you mean?	By x, I understand y.

All of these frames express either what the contributor means or what the respondent understands the contributor to mean. And they are all in the present tense, because they are directed at states of meaning and understanding at the moment of utterance.

These frames represent what speakers mean by these collateral signals, but what form do the signals actually take? A priori, we might expect them to exhibit four features:

1. *Backgrounding.* Signals in track 1, which are about the participants' official business, should be prominent. Signals in track 2 should be backgrounded.

2. *Simultaneity.* If the participants in a conversation take actions in both tracks at the same time, they should be performing signals in both tracks simultaneously. Two participants, A and B, might manage this in several ways. (a) A could perform signals in both tracks with the same behavior. (b) A could perform a signal in track 2 at the same time as the signal in track 1, but in a different medium – e.g., gesturing as against speaking. (c) B could signal in track 2 at the same time as A is signaling in track 1 – in the same or different medium. Or (d) A could perform signals in track 2 in the interstices of signals in track 1.

3. *Brevity.* Because most collateral signals carry so little information, they should be brief and limited in variety.

4. *Differentiation.* Signals in track 2 need to be distinguishable from those in track 1. They may well be created from a specialized, identifiable set of methods.

Among the signaling methods we saw in Chapter 6, some readily satisfy these four requirements, and they are often exploited in collateral signals. Here are some of the methods used for addressing meaning and understanding.

1. *Temporal placement*. Speakers can indicate they do or don't understand what was said by the placement of their utterance. Here are excerpts from previous examples:[7]

Track 2 signal	Example	Interpretation
Acknowledgment	A: it was a lovely day B: **yes**	"I understand what you have just now finished"
Uncertainty marker	A: Okay, the next one is the rabbit. B: **u::h**	"I don't yet understand what you have just now finished"
Collaborative completion	A: So I'd wanna- when I make a tape, B: **be able tuh speed it up.**	"Do you mean this: 'be able to speed it up'?"
Truncation	A: Where's the other - B: **On the back shelf.**	"I already understand your question so I am answering now."

In each case, B signals what he or she understands by the timing of the utterance. Acknowledgments are timed to overlap or abut the end of the phrase or clause they acknowledge. And although "yes" and "u::h" in the first two examples are signals in track 2, the words in the last two examples are not. For these, the collateral signaling is achieved entirely by their placement.

2. *Marked prosody*. Every utterance in track 1 has an expected prosody. One way to create a collateral signal is to superimpose an unexpected, or *marked*, prosody on that utterance. Here are extracts from previous examples:

---

[7] The uncertainty marker is from Clark and Wilkes-Gibbs (1986).

Track 2 signal	Example	Interpretation
Trial constituent	A: a man called **Annegra?** -	"Confirm that you know who I mean by Annegra."
	B: yeah, Allegra	
Installment	A: so **Mr. D. Challam,**	"Confirm that you understand this installment."
	B: yes	
Fade-outs	A: you know, **she's just gonna - -**	"I am sure you understand without my completing this."
	B: yeah	

Speakers mark trial constituents with a rising intonation and pause. They mark installments with a so-called list intonation and pause. They mark fade-outs with a drop in speed and volume. Remove these markings and you remove the collateral signals.

3. *Gestures.* Gestures are often ideal as collateral signals. They are easily distinguished from speech and can be performed simultaneously, briefly, in the background of that speech. Head nods, for example, are regularly used as acknowledgments. Respondents also display constru-als with motor mimicry, as when Nina grimaces as Roger describes a bad car accident (Chapter 6).

Other gestures have been identified as collateral signals by Janet Bavelas and her colleagues (Bavelas et al., 1992). Iconic and indicative gestures, they argue, divide into what they called *topic* and *interactive gestures*:

Topic gestures depict semantic information directly related to the topic of dis-course, and interactive gestures (a smaller group) refer instead to some aspect of the process of conversing with another person. (p. 473)

So topic gestures are in track 1, because they deal with official business, and interactive gestures are in the collateral track, because they serve a meta-communicative function. Among the interactive functions Bavelas and her colleagues noted is "seeking agreement, understanding, or help." (p. 473) Example: One person has just talked about looking up information in a library card catalogue, and a second person says:

then look up under the *appropriate* thing

On the word *appropriate* the speaker makes a quick hand movement toward the first person – an indicative gesture – meaning "you know, what you just said about looking up the author or title." Bavelas et al.'s narratives had many such gestures.

So collateral signals have identifiable forms – they are genuine signals. It is just that they are backgrounded to the primary signals: They are either simultaneous with or in the interstices of primary utterances. As a result, they are often realized with temporal placement, marked prosody, or gestures.

PROJECTING EVIDENCE

To complete a contribution, contributors need evidence that their respondents have understood what they meant, and the respondents try to provide that evidence. The *raison d'être* of track 2 is to deal with such evidence. Indeed, in the presentation and acceptance phases, the two partners are trying to complete this minimal joint project in track 2:

Proposal. I request you now to provide evidence of understanding of type *x*.
Uptake. I hereby provide evidence of understanding of type *x* (or stronger).

For such evidence to be of value, it must be valid, economical, and timely, and the two partners should exploit their collateral joint projects to make sure it is. That suggests the following principle:

Principle of projected evidence. With every presentation, contributors use signals in track 2 to project the type of evidence of understanding that they consider to be valid, economical, and timely enough for current purposes.

We have already seen evidence for this principle. When speakers decide how to present an utterance, they are simultaneously projecting the type of evidence they want. Here are extracts from previous examples:

Type of presentation	A's presentation	Evidence projected from B
Complete proposal	and what are you then	uptake of proposal
Continuing presentation	it was uh it was a lovely day	backgrounded acknowledgment
Installment	and through the gate, -	explicit confirmation
Verbatim installment	forty-nine Skipton Place	verbatim repetition
Constituent query	Annegra?	explicit confirmation
Backgrounded acknowledgment	uh huh	continued attention

When Alan asks "and what are you then," he is projecting Burton's uptake, which will display that understanding. Each type of presentation projects a different uptake in track 2 – from continued attention to verbatim displays. Indeed, in the examples cited here, the respondents' uptake is as expected.

Economy. In choosing a type of presentation, contributors project the most economical evidence they think they need for current purposes. One part of this cost is processing time (Chapter 3): The participants try to minimize total joint processing time. Other things being equal, the briefer the evidence, the better. Contributors won't request elaborate evidence unless they need it, nor will their respondents be more elaborate than they think is needed. Here is the principle of opportunistic closure at work.

The most economical evidence is uptake or backgrounded acknowledgments. Uptakes, like answers to questions, take no time out from the progress of the conversation. They carry it on without a break. Backgrounded acknowledgments also take no time out. They are produced in track 2 without respondents taking extra turns or, because they overlap, additional time. These are precisely the forms of evidence projected in concluded and continuing contributions. That is one reason why they are so common.

Other evidence costs more. Contributors need a special reason to make a constituent query, requesting a nod or "uh huh"; for example, their need to check on a reference must be urgent. They also need a special reason to invite explicit "uh huh"s with more than one installment per utterance; it must be important to check on their respondents' understanding of each installment. They also need a special reason to invite a completion; the need for a name, word, or phrase to finish off their contribution must be great. In contrast, in using "uh huh," contributors project nothing more than continued attention. It would be odd to acknowledge "uh huh" with another "uh huh," or "I see," or "okay." The participants estimate how long it should take to reach joint closure and make choices to minimize that time.

Timeliness. Contributors also project *when* respondents are to give evidence. The usual point is the slot immediately after the presentation. Full turns are to be accepted with the initiation of the next turn; installments are to be accepted immediately in the following pause; trial constituents are to be accepted immediately after the constituent; and so on. There is good reason for this regularity. Speakers try to design presentations to provide all the material that is needed for complete understanding. So almost all presentations are full constituents – full sentences, clauses, or smaller phrases – and not fragments. Roger cannot present "do you and" and expect Nina to understand. She needs to know how he will finish. Full constituents are natural units of meaning and understanding.

But respondents should provide evidence in the projected slot as soon as reasonably possible. The reasoning is this. For two people to accumulate common ground in an orderly way, they must complete the current contribution before going to the next (Chapter 2). Most contributions depend on the previous ones for their success, so they are likely to go wrong unless the previous ones are complete. And to minimize joint processing time, respondents should give evidence of understanding as early in the projected slot as they can. The lack of timely evidence can be construed as a lack of attention, identification, or understanding. When I call out "Helen?" and Helen doesn't respond immediately, I may take that as evidence she didn't hear me. When A tells B "Okay, the next one is the rabbit," and B begins "u::h," A takes that as evidence that B cannot identify "the rabbit" so A adds "that's asleep, you know, it looks like it's got ears and a head pointing down?" to which B says "okay" (Clark and Wilkes-Gibbs, 1986). We use the promptness of a response as part of its evidence of understanding.

In special circumstances, evidence of understanding is also provided within presentations. When Justin went on and on with his description of a girl named Polly, he was inviting Ken to interrupt when he understood. When Eve cut off Herb's question "Where's the other -" with her uptake "On the back shelf," she used the placement of her utterance to signal she already understood. Josh used a similar signal when he completed Marty's nonconstituent utterance, "So I'd wanna- when I make a tape," with "be able to speed it up."

Conclusions

In conversation, speakers don't just speak, and listeners listen. They demand closure on their actions – even their joint actions. According to the grounding hypothesis, people work hard to ground their joint actions – to establish them as part of their common ground. If so, contributing to a conversation should take the efforts of both contributors and their respondents, and it does. Contributors present signals to respondents, and then contributors and respondents work together to reach the mutual belief that the signals have been understood well enough for current purposes.

In this picture, contributions can emerge in many forms. Two forms predominate. In concluded contributions, respondents presuppose they understand a presentation by proceeding to the next relevant contribution. When asked a question, they take it up, their answer displaying their construal of the question. In continuing contributions, respondents assert they understand with an acknowledgment like "uh huh" or "yeah" or a nod. Other forms of contributions depend on how contributors design their presentations (in installments, with rising intonation, with fade-outs) and how respondents respond to them (with queries, evidence of misunderstanding, collaborative completions). There is no end to the variety of forms of emergent contributions.

People in conversation are therefore engaged in two tracks of actions at once. They talk about official business in track 1 and about their communicative acts in track 2. It is in track 2 that contributors ask for confirmation or invite completions, and respondents provide acknowledgments and other evidence of understanding.

9 | Utterances

Utterances are the most tangible products of language use. They have traditionally been treated as autonomous acts by speakers, but that isn't right. Although speakers may assume the major responsibility, they cannot present utterances without the coordination of their addressees. When Connie presents an utterance to Duncan, she is trying to get him to identify her words, constructions, and gestures, and that takes his actions too. Getting utterances attended to and identified is just as much a joint action as getting them understood.

We also tend to think of utterances as single, linear threads of talk. Connie begins with an intention, formulates an utterance piece by piece, and presents each piece to Duncan as she completes it. In reality, utterances are nonlinear and have more than one track. Connie may produce an expression, change her mind, and start over. She may make a mistake and repair it. She may realize she didn't have Duncan's attention and repeat what she said. She may interrupt herself to explain a pause or disfluency, or to apologize for a gaffe. Duncan may add his own bits to her utterance. These phenomena aren't rare. In spontaneous utterances, speakers and addressees have many intricate issues to manage.

In the last two chapters we looked at how people carry out joint projects and establish what the speaker is to be taken as meaning, the top two rungs of this ladder (Chapter 5):

	Speaker A's actions	Addressee B's actions
4	A is proposing joint project w to B	B is considering A's proposal of w
3	A is signaling that p for B	B is recognizing that p from A
2	A is presenting signal s to B	B is identifying signal s from A
1	A is executing behavior t for B	B is attending to behavior t from A

In this chapter we will see how people manage utterances, and for that we will look at the bottom two rungs – level 2, presentation and identification, and level 1, execution and attention.

Presentations

In every communicative act, speakers present signals for their addressees to identify. Roger, for example, presents the utterance "now, - um do you and your husband have a j- car" in order to ask Nina whether she and her husband have a car. To complete his question (at level 3), he has to get Nina to identify his presentation (at level 2), but doesn't quite manage the first time around:

Roger: now, - um do you and your husband have a j- car
Nina: - have a car?
Roger: yeah
Nina: no -

Apparently, Nina isn't sure of the last phrase, "have a car," so she asks Roger to confirm it. Only once that identification is complete (at level 2) does she understand the question (level 3) and take it up with "no" (level 4). The joint process of presenting and identifying signals is essential to communicative acts.

Every use of a word, phrase, or sentence has an *ideal delivery* – a flawless presentation in the given situation (Clark and Clark, 1977). It is flawless in that it is fluent, and the pronunciation, intonation, speed, and volume are appropriate to the circumstances. It is the delivery speakers would make if they had formulated what they were going to say before speaking and could follow through on that plan. Something close to an ideal delivery is produced by radio and television announcers and stage actors. But as Roger's utterance illustrates, speakers in conversation achieve ideal deliveries only in spurts. As hard as they try, they cannot sustain fluency for any length of time.

The problem is human limitations. Roger commits to speaking with "now," but then has to pause to formulate the next word. Later, he begins a word "j-" but cuts himself off and uses the word "car" instead. Speakers have trouble deciding on, formulating, and articulating what they want to say and that interferes with their ideal delivery. To account for these problems and their repair, we must return to the notion of tracks of talk.

PRIMARY AND SECONDARY PRESENTATIONS

As we saw in Chapter 8, signals divide into tracks 1 and 2. Signals in track 1 are addressed to official business, and those in track 2, to the communicative acts themselves. The side sequence in Roger and Nina's exchange was an example of a collateral project:

Nina: - have a car?
Roger: yeah

Nina's question, "Was the phrase you just presented 'have a car'?" is about Roger's communicative act, not about the official business of their conversation, so this exchange belongs to track 2.

Roger's gross presentation "now, - um do you and your husband have a j- car" also divides into two tracks. Roger's "now, do you and your husband have a j- car?" is in track 1 because it is "official" or "for the record." The status of Roger's "j-," however, changes midutterance when he replaces it by "car" and then considers it "*no longer* for the record." In contrast, Roger's "um" is never "official" or "for the record" in this sense. It deals with the communicative act, so it belongs to track 2. And, finally, there are incidental elements in the gross presentation that are not intended. One may be the pause after "well," since Roger deals with it by saying "um."

We can therefore partition a gross presentation into four distinct classes of elements, as follows:

Primary presentation. Those parts of the gross presentation that the speaker intends as signals about the official business of the discourse (e.g., Roger's "now, do you and your husband have a j- car"). These belong to track 1.

Secondary presentation. Those parts of the gross presentation that the speaker intends as signals about the communicative acts themselves (e.g., Roger's "um"). These belong to track 2.

Ex-official elements. Those elements of the primary presentation that the speaker later intends to be preempted by other elements (e.g., Roger's "j-"). These were part of track 1 when they were produced.

Incidental elements. Those elements of the gross presentation that the speaker doesn't intend to be part of any communicative acts (e.g., Roger's pause after "well").

Speakers design presentations so their addressees can distinguish among these four types of elements. If they didn't, their addressees couldn't understand.

GESTURES

Gross presentations contain nonlinguistic as well as linguistic signals (Chapter 6). Speakers gesture with their voice, hands, arms, face, eyes, and body in order to describe, indicate, and demonstrate an indefinitely wide range of objects, events, states, and properties. Gestures divide into primary, secondary, and ex-official elements as well.

The commonest gestures in track 1 are indicative gestures, iconic gestures, and beats. Many demonstrative references aren't complete without indicative gestures, as in this example (Schegloff, 1984, p. 280):

Frank: why:nchu put that 't the end uh the ta:ble there

Frank refers to the dish "that" in front of Marge without a gesture, but refers to the end of the table "there" by pointing at it. Without the gesture, he couldn't get Marge to recognize where precisely on the table he meant. Indicative gestures are parts of other communicative acts too, as here (Schegloff, 1984, p. 284):

Linda: en I'm getting a sun tan

As Linda says this, she points first at her left cheek and then at her right, asserting she is getting a tan on her cheeks even though she never mentions her cheeks verbally. These, too, are part of her primary presentation.

So are most iconic gestures and beats. Recall the joke Fran told about the movie *Some Like it Hot* (Chapter 6). In the course of that joke, she says:

Fran: they wheel a big table in, with a big with a big [1.08 sec] cake on it, and the girl, jumps up.

In the pause before "cake," Fran produces an iconic gesture, depicting the cake as large and round. Her addressees would have missed part of what she meant if they didn't understand that. Beats, in their purest form, reinforce major stresses in a presentation, as here (Schegloff, 1984, p. 273):

Sam: I mean it's like Eddie says, (1.0 sec) as time goes on it gets worse 'n worse 'n worse 'n worse

Sam makes a thrusting gesture on the word *time* and on each of the four instances of *worse*. He is apparently emphasizing these five words to help mark them as new information, making the beats part of track 1.

Speakers use descriptive, indicative, and iconic gestures in track 2 as well (see Chapter 8). They use indicative gestures to designate their current addressee. The commonest gestures are eye gaze or body orientation, as Charles Goodwin (1981) noted in this utterance:

Elsie: See first we were gonna have [**gazing at Ann**] Teema, Carrie and Clara, (0.2) a::nd myself. [**gazing at Bessie**] The four of us. The four [**gazing at Clara**] children. But then – uh:: I said how is that gonna look.

As Elsie gazes successively at Ann, Bessie, and Clara, she repeats and expands on her references, designing "Teema, Carrie, and Clara," for Ann, "the four of us" for Bessie, and "the four children" for Clara. She tailors each reference for the particular woman she is addressing, indicating that woman by her gaze. Gestures like these are indispensable to indicating the addressees for particular utterances (see also Goodwin, 1986b, 1987).

For an example of iconic gestures in track 2, consider what Marjorie Harness Goodwin and Charles Goodwin (1986; Goodwin, 1987) have called the *thinking face* in this presentation:

A: He pu:t uhm, (0.7) tch! Put *crab*meat on th'bo:dum.

Beginning at "uhm" and ending at "tch!" A turns away from the addressee with a distant look in his eyes in a stereotyped facial gesture of someone thinking hard. Speakers use the thinking face to signal that they are doing a word search and to account for why they aren't proceeding with their utterance. In this example, A ended his thinking face when he was able to proceed to the word *crabmeat*. Other times, speakers end the thinking face by turning to their addressees for help in finding the word they were searching for.

The commonest gestures in track 2, according to Bavelas (1994; Bavelas et al., 1992; see also Cassell and McNeill, 1991), fall into these main categories:[1]

---

[1] Bavelas and her colleagues called these *interactive gestures*, which contrast with *topical gestures* (part of the primary presentation).

Type of gesture	Function of gesture	Example
Delivery gesture	to refer to the delivery of information by speaker to addressee	speaker "hands over" to addressee new information relevant to main point
Citing gesture	to refer to a previous contribution by addressee	speaker points at addressee to indicate "as you said earlier"
Seeking gesture	to elicit a specific response from addressee	speaker looks at addressee as if to say "Can you give me the word for...?"
Turn gesture	to deal with issues around the speaking turn	speaker "hands over" the turn to addressee

Among gestures in track 2, we find symbols (e.g., head nods, head shakes), indexes (eye gaze, pointing, nodding), and icons (thinking face, smiling, frowning). The full range of gestures is exploited in both primary and secondary presentations.

Gross presentations, then, divide into primary and secondary signals. To see how and why, we must examine how speakers and addressees manage presentations that are less than ideal.

Disruptions

When speakers cannot manage an ideal delivery, they usually *disrupt* their presentations. Most disruptions can be divided into three intervals whose boundaries are fixed by two points (Levelt; 1983, 1989; Shriberg, 1994). I will call this the *disruption schema*:

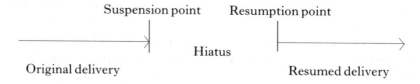

The five parts of the schema are defined as follows (illustrated for Roger's "j-"):

1. *Original delivery.* This is the smooth delivery before the disruption (here, "have a j-").
2. *Suspension.* This is the first outward sign of the disruption, the point at which the speaker suspends the original delivery (here, in the middle of the word beginning "j"). I will denote the suspension point with a left curly bracket {.

3. *Hiatus.* This is the interval from the point of suspension to the point at which the speaker resumes the primary presentation, here the interval between "j-" and "car." In some cases, the time between suspension and resumption is zero (Blackmer and Mitton, 1991). Other times, it may contain such elements as "uh" or "I mean." Whatever its length, I will call it a hiatus.[2]

4. *Resumption.* This is the point at which the speaker resumes the official presentation, here the beginning of the word "car." I will denote the resumption point with a right curly bracket }.

5. *Resumed delivery.* This is the delivery after the resumption.

In my notation, Roger's presentation is this: "do you and your husband have a j- {} car."

Although disruptions are usually associated with disfluencies, they need not be. Speakers can suspend their delivery for any purpose whatever – to laugh, to take a sip of coffee, to clear one's throat. Here is a good example (1.3.1):

Nancy: I'm not {- oh, thanks, .} not really comfortable, {.} like this

When Nancy's companion offers her tea, she suspends her current utterance to accept it.

Disruptions often come in spates. Here are two spontaneous utterances marked with the notation just introduced (1.2.370; 1.2.787):

well {. I mean} this {. uh} Mallet said {} Mallet was {uh} said something about {uh you know} he felt it would be a good thing if {u:h .} if Oscar went

well, they've accepted th- {uh} this as a commitment {-} because it's a {} it's a {} it's a m {} he's done a {} he's on a Ph.D. {- you see}

In the first example, the seven words after "well" encompass two disruptions, each with several parts. The hiatus in "well {. I mean} this" contains a pause and an editing phrase ("I mean"). The hiatus in "this {. uh} Mallet" contains a pause and a filler ("uh"). Despite the disruptions, these two examples posed no problems for the addressees. The reason lies in the way the speakers and addressees managed them. In each disruption, the speakers added signals in track 2 telling the addressees exactly what they were doing and why. To see how, let us examine the three parts of the disruption schema – the suspension, the hiatus, and the resumption.

SUSPENSION

The point of suspension is usually clear. Speakers cease their presentation at a point where, in the ideal delivery, they should not be ceasing.

[2] Shriberg (1994) calls this interval the *interregnum.*

This is really what defines the point of suspension. The cessation of speech is often accompanied by one or more *suspension devices*. Here are five common devices (1.1.819; 8.2a.335; 1.12.661; 1.2.229; 1.1.1164):

Suspension device	Example
Pause	there's another {-} fight I've got on my hands
Word cut-off	have a j- {} car
Elongation	and **thuh:** {} the parish church is beginning to go boing boing,
Nonreduction	come to look at **thiy** {.} the literature
Filler	and then you'll get {**uh**} difficulties about marking

    1. *Pause.* The simplest accompaniment to cessation is a pause. It is often the only sign indicating the point of suspension.

    2. *Word cut-off.* Speakers can deliberately suspend their delivery in the middle of a word. They often do this with an audible closure of the glottis, so that listeners hear not only the cessation of speech, but the glottal stop.

    3. *Syllable elongation.* Sometimes speakers elongate the syllable just before the suspension, as in this example:

and thuh: {} the parish church is beginning to go boing boing,

In the ideal this speaker would have delivered "and the parish church is beginning ..." producing *the* only once with the reduced vowel schwa. Instead, he pronounced *the* with a lengthened schwa (as marked by the colon), suspended his delivery, and, on resuming, repeated *the* with a normal length. In repeated "the"s, the first token tends to be longer than normal, and the second, normal (Shriberg, 1994).

    4. *Nonreduced vowel.* In the ideal delivery, many unaccented syllables are pronounced with reduced vowels. If you deliver "The dog found a bone" fluently, you will produce both *the* and *a* with the reduced schwa "uh." But speakers sometimes mark suspensions by producing vowels *without* reducing them. They pronounce *the* and *a* as "thiy" and "ai" (rhyming with *me* and *day*), as in this example:

come to look at thiy {.} the literature

In the London–Lund corpus, 81 percent of the tokens of "thiy" were at points of suspension, whereas only 7 percent of the tokens of "thuh" were. Clearly, "thiy" can be used for signaling points of suspension (Fox Tree and Clark, 1994). Likewise, speakers may produce *to*, ordinarily pronounced "tuh," as a nonreduced "too," and the same for other schwas. Note that producing a nonreduced vowel ("thiy") is not the same as lengthening a vowel ("thuh:").

5. *Fillers*. Another way to mark suspensions is by placing a vocal or visual element in the hiatus. Two common elements in English hiatuses are "uh" and "um," but there may also be throat clearing, laughter, and gestures.

Suspension devices aren't produced accidentally. They are the result of the speakers' own actions – they are *self*-suspensions – and are signs in Peirce's sense (Chapter 6). But Peirce's signs can be either signals (actions by which speakers mean something for their addressees) or symptoms (such as spots for measles). At least some suspension devices are signals.

Take "thiy." Whenever speakers use "thiy," they choose it over "thuh." They cannot pronounce *the* as "thiy" simply by lengthening the vowel, as if they were accidentally slowed down in speaking. Their choice of "thiy" over "thuh" is like any other lexical choice – for example, *the* over *a*, or *in* over *at*. It is part of the signal they have planned. What they signal with their choice of "thiy" is not official business (track 1), but a suspension of the presentation of the utterance (track 2). With it they mean, "I am suspending the primary presentation at this point for a moment." That makes the vowel choice in "thiy" a collateral signal.

The logic here is based on a *principle of choice*: Whenever speakers have more than one option for part of a signal and choose one of the options, they must mean something by that choice, and the choice is a signal. By this logic, the word cut-off is a signal: Speakers could have chosen to complete the word as formulated. To cut it off is to signal they have changed their minds about it. The same argument applies to elongation, nonreduction, and suspensions by fillers.

What about mere cessation, as in this example:

there's another {-} fight I've got on my hands

On one view, the cessation after "another" and the pause "-" aren't signals, but symptoms – *unintended* consequences of not yet having formulated the next piece of the utterance. On another view, this speaker chose to begin "there's another" *before* he had formulated that next piece. He could have waited until he had formulated the entire clause, but he chose not to. At some level of planning, he intended to suspend his delivery after "another" and to pause until he could continue. By this logic, cessations and pauses are signals. It is as if speakers were saying: "I am suspending the primary presentation now because I haven't yet formulated the next piece of the utterance." There are strengths and weaknesses in both of these views. For now, I will be conservative and treat mere cessation as a symptom – an unintended sign. Still, I will place pauses in track 2, for whatever their status, they do not belong to the primary presentation.

HIATUS

The hiatus in fluent speech – the interval between the suspension and resumption points – is often filled with more than silence. Here are six common types of content (8.2a. 335; 1.1.819; 1.1.1164; 1.3.253; 2.7.692; Goodwin and Goodwin, 1986):

Contents	Example	
No pause	have a j-	{} car
Pause	there's another	{-} fight I've got on my hands
Filler	and then you'll get	{uh} difficulties about marking
Editing expression	I'd	{I mean} I haven't had any {.} results
Elongation	I think he th	{o:} he'd realized then
Iconic gesture	He pu:t	{uhm (0.7) [thinking face] tch} put crabmeat on th'bo:dum

Hiatuses may contain nothing, silence, sound, or gestures. They often contain more than one type of content – pauses, fillers, editing phrases, elongations, gestures. Which of these elements are signals, and if they are signals, what do speakers mean by them?

Editing expressions are clearly signals (DuBois, 1974; Erman, 1987; Hockett, 1967; Holmes, 1986; James, 1972, 1973; Levelt, 1983, 1989; Schiffrin, 1987). Here are a few examples with interpretations of some of their uses:

Editing expression	Interpretation of some uses
I mean	"Instead of that I mean this"
you know	"I am about to tell you something you already know"
sorry	"I'm sorry for that error"
oh	"I have just thought of a way of expressing this"
like	"I mean this only approximately"
no	"That was in error"
that is	"I am specifying that further in this way"

All these expressions make reference to the communicative acts they are placed within. Take the example with "I mean":

I'd {**I mean**} I haven't had any {.} results,

What the speaker means by "I mean" is roughly this: "Instead of what I would have meant from 'I'd' onward, I mean 'I haven't had any results.'" In each of these interpretations, the terms "that" and "this" refer to particular preceding and following acts. So editing expressions are genuine signals in track 2.

Fillers are also genuine signals in track 2. In British and North American English, speakers have a choice between at least *uh* and *um*, and even between normal and elongated versions of these expressions. These also contrast with the simple pause. What are they used for? In a study by Smith and Clark (1993), respondents were interviewed in a conversational setting and asked a series of factual questions that each had one-word answers. Here is a typical exchange (the numbers in parentheses denote pause lengths in seconds):

Experimenter: In which sport is the Stanley Cup awarded?
Respondent: {(1.4) **um** (1.0)} hockey

When the respondents didn't have the answer on the tip of their tongue, they would delay, sometimes introducing *uh* or *um* into the hiatus. The average time to answer was 2.23 seconds when they didn't use a filler, 2.65 seconds when they used *uh*, and 8.83 seconds when they used *um*. The respondents used *uh* to signal that they were having a minor problem and *um* to signal they were having a major one. Speakers recorded in the London–Lund corpus also distinguished between *uh* and *um*.[3] They were much more likely to pause after *um* than after *uh* – 55 percent to 20 percent of the time. They too used *uh* to signal a minor break and *um* a major one.

By the principle of choice, elongated vowels are also signals in track 2. Consider this example:

I think he th{**o:**} he'd realized then

Here the speaker began saying "he thought" but suspended his delivery midword and restarted again with "he'd realized." In suspending his delivery, the speaker had these choices, among others:

1.   full word + pause: thought {-}
2.   word fragment + glottal stop + pause: tho- {-}
3.   word fragment + elongated vowel + no pause: th{o:}

[3] H. H. Clark and J. E. Fox Tree, unpublished study.

In choosing the elongated vowel, the speaker therefore meant something – roughly, "I am suspending the primary presentation for a brief time while I formulate a repair for this word."

Hiatuses aren't just idle moments in speaking. They may contain a variety of actions, many of which are signals in track 2.

RESUMPTION

When speakers resume speaking after the hiatus, they present further official content of their utterances, more signals in track 1. But what is the relation of the resumed delivery to the original delivery? Here are the five basic patterns (1.1.819; 1.2.1304; 1.2.80; 1.2.231; 1.1.748):

Type		Example
Continuation	there's another	{-} fight I've got on my hands
Repetition	surely, your	{} **your** committee is not going to come to that conclusion
Substitution	what is	{.} **has** happened since then
Deletion	I don't think they've	{.} they ever in fact embodied
Addition	one of the things that	{- uh} one of the **many** things

In the first pattern, the speaker continues the utterance he had suspended. In the next three, the speakers repeat, substitute for, or delete one or more of the original words, and in the fifth, the speaker adds a word to the original. The last three patterns are often called *self-repairs*.

All these resumptions reflect a single operation I will call *replacement*: The resumed delivery is intended to replace – take precedence over – a continuous portion of what has been produced up to the point of resumption. Here is what got replaced in the five examples:

Type	Elements replaced	Resumed delivery
Continuation	{-}	fight I've got on my hands
Repetition	your {}	your committee is not going to come to that conclusion
Substitution	is {.}	has happened since then
Deletion	they've {.}	they ever in fact embodied
Addition	one of the things that {- uh}	one of the many things

A continuation replaces only the hiatus; the rest replace the hiatus plus some final portion of the original delivery. Note that to delete a word or other element (e.g., *'ve*), speakers must return to an earlier point (*they*) to show what is to be deleted. And to insert a word (e.g., *many*), they must show where it is to be inserted (before *things*). Replacement is a single method by which speakers can perform all five functions.

Resumptions, therefore, work at the level of presentation and identification (level 2). Replacements are simply *re-presentations* of what the speakers, on reconsideration, would prefer to have presented in the first place.[4] Take an utterance examined earlier:

Type of resumption	Example	
	well, they've accepted **th-**	**{uh}**
repetition	this as a commitment	**{-}**
continuation	because **it's a**	**{}**
repetition	**it's a**	**{}**
repetition	**it's a m**	**{}**
substitution	**he's done a**	**{}**
substitution	he's on a Ph.D.	**{- you see}**

Although Sam changed his mind six times and for three different reasons (repetition, continuation, substitution), he signaled each change in the same way: He returned to a previous point (the onset of boldface elements) and started over. If we delete the boldface elements, we get what Sam, afterward, would prefer to have presented: "Well, they've accepted this as a commitment because he's on a Ph.D." In most resumptions, the continuity is not just in wording, but in prosody. If we excise the boldface elements in a *recording* of Sam's utterance, we get an utterance that is prosodically well formed, that sounds natural (Fox Tree, 1995; Levelt, 1984).

Replacements, especially with prosodic continuity, are optimal for both speakers and addressees. When speakers resume speaking, they must indicate what they are doing, and replacements offer a simple, uniform method. It is easy to return to a previous point in the formulation and start again. As for addressees, they must be able quickly to identify what is being repaired. Replacements allow them to match the syntax and prosody of the resumed delivery against a portion of the original delivery with great precision. Not all repairs are achieved by replacement (Van Wijk and Kempen, 1987), but almost all resumptions are.

"To replace," however, doesn't mean "to obliterate." When the one speaker says "what is {.} has happened since then," he intends "has happened..." merely to *take precedence* over "is" in the original delivery. The point is illustrated here (1.3.305):

---

[4] Although not always. See Polanyi (1978).

Nancy: {um - - -} the interview, was {-} it was all right

After replacement, Nancy says "it was all right." But "it" is "the interview." To see this, Nancy's addressees must appeal to the reference in
what she has just replaced. So replacements take precedence over the elements they replace, but without obliterating them.

Resumptions, therefore, don't substitute, delete, or add elements per
se. They *re-present* elements that speakers, on second thought, would
prefer to have presented in the first place. It just happens that
re-presenting these elements has the effect of continuing, repeating, sub-
stituting for, deleting, or adding to portions of the original delivery.

Strategies of presentation

Primary presentations should and do have a privileged status. The most
striking evidence of this is the ubiquity of replacement. Almost all
presentations are continuous and well-formed once we do all the replacements. From "well {. I mean} this {. uh} Mallet said {} Mallet was {uh}
said something about {uh you know} he felt it would be a good thing if
{u:h .} if Oscar went," we get "well, Mallet felt it would be a good thing if
Oscar went." We have seen some of the devices for creating such presentations, but when and why do speakers choose the devices they do? The
answer lies in the joint nature of language use.

Speakers' actions in talk aren't independent of their addressees'
actions, or vice versa, and that goes for their problems as well. When
speakers need extra time to plan an utterance, that isn't their problem
alone. The time they need belongs to them and their addressees together,
so they have to coordinate with their addressees on the use of that time.
Or when speakers present the wrong word or phrase, that problem isn't
theirs alone either. It belongs to them both, and it takes the two of them
together to fix it. Most problems in using language are *joint* problems,
and dealing with them requires *joint* management (Clark, 1994).

TWO IMPERATIVES

Time is inexorable, irreversible. We cannot turn the clock back, erasing
a time interval and claiming that it didn't occur. Whatever we do or don't
do in a time interval is irrevocable, and we must deal with the consequences. In joint actions, time is doubly important. When Roger and
Nina talk to each other, what he does in his time is also done in her time,
and vice versa. That places them under the following constraint:

The temporal imperative. In a joint action, the participants must provide a public account for the passage of time in their individual parts of that action.

Because of this imperative, participants try to act in a timely fashion. They are also subject to a second imperative:

The formulation imperative. Speakers cannot present an expression before they have formulated it.

Although the formulation imperative is a truism, it is an important truism. In order to present a signal of any kind, speakers must formulate it first, and that may prevent them from acting in a timely fashion.

Speakers are continuously pressed by these two imperatives. So long as they speak with an ideal delivery, they are providing the best possible account of what they are doing with their time: They are doing their part in the joint action of presenting and identifying an utterance. They should strive for the ideal delivery for this reason alone. On the other hand, formulating a presentation is a fitful, cyclic process, and speakers rarely have a presentation entirely formulated before they start speaking. They generally have only a vague plan and formulate one short phrase at a time (Bock and Levelt, 1994; Levelt, 1989).

Once speakers embark on a presentation, they place themselves on a tight schedule. At each point they have two choices: (1) continue speaking, or (2) stop speaking. The ideal is to continue – *prima facie* evidence they are doing their part. The non-ideal choice is to pause. When they pause, they no longer have a public justification for their actions. They may still be busy formulating; they may have aborted their presentation; they may be reconsidering what they have just presented; they may have been distracted. Stopping midutterance is *not* part of the joint action. In short, continuing to speak doesn't need an explanation, but stopping does. The preference for continuing over stopping leads to three broad strategies.

STOP-AND-CONTINUE STRATEGIES

Speakers can pause in an ideal delivery, but only briefly at certain phrase boundaries. One unit of presentation is the *intonation unit*, a stretch of talk spanned by a single prosodic contour.[5] Each line from this narrative by Nancy is an intonation unit (1.3.100):

5 These units have been variously named *tone groups* (Halliday, 1967), *tone units* (Crystal, 1969, Crystal and Davy, 1975; Svartvik and Quirk, 1980), *intonation groups* (Cruttenden, 1986), *intonation units* (Chafe, 1992), *information blocks* (Grimes, 1975), *idea units* (Chafe, 1979, 1980), and *lines* (Gee, 1986).

well when I was {.} doing freelance advertising,
- thiy: {} advertising agency,
that I {.} sometimes did some work for,
. rang me,
and said {um -} we've got a client,
who wants {um - -} a leaflet designed,
. to go to s- {uh} instructions how to use a sewing-machine,

There are pauses before three intonation units, yet they are heard not as disruptions, but as parts of Nancy's official presentation. In narratives studied by Wallace Chafe (1979, 1980, 1992), there were pauses before 88 percent of the intonation units, and they averaged about 1 second in length.[6] Speakers apparently pause at these boundaries to help formulate the next intonation unit.

The six hesitations that arise mid-unit in Nancy's narrative, however, *are* heard as disruptions. The first five of these are *pure hesitations*: They are followed by continuations, the simplest form of resumption. Hesitations take two main forms – pauses (as in four of Nancy's disruptions) and elongated syllables (as in Nancy's "thiy:"). Both give speakers extra time mid-unit to formulate what to say next. Elongations give the added illusion of fluency, as if the speakers weren't truly disrupted. Speakers may choose elongations over pauses when they think the disruption will be brief.

There is a limit to how long speakers can pause without discomfort. According to Gail Jefferson (1989), who examined more than a thousand examples, speakers tend to limit initial pauses midutterance to about one second. They tend to resume talking, produce a filler, or clear their throat – something to signal they will continue – after only one second of silence. It isn't surprising that there is such a limit if speakers are pressed by the temporal imperative. What is remarkable how little silence is tolerated. Let us call this the *one-second limit*.[7]

If midutterance silences over a second are a problem, speakers must monitor for this possibility. Nancy's first three hesitations don't cause problems because she resolves them within one second, but the next three do. Apparently, anticipating a hiatus longer than one second, she produces

---

[6] Compare Boomer's (1965) average for juncture pauses of 1.03 sec.
[7] Jefferson (1989) called this the "standard maximum tolerance." Other cultures may tolerate much longer silences or only shorter silences. Jefferson's data seem to come from urban North American and British speakers of English.

"um." She does so not to help her formulate the following words more quickly, but to tell her audience what she is doing and help them deal with the disruption (Brennan and Williams, 1995; Smith and Clark, 1993).

Even between intonation units, silences become a problem when they grow too large. Take this exchange:

Reynard:	i- {} is {.} is it this year, that {u:h} Nightingale goes
Sam:	{- - **u:h**} no next year,
Reynard:	{- - **u:m** . -} sixty-f- {}
Sam:	sixty-five
Reynard:	- four {} sixty-five
Sam:	yeah

When Sam is asked "Is it this year that Nightingale goes?" he must respond. If he delays too long, he may be misconstrued as unable or unwilling to answer, as waiting for more of the question, or as distracted. To show he is preparing a response, he cuts off the silence with "u:h" (in track 2). Reynard does much the same with "u:m."

In the stop-and-continue strategy, therefore, speakers stop until they have formulated the next element and then continue. Pure hesitations are by far the commonest disfluency. But if their hesitations are too long, speakers need to justify them with fillers, editing expressions, and other signals.

COMMIT-AND-REPEAT STRATEGY

Another way speakers can justify a stoppage is to present the first word or words of the phrase they are formulating even though they cannot present the rest of it. Suppose Duncan is trying to formulate "he may be qualified." Once he decides it begins with "he," he can present "he" and stop. This way he shows he is committed to presenting a phrase beginning with *he*. But that raises a secondary problem. If he simply continues after the interruption, as in "he {[pause]} may be qualified," the phrase won't be fluent or easy to identify. The solution is to repeat "he," as in this example (1.2a.985):

Duncan:	{u:m .} and that **he** {} **he** {uh} **he** may be qualified **to** {} **to** be recognized as a teacher of French

The *commit-and-repeat strategy* accomplishes two things. The first "he" provides advanced evidence that Duncan is committed to a constituent beginning with "he." The last "he" allows for the fluent delivery of the phrase "he may be qualified."

With the commit-and-repeat strategy, repeats should be common on the first words of major constituents, and they are. Compare nominative versus accusative pronouns – e.g., *he* versus *him*. *He* is almost always the first element in a larger constituent, such as the clause "*he* may be qualified," but *him* is usually its own constituent, as in "everyone saw *him*." In a large sample of telephone conversations studied by Thomas Wasow and myself,[8] nominative pronouns were repeated 5.2 percent of the time, and accusative pronouns, only 0.04 percent of the time – a difference of more than 100 to 1.

The constituent being planned can also be large or small. Consider the most inclusive phrase initiated by the noun phrases in these four roles:

Role of noun phrase	Example	Percentage of "the"s repeated
Topic	**the van that we've got** the gentleman who owned it had died	7.9
Subject	**the dog I have** is a German shepherd	5.0
Object of verb	I managed to find **the stereo I wanted** in Austin	3.4
Object of preposition	my wife parked her car in **the garage across from our house**	1.8

On average, topics initiate the longest major constituent, subjects the next longest, objects of verbs the next, and objects of prepositions the shortest. In the same sample of telephone conversations, the longer this constituent, the more speakers repeated *the*, the initial word in the noun phrase. The noun phrase initiated by *the* may itself be simple or complex. For example, *the stereo I wanted* is complex because it has a modification after the head noun *stereo*, whereas *the stereo* is simple. In the same telephone conversations, speakers repeated *the* more often in complex than in simple noun phrases, 4.1 to 2.7 percent of the time. In general, constituents tend to begin with function words (pronouns, prepositions, articles, auxiliary verbs, etc.) and not content words (nouns, verbs, adjectives, adverbs), and function words were ten times as likely to be repeated as content words.[9]

The commit-and-repeat strategy, therefore, has two main advan-

---

[8] H. H. Clark and T. Wasow, unpublished data.
[9] H. H. Clark and T. Wasow, unpublished data.

tages. It provides early evidence of what speakers are doing, and it results in fluent constituents, and indeed, that helps addressees (Fox Tree, 1995). Except for pure hesitations, repeated words are by far the commonest disfluency in spontaneous speech.

COMMIT-AND-REPAIR STRATEGIES

Speakers often change their minds about what they are presenting. As Willem Levelt (1989) has argued, they monitor their presentations for these (among other) problems (1.2.33; 1.2.787; 1.13.246; 2.13.1204; 2.8.304):

Question	Example of repair
1. Is this the message or concept I want to express now?	we **must ha-** {} we're {.} big enough to stand on our own feet now
2. Is this the way I want to say it?	he**'s done a** {} he's on a Ph.D.
3. Am I making a lexical error?	if **she**'d been {} he'd been alive,
4. Are my syntax and my morphology all right?	he think **E-** {} thinks Ella's worried about something
5. Am I making a sound-form error?	everything is **mitch** {} much more complex

And when they find something they want to change, they repair it. The element to be repaired (marked here in boldface) is the *reparandum*. In principle, speakers could avoid repairs if they took enough time before speaking, but in practice, repairs are inevitable. In conversation at least, speakers can never anticipate everything they might change their mind about. They are forced to proceed by a *commit-and-repair* strategy.

Although speakers should be able simply to replace the reparanda and then proceed, they often replace entire stretches of the original presentation in addition to the reparanda. We can distinguish four types of resumption:

1. *Instant replacements*. In these, the speaker replaces the reparandum and nothing more, as here (1.14a.124):

have I ever **tel-** {} talked to you about Cookstown County Tyrone?

2. *Trailing replacements*. When speakers don't suspend their delivery immediately after the reparandum, they need to replace the reparandum plus the trailing elements, as here (3.4.707; 1.13.246; 1.2.29):

- to buy any more sites, {.} **in the college, {.}** for {.} the college
- if **she'd been** {} he'd been alive
- **we're not prepared, to go on being part,** {} I'm not prepared to go on being part of Yiddish literature

In these examples, the trailing elements are "the college," " 'd been," and "not prepared to go on being part." In the operation of replacement, trailing replacements are obligatory.

3. *Anticipatory replacements.* Speakers often replace not only the reparandum, but elements before it as well. Sometimes the process is obligatory, as in these examples:

- he **think E- {}** thinks Ella's worried about something
- everything is **mitch {}** much more complex

The first speaker couldn't add "-s" to "think" without re-presenting "thinks," and the same goes for the second. More often, the process is optional, as here (1.1.750):

this is {} this is **one of the things that {- uh}** one of the many things, {- uh} in English structure, which is {- u:m - - -} an item in a closed system

4. *Fresh starts.* Speakers sometimes abandon an entire presentation and make a fresh start, as here (1.2.33):

we must ha- {} we're {.} big enough to stand on our own feet now

In fresh starts, it is hard to single out particular elements that are being repaired. The entire fragment is simply abandoned.

Each resumption is a signal in track 1, just as each original presentation is: It is part of the official presentation. But the speakers' *choice* of resumption is also a signal in track 2: It tells addressees what the speakers are replacing and, often, why. Speakers indicate what they are replacing, as Levelt (1989) has argued, by two main strategies.

1. *Word-identity.* When the first word of the resumption is identical to a recent word in the original presentation, the resumption is to replace everything from that word on. This works for repeats and anticipatory replacements:

- and that **he {} he** {uh} he may be qualified to {} to be recognized as a teacher of French
- this is **one of the** things that {- uh} one of the many things, {- uh} in English structure, which is (etc.)

Addressees can identify what is to be replaced as beginning with "he" and "one of the."

2. *Category-identity.* When the first word of the resumption is a member of the same category as a recent word in the original presentation, the resumption is to replace everything from that word on. This is illustrated in these earlier examples:

- if **she**'d been {} he'd been alive
- to buy any more sites, {.} **in** the college, {.} for {.} the college

In the first example, "she" and "he" are both personal pronouns, so the resumption is to replace everything from "she" on. In the second example, "in" and "for" are both prepositions, with an analogous result. Although fresh starts don't always adhere to these two strategies, most other replacements do. For speakers working under pressure, that is a remarkable feat.

EDITING EXPRESSIONS

By the temporal imperative, speakers in trouble need to account for their actions. When Roger makes an error, Nina is entitled to ask, "Why did he make an error? Does he realize he has made it? Is he going to repair it?" Even when he merely suspends his presentation, she can ask, "Why is he stopping? Will he resume and, if so, when? What should I expect next?" One way speakers provide these accounts is with editing expressions produced in track 2. We have already seen how *uh* and *um* are used to signal length of hiatus. Other expressions have more specific uses.

Editing expressions like *no, or rather, I mean*, and *that is* are used for characterizing the trouble a speaker is in and its relation to the repair. With *no*, speakers characterize the reparandum as "incorrect", and with *or rather*, they compare it with the new expression to be offered. Each term is appropriate for a different type of trouble or repair. For example, the Dutch equivalents of *no* and *or rather*, which describe something as incorrect, are used for error repairs and not appropriateness repairs (Levelt, 1984), and the English expression *you know* is reserved for appropriateness repairs (Clark and Gerrig, 1990).

Editing expressions like *well, oh, ah, aha*, and *let me see*, in contrast, comment on the *source* of the speaker's troubles (Heritage, 1984; James, 1972, 1973; Schourup, 1982). With each, speakers disclose their current thinking about what they are about to say, as when Elizabeth is talking to Ned (1.6.232):

Elizabeth: he {} I think he thinks it's all a little bit {uh: - **well**,} stupid but {uh:, .}
[continues]

With "well," Elizabeth tells Ned, in track 2, that she is consulting her thoughts about how best to express the next trait. She accounts for the hiatus and implies she considered other (perhaps weaker) adjectives.

Still other editing expressions address interpersonal problems caused by disfluencies. Speakers may apologize for an error, as when a radio announcer said (Goffman, 1981b, p. 291):

And now, Van Cliburn playing Tchaikovsky's Piano Concerto Number One in Blee Fat Minor...**I beg your pardon**, that should be Fee Blat Minor

They may explain why they aren't as incompetent as they appear to be, as when another announcer said (Goffman, 1981, p. 294):

Stay tuned for Aeolia where they will be reading – **if you wait a moment I'll be able to tell you...here it is...**

They may even make light of the error, as this disc jockey did (Goffman, 1981b, p. 299):

We hear now a song from the new Columbia album featuring Very Jail...**Oops, I ought to be in jail for that slip...**of course, I mean Jerry Vale!

As Goffman suggested, pauses and errors can make speakers look incompetent, and speakers can use editing expressions to mitigate the damage.

Speakers work hard, then, to deal with the temporal and formulation imperatives. They cannot speak until they have something formulated, but they must also provide a public account of what they are doing. The optimal strategy is to produce a fluent, ideal delivery. When that isn't possible, speakers commonly resort to three strategies: stop and then continue (with an explanation, if necessary); commit to the beginning of a phrase and then repeat it; and commit to an expression and then repair it if necessary. Whenever speakers pause beyond the one-second limit, they say why they are pausing. And they use editing expressions to help addressees prepare for and identify the repairs they make. By explaining the trouble, they help addressees understand what they intend to say and mitigate any interpersonal damage they might have caused.

Execution and attention

In order to signal anything, speakers must execute audible and visible behaviors for addressees to attend to. In the action ladder, success at level 2, presentation and identification, depends on success at level 1, execution and attention, just as success at level 3, meaning and understanding, depends on success at level 2. What does it take to succeed at level 1? Roger may produce the sounds "now, - um do you and your husband have a j- car" yet not get Nina to attend to them. Roger and Nina face the *attention problem*: how to coordinate his articulating those sounds with her attending to them in the right way. Coordination of attention is taken for granted in most theories of language use, but in fact isn't easy to achieve. People have a battery of techniques for achieving it, techniques that shape language use at its very core.

THE ATTENTION PROBLEM

Speech is evanescent – it fades immediately. If Roger is to succeed in telling Nina something, he must make sure she is trying to attend to his sounds *at the very instant* he is articulating them. Executing behaviors to be attended to and attending to those behaviors, then, are participatory acts: Roger cannot do his part without Nina doing hers, and vice versa.

What is attention? If we think of people as attending to a strand of events over a period of time, attention has three notable properties:

1. *Selectivity*. People can attend to only *one* level of *one* strand of events at a time.
2. *Redirectability*. People can redirect their attention to a second level or strand of events very quickly, often within milliseconds.
3. *Vulnerability*. Attention to one strand of events is fragile and easily captured by another strand of events.

At an orchestra concert, I can attend to the music as a whole, or to the violins alone, but not to both at once. Still, I can shift attention from one to the other so quickly that, if neither strand is too complicated, I can keep track of both at once. I can also redirect my attention from the music to what I am doing tomorrow. Yet, my attention to any of these strands is fragile. If my neighbor coughs, my attention may shift to the coughing despite my best efforts. Orienting reflexes shift our attention automatically, so certain events appear to capture our attention regardless of our intentions.

These properties are easy to demonstrate in listening to speech (Clark and Clark, 1977). If you listen through earphones to two people speaking at once, you can shadow – repeat immediately – what one of them is saying. But soon you cannot report whether the unattended voice is male or female, or speaking English or French, or even that it has repeated your own name twenty-five times. This is selective attention. Still, you can switch your attention to the other voice when you choose to. And if the voices are too similar – both male, both speaking English, both coming from right in front of you – it becomes more difficult to shadow either one of them, to maintain selective attention. When you are attending to one voice, it is also harder to carry out other tasks.

People implicitly take these properties into account in monitoring each other's states of attention. If Ann and Bob are the current speaker and addressee, Ann must monitor Bob's state of attention as she executes her utterance, and Bob must help her do that. They recognize both positive and negative evidence of B's attention to A:

Evidence that B is attending to A's execution now
  B is gazing at A.

Evidence that B is *not* attending to A's execution now
  B is doing something that takes too much competing attention.
  B is making a primary presentation himself.
  B is attending to another speaker.
  B is trying to think about or do something else.
 The situation may potentially interfere with B's attention.
  B isn't in a position to hear or see A's execution.
  A nearby event is so loud or bright that B cannot hear or see A's execution.
  A nearby event is likely to capture too much of B's attention.

And this list is hardly complete.

Face to face, listeners generally signal attentiveness with eye gaze (see Argyle and Cook, 1976). While Bob is listening to Ann speak, he gazes at her much of the time, apparently to signal that he is attending to her (Kendon, 1967). She gazes back at him, but for much shorter periods, apparently to check whether he is already gazing – to acknowledge his signals (Goodwin, 1981; Kendon, 1967). As Goodwin (1981) argued, the preferred condition in gazing is this: "When speaker's gaze reaches a recipient, that recipient should be gazing at the speaker" (p. 76). These signals – gazing and acknowledging gazes – are collateral to the official business at hand, so they are in track 2.

Eye gaze ordinarily provides valid, economical, and timely evidence of a person's full attention (see Chapter 8). While Bob is gazing at Ann, he cannot be looking at something else, and if he is also silent, he isn't overtly engaged in a competing activity.[10] Not only is his gaze valid evidence, but it is cheap to provide and available precisely when it is most useful to Ann. But Bob's unilateral gaze isn't enough – Ann must acknowledge it. Mutual gaze is just what the two of them need as a shared basis for the mutual belief that he is attending to her at that moment.

[10] He could be thinking of something else, of course, but people appear to believe they can distinguish attentive from inattentive gazes.

ONE PRIMARY SPOKEN PRESENTATION AT A TIME

People in conversation do more than monitor each other's attention: They anticipate interference and try to work around it. If one of them coughs or pounds a hammer, the noise could interfere with hearing, so they time their actions – both their speech and the interfering actions – so as not to overlap (Jefferson, Sacks, and Schegloff, 1987). Likewise, public speakers time their oratory to be clear of their audience's applause or laughter, and audiences accommodate their applause and laughter to the speaker's talk (Heritage, 1984). Accidental overlaps are repaired too, as here (1.1.531):

Sam: well, {uh} *I put* {} I put the linguistic jargon in, Reynard
Reynard: *(coughs)*

The ideal is to talk clear of serious auditory interference – to speak *in the clear*.

The commonest source of interference in conversation is other talk – overlapping speech. When Ann considers starting an utterance while Bob is speaking, she should consider these factors:

1. Auditory interference   A's and B's utterances may obscure each other auditorily.
2. Conflict of attention   A and B may be unable to give each other their full attention while they are deciding on, formulating, and presenting their own utterances.
3. Distraction   A and B may be distracted by the other's utterance and make errors in their own presentations.
4. Shift of attention   Still, A and B may each be able to shift their attention to the other's utterance – if one of the two presentations is short enough or easy enough to process.

Ann should conclude that she can present an overlapping utterance if it takes Bob's attention only briefly. That would allow secondary presentations – head nods, gestures, "uh huh"s, utterance completions – but not, ordinarily, primary spoken presentations.

Speakers, therefore, generally observe a *one-primary-spoken-presentation-at-a-time* limit during conversations. To do this, they need to manage who speaks when, and the result is an emergent system of turn taking, which I will return to in Chapter 11. To avoid overlaps in primary speech, they try to project the end of the current speaker's presentation before starting their own, and they are extraordinarily precise in doing this (Jefferson, 1973; Sacks, Schegloff, and Jefferson, 1974). For most turns, the current speaker begins his or her official presentation with (1) no overlap with the previous speaker, (2) overlaps of only one or two syllables, or (3) very brief pauses (Beattie, 1983; Beattie and Barnard, 1979; Schegloff et al., 1977). All three are heard as smooth transitions between speakers – as no pause or overlap. On the other hand, speakers are perfectly happy for secondary presentations such as "uh huh" to overlap with a primary spoken presentation. So overlap is common, but mostly of track 2 presentations with track 1 presentations.

Accidental overlaps in primary presentations are often considered problems, as in this example (1.3.222):

Nancy: I mean this whole system, of being invited somewhere for lunch, and
then for dinner, {-} and overnight, {.} *and breakfast,*
Nigel: *oh you st- {}* you {} you did stay

Nigel projected Nancy's utterance to end after "overnight" and started to present "oh you stayed." Once he discovered his error, he stopped and, omitting "oh," repeated his primary presentation "you {} you did stay" in the clear. Speakers use much the same technique when two people initiate turns simultaneously.

So speakers tacitly recognize how much they can overlap and still be attended to, identified, and understood. Here is a rough ordering of speech overlaps from least to most interfering:

1. There is no overlap; A's primary presentation is in the clear.
2. A's primary presentation is partly overlapped by B's secondary presentation.
3. The end of A's primary presentation is overlapped with pre-placed expressions like "well" and "in other words" of B's primary presentation (Schegloff, 1987).
4. A's primary presentation is partly or entirely overlapped by B's primary presentation.

Overlapping speech should be tolerated only so long as both parts can be attended to well enough for current purposes.

GAINING ATTENTION

At level 1, Ann and Bob must go through an attention cycle for each presentation. This cycle has the entry–body–exit format of all joint actions:

Entry. A must get B's attention in advance.
Body. A must hold B's attention throughout the presentation.
Exit. A may relinquish B's attention afterwards.

For entry into this cycle, Ann needs to get Bob's attention. She can get it by requesting it, by capturing it, or even by making it impossible for him not to attend. Here are five common techniques:

1. *Summons.* Ann can initiate a summons–answer exchange with Bob – a minimal joint project – in this way (Schegloff, 1968; Schegloff and Sacks, 1973):

Ann: Bob?
Bob: Yes?

With "Bob," she designates Bob as the person whose attention she wants, and with her rising intonation, she asks him to respond. This way she requests his attention. Bob takes her up by responding "yes" and, with his rising intonation, turns the conversation back to her. Vocatives like "Bob" are useful when gaze is ineffective. When I enter a house, I can yell "Sam" to request Sam's attention if he's there. In a large lecture, I can address one of the students, "Mr. Kaplan," to request his attention in particular. Summons can also take the form of telephone rings, doorbells, and whistles.

2. *Turn restarts.* When Ann starts speaking to Bob, she will ordinarily check to see whether he is gazing back. If he isn't, she must secure his attention. One technique for doing that, as Goodwin (1981) argued, is the turn restart, as in this example (p. 61):

Track 1	Track 2
Lee:	Can you bring (0.2)
Ray:	*[starts to turn head]*
Lee: *Can* you bring me here that nylon	

Lee starts in on "Can you bring," but merely to request Ray's attention. Once Ray gazes back, Lee restarts his presentation to be sure Ray hears it from the beginning. On Goodwin's videotape one can see Lee's restart begin precisely as Ray begins turning his head. Lee's initial fragment is a natural way of requesting Ray's attention, yet it is up to Ray to signal that he is actually attending. Both signals are in track 2.

3. *Mid-turn delays.* Ann can also request Bob's attention by delaying mid-presentation, as in this example from Goodwin's videotapes (p. 76):

Track 1	Track 2
Barbara:	uh
Barbara: my kids	*(0.8 sec pause)*
Ethel:	*[starts to turn head]*
Barbara: had all these blankets, and quilts and sleeping bags.	

Barbara starts her presentation and then pauses, all to request Ethel's attention. By the start of the 0.8-second pause, Ethel starts turning her head toward Barbara, and by its end, she is gazing at Barbara. Unlike Lee, Barbara doesn't restart her presentation. Speakers tend to choose mid-turn delays when they haven't yet gazed at their addressees, but turn restarts when they have (Goodwin, 1981).

4. *Recycled turn beginnings.* Speakers can also request the other participants' attention before the previous speaker has completed his or her presentation. To do this, they need a special technique, as illustrated here (Schegloff, 1987, pp. 80-81):

A: Yeah my mother asked me. I says I dunno. I haven't heard from her. I didn't know what days you had *classes or anything.*

B: *Yeah an I didn' know* I didn't know when you were home or - I was gonna.

As Schegloff argued, even though B projects the end of A's turn, he starts his presentation early in order to claim the right to speak next. Since B realizes that he cannot be attended to fully – the one-primary-spoken-presentation-at-a-time limit – he recycles the beginning of his turn to present it in the clear. B is remarkably precise at starting his full recycle in the clear. Also, he drops "yeah" in the recycled presentation perhaps because it demands so little attention or carries so little information. So with recycled turn beginnings, speakers request their addressees' attention and yet articulate their entire presentation in the clear.

5. *Strategic interruptions.* Speakers can also exploit the one-primary-spoken-presentation-at-a-time limit with strategic interruptions, as here (1.9.804):

Wendy: and as long as I'm in my own {-} little nit and nobody's telling me what to do

Ken: yes

Wendy: there doesn't really seem *anything*

Ken: *but how* long do you think it'll take them to finish?

In the last line, Ken initiates a primary presentation – marked by "but how" – before Wendy can finish hers. Since the two of them cannot make primary presentations at the same time, one has to give way, and Wendy does. Indeed, this is the goal of Ken's strategy. He tacitly reasons: "She and I cannot make primary presentations at the same time. So by beginning mine in the middle of hers, I am signaling that she should stop because what I have to say is more important now than what she has to say." Wendy accedes, though she needn't have.

RETAINING ATTENTION

In the second step in the attention cycle, speakers need to keep their addressees' attention on their execution. Ann must hold Bob's attention throughout her presentation, and Bob needs to reassure her of his continued attention. How do they do this?

Once Ann has got Bob's attention and begun a presentation, she can ordinarily assume he will continue to attend until she is finished. So it is important for her to keep him informed of her progress: Is she continuing, or is she done? We have already seen three broad strategies for letting him know: stop-and-continue, commit-and-repeat, and commit-and-repair. With all three, she signals that she is still working on a piece of her presentation and intends to continue. And Bob signals that he is still attending by (1) continuing to gaze back, (2) not initiating an official presentation, and (3) not performing an action that competes for his attention.

Still, these signals aren't always clear. One problem is projecting the end of a presentation. In an earlier example, Calvin misprojected the end of Nancy's utterance and began on his own presentation "oh you stayed." He resolved the competing attention by stopping. Other times the second speaker doesn't abandon his or her new presentation, and if the first speaker wants to continue, he or she has to take positive actions to retain the addressee's attention. Here, British prime minister Margaret Thatcher is interrupted by a television interviewer, Dennis Tuohy (Beattie, 1983, p. 137):

Thatcher:	...there are comparatively few people they could be measured in thousands who wish to destroy the kind of society which you and I value destroy the free society
	*Please, please this is the most
	please this is the most
	please this is*
Tuohy:	***You were talking about striking ambulance workers**
	you were talking about ancillary workers in hospitals*
Thatcher:	the most important point you have raised there are people in this country who are the great destroyers.

Tuohy misprojected the end of Thatcher's response and initiated his next question before she was finished. But when Thatcher was interrupted, she recycled "please this is the most" three times before she got Tuohy's full attention again. Just as determinedly, Tuohy recycled his utterance once before giving up. Both recognized that the other – and the viewing audience – couldn't be attending fully to both primary presentations. They each recycled to force the other to abandon their presentation and to attend to the other.

RELINQUISHING ATTENTION

At the end of a presentation, speakers can relinquish their addressees' attention. But to complete the presentation phase of a contribution is to be prepared for the acceptance phase, which is ordinarily initiated by the addressees. So speakers often let their addressees know they are relinquishing their attention by turning their own attention to their addressees.

One technique is to use eye gaze. Recall Goodwin's preferred condition for gazing: "When speaker's gaze reaches a recipient, that recipient should be gazing at the speaker." When Ann wants to show Bob that she is done with her presentation and ready to attend to his, she can turn her gaze to him. This is what people generally do (Kendon, 1967). Other techniques are to use an intonation appropriate for the end of an utterance, or deliberately *not* to rush into the next utterance to signal an intention to continue. All these techniques make room for the next speakers to execute their presentations in the clear.

Executing a presentation and attending to that execution, then, takes continuous coordination. Ann and Bob need to coordinate their entry, continuation, and exit from these actions. For her part, Ann needs valid, economical, and timely evidence that Bob is attending to what she is producing, and he needs to attend to her and give her evidence that he is doing so. They manage this coordination by exchanging gazes, managing sources of interference, and making repairs when coordination goes wrong. Actions at the level of execution and attention are just as much joint actions as those at higher levels of talk.

MONITORING AND COMPLETION

When does an utterance become complete? That depends on the level. We can divide a conversation into intervals relative to the moment of speech (time o). This diagram depicts turns by A, then B, then A, with six intervals labeled *a* through *f*:

	A's turn			B's turn		A's turn		
Intervals	a	b	c	d		e	f	

Time o

At time o, during Ann's presentation, Ann is trying to get Bob to attend to her execution (level 1), identify her presentation (level 2), understand what she means (level 3), and consider her proposed joint project (level 4). To reach closure on each of these joint actions, the two of them need the right evidence, and that becomes available in different intervals for the four levels.

AVAILABILITY OF EVIDENCE

The evidence Ann and Bob need for closure can be divided initially into *self-* and *other-evidence*. Self-evidence comes from monitoring oneself – Ann monitoring her actions in speaking, and Bob monitoring his mental states in reception. Ann and Bob also monitor for other-evidence, and that takes coordination. Bob must present evidence about his mental states at just those moments he believes Ann is monitoring for it, and Ann, knowing this, should monitor him closely at these points.

At level 1, both self- and other-evidence tend to be available *continuously*. Ann listens to herself speak and sees herself gesture in interval *b*, precisely as Bob is attending to her behavior. Ann is able even in interval *a* to monitor a pre-spoken version of what she is about to deliver (Levelt, 1989). As for other-evidence, Bob shows his attention by gazing at Ann, and she returns his gaze, all in interval *b*. So at level 1 Ann and Bob ordinarily reach joint closure almost immediately.

At levels 2, 3, and 4, in contrast, both self- and other-evidence become available only *periodically*. At level 2, self-evidence is available in interval *b*, but only a word or phrase at a time. Bob can be certain of Ann's presentation only after major phrases, after all her replacements, and she cannot be certain of his identification until he has nodded, smiled, said "uh huh," or given other evidence, sometimes in interval *b*, but often in interval *c* or *d*. At levels 3 and 4, self-evidence is available only as Ann completes larger units in interval *b* – phrases or entire sentences. But other-evidence usually isn't available to Bob until interval *c*, or to Ann until interval *d*, when Bob takes up what Ann has proposed.

To gather up these points, self-evidence is generally available before other-evidence. And the higher the level, the later either type of evidence is available. Ann and Bob ordinarily reach joint closure at level 1 in interval b, at level 2 in interval c or d, at level 3 in interval c or d, and at level 4 in interval d but sometimes not until interval e or f. That is, the higher the level, the later the closure.

REPAIRS

According to the principle of opportunistic closure (Chapter 8), Ann and Bob should consider an action complete at the first opportunity – at the first evidence of completion. On the same grounds, they also should consider an action in need of repair at the first evidence of failure, as expressed in this principle:

Principle of repair. When agents detect a problem serious enough to warrant a repair, they try to initiate and repair the problem at the first opportunity after detecting it.

By this principle, repairs should be initiated and completed as soon as possible. Just how soon depends on the availability of evidence and the opportunities for initiating and for making a repair.

Most repairs are probably invisible. Ann can detect and correct a problem in her actions without Bob ever knowing; likewise, Bob can detect and correct a problem in his reception without *Ann* ever knowing. These problems are private, and so are the repairs. Although the repairs are invisible, they are in line with the principle of repair because they are initiated as soon as a problem is detected.

Whenever a problem becomes public, however, it becomes a *joint* problem. Public problems are joint problems for two reasons. First, it is often impossible to identify who in the conversation is responsible for them. The point is illustrated in the exchange between Roger and Nina:

Roger: now, - um do you and your husband have a j- car
Nina: - have a car?
Roger: yeah
Nina: no -

Who is at fault for the problem repaired with "- have a car?" "yeah"? Is Roger to blame for a muddy pronunciation, or is Nina to blame for not listening closely enough? The source of the problem is often indeterminate.[11] Second, regardless of source, public problems require joint solutions. Nina and Roger have to act jointly even to repair problems that only one of them is really responsible for. Roger, for example, repairs the problem caused by the pause after "now" by using "um" to tell Nina that he is still formulating the next word. Public repairs are joint actions (Clark, 1994).

Public repairs are part and parcel of the process of joint closure. As discussed in Chapters 7, 8, and 9, they characteristically occur in different intervals for levels 1, 2, 3, and 4:

Intervals	a	b	c	d	e	f
Level 4				[———	———	———]
Level 3		[———	———	———]		
Level 2		[———	———]			
Level 1	[———	———]				

Repairs like these are simply part of the joint actions Ann and Bob carry out at each of the four levels. It is impossible to reach joint closure without the availability of repair.

People in conversation, in sum, are opportunistic in trying to reach closure on their actions. They try to repair problems as quickly and as efficiently as possible. Doing this, however, isn't easy. It requires the participants to monitor both themselves and their partners at all levels of action – from execution and attention upward – and to be prepared to initiate and make repairs at the first opportunity.

Conclusions

Utterances are often viewed as the prerogative of speakers – products that speakers formulate and produce on their own. Nothing could be further from the truth. Uttering things involves two levels of joint actions. At level 1, speakers execute certain behaviors – vocalizations and gesticulations – for addressees to attend to. At level 2, speakers present signals for

---

[11] According to Schegloff et al. (1977), repairs can be classified by who initiates them, as *self-* or *other-initiated* repairs, and by who makes them, as *self-* or *other-corrections*. For this classification to work, one must be able to identify the source of the problem, and for repairs like Nina's and Roger's, that seems impossible. If we attribute the problem to Roger, the repair is *other*-initiated and *self*-repaired. If we attribute it to Nina, it is *self*-initiated and *other*-repaired. If we view it as a joint problem, or as indeterminate, as it seems proper to do, the terms don't apply at all.

addressees to identify. There can be no communication without tight coordination at both levels.

Speakers and addressees have a battery of strategies for coordinating at these two levels of action, strategies that exploit signals in track 2. At level 1, the main issue is how to establish, hold, and relinquish the addressees' attention to the speakers' vocalizations and gesticulations, and one of the most useful signals is eye gaze. At level 2, the main issue is how to deal with disruptions in the speakers' delivery, and speakers use special signals to mark suspensions in delivery, to account for the disruptions, and to indicate what is to be replaced. Utterances are truly products of speakers and addressees acting jointly.

PART V

Discourse

10 | Joint commitment

Kindness, n. A brief preface to ten volumes of exaction.
Ambrose Bierce, *The Devil's Dictionary*

Autonomous actions are things that individuals have to be willing and able to do, but joint actions take the commitment of *all* the participants. I may be willing and able to ask a stranger on the street for his name, but he may be unwilling to tell me. I may be willing and able to ask him how to find City Hall, but he may be *unable* to tell me. When I propose these joint projects, I am committing myself, but that doesn't mean the stranger will commit himself too. Recall that joint projects require joint purposes, which have four conditions (Chapter 7):

For A and B to commit themselves to joint purpose r:
1. *Identification.* A and B must identify r
2. *Ability.* It must be possible for A and B to do their parts in fulfilling r
3. *Willingness.* A and B must be willing to do their parts in fulfilling r
4. *Mutual belief.* A and B must each believe that 1, 2, 3, and 4 are part of their common ground

It is one thing to propose a joint project and quite another to establish a joint commitment to it.

This chapter is about reaching joint commitments in the transfer of goods, as in a request and its compliance. Reaching such a commitment isn't merely a matter of getting the mechanics right – establishing what is expected of whom and when. Transferring goods is a social process that requires the management of the participants' feelings, emotions, and identities. It is shaped by some of the most intimate features of social life.

Equity and face

People engaged in joint activities create what George Herbert Mead (1934) called *social objects*. When I bought a bottle of shampoo at the drugstore (see Chapter 2), the clerk and I construed it not just as shampoo, but as property, first the drug store's and then mine. In the course of our transaction, we took other social objects for granted as well (the drugstore, the value of money, our roles as clerk and customer), and through our joint actions, we created still others (the price of the goods, the sale, the transfer of money). A twenty-dollar bill, Searle (1969) once observed, is merely a rectangular bit of paper with green, red, and black ink on it: This is a *brute fact* about the bill. But it also has the value of twenty-dollars within a monetary system: This is an *institutional fact*. Brute objects become social objects by virtue of social institutions. Social objects are what people jointly construe them to be, nothing more and nothing less. They are both presupposed and created in every joint activity.

One type of social object is the *social situation* itself, the set of conditions in which particular joint activities are carried out. It has long been noted that people compare what they put into a social situation with what they get out of it – their perceived costs and benefits. In many situations they aim for equity. When the drugstore clerk gives me shampoo, she bears a cost and I gain a benefit. To restore equity, I give her money so that I bear a balancing cost and she gains a balancing benefit.

Balancing costs and benefits lies at the foundation of a family of influential social theories. Two members of this family are the theories of *reciprocity* (Gouldner, 1960) and *social exchange theory* (Homans, 1950, 1958), which have been well established in empirical research (see, e.g., Cialdini, 1993). Another member of this family is *equity theory* as described by Elaine Walster and her colleagues (Walster, Berscheid, and Walster, 1976; Walster, Walster, and Berscheid, 1978). It is this theory I will use as a basis for the joint project of transferring goods.

EQUITY

The basic assumption of equity theory is that people in social situations try to maximize their outcomes – their benefits minus their costs. But if everyone were utterly selfish without restraint, the result would be social chaos and everyone would suffer. So social groups have evolved systems for apportioning costs and benefits equitably and for penalizing members who don't adhere to these systems. There is the market system for exchanging money for goods; there is the system of justice in which wrongdoers pay for their crimes; there is a system of employment in which employers pay employees for their labor.

For us, the crucial point of equity theory is that when people find themselves in inequitable situations, they feel distress, and the more inequitable the situation, the more distress they feel. To eliminate this distress they are motivated to restore equity. This has a range of well-documented consequences. Let us look at the two primary cases of inequity, one resulting from beneficial acts and the other from harmful acts. How, then, is equity restored?

Dealing with benefits. Suppose Alan and Barbara – A and B – begin in a state of equity, but then A benefits B by doing act k. A might give or loan B money, give B information, or do some other favor. This generally places B under an obligation to benefit A in equal measure. B should return money or goods to A, give A equally valuable information, or the like. Consider the ways A can restore equity. He can hold B under an obligation to do something in return; this is a common technique for exploiting people – doing them a favor to make them obligated. If A recognizes that B can never make the repayment, he can do other things. He can belittle the value of act k, saying it wasn't worth much anyway. Or he can use the occasion to humiliate B, to show his moral or social superiority over B.

What B does in response to A's benefit is motivated in part by A's techniques for restoration. The simplest response is to reciprocate the benefit, as when I pay the clerk for the shampoo. So B is more likely to accept a gift she can reciprocate than one she cannot. B apparently realizes how discomfiting it is to be left with an unfulfillable obligation, how it can be used to exploit or humiliate her. Even when B accepts a benefit she cannot reciprocate, she has several ways out. She too can belittle A's act k, saying it didn't cost A much. Or she can deny that A and B were in equity before A's beneficial act, and that it was owed to her.

Dealing with costs. Suppose instead that A and B begin in a state of equity, but then A costs or harms B by doing act k. A might step on B's foot, take B's money, or otherwise exploit her. Here A can restore equity in several ways. He can compensate B for the costs of act k. He can punish himself, placing equal costs on himself. He can minimize B's suffering, convincing himself that what he did was actually equitable. He can blame or derogate B, saying she deserved the harm she incurred. He can even deny having done k. Finally, he can apologize to B. As Walster and her colleagues note, apologies can restore equity in several different ways. They may restore actual equity by humbling A and exalting B. They may explain how much A has already suffered, and so equity has already been restored. They may be attempts to convince B that A's act was justified. Or they may be attempts to convince B to forgive A since there is no other way to restore equity. In brief, Walster and her colleagues conclude, "exploiters tend to use either justification techniques or compensation techniques to restore equity" (1978, p. 35).

As the harmed or exploited party, B also has techniques for restoring equity. Victims, it has been found, are especially motivated to right inequities. B can demand compensation – a benefit to match the cost. B can retaliate, returning the cost to A. When impotent to do either of these, B can justify the inequity other ways. Victims of an injustice, for example, sometimes convince themselves that the exploiter deserved the benefits he got, or that they deserved the harm that was done to them. B can also devalue A's act – it wasn't really as costly as it appeared.

The thrust of equity theory, in brief, is that A and B try to maintain equity, and empirical evidence shows that they will go to extraordinary lengths to do that. Assume that A causes an inequity with B by doing k. The techniques they have for restoring equity fall into three basic types:

1. *Compensation.* A and B can perform acts to equalize the costs and benefits of k.
2. *Reevaluation.* A and B can change the perceived value of k.
3. *Redefining the situation.* A and B can redefine the situation to make k equitable.

FACE

Equity theory rests on the assumption that people try to avoid the distress they feel in inequitable situations. But why should they feel distress? One answer can be found in Erving Goffman's (1967) analysis of the folk notion of *face*. In Goffman's view, face is the positive image, or respect, that one claims for oneself in the *line* of actions one takes with others in an encounter. People can maintain, gain, or lose face in such encounters, but any change in face arouses emotion. When Alan is talking to Barbara, he can feel confident and assured as long as he maintains face. But if he loses face, he may feel ashamed, embarrassed, or chagrined, and if he thought Barbara was to blame, he may feel angry at her. We each exhibit a certain self-respect in dealing with others. Whenever it is enhanced or undermined, we react immediately with positive or negative emotions, and these emotions are something we try to manage.

Face, in Goffman's view, is a social object. It is determined not only by its owner, but by the others in an encounter – it is jointly determined.

In an encounter between Alan and Barbara, Alan is expected to exhibit self-respect, but also to be considerate of Barbara; the same goes for her. They are "expected to do this willingly and spontaneously because of emotional identification" (p. 11) with each other and their feelings; if they didn't, they would be considered heartless and unfeeling, to be acting without shame.

> The combined effect of the rule of self-respect and the rule of considerateness is that the person tends to conduct himself during an encounter so as to maintain both his own face and the face of the other participants. (p. 11)

That takes cooperation. One result is that Alan and Barbara tend to mutually accept the lines of actions they each have chosen. As Goffman argued, "Ordinarily, maintenance of face is a condition of interaction, not its objective" (p. 12).

In social encounters, the participants are expected to act with *deference* toward each other – to display their appreciation *of* each other *to* each other. According to Goffman, they rely on two broad strategies. The first he called *presentation rituals* "through which the actor concretely depicts his appreciation of the recipient" (p. 73). Alan, for example, may provide Barbara with salutations, invitations, compliments, or other minor services. The second type of strategy Goffman called *avoidance rituals*, "taking the form of proscriptions, interdictions, and taboos, which imply acts the actor must refrain from doing lest he violate the right of the recipient to keep him at a distance" (p. 73). Alan will try to avoid interfering with Barbara's normal activities or invading her privacy. Presentation rituals are designed to maintain the partners' feelings of *self-worth*, and avoidance rituals, their feelings of *autonomy*, or freedom of action. These two sides of a person's face, self-worth and autonomy, have sometimes been called *positive* and *negative face*.

In using language, people are therefore motivated to maintain their own and their partner's face. That is the basis for Penelope Brown and Stephen Levinson's (1987) analysis of politeness. Following Goffman, they have pointed out that some speech acts tend to affect self-worth, and others tend to affect autonomy – either the speaker's or the addressee's. Suppose Alan is speaking to Barbara, making A the speaker and B the addressee:

1. *Acts that lower B's self-worth.* A may show disapproval or disrespect for B by his actions. These include criticism, contempt, and ridicule; disagreements and challenges; and raising embarrassing topics.

2. *Acts that lower B's autonomy.* A may reduce B's freedom of action in many ways. These include requests, orders, suggestions, and warnings, since A is getting B to do something, and that will restrict her actions.
3. *Acts that lower A's self-worth.* Any action by A may lead to a lowering of his own self-worth, as when he apologizes, accepts criticisms, or admits responsibility for actions that are disapproved of.
4. *Acts that lower A's autonomy.* When A makes promises, expresses thanks, or accepts offers, apologies, or thanks, he is limiting his own future course of action, reducing his autonomy.

Any particular action by A toward B may affect both A's and B's face.

Goffman's proposals about face really constitute a type of equity theory. The steps people take in displaying deference, maintaining demeanor, and dealing with loss of face are almost identical to the strategies I outlined earlier for maintaining and restoring equity. Indeed, Goffman often spoke of reciprocity, balance, mutuality, and compensative effort in discussing these strategies. Clearly, equity and face are on intimate terms.

THE EQUITY PRINCIPLE

Every joint project raises issues of equity and face. The point can be illustrated in the following exchange (1.9.36):

Alan: Manzanilla?
Barbara: yes please, that'd be lovely

Here Alan offers Barbara some Manzanilla sherry, and she accepts. When Alan proposes the offer, he puts his face at risk. What if she takes the sherry without adequate recompense? And when Barbara takes up his proposal, she puts her own face at risk. What if she cannot repay him for the favor? Promises, threats, requests, apologies, assertions – all these create costs and benefits that the participants must attend to.

Many of these costs and benefits come from Alan's and Barbara's commitments to each other. Note that simple commitments vary in degree. Alan's commitment to reading *War and Peace* may range from strong to weak, influencing what he does about reading it. When there are two people involved, commitments also vary in form, as in this series:

1. A commits himself to doing *k*.
2. A commits himself *in front of* B to doing *k*.
3. A commits himself *to* B to doing *k*.
4. A commits himself to B to *doing his part* of *k*, a joint action by A and B.

Suppose Alan commits himself to quitting smoking, but then reneges. If his commitment was private, as in 1, he may be disappointed, but he won't suffer any loss of face to Barbara, who may know nothing about it. If he made the commitment in front of Barbara, as in 2, his failure should lead to loss of face – he is embarrassed for her to see he doesn't have the self-control to stop. If he made his commitment directly to Barbara, as in 3, a failure should lead to even greater loss of face because he fails not only himself but Barbara. *Participatory commitments*, as in 4, are the most demanding. If Alan and Barbara have promised each other to quit smoking so long as the other does too, Alan's failure will undermine not only his goal, but hers: He will be partly responsible for her continuing to smoke. Failure here should lead to the greatest loss of face. All joint projects require participatory commitments, and that is why equity and face are so important to them.

How do people maintain equity in completing joint projects? The hypothesis I wish to entertain is that they follow this principle:[1]

The equity principle. In proposing a joint project, speakers are expected to presuppose a method for maintaining equity with their addressees.

When Alan offers Barbara sherry, he takes for granted that they can reach an equitable outcome, and that Barbara will coordinate in reaching it. Indeed, Barbara goes beyond accepting Alan's offer with "yes." She defers to his autonomy with the concession "please" (meaning "if you like") and to his self-worth with the compliment "that'd be lovely." These gestures appear to be partial recompense for the benefits she receives at Alan's cost. Of course, not all joint projects are designed to maintain equity. If Alan wants to insult, put down, embarrass, or flatter Barbara, he will deliberately violate the equity principle. Although the equity principle applies to both equitable and inequitable joint projects, I will focus on the equitable ones.

People have a vast array of techniques for maintaining and restoring equity in using language. Many of these have been documented by Brown and Levinson (1978, 1987), who have argued that they are universal, or nearly universal, in languages of the world. But precisely how do these techniques work? For a full account, let us see how they arise in joint projects within larger social situations.

---

[1] Compare Goffman (1967): "Ordinarily, maintenance of face is a condition of interaction, not its objective" (p. 12).

Transfers of goods

When Alan directs Barbara to do something, and she complies, they complete a joint project I will call a *transfer of (symbolic) goods*. Alan's directive may range from a hint to an order, and Barbara's compliance, from a tentative to a strong commitment. The result may be a question and answer, order and obedience, request and compliance, suggestion and uptake, or a more extended sequence. These procedures are important because they bring into focus all the problems we have noted for joint projects. It isn't that Alan merely issues a directive and then Barbara complies. The two of them (1) negotiate a joint purpose and (2) find a way of fulfilling it equitably. Both processes help determine the mutual construal of Alan's utterance and Barbara's response to it.

Most transfers of goods have the potential of creating inequities. All other things being equal, when Alan asks Barbara to stand up, and she stands up, they create an inequity. He has gained a benefit by having his desire fulfilled (he wanted her to stand up), and she has paid a cost by doing something she wouldn't otherwise have done (she stood up). These costs and benefits are linked. Alan intended his benefit to come at a cost to Barbara, and she intended her cost to benefit him. Potentially, he gains face, and she loses face. The issue is how to complete the transfer of goods and yet maintain equity, and that depends on the social situation. Let us first consider one end of a continuum of social situations – closed situations.

ROUTINE PROCEDURES

In *Philosophical Investigations*, Ludwig Wittgenstein designed a primitive language that he described this way:

The language is meant to serve for communication between a builder A and an assistant B. A is building with building-stones: there are blocks, pillars, slabs and beams. B has to pass the stones, and that in the order in which A needs them. For this purpose they use a language consisting of the words "block," "pillar," "slab," "beam." A calls them out; – B brings the stone which he has learnt to bring at such-and-such a call. – Conceive this as a complete primitive language. (1958, p. 3)

A and B achieve a transfer of goods with what I will call a *routine procedure*, one that is almost entirely prescribed by the social situation. A simply calls out "Slab," and B brings one. How are routine procedures possible?

A and B's social situation is tightly circumscribed, fixed, or what I will call *closed*. In their roles as builder and assistant, A has the authority to order B to pass stones, and B has the duty to obey. Although Wittgenstein doesn't say, the situation presupposes a method of maintaining equity; for example, A may have contracted with B to do the work for pay. Further, A has no authority or ability to issue other orders. And in his role B is assumed capable of passing stones, and there are no physical barriers to his work. The situation is so tightly circumscribed that the only condition of their joint purpose left to establish is its *identity*, and that has two parts: (1) that A is now ordering B to pass a stone; and (2) which of the four types of stone A wants B to pass. A can achieve 1 by uttering any of the four words he knows. He can achieve 2 by the word he chooses. All of this, of course, is part of A and B's common ground.

Closed situations are defined by the *parameters* and *values* taken for granted in them. In this situation, A and B take it as common ground that there is one parameter (type of block) with four possible values (block, pillar, slab, beam), and A's utterance specifies the intended value. The joint project is completed by B's doing what is specified by the value of that parameter. The result is a highly routine procedure, a standard action–response pair – a completed joint project:

A: Slab
B: [brings a slab]

Other situations have more than one parameter each with its own possible values, but the result is still a routine procedure.

Life is full of closed situations with routine procedures. Here are a few examples:

Army — A sergeant on a parade field can yell out "March," "Left," "At ease," "Parade rest," and a private under his or her command will comply. The parameter is what the private is to do next, and the value is specified via a small class of phrases. Compare a ship captain's orders to the ship's crew, "Full speed ahead," "Hard astern," and "Bearing 20 degrees starboard."

Ticket booth — When customers approach the ticket window at a theater, they take it as common ground that the ticket seller is available for requests for tickets and little else. All they need to specify is the number and type of tickets, as in "Two adults and one child."

Surgery — During an operation, surgeons can issue one-word commands – "Scalpel," "Sponge," "Scissors" – and their assistant's job is to hand them the right instrument. The parameter is the instrument wanted. Its value is specified by a bare noun.

Bar   Some situations present more than one parameter, so speakers must specify the parameter as well as its value. With a bartender, customers could specify the drink wanted, "Two gin and tonics," or other information, "The men's room?" all with phrasal utterances.

In these situations, equity is taken for granted. In the army, a soldier's rights and duties are established institutionally. Sergeants have the right to order privates to do certain things, and privates have the duty to obey. For each permitted order, the sergeant and private don't need to deal further with equity – say, through mitigating devices such as "Would you mind standing at ease?" That has already been taken care of. The same goes for the ticket seller, surgeon, and bartender.

In other situations, equity is well defined, but the range of goods that can be transferred is greater. Examples:

Classroom   Teachers have the right to ask many things of their students. Because the situation is closed, they can do so in routine ways: "Sit down, Alan"; "What is the capital of the Netherlands, Ned?"; "Class is dismissed." No extra negotiations are ordinarily needed.

Restaurant   A waiter's job is to take customers' orders, so customers can do this simply: "A hamburger." All the waiter needs to know is the customer's wants or expectations, so we also find "I want a hamburger" or "I'll have a hamburger."

Friends   Suppose Ned gets Julia to help him compute square roots. Once they have defined the situation, Ned can make his requests simply – "Give me the square root of 7" or "Now I need the square root of 7" or even "Seven" – and Julia will give the square root.

In closed situations, the participants know their roles, rights and duties, and potential joint purposes. All they need to establish is the joint purpose for that occasion. That they can do with a routine procedure. The first partner initiates the routine, often with a phrasal utterance, and the second partner completes it by complying.

REGULAR PROCEDURES

When the situation isn't so closed, the participants cannot rely on routine procedures. Suppose I ask Verona, an acquaintance, "Do you know where Goldberg's Grocery is?" and she answers "Yes, it's around the corner." She and I have carried out something more than a routine procedure, yet we didn't create it from scratch. It is semi-routine, or what I will call a *regular procedure*. Many regular procedures have evolved for situations that are recurrent but not fully routine.

A transfer of goods, like any joint action, is subject to the principle of closure. When the transfer isn't routine, there are potential obstacles to its completion. I may want Verona to tell me where Goldberg's Grocery is, but she may not be able to, or want to, or be allowed to, or find it equitable to, or recognize that I want her to. That is, we may not be able to satisfy the identity, ability, and willingness conditions in establishing a joint purpose. To achieve the transfer, she and I must overcome any such obstacles. The general pattern consists of two tasks:

I.   A and B prepare for transfer of goods
II. A and B make the transfer of the goods proper

Ordinarily, A and B deal with potential obstacles to a transfer of goods and then make the transfer.

So, many transfers of goods get accomplished in *extended* joint projects. Recall that extended joint projects are created in three basic ways – embedding, chaining, and pre-sequencing (Chapter 7) – and all three are exploited in extended transfers of goods. Here are four common patterns that emerge.

Pattern 1. Preparation plus request. In the simplest form of the general pattern, A and B carry out two minimal joint projects in a chain, as here (Merritt, 1976, p. 324):

Customer: Hi. Do you have uh size C flashlight batteries?
Server: Yes, sir.
Customer: I'll have four please.
Server: [turns to get]

In the first adjacency pair, C and S establish that S has the requisite batteries, a potential obstacle to C's getting S to sell him batteries. Only when they have completed the preparatory joint project do they turn to the transfer proper.

A and B should be opportunistic about completing their transfer and, all other things being equal, try to minimize their effort. So when C said, "Do you have uh size C flashlight batteries?" S might have tried to short-circuit the process by anticipating C's next move. That is the basis for the next three patterns.

Pattern 2. Preparation plus offer. When C initiates the preparatory joint project, he may also elicit an offer, as here (Merritt, 1976, p. 324):

Customer: Do you have the pecan Danish today?
Server: Yes we do. Would you like one of those?
Customer: Yes, please.
Server: [turns to get]

In the first two turns, C and S establish that S has the requisite pecan Danish. But in turn two, S anticipates that he and C are likely to transfer goods and *offers* him a Danish ("Would you like one of those?") before C requests one. S, in effect, construes C's first turn as a pre-request and preempts the anticipated request with an offer.

Preparation-plus-offer is beneficial to C because he would rather S offer him goods in the second turn than request the same goods himself in turn three. This follows from the equity principle. It costs me less if you offer to lend me a book than if I ask you to lend it. Your offer shows you are willing and able, so that is no cost to overcome. When, instead, I request you to lend it, I don't presuppose that you are willing and able, so I bear an additional cost. Questions like "Do you have the pecan Danish today?" are useful for turning potential requests from C into offers from S.

Pattern 3. Condition plus request. Often, A initiates a sequence in such a way that he or she is construed as making the request too – an elective construal. An example (Clark, 1979):

Susan: Do you have a price on a fifth of Jim Beam?
Manager: Yes, I do. It's five dollars and fifty-nine cents.

Here the manager construed Susan as intending her utterance to serve double duty. He took it both as a question, which he answered "Yes, I do," and as a request, to which he responded "It's $5.59." Note that he didn't skip anything he would have done in the chain. He simply eliminated Susan's second turn. Of 100 merchants faced with this pre-request, about 40 did answer "Yes." The manager, in effect, construed Susan's utterance as a *conditional* request, roughly, "Do you have a price for Jim Beam, and, if you do, what is it?" The condition is expressed in Susan's pre-request, and the request proper is an elective construal.

Pattern 4. Pro forma condition plus request. In many situations, A makes a pre-request that is to be taken as *pro forma*, as in this example (Clark, 1979):

Susan: Can you tell me what time you close tonight?
Manager: Six o'clock.

Here, the manager doesn't take Susan's apparent question seriously at all. He construes Susan's utterance solely as a request for the closing time and responds "Six o'clock." Of thirty merchants presented with this pre-request, none answered the question before giving the closing time. It is irrelevant whether Susan intended her pre-request to be *pro forma* or not. What counts is that the manager takes it to be *pro forma*, and she accepts his construal.

These four patterns may also include embedded joint projects. Here, for example, is a condition plus request (pattern 3) with an embedded side sequence to deal with further preparatory conditions (Merritt, 1976, p. 325):

Customer: Do you have Marlboros?
Server: Yeah.
Server: Hard or soft pack?
Customer: Soft please.
Server: Okay. [turns to get]

S takes C's initial utterance as projecting two joint actions, a transfer of knowledge and a transfer of cigarettes. He makes both projects explicit. The embedded joint project ("Hard or soft pack?" "Soft please") is preparatory for completing the second. The next sequence is similar, but is an instance of *pro forma* condition plus request (pattern 4) (Merritt, 1976, p. 343):

Customer: Do you have Marlboros?
Server: Hard or soft pack?
Customer: Hard.
Server: [Turns to get]

Patterns 1 through 4 lie on a continuum. A and B's total effort is greatest in pattern 1 and least in pattern 4. On the other hand, B makes the weakest assumptions about A's request in pattern 1 and the strongest in pattern 4. For A and B to short-circuit the full process in pattern 1, it must be mutually obvious what A's next step is likely to be. For that B must be able to infer A's larger purpose.

LARGER PURPOSES

Whenever Alan broaches a new issue with Barbara, they take for granted he has some larger purpose as part of their overall joint activity. He didn't ask "Where do you live?" or "What time is it?" just to discover where she lives or what time it is. He did it because he wanted to mail her a brochure or catch a bus. If they are ever to short-circuit their exchange – as in patterns 3 or 4 instead of 1 or 2 – they need to appeal to that larger purpose.

Speakers intend their larger purposes to be inferred from their utterances as construed in the current situation. This is nicely illustrated by the study, mentioned in Chapter 7, in which a woman named Susan telephoned 150 San Francisco area restaurants and asked the manager one of three questions (Clark, 1979):

Question 1   Do you accept American Express cards?
Question 2   Do you accept credit cards?
Question 3   Do you accept any kinds of credit cards?

The managers could have given a simple "yes" or "no," but that wasn't their approach. They went on to infer Susan's larger purpose.

"Why," the managers asked themselves, "is this woman calling the restaurant now to ask if we accept American Express cards (or credit cards, or any kinds of credit cards)?" They could infer roughly this hierarchy of purposes (from general to specific):

1. She wants to decide whether or not to eat at the restaurant, probably that night.
2. She wants to decide how to pay for the meal.
3. She wants to know whether she can pay with a credit card.
4. She wants to know whether any of the credit cards that the restaurant accepts matches any of the cards she owns.

And, depending on her question, they could infer that her most specific purpose was one of these two:

5a. She wants to know whether the restaurant accepts American Express cards.
5b. She wants to know whether the restaurant accepts any credit cards.

They could go further. If she asked about "American Express cards" (question 1), she must own an American Express card and perhaps others. If she asked about "credit cards" (question 2), she probably owns all major credit cards – otherwise she would have been more specific. If she asked about "any kinds of credit cards" (question 3), she probably owns several but not all major credit cards – otherwise why mention "*kinds* of credit cards."

Armed with these inferences, the managers should try short circuiting for some of Susan's questions, and they did. Take the managers who were able to say yes to her question. Those who were asked "Do you accept American Express cards?" should assume Susan had only the one card and wanted to know whether it was acceptable. They should answer simply, "Yes, we do," as if they were initiating pattern 1, and they did:

Caller's utterance	Manager's response	Percent
Do you accept American Express cards?	1. Yes, we do	100

The managers who were asked "Do you accept credit cards?" might assume she had all major cards and respond "Yes" (pattern 1). But since she might not have all of them, they might give her their list of the acceptable credit cards too, "Yes, we accept Mastercard and Visa" (pattern 3). Here is what they did:

Caller's utterance	Manager's response	Percent
Do you accept credit cards?	1. Yes, we do	44
	3. Yes, we accept Mastercard and Visa	38
	4. We accept Mastercard and Visa	16

And the managers who were asked "Do you accept any kinds of credit cards?" should be fairly sure she needed a list of the acceptable credit cards (she probably didn't own them all), so they should initiate pattern 3 or 4. Here are their responses:

Caller's utterance	Manager's response	Percent
Do you accept any kinds of credit cards?	1. Yes, we do	10
	3. Yes, we accept Mastercard and Visa	56
	4. We accept Mastercard and Visa	33

When managers were asked the follow-up question, "Do you accept any other credit cards?" almost all responded "We accept Mastercard and Visa," initiating pattern 4. The managers initiated patterns 1, 3, and 4 depending on their inferences of Susan's larger purposes.

Managers made the same inferences when they were not able to answer yes to Susan's question. Many managers who were asked "Do you accept American Express cards?" initiated pattern 3 and answered "No, but we accept Mastercard and Visa," anticipating a follow-up question about other credit cards. And many managers who were asked

"Credit cards?" or "Any kinds of credit cards?" moved further up the hierarchy of purposes and answered "No, we just take checks or cash." Two managers even dealt with Susan's most general purpose, her patronage at the restaurant. When asked "Do you accept credit cards?" one of them answered, "Uh, yes, we accept credit cards, but tonight we are closed."

EXTENDED PROCEDURES

The joint projects that emerge in many open situations are even more extended. When there is too much that Alan and Barbara cannot take for granted, they must establish their roles, rights, and obligations as well as the means by which equity will be maintained.

Once again the issue is equity. If Alan wants Barbara to do something for him, the two of them must negotiate a joint purpose equitable to them both. Alan must identify not only what he wants Barbara to do for him, but also what he will do in return. As Dale Schunk and I found, more complicated transfers of goods regularly divide into these two parts:[2]

1. A's acquisition of goods from B
    a. A's justification of the need for the goods
    b. A's minimization of the cost of the goods
    c. A's request of the goods proper

2. A's return of goods to B
    a. A's future obligation of other goods.
    b. Other benefits for B.

If Alan wants to borrow $100 from Barbara, he might proceed this way: "Say, Barbara, I need $175 to pay the mechanic for fixing my car, and I have only $75 [a justification]. Could you lend me $100? [the request proper]. I'll pay you back in the morning [future obligation]." In sequences like this, acquisition almost always comes before return of goods, as it should. If I were to make a request of Verona, she would need to know what goods she was to deliver before she could evaluate the goods I was committing in return.

If such a transfer of goods is subject to equity, it should include equalizing devices of the expected types, and it does. A should try to define the situation as one in which one or more of these conditions hold:

---

[2] D. H. Schunk and H. H. Clark, 1984, unpublished research.

1. *Justification.* It is reasonable for B to do the act for A. Examples: "I really need the money," "I can't get to the bank," and "You still owe me $5, don't you?"
2. *Minimization of request.* The act B is to do is not very costly. Hence: "I'm not really asking for much," "It's not out of your way," and "You don't have to do it right away."
3. *Future obligation.* A intends to do something in return, as made explicit in "I'll pay you back," "I'll remember this," and "I'll return the favor."
4. *Maximization of B's benefit.* B will benefit from doing the act, as expressed in "You'll enjoy it" and "It'll do you good."

These devices each regularly occur in open transfers of goods.

Which devices are needed depends on the situation. Large requests threaten to cost B dearly, and indeed they lead to more justifications, minimizations, obligations, and benefits than small requests (see also Brown and Levinson, 1987). I don't need to justify asking Verona for the time, but I may need to justify asking her for money or for the loan of her car. Also, requests among friends tend to be repaid in kind – real goods for real goods, favors by favors. I wouldn't pay Verona to mail a letter, or try to convince her that mailing the letter will do her good. There are strong social constraints on how one person's acts are to be justified and compensated for.

The social situation in which people carry out a joint activity is all-important. Closed situations allow routine procedures; less circumscribed situations allow regular procedures; and even less circumscribed situations may require extended procedures. In open situations, the participants have a great many options. The procedure they develop depends on the situation as they construe it – especially the larger purposes they take for granted and the equity they need to maintain.

Framing situations

In proposing a transfer of goods, speakers often frame the situation in which the joint project is to be carried out. When I asked Verona "Do you know where Goldberg's Grocery is?" I framed a miniature social situation with two highlighted components:

1. I wasn't certain whether she knew where Goldberg's Grocery was; and
2. I wanted to know where Goldberg's Grocery was.

Component 2 would belong to any procedure I would use for that request, but I had a choice with component 1. I could have framed the situation as one in which she wasn't allowed to tell me, or hadn't heard of Goldberg's Grocery, or was in a hurry, or many other things. People initiating a regular procedure have options about the situation to frame, and take that option in their choice of pre-request.

TYPES OF PRE-REQUESTS

For a transfer of goods, there are many potential obstacles to negotiating a joint purpose everyone can agree on. These obstacles follow from the four requirements on any joint purpose – identification, ability, willingness, and mutual belief – but take a special form in the transfer of goods:[3]

1.	Identification	B is to do k for A.
2.	Ability	
	a. A's future act	K is a future act of B for A.
	b. B's physical possibility	It is physically possible for B to do k for A
	c. B's competence	B is competent to do k for A.
3.	Willingness	
	a. A's desire	A wants B to do k for A.
	b. B's intention	B intends to do k for A.
	c. A and B's equity	A and B recognize the consequences on equity of B's doing k for A.
4.	Mutual belief	Conditions 1 through 4 are part of A and B's common ground.

If A uses his pre-requests to frame the situation, and if he must frame it to overcome potential obstacles, then he should design pre-requests that deal with identification, ability, and willingness in the transfer of goods. And this is what people do (e.g., Ervin-Tripp, 1976, 1981; Gordon and Lakoff, 1971; Searle, 1975b).

Whatever else A and B do, they must identify the joint purpose they are committing themselves to – the transfer of certain goods. In many pre-requests, the goods to be transferred are mentioned explicitly, as in the italicized portions of these pre-requests:

Do you have *the pecan Danish* today?
Can you tell me *what time you close tonight*?
Could you possibly *shut the door*?
May I ask *who's coming to the party tonight*?

---

[3] These conditions are related to Austin's (1962) and Searle's (1969) felicity conditions, and Bach and Harnish's (1979) success conditions, on requests, but go beyond them in several ways. The point is that these conditions derive from general requirements for any joint purpose.

In other pre-requests, they have to be inferred from A's utterance as construed in the current situation, as here:

This soup needs salt. [B is to pass the salt.]
Don't you think the room is a little warm. [B is to open a window.]
Benny, the door's open. [B is to close the door.]
Waiter, there is a fly in my soup. [B is to replace soup.]

Depending on the situation and utterance, what B is to do could be almost anything.

What B is to do for A must also be (1) a future act, (2) physically possible, and (3) within B's competence. Many pre-requests check on these obstacles:

B's future act	Students are to bring number 2 pencils to the exam.
B's possibility	Do you have uh size C flashlight batteries?
	The door is open for you now.
	Isn't the water for the coffee boiling?
	Can you reach the salt?
B's competence	You can be a little more quiet now.
	Did you happen to see in the newspaper when the concert is tonight?

And there are many more types.

Finally, there are conditions on A's and B's willingness to commit to a transfer of goods. It requires (1) A to want B to take an action, (2) B to intend to do it, and (3) A and B to recognize the equity of B's doing it. Pre-requests are often designed to address these obstacles:

A's desire	I want you to leave right now.
	I'd like to hear what happened the other day at the office.
B's intention	Will you tell me where Ken is?
	Do you want to pour me a cup of coffee?
	Would you mind holding this for me a second?
	You are allowed to go in now.
A and B's equity	I'd appreciate it if you didn't do that.
	It'd be a great help if you read to Benny for a while.

Many other pre-requests fall into these categories.

The situations framed by these pre-requests differ in equity. By equity theory, whenever the situation, as A frames it, increases B's self-worth or autonomy, A should be judged polite. Whenever it lowers either one, A should be judged less polite. There is good evidence for these predictions (Brown and Levinson, 1987; Clark and Schunk 1980; Lakoff, 1973, 1977).

B's autonomy, or freedom of action, tends to be restricted by transfers of goods, since B is being asked to do something she wouldn't otherwise do. Pre-requests that are polite generally give back some of this autonomy: They give B the option of not complying, or a legitimate excuse if he takes that option. In the situation framed by "Do you know who's coming tonight?" B isn't necessarily expected to have the information and is being offered the chance to say she doesn't. She is being offered a legitimate reason *not* to agree to the transfer of goods. Questions tend to make pre-requests polite because they give, or appear to give, B some autonomy about complying. And that makes pre-requests such as "I want you to hand me the knife" or "I'd like you to hand me the knife" less polite.

B's self-worth should also go up with some pre-requests and down with others. With "May I ask you where Jordan Hall is?" the situation that A frames is one in which A is so subordinate to B that he has to ask B's permission even to make a request. With "Shouldn't you tell me where Jordan Hall is?" in contrast, the situation framed is one in which A can remind B of her obligations and hold her to them. B's self-worth is raised in the first situation but lowered in the second. By equity theory, the first pre-request should be judged more polite than the second, and it is. There are many ways that B's self-worth can be raised or lowered, and each affects politeness.

These examples give us only a glimpse at the obstacles A and B may prepare for in a transfer of goods. The point is that most pre-requests frame a situation with two joint projects: a preparatory one and, if that succeeds, the transfer of goods proper. It is this property that often allows for an opportunistic short-circuiting of the process.

GREATEST OBSTACLES

What situation should people frame for an effective transfer of goods? With so many potential obstacles, they need a strategy, and the opportunistic strategy would be to check on the most likely obstacles first – all else being equal. That is the same strategy I would use in fixing a computer program that wouldn't run, or a car that wouldn't start. The principle is this:

Principle of greatest obstacle. All else being equal, two people trying to establish a joint purpose will try first to overcome the greatest, or most likely, obstacle to reaching it.

The obstacle principle should apply to any joint purpose. Let us see how it applies to the transfer of goods.

Suppose Alan wants to know the time of a lecture announced that morning in the newspaper and thinks his friend Barbara would be perfectly willing to tell him if only she had seen the announcement. He should judge this to be the greatest potential obstacle and frame the situation around it: "Did you happen to read in the newspaper this morning what time the governor's lecture is today?" If he were to say, instead, "*Do you want to tell me* what time the governor's lecture is today?" he would have framed a situation in which Barbara surely knows the time but may be unwilling to tell him, and this would go against his assumptions.

By framing the situation he does, he accomplishes several things. First, he helps Barbara overcome the greatest obstacle. In effect, he tells her how to find the information he wants – by recalling what she had read in the morning newspaper. Second, he helps retain equity. By helping Barbara find the right information, he makes it easier for her to comply. He also gives her a face-saving way out if she doesn't know the information. All she need do is say, "Sorry, I didn't see the paper," a justification Alan indicates is perfectly reasonable. The optimal pre-request not only overcomes the greatest potential obstacle to compliance, but also helps maintain equity if it is impossible to comply.

People appear to follow this principle (Francik and Clark, 1985; Gibbs, 1986b). In several experiments, people were placed, or were asked to imagine themselves, in a variety of situations and asked to make requests. When there were no obvious potential obstacles, they tended to use simple requests or questions, like "What time is the governor's lecture tonight?" When there were obstacles, their requests tended to be directed at the greatest obstacle – whether it was B's potential ignorance, inability, unwillingness, or lack of memory.

Pre-requests vary in how *specific* they are in identifying an obstacle. Alan could have asked Barbara any one of these questions:

1. Can you tell me when the governor's lecture is?
2. Do you know when the governor's lecture is?
3. Do you happen to know when the governor's lecture is?
4. Did you happen to see when the governor's lecture is?
5. Did you happen to read in the newspaper this morning when the governor's lecture is?

These are ordered from general to specific. To answer yes to question 5 is to entail yes to questions 1 through 4, but not vice versa.

Which pre-request should Alan use? By the greatest obstacle principle, he should be as specific as reasonable. Question 1 wouldn't pinpoint the potential obstacle as precisely as 5 would: It wouldn't help Barbara find the wanted information nor would it give her a convincing excuse if she didn't have it. Yet it isn't always advisable to be specific. If Alan were trying to find out how much weight Barbara had gained, the greatest potential obstacle might be Barbara's being too embarrassed to say. To identify this obstacle publicly ("Would you be too embarrassed to say how much weight you have gained?") could be very threatening indeed, so it might be better to hint obliquely at the obstacle, as with "People often gain a bit of weight when they turn forty – has that been a problem with you?" People appear to follow this advice (Francik and Clark, 1985; Gibbs, 1986b).

So it isn't the pre-request itself that is effective or ineffective, equitable or inequitable. It is the situation that the speaker frames with it. Pre-requests are chosen for the situations they help create.

GENERIC OBSTACLES

People often have only a vague idea of the potential obstacles to compliance, yet have to frame a situation of some sort. One strategy is to select a general yet plausible obstacle and frame a situation to overcome it. You want Susan to hand you a pencil, believing she is able and willing to if asked. If you order her, "Hand me a pencil," that implies you have authority over her. Your tactic, instead, is to identify an innocuous obstacle – an unspecified inability or unwillingness to hand you a pencil – and frame the situation to overcome it, as with "Can you hand me a pencil?" or "Could you hand me a pencil?" This way you frame an equitable situation.

The tactic is to assume one of a small set of *generic obstacles* that are useful in situation after situation. Here are some examples with illustrations:

Generic obstacle	Conventional pre-request
B's ability and willingness	Can you hand me a pencil?
	Could you hand me a pencil?
B's knowledge	Do you know where Irene is?
B's physical ability	Do you have uh size C flashlight batteries?
B's intention	Will you try this shirt on?
	Would you try this shirt on?

| Imposition on B | Would you mind passing the salt? |
| A's permission to make a request | May I ask you where you bought that tie? |

The vaguer the obstacle, the more useful it should be, and indeed, "Can you...?" and "Could you...?" are among the commonest pre-requests in English.

Generic obstacles are so useful that *conventional pre-requests* have evolved for dealing with them. The first obstacle, for example, is usually handled with "Can you" or "Could you hand me a pencil?" and not "Are you capable of handing me a pencil?" or "Would you be able to hand me a pencil?" "Can you...?" and "Could you...?" have become the idiomatic or conventional linguistic devices for framing these situations. Other devices that could have evolved didn't (see Morgan, 1978; Searle, 1975b). Conventional pre-requests have apparently evolved in most languages for dealing with generic obstacles (Brown and Levinson, 1987).

What does it mean for "Can you?" to be a conventional pre-request? First, A can expect B to be able to construe "Can you?" as a request – by assuming a generic obstacle. B doesn't have to identify a specific obstacle in order to construe A as asking her to do something and what that something is. People have been shown to understand expressions like "Can you?" more quickly when construed as pre-requests than as mere questions about ability (Gibbs, 1979, 1981, 1983; Schweller, 1978). It is the other way around for non-conventional pre-requests like "Are you capable?" These are easier to construe as questions about ability than as preparations for requests.

It also means that "Can you?" is readily used as a *pro forma* condition for a request. When I ask a bank clerk "Can you tell me the current interest rate on savings accounts?" I am signaling that I don't expect her to take my pre-request seriously. I'm not really interested in whether or not she can tell me the interest rate. She can answer simply "Six percent." But when I word my pre-request "Are you able to tell me the current interest rate?" using a non-conventional form, I signal that she is to take the condition on my request seriously. In one study, here is how often bank clerks said yes to these two questions (Clark, 1979):

Caller's utterance	Clerk's response	Percent
Can you tell me...?	Yes, six percent	16
Are you able to tell me...?	Yes, six percent	35

The other clerks responded simply "Six percent." So to use a conventional pre-request, such as "Can you tell me?" over "Are you able to tell me?" is ordinarily to signal that the condition is to be taken *pro forma*.

But pre-requests aren't empty gestures just because they are *pro forma*. It is tempting to treat "Do you know who's president of Mexico?" or "Do you know when the concert begins?" merely as polite equivalents to "Who's president of Mexico?" and "When does the concert begin?" It is tempting to think they have no real content – that people respond to them mindlessly (Langer, Blank, and Chanowitz, 1978). But if that is all they are, I should be able to ask for your middle name by saying "Do you know your middle name?" and I can't. You don't respond mindlessly. For my pre-request to satisfy a preparatory condition, I must have reason to believe you wouldn't know your middle name, and it is odd even to pretend you wouldn't. The generic obstacle I frame with my pre-request counts.

Compliance

The ultimate test of the situation Alan frames with his pre-request is whether it gets results: Does Barbara comply or not? For situations framed one way, B should be willing to commit herself to the joint purpose A is proposing, and for others, she should decline or withdraw. Equity theory makes one particularly strong prediction: The more costly the goods (all other things being equal), the less equitable the situation is for B and the less likely it is that she should comply. In one study (Latané and Darley, 1970), Columbia University students made one of five requests of hundreds of people on the streets of New York, and New Yorkers complied in the following percentages:

Excuse me, I wonder if you could
1.	tell me what time it is?	85%
2.	tell me how to get to Times Square?	84%
3.	give me change for a quarter?	73%
4.	tell me what your name is?	39%
5.	give me a dime?	34%

Very roughly, it should cost New Yorkers less to give the time, directions, or change than to give their name or a dime. As predicted, the more costly the request, the fewer New Yorkers complied. Unfortunately, we are not told how the rest of the New Yorkers declined or withdrew.

By the same principle, New Yorkers should comply more readily when they are given something first. In the same study, students also made these four requests, with the following rates of success:

1. Excuse me, I wonder if you could give me a dime?   34%
2. Excuse me, my name is—. I wonder if you could give me a dime?   49%
3. Excuse me, could you tell me what your name is?   39%
4. Excuse me, my name is—. Could you tell me what your name is?   59%

When the students stated their names, they were divulging something of value, and to satisfy equity, their addressees should have felt obliged to repay that cost. They did, for they complied more often in 2 and 4 than in 1 and 3.

Equity principles say that it should also make a difference how well the request is justified. Generally, A should try to frame a situation in which there is a legitimate justification for B to comply. The more legitimate the justification, the more likely B should comply. That was confirmed in the New York study with these four requests and their rates of compliance:

Excuse me, I wonder if you could give me a dime?
1. [No additional justification]   34%
2. I've spent all my money.   38%
3. I need to make a telephone call.   64%
4. My wallet has been stolen.   72%

Compliance was lowest for no justification and highest for the most legitimate justification (see also Langer and Abelson, 1972).

Justifications can be effective even when they are *pro forma*. In one well-known study (Langer et al., 1978), a student experimenter approached people at a copying machine in a university library and made one of these two requests:

1. Excuse me, I have five pages. May I use the Xerox machine?
   [No further justification]   60%
2. Excuse me, I have five pages. May I use the Xerox machine,
   because I have to make copies?   93%

In 1 the student offered no justification and succeeded only 60 percent of the time. In 2 she framed the situation as one in which she had a legitimate justification, even though the justification was in fact *pro forma*, and then she succeeded 93 percent of the time. A *pro forma* justification is more effective than no justification because it displays the speaker's intent to make the situation equitable.

All of these situations deal with B's face. B has the free will to comply or withdraw, and her choice depends in part on how she thinks it will affect her self-worth and autonomy. Large requests and requests without legitimate justification tend to lower self-worth and autonomy. To comply, she has to take time from her affairs, which restricts her autonomy. She also cannot expect an adequate return for her pains, which eats into her self-worth.

POLITE RESPONSES

Compliance isn't all or nothing. When New Yorkers are asked "Excuse me, I wonder if you could give me a dime," they may comply and yet complain: "I'll give you a dime, but not one cent more." If they decline, they may do it only half-heartedly: "Sorry, I don't have one on me." Or they may show how offended they are by the proposal: "Not on your life." Comments like these are attempts to deal with equity beyond mere compliance, declination, or withdrawal. They display just how committed B is to the joint project proposed by A.

As we have seen, politeness has to do with how Alan and Barbara deal publicly with each other's self-worth and autonomy. We have already looked at A's politeness. All else being equal, the less threatening the joint task A is proposing is to B's self-worth or autonomy, the more polite A is judged to be. But much the same principle should apply to B's response: All else being equal, the less threatening B's response is to A's self-worth or autonomy, the more polite B is judged to be. If B complies, she should be judged more polite the more committed she is. If she declines, she should be judged more polite the more legitimate her justification.

These predictions are confirmed in judgments of politeness. In one study, people were asked to judge alternative responses to a series of requests (Clark and Schunk, 1980). One of these requests was "Can you direct me to Lost and Found?" Here A is proposing both a preparatory project ("Can you direct me?") and, electively, a transfer of information ("Please direct me"). So B is being asked to commit to two projects. She should be considered most polite when she commits to both, and less polite the less committed she is to either one. Here are four alternative ways of complying:

Can you direct me to Lost and Found?
1. Certainly. It's around the corner.
2. Yes, I can. It's around the corner.
3. Yes. It's around the corner.
4. It's around the corner.

Of the responses that deal explicitly with the preparatory task, 1 is the most enthusiastic, and 2 is more explicit than 3. As predicted, 1 was judged most polite, 2 next most polite, 3 next most polite, and 4 least polite. If, instead, B declines either project, she should be judged more polite the more legitimately she accounts for her declination. Here are three alternative ways of declining:

Can you direct me to Lost and Found?
  5. No, I'm sorry. I can't.
  6. No, I can't.
  7. No.

Both 5 and 6 offer a legitimate reason for declining, and 5 offers an apology in addition. As expected, 5 was judged most polite, 6 less polite, and 7 least polite.

Traditionally, politeness is viewed as a property of A's and B's unilateral actions (e.g., Brown and Levinson, 1987; Lakoff, 1973). But like most aspects of transfers of goods, it too is determined jointly. As an illustration, suppose Verona has made a request of me, and I consider three alternative responses:

Did you tell me what time the party is tonight?
  1. Yes, I did, five minutes ago. It's at nine.
  2. Yes, I did. It's at nine.
  3. Oh – it's at nine.

Verona uses her pre-request to frame a situation in which she cannot recall whether or not I told her the time of the party tonight – hence she needs the time of the party. If I haven't told her, then I should now. If I have, then she is giving me the opportunity to chasten her for her lapse of memory. Now although it is polite for her to *offer* me this opportunity, it would be impolite for me to *take up* the offer, as with response 1 or 2. The polite thing to do is forgo the chastening and give her the time, as in response 3.

How polite Verona and I are here depends on the cooperation of the other. She is polite if I respond with 3. She has offered me the opportunity to chasten her even if I don't take it. But if I respond with 1 or 2, I also make *her* seem less polite. It would be as if I were to say, "You tried to make me responsible for your not knowing the party time, but I'm not. I told you five minutes ago. Shame on you for not remembering. Here is the time again." With response 1 or 2, I might even force her to apologize, as with "Sorry, thanks." So although I may be impolite in responding with I, I make her out to be impolite too. Politeness is determined by how Verona and I choose to view each other, and we establish that through our joint actions.

For requests introduced by pre-requests, then, B is judged to be polite when she deals with both proposed projects (Clark and Schunk, 1980). For the proposed transfer of goods (e.g., "Can you direct me to Lost and Found?"), she is judged more polite if she:

1. complies fully ("It's around the corner")
2. does so clearly ("It's around the corner" instead of "Around the corner")
3. apologizes when she cannot ("Sorry")
4. justifies herself when she cannot ("I can't")

For the preparatory joint project, she is judged more polite if she:

1. commits herself to it explicitly ("Yes")
2. does so with clarity ("Yes, I can")
3. makes the commitment especially serious if it is not *pro forma* ("I'd be happy to")
4. deals with any negative repercussions of its completion

Every choice A makes affects the force of B's options, and vice versa, so even politeness is determined jointly.

Conclusions

Joint projects require people to commit to doing things with each other. When Alan commits himself to riding a tandem bicycle with Barbara, his commitment is special. He is committing himself to her only on condition that she is committing herself to him. If he fails to do his part, not only does he renege to Barbara, but he undercuts her own commitment to him. It is no wonder joint commitments affect equity and face. Alan's actions affect the public perception not only of his own self-worth and autonomy, but of Barbara's.

Exchanges of goods are generally engineered to maintain the face of the participants. When Alan proposes an exchange with Barbara, he is expected to presuppose a method for maintaining equity with Barbara. In closed situations, like buying a ticket at a movie theater, he can accomplish that by calling on a routine procedure ("One, please"). In other situations, he has to do something more. A common method is to use a pre-request (e.g., "Do you happen to know where Goldberg's Grocery is?") to frame a situation that makes the exchange equitable. The goal is to overcome the most likely, or greatest, obstacle to Barbara's commitment, and that is often done by framing generic obstacles (as with "Can you tell me where Goldberg's Grocery is?"). Still, Alan's success in maintaining equity depends on what Barbara does in response. The politeness of each depends on the actions of both.

Other joint projects manage face in other ways. Indeed, managing face is the primary purpose for many. Compliments, offers, thanks, congratulations, greetings, and apologies increase the self-worth or autonomy of one or both of the participants, whereas insults, reprimands, censures, and criticisms do just the opposite. Exchanges of goods are different in that their primary purpose is to effect the transfer of goods, yet they cannot be carried out without managing face. Equity and face appear to constrain all actions that require joint commitments.

11 | Conversation

The fundamental site for language use is conversation, spontaneous dialogue among two or more people. Although conversations are created
from utterances, they are more than the sum of their parts. Let us return
to the telephone conversation discussed in Chapter 7 (8.11.851):

Jane: (rings C's telephone)
Kate: Miss Pink's office - hello
Jane: hello, is Miss Pink in .
Kate: well, she's in, but she's engaged at the moment, who is it?
Jane: oh it's Professor Worth's secretary, from Pan-American College
Kate: m,
Jane: could you give her a message *for me*
Kate: *certainly*
Jane: u:m Professor Worth said that, if . Miss Pink runs into difficulties, . on
        Monday afternoon, . with the standing subcommittee, . over the item
        on Miss Panoff, - - -
Kate: Miss Panoff?
Jane: yes, that Professor Worth would be with Mr Miles all afternoon, - so
        she only had to go round and collect him if she needed him, - - -
Kate: ah, - - - thank you very much indeed,
Jane: right
Kate: Panoff, right *you* are
Jane: *right,*
Kate: I'll tell her, *(2 to 3 syllables)*
Jane: *thank you*
Kate: bye bye
Jane: bye

Here Jane and Kate complete one main task, passing a message from
Professor Worth to Miss Pink. They do this through a series of smaller

sections – opening the conversation, exchanging information about Pink, exchanging the message from Worth, and closing the conversation. They complete each section by means of adjacency pairs (e.g., questions and answers), and complete each adjacency pair turn by turn. Viewed as a whole, the conversation consists of a hierarchy of parts: conversation, sections, adjacency pairs, and turns.

Where does this structure come from? It is tempting to answer "the participants' goals and plans." In this view, the participants devise plans for each conversation, section, adjacency pair, and turn, where each plan is designed to achieve a specific goal. The *goals-and-plans view* of conversation is the received view for many students of language use.

Actual conversations pose problems for this view. Although people talk in order to get things done, they don't know in advance what they will actually do. The reasons are obvious: They cannot get anything done without the others joining them, and they cannot know in advance what the others will do. Jane and Kate's conversation is a good example. Jane called to tell Miss Pink where Professor Worth would be that afternoon. When she discovered Miss Pink was busy, she recruited Kate to pass on the information. Kate had her own purposes in answering the telephone – to take messages and keep callers from interrupting Miss Pink – but she had no idea who was calling or what they would say. Jane and Kate entered the conversation with certain purposes, but without specific plans about how they would achieve them.

Conversations, therefore, are *purposive* but *unplanned*. People achieve most of what they do by means of joint projects, both large and small, in which they establish and carry out joint purposes they are willing and able to commit to (see Chapters 7 and 10). To complete these, they have to work at the level of minimal joint projects, for it is with these that they negotiate broader purposes and complete extended joint projects. What emerges are sections and, ultimately, the entire conversation itself. Conversations look planned and goal-oriented only in retrospect. In reality, they are created opportunistically piece by piece as the participants negotiate joint purposes and then fulfill them. Let me call this the *opportunistic view* of conversation.

In the opportunistic view, the hierarchical structure of conversation is an emergent property. It appears because of principles that govern any successful joint activity. Conversations cannot work without coordination of both content and process. So the participants try to complete each joint action in accordance with the principle of closure and its corollaries.

They work together to complete the levels of execution and attention, presentation and identification, signaling and construing, proposal and uptake, and more extended joint projects. Once the participants apply these principles, adjacency pairs, conversational sections, and entire conversations simply emerge. So do turns. Let us consider turn taking first.

Turn taking

In one folk view of conversation, people take turns talking. Only one person speaks at a time. This view, of course, hardly does justice to what actually happens. In the last four chapters, we have seen a much more complicated account of how people proceed, including who speaks when. How does this account fit with the view that people take turns? For an answer let us turn to a landmark paper on turn taking in 1974 by Harvey Sacks, Emanuel Schegloff, and Gail Jefferson.

TURN ALLOCATION

Sacks et al.'s proposal was that turn taking is governed by rules. The rules they proposed were designed to account for common observations about everyday conversations such as these (pp. 700-701):

1. Speaker change recurs, or, at least, occurs.
2. Overwhelmingly, one party talks at a time.
3. Occurrences of more than one speaker at a time are common, but brief.
4. Transitions from one turn to a next with no gap and no overlap between them are common. Together with transitions characterized by slight gap or slight overlap, they make up the vast majority of transitions.
5. Turn order is not fixed, but varies.
6. Turn size is not fixed, but varies.
7. Length of conversation is not fixed, specified in advance.
8. What parties say is not fixed, specified in advance.
9. Relative distribution of turns is not fixed, specified in advance.

These observations are mundane, but they are difficult to account for. Sacks et al.'s rules offer an ingenious account.

A system of turn taking must specify, first, what it is to be a turn. For Sacks et al., a turn consists of one or more *turn-constructional units*. These range in size from a single word (e.g., Kate's "certainly") to clauses filled with many embedded clauses (e.g., Jane's "u:m Professor Worth said that, if . Miss Pink runs into difficulties, . on Monday afternoon, . with the standing subcommittee, . over the item on Miss Panoff, - - - that

Professor Worth would be with Mr. Miles all afternoon, - so she only had to go round and collect him if she needed him, - - -"). Each unit ends at a *transition-relevance place* – a point at which the next speaker could begin a turn. Sacks et al. said little about these units. All we have to go on is an intuitive but circular notion: A turn-constructional unit is a unit that could constitute a complete turn at that moment in the conversation.

A system of turn taking must also specify the allocation of turns. In Sacks et al.'s system, the current speaker may "select" the next speaker, for example, by asking a question that obliges the addressee to take the next turn. Otherwise, a party may "select him- or herself" by speaking before anyone else begins. If neither of these actions occurs, the current speaker can resume speaking. The rules Sacks et al. proposed are as follows (p. 704):

1. For any turn, at the initial transition-relevance place of an initial turn-constructional unit:
   a. If the turn-so-far is so constructed as to involve the use of a "current speaker selects next" technique, then the party so selected has the right and is obliged to take next turn to speak; no others have such rights or obligations, and transfer occurs at that place.
   b. If the turn-so-far is so constructed as not to involve the use of a "current speaker selects next" technique, then self-selection for next speakership may, but need not, be instituted; first starter acquires rights to a turn, and transfer occurs at that place.
   c. If the turn-so-far is so constructed as not to involve the use of a "current speaker selects next" technique, then current speaker may, but need not continue, unless another self-selects.
2. If, at the initial transition-relevance place of an initial turn-constructional unit, neither 1a nor 1b has operated, and, following the provision of 1c, current speaker has continued, then the rule-set a–c reapplies at next transition-relevance place, and recursively at each next transition-relevance place, until transfer is effected.

These rules result in an orderly sequence of turns. Let me call the rules *turn-allocation rules*. Sacks et al.'s claim is that they govern the allocation of turns.

These rules readily account for the observations they were intended to deal with. They allow for variation in turn order, turn size, and number of parties. They also allow certain biases to operate. There is, for example, a bias for the just prior speaker to be selected as the next speaker. So when there are three parties, one of them tends to be left out, and when there are four, the conversation tends to split up into two two-party conversations. With rule 1b, there is also a bias toward turns of only one turn-constructional unit – a bias toward brief turns (Schegloff, 1982). That makes it difficult to take extended turns, as in telling a story, without special techniques. The rules also leave open the length of the conversation, what is said, and the relative distribution of turns.

These rules, Sacks et al. emphasized, are *projective*. Speakers use evidence from the current turn to project its completion and to time their next turn to begin at that point. The traditional view is that turn taking is *reactive*. Speakers wait until the current turn has ended before initiating their next turn (e.g., Duncan, 1972, 1973). The evidence favors the projective view. If speakers project turn completions, speaker switches should often be accomplished with little or no gap at all, and they are. In one study (Beattie and Barnard, 1979), 34 percent of all speaker switches in both face-to-face and telephone conversations took less than 0.2 seconds. There should also be overlaps when next speakers misproject the end of the current speaker's presentation, and there are, as in this example:

Jane: could you give her a message *for me*
Kate: *certainly*

Kate projected Jane's turn to finish after "message," so her "certainly" overlapped with Jane's "for me."[1] If turn taking were reactive, these brief transitions and slight overlaps should not have occurred. It is cognitively impossible to react to a stimulus in less than 0.2 seconds and logically impossible to do so before the stimulus even exists.

If listeners project the current turn's end before it is reached, how do they do it? Not much is known about the process, but they probably rely on many sources of information. They may use eye gaze, gestures, and intonation. Speakers tend to gaze away from their listeners during their turn and to gaze back as they finish it, whereas listeners tend to gaze at the speaker throughout his turn (Chapter 9). These patterns are magnified in conversations among strangers or about difficult topics. At turn ends, speakers may also elongate the last syllable, drop the pitch of their voice, relax their bodies, and complete gestures they have been making.[2] Yet gaze and gestures aren't necessary. There are no more gaps, and no

---

[1] On the other hand, Kate may have chosen to overlap with Jane, with precision timing, to emphasize her eagerness to comply (Jefferson, 1973).

[2] For details, see Beattie (1981), Duncan (1972, 1973), Goodwin (1981), Kendon (1967), among others.

longer gaps, in telephone conversations than in face-to-face conversations (Beattie, 1983; Beattie and Barnard, 1979). In one study (Beattie, Cutler, and Pearson, 1982), people were asked to judge whether utterances from a television interview had occurred in the middle or at the end of the speaker's actual turns. These judges were quite accurate in distinguishing turn middles from turn ends when they were shown full video recordings of the utterances. They were still quite accurate with only the visual or audio portions. They failed entirely with only written transcripts. Listeners probably project the ends of turns from a combination of facial features, eye gaze, syntax, and intonation.

LIMITATIONS OF TURN-ALLOCATION RULES

The turn-allocation rules, however, have limitations. There are many conversational phenomena they were never intended to account for, and once we include these, we get a different picture of who speaks when and why. One presupposition behind the rules is that conversations are all talk, and once we include other forms of communicative acts, we get yet another picture.

The turn-allocation rules are really about *primary* presentations – that part of what speakers present that deals with the official business of the discourse (Chapter 9). They seem to be contradicted by most types of *secondary* presentations, such as these:

Acknowledgments, like "uh huh," by B of A's presentation
Constituent queries by A followed by B's response
Collaborative completions by B of A's presentation
Turn restarts by A to secure B's attention
Recycled turn beginnings by A to request B's attention

Acknowledgments such as "uh huh" often deliberately overlap with the primary speaker's current utterance (Chapter 6). That makes them a pervasive and systematic exception to the generalization "one party talks at a time" and apparent counterevidence to rules 1a through 1c. Other acknowledgments are presented after the pieces of installment utterances, where they mean "please continue" (Schegloff, 1982). So do mid-turn queries, as in this excerpt from Jane and Kate's conversation:

Jane: u:m Professor Worth said that, if . Miss Pink runs into difficulties, . on
        Monday afternoon, . with the standing subcommittee, . over the item on
        Miss Panoff, - - -

Kate: **Miss Panoff?**

Jane: **yes,** that Professor Worth would be with Mr. Miles all afternoon, - so she only had to go round and collect him if she needed him, - - -

Every secondary presentation that comes midturn is apparent counterevidence to the rules.

Why aren't acknowledgments and their kind considered counterevidence to the turn-allocation rules? They aren't considered genuine turns, apparently because they don't carry out official business. There is a danger here of circularity: Something is a turn only if it fits the turn-allocation rules. To decide whether the turn-allocation rules apply, we need to know whether the business is official or not, and that takes us back to more basic principles.

The turn-allocation rules, however, don't even cover all primary presentations. Take these strategies (Chapters 6 and 7):

Truncations. A invites B to interrupt, and B interrupts
Fade-outs. A leaves an utterance deliberately incomplete
Strategic interruptions. A deliberately interrupts B mid-presentation

All three phenomena violate the turn-allocation rules, although they aren't considered violations by the people who use them. Even strategic interruptions are legitimate when the speakers have the right to take over the floor whenever they want or need to – teachers, police interrogators, military officers. Again there is a danger of circularity: A strategy is a violation of turn taking if it violates the turn-allocation rules. But truncations, fade-outs, and strategic interruptions are not true violations of conversational practice.

The turn-allocation rules also don't fare well in conversations that aren't all talk. The point is nicely illustrated in a study by Susan Brennan (1990). Pairs of people, exemplified here by Ben and Charlotte, sat at separate computer terminals with maps of the Stanford University campus on their screens. Ben's job was to guide Charlotte as she moved a car (represented by her cursor and moved by her mouse) from one place on her map to another, clicking on the mouse when she reached the destination. Here is a brief example:

	Speech	C's cursor
Ben:	oooh! right in the muh- middle of Memorial Church	
Charlotte:	Memorial Church	
Ben:	*complete*ly enclosed	*[moves 300 pixels]*
Charlotte:	*complete*ly enclosed? okay	*[moves 20 pixels]*
	# I'm clicked in	[# = clicks mouse]
Ben:	awright	

Here Ben directs, and Charlotte confirms, in turns that fit the turn-allocation rules. But when Charlotte's cursor appeared on Ben's map as well as her own – and they both knew that – their talk looked very different. Here is a conversation with the same map and destination:

	Speech	C's cursor
Ben:	okay now we're at Mem Chu	
	no to your right	*[moves 80 pixels]*
Charlotte:	uhh	
Ben:	**no over by the quad**	**[moves 230 pixels]**
	right there yah right there	*[moves 10 pixels]*
	#	[# = clicks mouse]

Adjacency pairs took different shapes in the two conversations. They had a standard form when there was auditory evidence alone, as here:

Ben:	oooh! right in the muh- middle of Memorial Church
Charlotte:	Memorial Church

But their form changed when there was visual evidence as well, as in this comparable adjacency pair:

Ben:	okay now we're at Mem Chu
Charlotte:	[moves cursor 80 pixels]

In the first pair, Charlotte confirmed Ben's directions by saying "Memorial Church," but in the second, by moving her cursor to Memorial Church ("Mem Chu"). In the second pair, Charlotte's turn isn't speech, but a manifesting act of compliance, a different type of signal, but still a signal (Chapter 6). The turn-allocation rules don't recognize manifesting actions as turns and therefore treat the two sequences as fundamentally different. Yet as minimal joint projects, they are equivalent (Chapter 7).

Although speakers tend to avoid overlap in primary talk (Chapter 9), they are happy to overlap verbal and nonverbal presentations. With auditory evidence alone, Ben started his second instruction only after Charlotte stopped speaking:

Charlotte: Memorial Church
Ben: completely enclosed

But with visual evidence, he started his next instruction as soon as he saw her cursor move:

Charlotte: *[moves 80 pixels]*
Ben: *no* to your right

People don't have to take turns in primary presentations that are not spoken.

The most striking phenomenon with visual evidence is the continuous reformulation of utterances. When Ben had continuous evidence of Charlotte's understanding, he adjusted his utterance phrase by phrase to take account of it. What emerged was an utterance in four installments:

okay now we're at Mem Chu,
no to your right,
no over by the quad,
right there yah right there

Recall that in installment utterances, speakers seek acknowledgments of understanding (e.g., "yeah") *after* each installment and formulate the next installment contingent on that acknowledgment (Chapter 8). With visual evidence, Ben gets confirmation or disconfirmation *while* he is producing the current installment.

Utterances with visual evidence of understanding are common enough in everyday settings. Suppose Ben is getting Charlotte to center a candlestick in a display:

Ben: Okay, now, push it farther - farther - a little more - right there. Good.

Charlotte nudges the candlestick bit by bit as Ben is speaking, stretching vowels and repeating words to tell her how far. Ben's and Charlotte's actions are simultaneous, and deliberately so, whereas the turn-allocation rules, if applicable, allow only sequential actions. Ben and Charlotte, of course, are still observing the principle of closure. It is just that they aren't taking turns.

These examples bring out several problems for turns. Secondary presentations, like acknowledgments, regularly overlap with primary presentations, and primary presentations are often designed to overlap with each other as well. Also, many communicative acts in conversation aren't spoken, and these can overlap without causing difficulties for attention, identification, or understanding. And when there is external evidence of understanding, speakers may continuously reformulate their utterances without forming true turn-constructional units. The turn-allocation rules cannot account for these observations, so we need principles that do.

EMERGENT PHENOMENA IN CONVERSATION

The placement of speech and other actions in conversation really emerges from the way people try to advance joint activities. As we saw in Chapters 7 through 10, the participants in a joint activity work hard to get closure at all levels of talk – execution and attention, presentation and identification, meaning and understanding, projection and uptake. What emerges is a set of procedures that determine who speaks and acts when. These in turn account for Sacks et al.'s turn-allocation rules. To see this, let us look at three procedures: minimal joint projects, one primary presentation at a time, and presentation and acceptance phases.

Recall that the responses in minimal joint projects do double duty (Chapter 7). When Ben asks Charlotte a question, he (1) needs evidence that she has understood him and (2) projects as her next action an answer to it. Charlotte, by answering his question and by doing so immediately, both (1) provides that evidence and (2) takes up his proposed joint project. That accounts for turn-allocation rule 1a, the "current speaker selects next" rule. It explains both who is selected (Charlotte) and why she has the right and the obligation to begin the next turn at that point.

Joint projects also explain why Charlotte's next turn can be nonlinguistic. Often she can complete minimal joint projects without speaking at all – as when she opens a door at his request, or takes the program he has offered in a quiet concert hall, or nods when he pays her a compliment. It also accounts for why Ben's projection and Charlotte's uptake can be simultaneous rather than sequential. When Ben asks Charlotte to move the candlestick in the display, she can both give evidence of understanding and take up his request as he speaks. And, finally, the explanation also shows how rule 1a is related to other action–response pairs. Suppose Ben hands Charlotte a concert program and she says "Thanks." Although rule 1a doesn't apply, Ben may well expect Charlotte to provide evidence that she deems his deed a favor. That makes her "Thanks" like other next turns that are covered by rule 1a.

Next recall the argument for "one primary spoken presentation at a time" (Chapter 9). Speakers and addressees cannot coordinate execution and attention whenever the demands on their attention are too strong, so they generally restrict themselves to one primary spoken presentation at a time. That accounts for several main features of rule 1b. Charlotte cannot begin a primary spoken presentation after Susan has begun one and expect to succeed at the level of execution and attention. If Ben is speaking and Charlotte wants to contribute next, and if she sees Susan as a possible competitor, she must try to speak up before Susan does. That leads her to project the end of Ben's utterance and minimize the gap between their utterances.

The one-primary-spoken-presentation constraint yields other conversational strategies as well (Chapter 9). Charlotte can use a recycled turn beginning to preempt Susan for the next turn; this signals the beginning of a next primary presentation before the last one is ended. Also, Charlotte can use a deliberate interruption to take the floor from Ben when she believes her contribution takes priority at that moment over Ben's. Even if she uses these techniques exploitatively, what she does is accounted for not by rule 1b but by the one-primary-spoken-presentation constraint itself.

Recall, finally, that participants generally contribute to discourse in two steps – a presentation phase and an acceptance phase (Chapter 8). In the first phase, Ben presents Charlotte with an utterance, and in the second, she provides evidence that she has identified it and understood him well enough for current purposes. It is this process that determines Sacks et al.'s turn-constructional units and accounts for the workings of rule 1c.

Turn-constructional units are really primary presentations. When Ben begins speaking, he has some idea of what he wants to contribute, and he formulates and produces his presentation accordingly. For an assertion, he may produce the clause "I've just been up in Caribou"; for a request for repair, the phrase "Which woman?"; or for an acknowledgment, "uh huh." He realizes that he must get Charlotte to hear his presentation as complete and as offering her the chance to give evidence of acceptance. So his presentation must ordinarily be a complete syntactic unit appropriate to the work he wants it to do and marked with the right intonation and gestures. It can range from a simple "uh huh" to an extended assertion.

Primary presentations are needed in accounting for all three turn-allocation rules, but they are especially important in interpreting rule 1c. By that rule, "the current speaker may, but need not, continue unless another self-selects." Whenever Charlotte accepts Ben's presentation with a backgrounded acknowledgment, that falls under rule 1c. Whenever she accepts each installment of an installment utterance, that also falls under rule 1c. Whenever Charlotte hesitates in accepting Ben's presentation, so he expands on it until she does, that too falls under rule 1c. It isn't that Ben (the current speaker) simply continues unless Charlotte (another party) speaks first. The pattern arises from the several ways of managing the presentation and acceptance phases of Ben's contribution. The two phases of contributing account for who speaks when in ways that go beyond the turn-allocation rules.

Is there anything left for the turn-allocation rules to account for? Apparently not. There is no evidence that people try to preserve turns per se. If they seem to take turns in a conversation, it is because they are trying to contribute to the current joint activities, which leads to presentations and acceptances, one primary spoken presentation at a time, and minimal joint projects.

FORMAL TURNS

Many of the strategies that work in spontaneous conversations get changed or suspended in other types of discourse. In debates and church services, turns are allocated by predetermined formulas, and in formal meetings by the chair. In court rooms, turns are allocated by the judge and attorneys, with the judge having ultimate control. In school classrooms, teachers allocate turns and wield control over their length and content.

Even in these settings, the discourse is ultimately shaped by the attempts to contribute to it. Take strategic interruptions. In formal meetings, according to *Robert's rules of order* (Robert, 1970), a member who "has been assigned the floor and has begun to speak" can be legitimately interrupted by another member or the chair in order to raise a point of order, raise a question of privilege, make "a request or inquiry that requires an immediate response," make an appeal, or make an objection to the consideration of a question, among other things. In court, judges and attorneys can and do legally interrupt witnesses, preempting their testimony, on a variety of grounds (Atkinson and Drew, 1979). In classrooms, students and teachers can acceptably interrupt each other in the right circumstances. In a study of British university tutorials, strategic interruptions were used on 34 percent of all speaker transitions when there were three to six students plus the tutor, but on only 11 percent when there was only one student. In the larger tutorials, students interrupted the previous speaker on 51 percent of the transitions from other students and on 37 percent of the transitions from the tutor, whereas the tutor interrupted on only 26 percent of the transitions from the students (Beattie, 1981, 1982). Interruptions like these are legitimate in forums where the participants are encouraged to compete with their ideas.

In informal business meetings, university seminars, and briefing sessions, the participants often allocate turns by explicit agreement. They work out a formula for who is to talk on what for how long and then abide by it. They can agree to alter or limit turns in any number of ways.

Nor do all formal systems for allocating turns respect the one-primary-spoken-presentation limit. In religious services, the congregation often speaks simultaneously. But these utterances are formulaic litanies or prayers that make no extra demands on the speakers' attention. The one-primary-spoken-presentation limit only applies when having more than one primary speaker would demand too much competing attention. So although people don't always honor the one-primary-spoken-presentation limit, they do adhere to the more basic principles.

Who speaks when, in brief, has its origins in the joint activities that the participants are trying to complete. It often conforms to Sacks et al.'s turn-allocation rules, but not because the participants are trying to adhere to them. They are simply trying to succeed in advancing their joint activities. Other systems of turn allocation have evolved in formal settings, but they too work in service of completing contributions. The fundamental problem is how to act jointly and succeed.

Sections in conversations

Conversations tend to divide into sections, longer stretches of talk devoted to a single task, point of discussion, or subject matter. Jane and Kate's telephone call, for example, might be divided into (1) an opening, (2) an exchange of information about Miss Pink, (3) an exchange of information about Miss Panoff, and (4) a closing. At first, each section seems to follow a plan that is designed to achieve a specific goal, and together, these plans achieve Jane's and Kate's overall goal.

There are two complications for the goal-and-plans view, as Sacks et al. argued in their analysis of turns. First, conversations are managed locally. The rules of turn taking specify only two adjacent turns – the current turn and the next turn – and the transition between them. What gets said when is managed turn by turn. Second, conversations are controlled jointly. Each turn is shaped by all the participants as they engineer the selection of the current speaker, and influence the course and length of each turn. Both properties hold even when turns are viewed as emergent phenomena. What they amount to, in this framework, is that conversations are managed contribution by contribution. People may have general goals on entering a conversation, but they cannot prepare specific plans to reach them. They must achieve what they do contribution by contribution.

EMERGENCE OF CONVERSATIONS

If conversations emerge one contribution at a time, how does that happen? Recall that for any joint activity, the participants go from not being engaged in it to being engaged in it to not being engaged in it again (Chapter 2). If so, we should be able to identify three time periods of a conversation:

1. Entry into the conversation
2. Body of the conversation
3. Exit from the conversation

If a joint action is brief enough, the participants can manage its entry, body, and exit by coordinating on only three features: (1) the participants; (2) the entry time; and (3) the action each participant is to perform (Chapters 3 and 7). But conversations are too complicated. It is impossible to specify in advance what actions each participant is to take in a long conversation. How, then, are their actions determined?

The secret lies in establishing joint commitments. It takes Ben and Charlotte's joint commitment to enter a conversation, to continue it at each point, and to exit from it. And the commonest way to establish joint commitments is through joint projects – ultimately minimal joint projects. These enable Ben and Charlotte to coordinate on everything they need to – entry times, participants, and actions at each point in the conversation. If so, the entry, body, and exit of a conversation should ordinarily be achieved sequentially by means of minimal joint projects, and they are. What emerges on entry is an opening section and on exit is a closing section.

OPENING SECTIONS

Ben and Charlotte will never decide at the identical moment that they want to talk to each other. Rather, one initiates, and the other accedes. Ben, for example, might want to talk to Charlotte. He proposes a conversation and, if she is willing and able, she accepts. Both take for granted that he has a purpose in initiating the conversation, and her decision to accept depends ultimately on agreeing to that purpose. So opening sections are a type of joint project.

Opening a conversation has to resolve, among other things, the entry time, the participants, their roles, and the official business they are to carry out. One way to resolve these face to face is with a summons–answer pair, as here (Schegloff, 1968):

Ben: Charlotte?
Charlotte: Yes?

With his summons, Ben does several things. He proposes that moment as the entry time for a conversation. In using "Charlotte," he presupposes the other person to be Charlotte and to have a particular status (he could have said, "Miss Stone?" or "Madam?") and proposes that the participants of the conversation are to be Charlotte (in that status) and himself. By using rising intonation, he turns the floor over to Charlotte and asks her if she is tentatively willing and able to talk on a topic yet to be specified.

Charlotte now has several choices (see Chapter 7). She can take up the proposed joint project ("Yes?"), alter it ("It's Miss Stone. Yes?"), decline it ("Sorry, I can't talk now"), or withdraw from it (by turning away). Here she takes it up. In doing so, she accepts his utterance as marking the entry into a potential conversation. She also displays her recognition of Ben, accepting his identification of her as Charlotte and of the two of them as the participants. With the rising intonation on "Yes?" she proposes that Ben raise the first topic. This way she shows that her willingness to continue is conditional on what Ben specifies as the first topic. If she finds it unacceptable, she can still withdraw. So two people can coordinate on the entry time, participants, roles, and conditional content of a conversation with just a single adjacency pair. The summons is really a pre-topic opening designed for entry into a conversation.

Opening a telephone conversation is often more elaborate because, without vision, it takes more work to identify the participants, their roles, and their commitments (Schegloff, 1968, 1979, 1986). On the telephone, the summons takes a special form, the ringing of a telephone. Unlike "Charlotte?" it doesn't identify the proposed participants or their roles, so that has to be done in separate moves, as here (8.1f.624):

Jane: (rings Helen's telephone)
Helen: hello? . Principal's office
Jane: uh this is Professor Worth's secretary? from Pan-American College
Helen: yes?
Jane: u:m could you possibly tell me, what Sir Humphrey Davy's address is, -

Helen responds to the ring with "hello," marking her possible entry into a conversation with Jane. She immediately identifies the role she expects to play in the conversation (as the Principal's agent), and Jane reciprocates, as if requested, by identifying her own role (as Professor Worth's secretary). These professional identifications define their official duties and responsibilities and allow them to proceed to their official business. It is only then that Helen requests the first topic ("yes?"), and Jane obliges.

Other times it is personal rather than professional identities that are needed, and they may take time to establish, as here (7.2k.939):

Karen: (rings Charlie's telephone)
Charlie: Wintermere speaking? -
Karen: hello?
Charlie: he*l*lo
Karen: Charlie
Charlie: yes
Karen: actually it's
Charlie: hello Karen
Karen: it's me
Charlie: m
Karen: I (- laughs) I couldn't get back last night, [continues]

Although Charlie identifies himself on answering Karen's summons, she expects him to identify her from one small sample of her voice ("hello?"). He responds "he*l*lo," but doesn't appear to have identified her. She returns with a second voice sample, "Charlie," and by moving from his "Wintermere" to her "Charlie," she also displays an intimacy with him. Still, he doesn't seem to recognize her, and she is about to identify herself ("actually it's") when he recognizes her, interrupts, and greets her. Indeed, once he has identified her, he says "hello Karen" as if he hadn't already said "hello" to her, *qua* Karen, in the conversation. Establishing personal identities can be a delicate process (Schegloff, 1968, 1979, 1986).

Establishing a joint commitment to talk often requires a greeting, the social process of making acquaintance or reacquaintance. People coming together after a period of separation may make it common ground that: (a) they find pleasure in each other's company, or are willing to accept each other for this occasion; and (b) the separation now ending hasn't been out of ill will or lack of interest (Goffman, 1971), as here (7.2h.677):

Ken:	(rings Margaret's telephone)
Margaret:	extension five uhu two? ,
Ken:	(. giggles) hello? .
Margaret:	hello? .
Ken:	hi, .
Margaret:	**how are you**
Ken:	**me? . I'm very well, - . and you? - .**
Margaret:	**fine, -**
Ken:	**are you? .**
Margaret:	**yes, . aren't you? -**
Ken:	I'm sorry I haven't rung before, . this week [continues]

Ken and Margaret greet each other by inquiring ostensibly about each other's health – "how are you?" "me? . I'm very well" etc. (Sacks, 1975). What gets included in a greeting varies greatly from culture to culture (e.g., Irvine, 1974). The point is that greetings are joint activities of their own, to be entered and exited from, and that creates their own structure.

The opening section is closed, and the next section opened, by introducing the first topic. This is often accomplished with a pre-announcement such as "Did you hear what happened to Wanda?" or "Let me ask you about the party tonight." So the opening section emerges with the usual entry–body–exit structure:

Entry. Orienting to the possibility of conversing
Body. Establishing a joint commitment to converse
Exit. Opening of first topic

With the exit, the participants enter the conversation proper – talk on the first topic – and the opening section has accomplished just what it should have accomplished.

CLOSING SECTIONS

Exits from most conversations are as complicated as entries. Two partici-pants, Ben and Charlotte, cannot make their exit simply by stopping. They must exit from the last topic, mutually agree to close, and then coordinate their actual disengagement. If Ben exits without warning, he will threaten Charlotte's self-worth, offending her, because she is still committed to their *joint* activity in the mistaken belief that he is too (see Chapter 10). The closing section has an entry–body–exit organization of its own:

Entry. Terminating the last topic
Body. Taking leave
Exit. Terminating contact

As an illustration, I will consider the closing of urban American telephone calls (Schegloff and Sacks, 1973).

The first task is to agree that the last topic is complete. Ben may be ready to close a conversation when Charlotte isn't, because she has another topic to bring up, or vice versa, so reaching that agreement is tricky. The characteristic solution, Schegloff and Sacks argued, is for one person, say Ben, to offer a *pre-closing statement*, like "yeah" or "okay," to signal a readiness to close the conversation. If Charlotte has another topic to bring up, she can do that in response. If not, she can accept the statement with "yeah" or "okay," which opens up the closing section. A pre-closing statement and its response constitute a pre-sequence: They project the closing of the conversation.

Consider the end of a conversation between a mother and a daughter, June and Daphie (7.3h.1012):

June:	yes	
Daphie:	thanks very much	
June:	**OK?**	[*apparent* pre-closing statement]
Daphie:	**right**, *I'll see you this*	[response]
June:	*because* there how did you did you beat him?	[initiation of new topic]
Daphie:	no, he beat me, four one (. laughs)	
June:	four one .	
Daphie:	yes, . I was doing quite well in one game, and then then I I- I lost	
June:	oh, how disgusting	
Daphie:	yes .	
June:	**OK**, . *right*	[pre-closing statement]
Daphie:	*right*	[response]
June:	see you tonight	[proposal for future]
Daphie:	right,	[uptake]
	bye	[terminal exchange]
June:	bye love	[terminal exchange]
Both:	(hang up telephones)	[contact termination]

In the first two turns, June and Daphie complete a topic (not shown here), potentially their last topic. In the third turn, June seems to offer a pre-closing statement ("OK?"), which Daphie accepts ("right") in order to begin the closing section ("I'll see you this evening"). But June then raises another topic – Daphie's squash game – and that takes precedence. Once this topic has run its course, June offers a second pre-closing statement ("OK . right"), which Daphie accepts ("right"), and the two of them enter the closing section proper.

Once the last topic is closed, the participants still have to prepare for their exit. If they are acquaintances, they may reassure each other that the upcoming break isn't permanent, that they will resume contact in the future (Goffman, 1971). Here are five minor projects people often accomplish in taking leave, and in this order (Albert and Kessler, 1976, 1978):

1.   Summarize the content of the conversation just completed
2.   Justify ending contact at this time
3.   Express pleasure about each other
4.   Indicate continuity of their relationship by planning for future contact either specifically or vaguely ("see you tonight")
5.   Wish each other well ("bye")

The last two actions often get conventionalized as farewells. Action 4 is expressed in such phrases as *see you, auf Wiedersehen, tot ziens, au revoir,* and *hasta la vista,* and action 5 in *good-bye, good evening, guten Abend, goede dag, bon soir, bon voyage, buenas noches, adios,* and *shalom.* With these actions, the participants reach the mutual belief that they are prepared to exit the conversation.

The final problem is to break contact together. On the telephone, that means hanging up the receivers. If Ben hangs up before Charlotte, or vice versa, that may offend the other, so the two of them try to break simultaneously. They work up to saying "bye" together, at which moment they begin replacing their receivers. If they do this just right, neither of them hears the click of the other's receiver.

If the second section is expressly for leave-taking, then it should be absent when there is no need to reaffirm acquaintance. In routine telephone calls to directory assistance, callers and operators generally exchange "thank you" and "you're welcome" and hang up without an exchange of "goodbye"s. Yet when callers ask operators for less routine information and become even slightly more acquainted, they are more likely to initiate a "goodbye" exchange (Clark and French, 1981). And two friends breaking contact only briefly won't need "goodbye"s either. The "goodbye" exchange is for exiting from the optional process of leave-taking, not from the conversation per se.

What does and doesn't get included in closing sections, therefore, hangs on the joint actions needed for the participants to close the final topic, prepare to break contact, and then break contact. Each joint action emerges with a characteristic entry–body–exit structure.

Organization in conversation

Conversations often seem organized around a set plan, but that is an illusion. This organization is really an emergent property of what the participants are trying to do. When Ben talks to Charlotte, he has goals, some well defined and some vague, and so does she. Most of Ben's goals, however, require her cooperation. She has the power to complete, alter, decline, or withdraw from any joint project he proposes, and she can propose joint projects of her own. The broadest projects they agree on emerge as sections, and the narrower ones, as subsections or digressions. The organization of their conversation emerges from joint actions locally planned and opportunistically carried out.

One source for this illusion is the transcripts from which we ordinarily infer the organization of conversations. The problem is that transcripts are like footprints in the sand. They are merely the inert traces of the activities that produced them, and impoverished traces at that. The structure we find in a transcript only hints at how a conversation emerged.

ORGANIZATION OF ACTIONS

Most intentional actions, indeed, look organized. If we watch Ben bake a cake and record what he does, we might create a sequence of statements like these: "Ben gets out a mixing bowl"; "Ben measures two cups of flour"; "Ben puts flour into the mixing bowl"; "Ben answers the telephone." Each of these describes a small completed task – Ben wants a mixing bowl and gets one – and these are parts of larger tasks:

Task 1. Ben bakes a cake
  Subtask 1.1. Ben mixes ingredients
    Subtask 1.1.1. Ben gets out mixing bowl
    Subtask 1.1.2. Ben measures out flour
    Subtask 1.1.3. Ben puts flour into mixing bowl
    ...

Subtask 1.1.20. Ben pours mixture into baking pan

Subtask 1.2. Ben bakes mixture
Subtask 1.2.1. Ben sets temperature on oven
Subtask 1.2.2. Ben opens oven
...

Subtask 1.3. Ben frosts cake
Subtask 1.3.1. Ben gets out icing sugar
...

Ben, we infer, began with the project of baking a cake, and that entailed certain subtasks, which themselves entailed other subtasks and so on.

This trace, however, hides the local and opportunistic nature of these tasks and subtasks. What led to the action "Ben gets out a mixing bowl"? Ben needed something to prepare the ingredients in, so he projected a goal – getting a mixing bowl. How could he reach that goal? Knowing there is usually a bowl in the cupboard, he looked there, found it, and got it out. If it hadn't been there, he would have considered alternative methods and chosen the most opportune one. He might have looked for a bowl in the dishwasher, borrowed a bowl from his next door neighbor, or got out a saucepan instead. For all we know, Ben went to the cupboard only after failing to see a bowl on the counter. The trace tells us nothing about the choices he did *not* make – the *opportunities he did not take*. On the contrary, it lulls us into assuming that Ben's choices were there from the start.

What the trace does represent are the opportunities Ben *did* take, and these bear several relations to one another. Three of the commonest relations between two tasks *s* and *t* are these:

	Relation of *t* to *s*	Condition on *s*
Sequence	*t* is subsequent to *s*	*s* must be complete before *t* is begun
Part–whole	*t* is part of *s*	*t* must be complete for *s* to be complete
Digression	*t* is a digression from *s*	*s* need not be complete before *t* is begun or completed

In our example, baking the mixture is *subsequent to* mixing the ingredients, and measuring flour is subsequent to getting out a mixing bowl. In contrast, putting flour into the mixing bowl is *part of* mixing the ingredients, and setting the oven temperature is part of baking the mixture. Answering the telephone is a *digression from* making the cake, mixing the ingredients, and putting flour into the bowl. Each of these relations is subject to certain conditions. For sequence, Ben must have completed mixing the ingredients before baking the mixture. For part–whole, he must have completed measuring out flour in order to have completed mixing the ingredients. But for digression, Ben need not have completed putting flour into the bowl in order to answer the telephone – though he will probably complete the call before returning to making the cake.

The identical relations appear in *joint* actions. Anna is in the middle of Frankfurt trying to find Goethe House, a well known landmark, and asks a passerby, Bernd, for directions. Here is what they say, in English translation (Klein, 1982, p 171):

Anna: Excuse me, could you tell me how to get to Goethe House?
Bernd: (3.0) Goethe House?
Anna: Yes.
Bernd: Yes, go up that way, always straight ahead, first street to the left, first street to the right.
Anna: First left, first right.
Bernd: Yes.
Anna: Thank you.

The task structure of this conversation is something like this:

Project 1. A and B converse
   Subproject 1.1. A and B enter conversation
      Subproject 1.1.1. A and B agree to open conversation
   Subproject 1.2. A and B carry out business of conversation
      Subproject 1.2.1. A and B exchange route directions
         Subtask 1.2.1.1. A proposes that B give A route directions
         Subtask 1.2.1.2. B gives A route directions
      Subproject 1.2.2. A and B exchange thanks
         Subtask 1.2.2.1. A proposes to thank B
         Subtask 1.2.2.2. B acknowledges A's thanks
   Subproject 1.3. A and B exit from conversation
      Subproject 1.3.1. A and B break contact

Here, too, we find the relations of sequence and part–whole. The exchange of thanks, for example, is subsequent to the exchange of route directions. And these are each part of the joint action of carrying out the business of the conversation. At an even lower level, the confirmation of understanding ("Goethe House?" "Yes") is part of Anna's contribution of asking Bernd how to get to Goethe House. (There are no digressions in this conversation.) So Anna and Bernd carry out many joint actions, all bearing the relation of either sequence or part–whole.

What is the status of this structure? In the goals-and-plans view, it would reflect a plan Anna and Bernd adhere to in order to reach their goals, much as the syntax of a sentence is a structure that speakers try to adhere to in performing an illocutionary act. In the opportunistic view, the structure emerges only as Anna and Bernd do what they need to do in order to deal with the joint projects that get proposed in the conversation. It is a trace of the opportunities taken, not of the opportunities considered.

Like all conversations, Anna and Bernd's dialogue has an entry, body, and exit. Its entry is initiated by Anna when she says "Excuse me," makes eye contact, and establishes that Bernd is willing to talk to her. Its body consists of one main joint project: Anna proposes that Bernd tell her how to get to Goethe House, and he takes her up. Although she tries to make her proposal with "Could you tell me how to get to Goethe House?" it takes her and Bernd two more turns to ground it. Once it is grounded, Bernd commits himself to the joint project and gives Anna the directions; and the two of them take the next two turns to ground those directions. Finally, Anna thanks Bernd for the information, and they exit from the conversation by breaking contact.

As this conversation unfolded, it could have taken very different directions depending on what Bernd did. Here are two alternatives: (1) Bernd could have ignored Anna's "Excuse me," refusing to make eye contact, and they wouldn't even have entered a conversation. (2) Or Bernd could have entered the conversation but declined Anna's proposal because he didn't know where Goethe House was, as in this second conversation initiated by Anna (accompanied by a friend) (Klein, p. 180):

Anna: Could you tell us how to get to Goethe House?
Carl: Goethe House? No address?
Anna: No, it was Great Hirschgraben, I think.
Carl: Sorry?
Anna: Great Hirschgraben, the street. (5.0) You don't know. We'll ask someone else.

Even though Carl offers no directions, there is still an opening, a joint project proposed and considered, and a closing.

In this view, Anna's and Bernd's conversation is structured by their *attempted* joint projects and actions. Project 1 ("A and B converse") is the total conversation. Subprojects 1.1, 1.2, and 1.3 (the entry, body, and exit) are joint projects that are required of any conversation. Subprojects 1.2.1 and 1.2.2 (the exchange of route directions and the exchange of thanks) are two joint projects that are parts of Subproject 1.2. And so on. Although the task structure is hierarchical and may look as if it had been there all along, it emerges only utterance by utterance as Anna and Bernd complete one contribution after another, proposing and taking up one joint project after another.

Route directions aren't special. All conversations have entries, bodies, and exits, which account for some features of route directions. All contributions require grounding, which sets other features. All successful joint projects get proposed and taken up, which leads to still other features. Most of these features are mutable because they depend on the joint commitment and actions of the participants. Conversations take the course they do, not because they follow a prescribed scheme, but because they follow general principles of joint action.

TOPICS OF DISCOURSE

Conversations are often assumed to divide into topics. The topic, or *discourse topic*, of any section or subsection is what that section is about. The idea is that after two people open a conversation, the one who initiated it introduces the first topic. Once they have completed the first topic, they may take up new topics recursively until they decide to close the conversation. Discourse topics, in turn, are often assumed to be related to what each utterance is about – its *sentence topic*.[3]

The notion of topic is notoriously vague, with little consensus on how it is to be defined and applied. In classical rhetoric, it describes the subjects or themes of essays and speeches, and there the notion has a rationale. Essays and speeches consist mostly of assertions organized into arguments that are designed to persuade, so "what the discourse is about" is really "what the writer or speaker is talking about," which is readily identifiable for each argument. And because essayists and orators work alone, editing and practicing what they write and say, they can make their subjects and themes as clear, complete, and consistent as they want. Essays and speeches can be divided into topics, then, because they are (1) highly planned, (2) under unilateral control, and (3) comprised mostly of assertions.

Conversations, in contrast, are (1) opportunistic, (2) under joint control, and (3) comprised of much more than assertions. Here "what the

---

[3] For a review of the notion of discourse topic, see Brown and Yule (1983). For sentence topic, see Reinhart (1981).

speaker is talking about" has to be changed to "what the *participants* are talking about," a more slippery notion. Such a topic is negotiated by all the participants, and often gets altered in each new contribution. If asked, the participants may even disagree on what they take it to be. The greatest problem comes with nonassertions. What are Ben and Charlotte talking about in a request and compliance: "Please sit down" "Okay"? Or in an offer and acceptance: "Have some cake" "Thanks, I will"? Or in an exchange of gratitude: "Thanks" "Don't mention it"? Or in greetings: "Hi" "Hi"? The notion "what the participants are talking about" may apply to assertions or unilaterally designed sections with an assertive force. It doesn't apply to other joint projects.

The more basic notion, I suggest, is joint project. Suppose we take the topic of Anna's and Bernd's conversation to be Goethe House, the route to Goethe House, or even getting to Goethe House. Such a topic doesn't help us account for what Anna and Bernd actually said, or why they chose the subtopics they did. It doesn't tell us, for example, why Anna asked "Could you tell me how to get to Goethe House" and Bernd answered "Go up that way," etc. In contrast, if we describe the emergent joint project as "A and B exchanging route directions," we see how it got initiated with Anna's request and taken up with Bernd's response. Discourse topic is a static notion that doesn't do justice to the dynamic course of joint actions and what develops out of them.

Treating discourse topics this way isn't really new. According to proposals by Barbara Grosz (1981) and Rachel Reichman (1978), conversational sections are a direct reflection of the pieces of the task the participants are trying to carry out. Grosz called these pieces *focus spaces*, and Reichman, *context spaces*. Both are organized by the relations of sequence, part–whole, and digression. The notion of joint project covers many aspects of both notions.

DISCOURSE TRANSITIONS

Extended joint projects (like exchanging route directions) have a complication that extended autonomous projects (like baking a cake) do not – the coordination of entry into, and exit from, their parts. Recall that for many joint actions, exits from one are coordinated by entry into the next (Chapter 3), and that holds for extended joint projects.

Transitions from one extended joint project, s, to the next, t – traditionally called *topic shifts* – depend on the relation between s and t. With the three relations, we can distinguish five types of transitions:

	Description	Relation of t to s
Next	Enter next project	t is subsequent to s
Push	Enter subproject	t is part of s
Pop	Return from subproject	s is part of t
Digress	Enter digression	t is a digression from s
Return	Return from digression	s is a digression from t

There is a range of devices for accomplishing these transitions, and we have already seen some of them. Here are two major types.

Adjacency pairs. One standard way to enter an extended joint project (Chapter 7) is to initiate a minimal joint project – to produce the first part of an adjacency pair. One might make an assertion ("oh it's Professor Worth's secretary, from Pan-American College"), ask a question ("is Miss Pink in?"), or offer thanks ("thank you very much indeed"). The type of transition it brings about depends on its relation to the previous utterance. For examples of next, push, and pop, consider this exchange at a notions counter (Merritt, 1984, p. 140):

C: Hi, do you have uh size C flashlight batteries?
S: [**Next**] Yes sir.
C: [**Next**] I'll have four please.
S: [**Push**] Do you want the long life or the regular?
      [**Push**] See the long life doesn't last ten times longer than the regular battery.
      [**Next**] Usually last three times as long.
      [**Next**] Cheaper in the long run.
      [**Next**] These're eight-eight.
      [**Next**] These're thirty-five each.
C: [**Pop**] Guess I better settle for the short life.
S: [**Next**] How many you want?
C: [**Next**] Four please.
S: [**Pop**] Okay (picks four and puts on counter).
   [**Next**] That's a dollar forty and nine tax, a dollar forty-nine.

With "Do you have uh size C flashlight batteries?" the customer C initiates the joint project of exchanging information. The expectable next turn is an answer, so with "yes sir," the server S proceeds to the next project. With "I'll have four please," C initiates an exchange of goods, another next. But as part of that exchange, S needs more information. She initiates one subproject with "Do you want the long life or the regular?" (a push) and then a second with "How many you want?" (a next) before returning to the main project with "Okay" (a pop).

Digressions are a bit like subprojects in their entries and exits, as illustrated here (1.4.121):

Adam:	and uh so they're probably their own pictures, aren't they
Brian:	m - -
Adam:	well, I don't know -
Brian:	[**Digress**] is there any milk? - .
Adam:	yeah there's this this uh powdered milk
Brian:	ah yes, - what does that do in tea, does that dissolve in tea
Adam:	I've only just discovered that, uh a week ago
Brian:	we used to have that in the war,
Adam:	I had it in coffee, . *earlier*,
Brian:	*m*
Adam:	the thing is, that it's quite handy, if you run out of *milk*
Brian:	*quite,* yeah, will it ** melt** in tea though .
Adam:	**it keeps**
Adam:	j- I suppose so - - it's dehydrated milk .
Brian:	m - - - to make a pint it says
Adam:	[**Return**] actually, he caught me, on the hop, because uh when you rang up, unfortunately, I was speaking to the bee-est gasbag I've met for years

Adam and Brian are fixing tea as they talk, and Brian initiates a digression by asking "Is there any milk?" Adam eventually initiates a return by resuming their previous discussion.

Broader joint projects, as we saw before, are often entered with adjacency pairs called pre-sequences. Here are examples cited in Chapter 7:

Pre-sequence	Example
Pre-question	Oh there's one thing I wanted to ask you.
Pre-announcement	Tell you who I met yesterday -
Pre-invitation	What are you doin'?
Pre-request	Do you have hot chocolate?
Summons	Hey, Molly
Telephone summons	(rings telephone)
Pre-closing statement	Well okay
Pre-narrative	I acquired an absolutely magnificent sewing-machine, by foul means, did I tell you about that?

Each pre-sequence specifies the entry time and content of the larger joint project. Respondents can commit to both by taking up the pre-sequence as in:

A: Guess what?
B: What?

Or they can decline ("Sorry, I've got to run") or withdraw altogether, refusing to commit themselves.

Discourse markers. Another device for marking transition points is what have been called *discourse markers*.[4] Here is an example (1.6.387):

A: I mean the fact that you you - study a thing, doesn't mean to say, you can't also feel it, does it .
B: m .
A: **[Pop] but, anyway,** this is his line, and he's sticking to it, at the moment, till he changes next year.

In A's second turn, he uses the discourse marker "but anyway" to signal a pop from a subproject. It is the preface to the minimal joint project that constitutes the actual return, and tells B explicitly how the project is to be construed.

Different transitions are marked in different ways. Here are a few discourse markers that have been noted (see Reichman, 1978; Schiffrin, 1987).

Transition	Description	Examples
Next	Enter next project	and, but, so, now, then; speaking of that, that reminds me, one more thing, before I forget
Push	Enter subproject	now, like
Pop	Return from subproject	anyway, but anyway, so, as I was saying
Digress	Enter digression	incidentally, by the way
Return	Return from digression	anyway, what were we saying

Which marker gets used depends on the joint project being proposed. For example, *and* can mark a next proposal as a continuation of the current extended project, whereas *but* marks the next proposal as a contrasting project. And *now* is often used to mark next subprojects of a main project. In essays and formal speeches, we find such discourse markers as *let me begin by saying, first, for example, then, thus, finally,* and *in conclusion.*

Returns from subprojects and digressions reveal an important property of unfinished business. When the participants return to a project

---

[4] See Schiffrin (1987). Other terms that have a similar meaning are *disjunct markers* (Jefferson, 1978), *discourse operators* (Polanyi, 1985; Redeker, 1986, 1990), *clue words* (Reichman, 1978), *cue words* (Grosz and Sidner, 1986), *cue phrases* (Hirschberg and Litman, 1987), and *discourse particles* (Schourup, 1982).

they have yet to complete, they also reinstate their attention to the common ground required by that project. That often allows them to continue the earlier project as if they had never left it. The point is nicely illustrated in the digression about milk. Before the digression, Adam and Brian had been talking about a man named Tim. After the digression, Adam continued to refer to Tim with the pronoun *he* ("actually, he caught me on the hop"), even though the digression had been ten turns long. Adam treated Tim as if he was still in their focus of attention (see Grosz, 1981; Reichman, 1978). Joint projects that have been left incomplete can often be reinstated with a minimum of effort.

Stories in conversation

When people tell stories – jokes, personal anecdotes, narratives – in conversation, they talk for extended periods of time. It is tempting to treat these stories as autonomous performances. When I tell friends a joke, I do all the telling, and it looks as if I am working on my own. On closer examination, I am not. These stories are part and parcel of the conversation, with the audience participating as much as the narrators. They are extended joint projects that require coordination and joint commitment. If so, they should have an entry, a body, and an exit, and as Harvey Sacks (1974) argued, they do:

Entry. The preface
Body. The telling
Exit. The response sequence

This structure emerges for most types of stories told in conversation.

ENTRY

Most stories in conversation are "locally occasioned," as Jefferson (1978) put it. An issue reminds people of a story, so they methodically introduce it into the talk the way they would introduce any extended joint project. In some conversations, stories are told for entertainment as ends in themselves, either in rounds or in a series by one storyteller, and these have slightly different entries and exits (Kirshenblatt-Gimblett, 1974). All stories take time and effort, so the participants must be convinced that a proposed story is worth their time and effort or they won't make room for it. It is just this work that gets accomplished in the preface.

Stories need justification. People must agree that: (1) they want *this particular person* to tell a story; (2) they want *this particular story*; and (3) they want it told *now*. One way to establish these conditions is for a member of the prospective audience to ask for a particular story now, as here (1.3.215):

Kate: **how did you get on at your interview, . do tell us**
Nancy: . oh - - God, what an experience, - - I don't know where to start, you
         know, it was just such a nightmare - - [proceeds on long narrative]

Kate proposes a particular joint project – that Nancy tell them now how she got on at her interview – which Nancy takes up with a thirty-minute narrative. Questions and answers are a standard way of establishing joint commitments, and they are useful in making room for stories.

If the participants don't realize that someone has a particular story to tell now, it is up to prospective narrators to broach the possibility, and an effective way to do that is with pre-sequences. With these, they offer to tell a particular story now and justify the time and effort everyone will spend on it. In some pre-sequences, the potential narrator makes an offer while taking the justification for granted, as Sam does here in a conversation with Reynard (1.1.446):

Sam: **let me tell you a story - - -**
Sam: a girl went into a chemist's shop and asked for . contraceptive tablets - -
       [proceeds on a three-minute joke]

Sam offers to tell Reynard the story, gives Reynard time to accept or reject (in the pause after *story*), then goes ahead. The cardinal rule for telling stories is that one shouldn't knowingly tell people a story they've heard before. So in many pre-sequences, potential narrators preview their story and ask whether the listeners have heard it before, as Nancy does for this anecdote (1.3.96):

Nancy: I acquired an absolutely magnificent sewing-machine, by foul means,
        did I tell you about that
Kate: **no**
Nancy: well when I was . doing freelance advertising - [proceeds to give a
        five-minute narrative]

Conversational partners can of course decline a story, as here (2.14.600):

Connie: **did I tell you,** when we were in this African village, and *- they were
         all out in the fields, - the*
Irene: *yes you did, yes, - yes*
Connie: babies left alone, -
Irene: yes .

Connie aborts her story once she has described enough of it that Irene can say "yes" in a strategic interruption.

With jokes, the preface takes the same shape, but in this example, it became more elaborate (Sacks, 1974, simplified):

Ken: You wanna hear- My sister told me a story last night.
Roger: I don't wanna hear it. But if you must. (0.7)
Al: What's purple and an island. Grape, Britain. That's what his sister told him.
Ken: No. To stun me she says uh, (0.8) there was these three girls and they just got married?

In his first turn, Ken offers to tell a joke and justifies it by suggesting it is new – he has just heard it from his sister. Roger first feigns rejection and then accepts the offer, but Al suggests that the story will be immature – after all, Ken's sister is only twelve. So Ken feels obliged to justify it further ("to stun me") and describe it briefly ("there was these three girls and they just got married?"). By using a rising intonation, he is still requesting permission to proceed. Roger and Al finally agree, and he tells the joke. The preface, as Sacks analyzed it, is a textbook example of a coordinated entry into a joint project.

Stories may also be introduced as a part of a joint project already in play, as here (Jefferson, 1978, p. 224, simplified):

Ken: He was terrific the whole time we were there.
Louise: I know what you mean. When they- my sister and her boyfriend [continues anecdote]

Louise justifies her anecdote as a continuation of Ken's claim ("He was terrific the whole time we were there") and starts right in on it. There is a similar justification in this entry (Jefferson, 1978, pp. 224-225, simplified):

Fran: I feel sorriest for Warren - how he sits there an' listens to it I don' know? But, um.
Holly: Well he must've known what she was like before he married her.
Fran: I guess. And -
Holly: He can be a bastard too, he uh one- one day we [continues anecdote]

Holly introduces an anecdote to illustrate her claim that Warren too can be a bastard, and that appears to be justification enough. Stories can be introduced even more simply with discourse markers like "speaking of that" – even as digressions with "incidentally" or "that reminds me." The story, whatever its relation to the current discourse, requires an entry coordinated by all the participants.

TELLING

The telling proper may appear autonomous, but it is far from that. Narrators still coordinate with their audience at the levels of execution and attention, presentation and identification, and meaning and understanding (Chapters 5, 7, 8, 9). Although the entry gives narrators the opportunity to tell their story, they still need evidence of attention, identification, and understanding. Throughout Nancy's narrative about the sewing-machine, Kate provided just that evidence, with acknowledgments like *m*, laughs, and, presumably, eye contact and head nods. The mere possibility that narrators can be interrupted for clarification makes their telling collaborative.

Sometimes, the course of a story is explicitly shaped by both narrator and audience. Narrators look for interests in their audience in deciding which direction to go, as Margaret does here in a narrative about fainting on the subway (Polanyi, 1989, p. 95, simplified):

Margaret: I'm very scared of fainting again - um - I don't know if you've ever
Peter: um
Margaret: experienced -
Peter: I haven't
Margaret: There is *no* experience in the *world* [continues narrative]

Margaret might have gone another direction if Peter's answer had been different. Later, Peter adds a comment that explicitly prompts her to change direction:

Margaret: And it's just dehumanizing.
Peter: But people were pretty nice, hm?
Margaret: People - are - always nice when there's a crisis like that [continues]

Interlocutors aren't passive receptacles, even during the telling of a story. Their participation may add details, heighten the drama, or change the direction, making the stories more effective.

Some stories are narrated by two people together.[5] Here is part of an anecdote told by Nancy and Susan to Livia and Bill about being robbed (Polanyi, 1989, p. 68, simplified):

---

[5] Falk (1979) called this dueting.

Susan: I didn't hear the guy in the car talking. Right?
Nancy: But he was shouting out things the whole time and I couldn't under-
           stand a word
Bill: He stayed in the car or whatever and
Susan: Yeah, he was in the driver's seat
Nancy: He was driving the car and and [continues]

As Nancy and Susan proceed, they correct, elaborate on, or continue what the other has just said. They coordinate all this with evidence of understanding from their audience, as when Bill says "He stayed in the car or whatever and."

The story proper tends to be opened and closed in characteristic ways. It may be marked with a distinctive formula, such as "Once upon a time," which varies depending on whether the story is a parable, joke, legend, or whatever (Kirshenblatt-Gimblett, 1974). It may begin simply with a setting, as in Sacks' joke, "There were these three girls. And they were all sisters. And they had just got married to three brothers." Exits are usually distinctive too. The punch line of a joke tells the audience when the joke proper has ended and the response should begin.

RESPONSE SEQUENCE

When narrators tell a story, they are proposing a joint project for their audience to take up: a joke to laugh at, an anecdote to appreciate for the point it makes, a narrative to appreciate for its drama, relevance, or moral. So once a story is complete, the audience is expected to take it up, alter it, decline it, or even withdraw. The initial uptake may be simple, as in Reynard's remark after the punch line to Sam's joke (1.1.517):

Reynard: Sam . you're a wicked fellow - that's very nice

Or as with Nancy's sewing-machine anecdote (1.3.196):

Nancy: so I've got this fabulous machine
Kate: *oh*
Nigel: *how nice*
Nancy: *which I -* in fact and in order to use it I have to read my *instruction
           booklet cos it's so complicated*
Kate: *(laughs)* - marvelous

For jokes, the expected uptake is laughter, but, as Sacks (1974) noted, achieving laughter isn't simple. The place to laugh is immediately after the punch line, but there are opposing forces at work here. If the audience delays too long, they may be seen as slow-witted – the joke being a type of understanding test. But if they laugh too quickly, without understanding, and the joke isn't funny, they may suffer loss of face. The audience must attend not only to the joke, but to each other's laughter, a rather unexpected problem of coordination. They can also, of course, decline to laugh, objecting they don't get it, it is sexist, or it isn't funny. The audience to a political speech must also attend not just to the speech, but to each other to decide when and how long to applaud (Atkinson, 1984; Heritage and Greatbatch, 1986).

With the response sequence, the participants must initiate new activities as they reenter their turn-by-turn conversation. The story itself is often the source of new topics – new joint projects (Jefferson, 1978). Sam used his joke as a springboard for telling another joke about contraception. Nancy used her anecdote as a justification for talking about wanting a special room for her sewing-machine. Al and Roger used Ken's joke as a reason for talking about Ken's sister and her maturity. If the conversation is to continue, the exit from one joint project must lead to the entry into a next one. The participants accomplish that just as they would any transition: They initiate new joint projects.

Conclusions

Conversations aren't planned as such. They emerge from the participants' attempts to do what they want to do. When Ben strikes up a conversation with Charlotte, he will have things he wants to accomplish – certain joint projects. But each of these projects takes a joint commitment, and Ben can never take Charlotte's commitment for granted. He can propose a project, but it requires her uptake to complete it, and she can alter it into a quite different project, decline to take it up, or withdraw from it altogether. She can also propose joint projects of her own. The result is often a conversation that looks orderly even though each step of the way was achieved locally and opportunistically.

Much of the structure of conversations is really an emergent orderliness. Although the participants appear to follow rules in turn taking, they are merely trying to succeed in contributing to the conversation. Other phenomena emerge as the participants enter, complete, and exit from the joint projects that get proposed, taken up, or abandoned. These include the opening, closing, and other sections of conversations, and the hierarchical organization of their subsections. They also include stories. Although jokes, anecdotes, and other narratives may seem special, they are still joint projects that are proposed and taken up.

12 | Layering

People sometimes appear to say one thing when they are actually doing something quite different. Take this exchange between a husband and wife about his tutoring sessions (4.1.129):

Ken: and I'm cheap, - - -
Margaret: **I've always felt that about you, .**
Ken: oh shut up,
          (- - laughs) fifteen bob a lesson at home, -

When Margaret says "I've always felt that about you," she isn't really, actually, or literally asserting that she always felt Ken was cheap, a *serious* use of her utterance. She is only acting *as if* she were making that assertion in order to tease him, a so-called *nonserious* use of her utterance (Austin, 1962).[1] Nonserious language is the stuff of novels, plays, movies, stories, and jokes, as well as teasing, irony, sarcasm, overstatement, and understatement. Life is hard to imagine without it, yet it has been slighted in most theories of language use.

Common to all nonserious actions is a phenomenon I am calling *layering*. When Margaret merely pretends to assert that she always thought Ken was cheap, she is taking actions at two layers. On the surface, she is making the assertion, a nonserious action. Yet beneath the

---

[1] Nonserious language use has been excluded from traditional philosophical, linguistic, and psychological accounts of language. A good example is Austin (1962, p. 22): "Language in such circumstances [e.g., play acting, practice] is in special ways – intelligibly – used not seriously, but in ways *parasitic* upon its normal use...All this we are *excluding* from consideration" (Austin's emphases). The term *nonserious* belies the serious intent behind Margaret's tease, but captures the notion of pretense, so I will retain it.

surface, she is pretending to assert this and, by means of the pretense, teasing him for being so cheap. These are serious actions. All nonserious actions are created in the course of serious actions. But how does Margaret get Ken to see that her assertion isn't serious? How does she manage to tease him about his stinginess? Nonserious language warrants a serious analysis.

Layers of actions

It is San Francisco in 1952, and two ten-year-olds named Alan and Beth are playing a game of make-believe in Alan's back yard. From a book they have read, they decide to be Wild Bill and Calamity Jane, living in Deadwood, Dakota Territory, during the gold rush of 1876. They designate a pile of dirt in the corner of the yard as placer diggings and an old kitchen plate as a gold pan, and they pan for gold. Soon they find a few nuggets (small stones), go off to Saloon Number Ten (the patio), sit down at a poker table (a picnic table), and play a few hands with an invisible deck of cards. After a while Beth is called home, and their game ends.

Alan and Beth's game is an example of layered actions. At *layer 1*, Alan and Beth are playing make-believe in Alan's back yard in San Francisco in 1952. Simultaneously at *layer 2*, they are two people panning for gold and playing poker in Deadwood in 1876. The actions in layer 1 are serious, what Alan and Beth are really, or actually, or seriously doing. The actions in layer 2 are nonserious because Alan and Beth aren't *really* named Wild Bill and Calamity Jane, and they aren't *really* panning for gold or playing poker. The actions in layer 2 are created out of whole cloth as a joint pretense. Metaphorically, the layers look like this (Chapter 1):

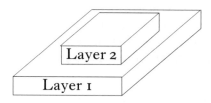

Layer 1 is the base or foundation, and layer 2 is like a theatrical stage created on top of it. More layers can be added recursively.[2]

What are these two layers of actions, and where do they come from? The analysis I offer is derived from three sources, with additions of my own. One is Erving Goffman's frame analysis, itself derived from Gregory Bateson's observations about play in humans and animals (Bateson 1972; Goffman, 1974). Another is Kendall Walton's arguments for make-believe as the basis for fiction (Walton, 1973, 1976, 1978, 1983, 1990).[3] The third is Bertram Bruce's analysis of levels in written fiction and the relation between authors and readers (Bruce, 1981). My analysis is an attempt to capture the spirit of the three sources, although it differs from all three.

DOMAINS OF ACTION

Alan and Beth's game is a game of imagination – becoming Wild Bill and Calamity Jane, panning for gold, playing poker. But Alan and Beth must coordinate their imaginings. If Alan imagined he was a future astronaut on Mars while Beth imagined she was Elizabeth I in sixteenth-century England, that just wouldn't do. Their game is a *joint activity*, and just as they are playing together in San Francisco, they must imagine themselves together in Deadwood.

Alan and Beth's actions take place in two worlds, or *domains of action*. Each domain is characterized by its participants, their roles, the place, the time, the relevant features of the situation, the possible actions, and other such things, as here:

---

[2] Layering is sometimes treated as a form of embedding, with layer 2 embedded within layer 1. In this view, Wild Bill and Calamity Jane's world would be embedded within Alan and Beth's daily activities in San Francisco in 1952. Although this metaphor is useful for some purposes, it can be misleading. To say that one clause (e.g., *that he left*) is embedded within another (e.g., *Veronica said that he left*) is to claim that the first clause is a proper part of the second. But layer 2 is not a proper part of layer 1 in this sense. Wild Bill and Calamity Jane are not part of the 1952 San Francisco scene, nor are any other elements of domain 2. This is just one of the reasons I prefer the metaphor of layering.

[3] See also Searle (1975b).

	Domain 1	Domain 2
Participants	Alan	Wild Bill
	Beth	Calamity Jane
Roles	players at make-believe	partners in placer mining
Place	San Francisco	Deadwood, Dakota Territory
Time	May 1, 1952	around 1876
Features	pile of dirt	pile of gold ore
	plate	gold pan
	patio	Saloon Number Ten
	picnic table	poker table
	etc.	etc.
Actions	sifting dirt on plate	panning for gold
	finding pebble	finding gold nugget
	etc.	etc.

Each domain is in principle a complete world, though only some of its elements are specified. Alan and Beth would assume Calamity Jane had parents even if they had never thought about it.

Actions take place in both domains, often based on the same behavior. Take this exchange:

Beth: Let's play gold rush.
Alan: Okay, Beth, I'll be Wild Bill.
Beth: And I'll be Calamity Jane.

Although Alan and Beth do things to establish domain 2, their actions are in domain 1. Next consider this series of events:

Alan puts dirt on the old plate and swishes it around, revealing a small pebble. He picks it out.
Alan: Look, Calamity Jane, I've found a gold nugget.
Beth: We're rich.

Here, events take place in both domains. Some, indeed, are simply different construals of the same behavior in the two domains, as here:

Domain 1: Alan picks a pebble out of the dirt.
Domain 2: Wild Bill picks a gold nugget out of the placer ore.

In domain 1, Alan's behavior is construed as an action by Alan, and in domain 2, as an action by Wild Bill. Other things have distinct construals in the two domains as well; for example, the plate in domain 1 is a gold pan in domain 2.

Many states and events in domain 2, then, *correspond to* states and events in domain 1. Alan and Beth jointly pretend that "Alan picking a pebble out of the dirt" is to be taken to be "Wild Bill picking a nugget out of the ore." We can think of the interpretation of elements in domain 2 as determined by a tacit *correspondence function* C(2) that maps elements of domain 2 into elements of domain 1 (where "=" means "is to be taken to be"):

C(2). Alan = Wild Bill; Beth = Calamity Jane; here = in and around Deadwood; now = 1876; this dirt = placer ore; pebbles in this dirt = gold nuggets; this action = panning for gold; this action = playing poker; etc.

The idea is that domain 2 depends on domain 1, but not vice versa. Domain 2 is created by Alan and Beth's joint interpretation, as represented by C(2), whereas domain 1 depends directly on what Alan and Beth take to be the case in San Francisco in 1952. It is by picking a pebble out of the dirt that Alan creates the action of Wild Bill picking a nugget out of the ore. The reverse is impossible.

The full correspondence function C(2) doesn't get established in a single stroke, but by coordination over time. Parts are established by explicit agreement. "I'll be Wild Bill, and you be Calamity Jane." "Okay." Other parts are established implicitly. "Look, I've found a gold nugget!" Alan says of the pebble he discovers in the dirt. Other parts are established by unplanned states and events in domain 1. When Beth finds a larger pebble in the dirt, it starts to rain, and a neighbor's dog barks, these events are given natural interpretations in domain 2 – that Beth has a larger nugget, that it is beginning to rain in Deadwood, or that a coyote is yelping. Many other aspects are taken for granted as consistent with everything else they have established. Some aspects may be disputed. Beth: "This nugget is on my claim." Alan: "No, it's on mine." C(2) isn't established all at once, or by a single method, or unambiguously. And like any construal, it takes Alan and Beth's coordination, and that isn't always successful.

Access to domains 1 and 2 is asymmetrical. The participants in 1 have access to elements of 2, but the participants in 2 have no access to the elements of 1. Alan and Beth create Wild Bill, Calamity Jane, and their world by their actions in domain 1. They know all they want to know about domain 2. Wild Bill and Calamity Jane, however, know nothing about Alan and Beth. At least, that is the pretense. Wild Bill, as Wild Bill, couldn't say, "I'm going back to being Alan." A log cabin stipulated to appear in domain 2 cannot cause a corresponding object to appear in domain 1. Interruptions too are asymmetrical. When Alan says, "Beth, your dad is here," Alan and Beth interrupt, or suspend, activities in layer 2 to return to layer 1. The reverse is impossible.

MEANING, IMAGINATION, AND APPRECIATION

Layering is essential to the use and interpretation of utterances. Let us consider two utterances by Alan:

1. Alan: Beth, your dad is here now, so I guess you have to go.
2. Alan: Look here, Calamity Jane, now you and I both have nuggets.

Although Alan uses the deictic terms "I," "you," "here," and "now" in both utterances, in 1 he is referring to Alan, Beth, San Francisco, and 1952, and in 2, he is referring to Wild Bill, Calamity Jane, Deadwood, and 1876. He intends the deictic terms in 1 to be interpreted in domain 1, and those in 2 to be interpreted in domain 2. We can represent the four main deictic elements of each utterance in what I will call a *deictic frame*:[4]

<layer,	I,	you,	here,	now>
<1,	Alan,	Beth,	San Francisco,	1952>
<2,	Wild Bill,	Calamity Jane,	Deadwood,	1876>

Utterances 1 and 2 are to be interpreted with different deictic frames.

Viewed another way, utterance 2 differs from utterance 1 in the speaker whose meaning is being expressed. Recall that speaker's meaning is that which fits Grice's formula "In doing *s*, S means that *p*." In uttering "Beth, your dad is here now," Alan means that Beth's father is there, so 1 represents what Alan means for Beth. In 2, however, if we took Alan literally, we would infer: In uttering "Look here, Calamity Jane, now you and I both have nuggets," Alan means that now he and Beth both have nuggets. But this isn't right. Instead, we must say: In uttering that sentence, Wild Bill means that now he and Calamity Jane both have nuggets. Utterance 2 represents what Wild Bill ("I") means for Calamity Jane ("you"). These examples illustrate an essential principle of layering:

Principle of layered meaning. The speaker who means what is expressed in an utterance, and the addressee for whom it is meant, belong to the highest current layer of action.

If you know the highest current layer of action, you can identify the deictic frame – e.g., the speaker who means what is expressed and his or her

---

[4] For a related notion, see Karl Bühler's (1982) concept of *origo*.

addressee. On the other hand, if you can figure out who means what for whom in an utterance, you can identify the highest current layer of action. The principle works both ways.

The principle of layered meaning is essential for interpreting talk in layered actions. When Alan says, "Look here, Calamity Jane, now you and I both have nuggets," Beth would be mistaken if she thought he, *qua* Alan, meant that he and she, qua Beth, both now have nuggets. Beth tacitly recognizes that Wild Bill means this for Calamity Jane. An over-hearer with no inkling of the joint pretense could get it wrong. Listeners, whoever they are, must distinguish appearance from reality in speaker's meaning, and that requires the principle of layered meaning.

Layers differ in the processes they require of the primary partici-pants. When Alan utters "Look, Calamity Jane, I've found a gold nugget," he is getting Beth to imagine him as Wild Bill taking the next turn in a conversation with Calamity Jane. Yet he also wants her to appreciate why he is getting her to do this. He is advancing their game. He is trying to help them simulate imaginary experiences. That is, we must distinguish between *imagining* actions in layer 2 and *appreciating* actions in layer 1. The principles I propose are these:

Principle of imagination. In layered actions, the primary participants are intended to imagine what is happening in the highest current layer of action.

Principle of appreciation. In layered actions, the primary participants are intended to appreciate the instigator's purposes and techniques in creating the highest current layer of action.

Alan and Beth are to imagine Wild Bill and Calamity Jane's world and, while doing that, appreciate their choices in creating that world.

SUMMARY

Let us gather up the properties of layering to come out of Alan and Beth's game of make-believe. The first properties all deal with the *duality* of lay-ering:

Relation	Layering is an asymmetric relation between joint actions in two domains.
Domains	Each domain is specified, principally, by its participants, roles, time, place, surroundings, and possible events.
Deixis	The joint actions in the two layers have distinct deictic frames.
Simultaneity	The two domains are present, or current, at the same time.
Recursion	Layering is recursive.

The next properties deal with the asymmetry between two adjacent layers, a primary layer 1 (with its primary participants) and a derivative layer 2:

Mapping	The primary participants jointly develop a correspondence function C(2) that maps entities of domain 2 into entities of domain 1.
Perspective	The primary participants may construe any entity (an object, state, or event) one way in domain 1 and, simultaneously, another way in domain 2.
Causality	Many entities in domain 2 are caused by the occurrence of the corresponding entities in domain 1, but not vice versa.
Access	The participants in layer 1 have informational access to entities in domain 2, but not vice versa.
Speaker's meaning	When there are two layers, the speaker who means what is expressed by a signal, and the addressee for whom it is meant, belong to layer 2.
Imagination	When there are two layers, the primary participants are to imagine the actions in layer 2, and appreciate the actions in layer 1.

Since layering is recursive, the primary and secondary domains are numbered 1 and 2, and further recursions have higher numbers. These properties may or may not be necessary to all layering.

In Alan and Beth's game of make-believe, layer 2 was created by joint pretense, but layers can be created in other ways too. Let us represent layers in a shorthand, as illustrated for Alan and Beth's two layers:

Layer 2	Wild Bill and Calamity Jane are doing things in Deadwood in 1876.
Layer 1	Alan and Beth jointly pretend in San Francisco in 1952 that the events in layer 2 are taking place.

The first statement describes the actions in layer 2, and the second describes how these actions are created in layer 1. As we will discover, the verb in layer 1, here *jointly pretend*, can change from one type of layering to the next.

Stories

Layering is a feature of all types of stories – from jokes and anecdotes to novels, plays, and operas. When you tell a friend a joke, for example, you describe an episode that didn't actually happen. You get your friend to join you in imagining the fictional world, the secondary domain, in which the events you describe actually happened. The two of you create that world as a joint pretense. All fiction requires a joint pretense.

STORIES IN CONVERSATION

Let us return to a joke discussed in Chapter 10. Here is Sam's preface, a few lines of Sam's joke, and Reynard's response:

Sam: let me tell you a story, - - -
          $_2$[a girl went into a chemist's shop, and asked for, . contraceptive
          tablets, - -
          so he said $_3$[well I've got . all kinds, and . all prices, what do you
          want,]$_3$
          ...
          $_3$[you may well have a baby,]$_3$ - -]$_2$
Reynard: Sam, . you're a wicked fellow, - that's very nice

With "Let me tell you a story," Sam asks Reynard to join in setting up the pretense that the episode he is about to describe actually happened. He then describes the episode as if it were real, beginning with "A girl went into a chemist's shop..." and ending with "you may well have a baby." Sam and Reynard leave the world of the joke when Reynard shows his appreciation with "Sam, you're a wicked fellow."

Sam's joke has three layers. The beginnings and ends of layers 2 and 3 are marked with numbered brackets such as $_2$[and]$_2$. When Sam says "Let me tell you a story," there is only one layer. But with "A girl went into a chemist's shop," he and Reynard create a second layer:

Layer 2   A reporter is telling a reportee that a girl went into a chemist's shop.
Layer 1   Sam and Reynard jointly pretend that the actions in layer 2 are taking
          place.

The joint pretense is that Sam is a reporter, and Reynard is his reportee, and that the reporter is telling the reportee about an actual happening in the chemist's shop. When the reporter uses direct quotation, "well I've got all kinds and all prices, what do you want," he creates yet another layer (Chapter 6):

Layer 3   The chemist is telling the girl he's got all kinds and all prices.
Layer 2   A reporter is demonstrating for a reportee the events in layer 3.
Layer 1   Sam and Reynard jointly pretend that the actions in layer 2 are taking
          place.

Jokes display all the properties of layering. For "A girl went into a chemist's shop," we can identify two concurrent layers: Sam and Reynard's world (domain 1), and the world of reporter and reportee (domain 2). There is a correspondence function with at least two elements: Sam = reporter, Reynard = reportee. These elements are each viewed under two perspectives: In domain 1, the two men are construed as Sam and Reynard, and in domain 2, as the reporter and reportee. As for causality, it is Sam and Reynard's actions that create layer 2, and while Sam and Reynard (in domain 1) have access to the happenings in domain 2, the reporter and reportee (in domain 2) have no access to the elements of domain 1. And there is recursion when the reporter creates domain 3 by demonstrating what the chemist said.

Sam and Reynard must keep track of this structure to establish who means what in each utterance. Here are the deictic frames, <layer, speaker, addressee, place, time>, for three selected utterances:

Let me tell you a story.	<1, Sam, Reynard, London, 1964>
A girl went into a chemist's shop.	<2, reporter, reportee, Britain, before 1>
I've got all kinds and all prices.	<3, chemist, girl, Britain, before 2>

Reynard must see that with "Let me tell you a story" Sam means something for Reynard, that with "A girl went into a chemist's shop" the reporter means something for the reportee, and that with "I've got all kinds and all prices" the chemist means something for the girl. Reynard can see that only if he and Sam coordinate. Sam does his part by announcing the story ("Let me tell you a story"), marking each quotation (with "he said" or a change in intonation), marking the punch line (with story final intonation), and using other such devices. It is remarkable how smoothly Sam and Reynard move from one layer to the next.

Jokes are only one type of layered story in conversation. There are also new stories, retellings of old stories, parables, and what-if narratives ("What if we do this. We go downtown," etc.) All of these have a layered structure much like Sam's joke.

NOVELS

Stories are the foundation of many genres of literature – novels, short stories, plays, operas, skits, parodies, satires – and layering takes much the same form in these as in conversation. Let us take the classic first line of Herman Melville's novel *Moby Dick*: "Call me Ishmael." With it, Melville invites us to join him in the pretense that the words are those of a man called Ishmael speaking to certain "landsmen" in the early 1800s. It has the deictic frame <2, Ishmael, landsmen, Boston, early 1800s>. We are to form two layers:

Layer 2   Ishmael is asking his landsmen audience to call him Ishmael.
Layer 1   Melville and readers jointly pretend that the events in layer 2 are taking
          place.

We continue to hold this joint pretense as Ishmael tells about Captain
Ahab and his obsession with a great white whale. Later, when Ishmael
quotes Queequeg "Who-e debel you?" we create still another layer:

Layer 3   Queequeg is asking Ishmael who he is.
Layer 2   Ishmael is demonstrating to his audience the event in layer 3.
Layer 1   Melville and readers jointly pretend that the events in layer 2 are taking
          place.

Novels differ from conversational stories in several ways. Readers are
normally far removed from authors in both space and time, and that has
consequences. Writing in the 1850s, Melville made certain assumptions
about his readers' knowledge and attitudes that are no longer true. And
when we set up layer 2 as a joint pretense, we do so not because of an
announcement like Sam's "Let me tell you a story," but because we know
the literary conventions for novels. (We might have come to the same
recognition on evidence internal to the book.) And in novels, we rarely
see utterances at layer 1. The only one in *Moby Dick* is Melville's dedica-
tion: "In token of my admiration for his genius this book is dedicated to
Nathaniel Hawthorne," which has the deictic frame <1, Melville, readers, Pittsfield Massachusetts, 1851>.

According to some literary theorists (e.g., Booth, 1983; Chatman,
1978), the actual author must also be distinguished from the implied
author.[5] Melville, for example, may have intended to look like an ordinary adventure story writer, whereas his real motives were very
different. If so, Moby Dick has three layers:

Layer 3   Ishmael is telling certain landsmen an autobiographical story.
Layer 2   The implied Melville and his implied readers jointly pretend that the
          events in layer 3 are taking place.
Layer 1   The actual Melville and his actual readers jointly pretend that the
          events in layer 2 are taking place.

For many novels, the added layer 2 is crucial for understanding the
author's tone, irony, symbolism, and other rhetorical effects.

[5] Booth (1961, p. 70): "As he writes, [the actual author] creates not simply an ideal,
  impersonal 'man in general' but an implied version of 'himself' that is different from
  the implied authors we meet in other men's works."

Novelists sometimes take pleasure in piling one layer upon another, yet we take them in stride. In Henry James' *The Turn of the Screw*, the first narrator quotes a story told to him by Douglas, who quotes a story told to him by a governess, who in turn quotes a child named Miles as saying "I took it." At that point, the novella has six layers:

Layer 6 Miles is telling the governess that he took a letter.
Layer 5 Governess is demonstrating for Douglas the events in layer 6.
Layer 4 Douglas is demonstrating for narrator the events in layer 5.
Layer 3 Narrator is demonstrating for fireside audience the events in layer 4.
Layer 2 Implied James and implied readers jointly pretend that the events in layer 3 are taking place.
Layer 1 Actual James and actual readers jointly pretend that the events in layer 2 are taking place.

There is similar multiple recursion in Washington Irving's *Rip Van Winkle* and many other literary works (Bruce, 1981).

Not only do novels create layer upon layer of actions, but these layers can be placed on further layers. Suppose that in 1921 in Edinburgh a schoolmaster begins reading *Moby Dick* aloud to his pupils and says "Call me Ishmael." For this utterance, we need to add a third layer to our original two layers (ignoring the distinction between actual and implied author):

Layer 3 Ishmael is asking his landsmen addressees to call him Ishmael.
Layer 2 Melville and his readers jointly pretend that the events in layer 3 are taking place.
Layer 1 Schoolmaster delivers to his pupils the wording of layer 2.

The schoolmaster's pupils must be alert to all three layers. They would be mistaken if they thought either Melville or the schoolmaster wanted to be called Ishmael. Layers are not a fancy bit of analysis. They are essential to interpreting the actions taking place.

DRAMAS

Plays, movies, operas, and television sitcoms have added complications. Suppose we read Samuel Beckett's play *Waiting for Godot*. It begins with a faceless, fictional narrator describing the scene: "Estragon, sitting on a low mound, is trying to take off his boot." Soon the narrator quotes Estragon, "Nothing to be done." In this utterance, we have three layers (again collapsing the two layers of authors):

Layer 3 Estragon is telling Vladimir there's nothing to be done.
Layer 2 Narrator is demonstrating for readers the event in layer 3.

Layer 1   Beckett and we readers jointly pretend that the events in layer 2 are taking place.

We read the play much as we read a novel, and the layers for Estragon's comment are much like those for Queequeg's question.

Something quite different happens when we see *Waiting for Godot* in a theater. Suppose we go to its premier English performance by the Arts Theatre Company, with Estragon and Vladimir played by Woodthorpe and Daneman.[6] Layer 1 now has us and the theater company as direct participants. As Jorge Luis Borges noted in an essay on Shakespeare, the actor "on a stage plays at being another before a gathering of people who play at taking him for that other person." But when Woodthorpe delivers the line "Nothing to be done," he and we don't accomplish that joint pretense alone. We are helped by the company and all of its theatrical tricks, from the direction to the scenery. Also, we are no longer aware of Beckett's narrator, although we do keep track of Beckett the playwright. One plausible analysis for "Nothing to be done" goes like this:

Layer 3   Estragon is telling Vladimir there's nothing to be done.
Layer 2   Beckett, actors, theater company, and theatergoers jointly pretend that the events in layer 3 are taking place.
Layer 1   Woodthorpe, theater company, and theatergoers jointly realize layer 2.

"Nothing to be done" represents what Estragon means for Vladimir, not what Woodthorpe means for Daneman or what Beckett means for the theatergoers. Estragon's action has been determined by both Beckett's script and Woodthorpe's realization of it. And we assume Beckett had some purpose in including the action at this point in the play, a purpose we are to appreciate, however dimly. We would have made very different assumptions if we thought the actors were improvising their lines.

Layering takes analogous forms in movies, television sitcoms, soap operas, radio plays, and even songs. In Franz Schubert's song "The Erlking" ("Erlkönig"), the baritone tells a story (by Goethe) with musical accompaniment (by Schubert). At layer 1, the baritone enacts for us layer 2, in which he and Schubert realize for us layer 3, in which we and Goethe jointly pretend that at layer 4 a narrator is telling an audience a true story about an elf king. Schubert's music deepens the emotions of the story. Just as "The Erlking" is like a narrated story, Mozart's opera

---

[6] The first production was held in the Arts Theatre in London in 1955 with Peter Woodthorpe and Paul Daneman playing Estragon and Vladimir.

Don Giovanni is like a play. It too needs separate layers to represent the performers and us, Mozart and us, the librettist Da Ponte and us, and the characters in the play.

IMAGINATION AND APPRECIATION

In stories, novels, and plays, we don't give all of the layers the same attention. Nor should we. As we read *Moby Dick*, we get engrossed in the world of Ishmael, Queequeg, Ahab, and the white whale (layer 2), and that is how Melville wanted it. As the novelist John Gardner (1983, p. 132) put it, "The writer's intent is that the reader fall through the printed page into the scene represented." Melville didn't want us engrossed, as we read, in his choice of words, actions, and characterizations (layer 1). These he wanted us to appreciate only once we had taken in Ishmael's world. Here again, we must distinguish imagination, which Gardner called "controlled dreaming," from appreciation.

Novels, plays, and stories are judged in part by how well they enable us to imagine the highest current layer – how well they transport us into the worlds of the stories. If an adventure story is good, we imagine its world so vividly that it is like a movie running off in our heads. We get so engrossed that we forget we are sitting in a chair, turning pages, and staying up too late. The same goes for a good play and a good movie.

Experiencing a story in imagination has surprising consequences. One is what Richard Gerrig (1989a, 1989b, 1993) called *anomalous suspense*. Ordinarily, suspense is a state in which we "lack knowledge about some sufficiently important target outcome (p. 79)." Yet when we read a suspense story for a second time, or when we read an account of a well-known historical event (for Americans, say, the assassination of President Lincoln), we often feel suspense even though we know precisely how the story turns out. We somehow get so thoroughly engrossed in our current imagining that we isolate ourselves from prior knowledge about the story. From the outside, the suspense seems anomalous, but in our imagination, it seems real.

Suspense is just one of many emotions we create in the process of imagining (see Walton, 1978). Novels, from pulp to the classics, are classified into genres largely by emotions they get us to experience. Mysteries evoke suspense, fear. Adventure stories evoke excitement, fear, anger. Horror stories evoke horror, loathing, fear. Romances lead to light sexual excitement, and pornography, to base erotic arousal. Satires evoke amusement. Movies belong to similar genres. We are as likely to cry at fictions in sad movies as at realities in daily life. Somehow, through the process of imagination, we experience emotions as if they were real. Such is the power of imagination.

The techniques by which novelists, playwrights, and film directors help us create these imaginings vary enormously. In novels, it is effective writing, and the best novelists have their secrets (e.g., see Gardner, 1983). In plays and movies, it is both an effective script and a skillful production. Good actors know how to get into character and help us imagine the actions, thoughts, and emotions of their characters. Good directors know how to place these characters and actions in readily imagined scenes and happenings. Nothing undermines a movie or play as quickly as bad acting, bad direction, or bad dialogue. Fostering our imagination is at the heart of literary art, and that makes it as much a subject for students of literature as for students of language.

Yet appreciation is also essential to most genres. Novelists, playwrights, and film directors want us to recognize *why* they are doing what they are doing. They may be trying to instruct, amuse, offer moral lessons, give insights into nature, or evoke an exciting experience. Some novelists and playwrights interrupt the highest current layer to make these purposes explicit. Classical Greek playwrights use a chorus to do that, Shakespeare uses a narrator to introduce his plays, and Bertolt Brecht uses voice-overs and narrators to comment on what is happening on stage.

To repeat, each layer is created and dealt with differently. The topmost layer (e.g., Ishmael's world) is the most explicit, representing what one person (Ishmael) means for others (certain contemporary landsmen) in that domain. In dealing with it, the primary participants (we and Melville) imagine those people taking those actions. The lower layers (e.g., Melville's world) are usually more obscure, more difficult to appreciate. Imagining the topmost layer is what immediately engrosses us, yet it is often our appreciation of the lower layers that make us understand what we have imagined.

Imagination and appreciation have long been recognized in literature. From the beginning, writers, playwrights, and musicians have exploited layering to achieve a wide range of rhetorical effects. Literary theorists have offered sophisticated, detailed analyses of those effects, and it is to them that we must turn for a more refined theory of layering, imagination, and appreciation in literary genres. My suggestions here are only a start, but no account of language use can really be complete without one.

Staged communicative acts

In stories, layering comes in extended stretches of language use, but there is also layering in single communicative acts. Recall the exchange between the husband and wife about the husband's tutoring:

Ken: and I'm cheap, - - -
Margaret: **I've always felt that about you, .**
Ken: oh shut up,
            (- - laughs) fifteen bob a lesson at home, -

Margaret is only *pretending* to claim she always thought Ken was cheap, and Ken shows that he recognizes this with his brisk comeback and laugh. Margaret's action has two layers:

Layer 2   Implied Margaret claims she always thought implied Ken was cheap.
Layer 1   Margaret and Ken jointly pretend that the event in layer 2 is taking place.

In creating the joint pretense, Margaret demonstrates a hypothetical situation (in layer 2) that blatantly contrasts with the actual situation (in layer 1). She intends Ken to appreciate why she is highlighting the contrast and see she is making fun of him.

Acts like this are what I will call *staged communicative acts*. The idea is that the speaker, say Ann, stages for Bob a brief improvised scene in which an implied Ann (like an implied author) performs a sincere communicative act toward an implied Bob. As playwright, Ann expects Bob both to imagine the scene and to appreciate her purpose in staging it. Let us denote implied A and implied B by Ai and Bi. A staged communicative act by A toward B has several properties:

1.   *Joint pretense.* A engages B in a joint pretense.
2.   *Communicative act.* The joint pretense is that Ai is performing a sincere communicative act toward Bi.
3.   *Correspondence.* A is to be taken as Ai, and B as Bi.
4.   *Contrast.* A intends A and B to mutually appreciate the salient contrasts between the demonstrated and actual situations.
5.   *Deniability.* If asked, A would deny meaning for B what Ai means for Bi.

Property 1 distinguishes staged from insincere acts. If Margaret had pretended by herself to make a sincere claim, her statement would be described as a lie, and a tease is different from a lie. Property 2 distinguishes staged acts from extended stories and jokes. Property 3 distinguishes staged acts from joint pretenses in which the primary participants play no roles. Property 4 expresses the purpose of staging a communicative act. And property 5 distinguishes staged from ostensible acts, a point I will take up later.

Staged communicative acts constitute a large family of actions that are common in conversation: irony, sarcasm, teasing, overstatement, understatement, rhetorical questions, and their relatives. They also occur in literature, but it is useful to start with conversation where we can examine the entire staging.

IRONY AND SARCASM

Irony is common in face-to-face conversation.[7] Let us begin with an example analyzed by Linda Coates (1992). Two strangers – call them Susan and Ellen – were videotaped in a session arranged by Coates as they discussed several topics, one of which was to plan a meal of foods they hate. In this example, they are discussing who they would invite to it. They have already agreed on foods to include, and Ellen has said who she would invite. The example starts when Susan remembers someone she could invite:

1. Susan: Ahh. Okay. Th- the sergeant that I know who was really nasty. He didn't want any women on his course so he did his best to get them off. [At "on" Susan begins nodding to mean "you understand the situation" and at "so" Ellen begins a face of disapproval of the sergeant.]
2. Ellen: Ah. Okay. [At "okay," Ellen begins nodding]
3. Susan: **Yes to thank him for all of his help in training.** [Over "thank" Susan raises her brow to signal "not really"; over "of his help in" she raises her brow to signal "unhelpful"; at the end, she laughs and smiles in humor. Meanwhile, over "of his help in train-" **Ellen smiles to signal understanding.**]
4. Susan: Yeah. Yeah. [Over "yeah yeah" Susan smiles in acknowledgment, and Ellen smiles to signal understanding.]
5. Susan: Okay. [At "okay" Susan picks up card on table to signal they should move on to next topic.]

When Susan says, "Yes to thank him for all of his help in training," she isn't really inviting the sergeant to thank him. Nor is Ellen serious in endorsing Susan's apparent suggestion. Both Susan and Ellen are being ironic in saying what they say.

[7] By irony, I mean what is sometimes called *verbal* or *discourse irony* and not *situational irony*, although the two are related (Fowler, 1965; Gibbs, 1994; Lucariello, 1994).

How do Susan and Ellen achieve this? As Coates argued, the full episode can be divided into four phases:

1. *Calibration.* The participants agree to a shared viewpoint or understanding of a topic. This is what Susan and Ellen do in utterances 1 and 2. The shared viewpoint needs to be clear for the next phase to succeed.
2. *Delivery.* The ironist delivers the utterance that is to be understood ironically. This is what Susan does in 3. But she does more than speak. She signals with her eyebrows that "thank" and "help" aren't to be taken seriously, and with her laugh and smile that the entire suggestion is a joke.
3. *Acknowledgment.* The participants let each other know that the irony has been understood. Susan and Ellen do this in 3 and 4 with two exchanges of smiles.
4. *Closure.* The participants signal to each other that the ironic episode has ended and that serious discussion is resuming. This Susan does in 5 and Ellen goes along.

In the large sample of cases videotaped by Coates, 84 percent of them had explicit calibration phases, all had delivery phases, 92 percent had at least one form of acknowledgment (like nodding or smiling), and 84 percent signaled the closure with a discourse shift marker like "so" or "anyway." What is remarkable in Coates' data, then, is how closely the two participants coordinate in setting up, carrying off, and closing these episodes.

But what is irony? What are Susan and Ellen trying to do with their actions? One traditional answer is *mere inversion.* When Susan says "To thank him for all of his help in training," she simply means the opposite of what she appears to mean. Ellen is to see that she couldn't want to thank the sergeant for his help – he's nasty and sexist – so she must mean the opposite. But this account isn't complete. Why did Susan use inversion here and not elsewhere? And why did Ellen go along with the inversion? Worse, many instances of irony and sarcasm don't entail inversion. Mere inversion offers no answers.

Another answer, offered by Dan Sperber and Deirdre Wilson (1981),[8] is that irony is *echoic mention.* The idea is this. When speakers say something ironic, they aren't using their sentences in the normal way. They are merely *mentioning* those sentences. In particular, they are mentioning, or echoing, earlier uses of the same sentences as a way of expressing an attitude such as contempt or ridicule. According to the echoic mention theory, when Susan says "To thank him for all of his help

---

[8] See also Jorgensen, Miller, and Sperber (1984) and Sperber and Wilson (1986).

in training," she is echoing an earlier utterance in order to show her ridicule or contempt for what it expresses.

The echoic mention theory is unsatisfactory too, and that is easy to see in the example. Because Susan and Ellen were strangers before their conversation, all that Ellen knows about the sergeant is what Susan has just told her – that he "was really nasty" and "didn't want any women on his course." There was no previous talk about thanking the sergeant for his help – nothing to echo – yet Susan is clearly heard as being ironic. The echoic mention, Sperber and Wilson argued, needn't be of a particular utterance, but merely of "popular wisdom or received opinions." It is difficult to see what popular wisdom or received opinions Susan might be echoing. Although some cases of irony allude to previous events, many do not. One of the most celebrated examples of irony is Jonathan Swift's 1729 essay "A Modest Proposal" in which he lays out, methodically and with dead seriousness, a proposal to use starving Irish children as food for the rich. It is implausible to say that anyone had ever uttered the entire essay before or that dining on Irish children was ever a part of popular wisdom or received opinion. Surely, Swift's irony works precisely because the "modest proposal" is so absurd that it could never have been entertained seriously. There was never anything like it to echo.

Another problem is with the technical notion of mentioning, which comes from traditional theories of quotation. The idea is that in quoting a sentence, one is not *using* the sentence, but merely *mentioning* it, as when I say " 'Morris is here' contains three words." But quotation is really a type of demonstration (Chapter 6), and demonstrating is a type of joint pretense (Clark and Gerrig, 1990). Any account of mentioning must appeal to joint pretense anyway.

Irony is better viewed as joint pretense (Clark and Gerrig, 1984).[9] As Grice (1978, p. 124) noted, "irony is intimately connected with the expression of a feeling, attitude, or evaluation. I cannot say something ironically unless what I say is intended to reflect a hostile or derogatory judgment or a feeling such as indignation or contempt." He went on: "To be ironical is, among other things, to pretend (as the etymology suggests), and while one wants the pretense to be recognized as such, to announce it as a pretense would spoil the effect." What is the pretense?

---

[9] For related views, see Gibbs (1986a, 1994), Kreuz and Glucksberg (1989), Kumon-Nakamura, Glucksberg, and Brown (1995).

An intuitively satisfying answer was offered by Fowler (1965, pp. 305–306) in his *Dictionary of Modern English Usage*:

Irony is a form of utterance that postulates a double audience, consisting of one party that hearing shall hear and shall not understand, and another party that, when more is meant than meets the ear, is aware both of that more and of the outsiders' incomprehension. [It] may be defined as the use of words intended to convey one meaning to the uninitiated part of the audience and another to the initiated, the delight of it lying in the secret intimacy set up between the latter and the speaker.

Combine Fowler's and Grice's suggestions and we have the *pretense theory of irony*.

Let us return to Susan's ironic statement, "To thank him for all of his help in training." In saying this, Susan and Ellen stage a brief scene in layer 2:

Layer 2 Implied Susan tells implied Ellen that she wants to thank the sergeant for all of his help.

Layer 1 Susan and Ellen jointly pretend that the event in layer 2 is taking place.

Susan invites Ellen (in layer 1) to imagine a particular scene (scene 2) in which the sergeant has been so helpful that Susan will thank him by inviting him to a nice meal. In the actual world, they know they are inviting the nasty and sexist sergeant to a disgusting meal (scene 1). So in creating layer 2, Susan has highlighted several contrasts between the two scenes:

Scene 2 Susan is inviting the sergeant to a *nice* meal to *thank* him for being so *helpful*.

Scene 1 Susan is inviting the sergeant to a *disgusting* meal to *chasten* him for being so *nasty and sexist*.

Actual Susan and actual Ellen (in layer 1) appreciate these contrasts, and, as Fowler noted, take delight in the secret intimacy (or "inner circle") they set up with them. What are they delighted at? At their recognition that the sergeant would think he was being thanked when actually he was getting his just deserts.

In the pretense theory, then, irony has two layers. A and B are at layer 1, and their implied counterparts Ai and Bi are at layer 2:

Layer 2 Ai is performing a serious communicative act for Bi.

Layer 1 A and B jointly pretend that the event in layer 2 is taking place.

A and B play the roles of Ai and Bi at layer 2, so the correspondence function C(2) specifies (among other things): $A = Ai$; $B = Bi$. They take delight in their recognition of the contrast between the two layers. Indeed, A and B often make fun of their characters by speaking in mock, exaggerated, or caricatured voices. They also take delight as A lets B show how sophisticated, knowledgeable, or savvy she is in catching on to A's pretense. An exaggerated performance by A helps B do that, and an exaggerated performance by B helps her show that she has caught on.[10]

Staged communicative acts that are classified as irony cluster around several attitudes. The point of an ironic act is generally to call attention to an *unexpected incongruity* between what might have been (scene 2) and what is (scene 1). It is common for speakers to comment on unexpected situations, especially negative ones, by "alluding" to what is normal or expected or by "echoing" "popular wisdom or received opinions" (Gibbs, 1994; Kumon-Nakamura et al., 1995; Sperber and Wilson, 1981; Wilson and Sperber, 1992). Here is a standard though contrived illustration:

Utterances	A: **"What a gorgeous day!"**
	B: **"Yes, isn't it!"**
Actual situation	There is heavy rain, when A and B had expected a nice day.
Staged situation	The day is gorgeous, and A and B are ecstatic about it.
Contrast	The weather is not at all what A and B expected.
Attitude	A and B are unhappy that the weather is not as expected.

Staged acts tend to be called ironic whenever, as Grice said, they "reflect a hostile or derogatory judgment or a feeling such as indignation or contempt."

"Sarcasm," Fowler (1965, p. 535) noted, "does not necessarily involve irony, and irony has often no touch of sarcasm...The essence of sarcasm is the intention of giving pain by (ironical or other) bitter words." So when sarcasm does involve irony, it works much the same as irony. A and B jointly pretend that implied A is performing a serious communicative act to implied B. It is just that the point is to cause B pain. Here is an example from a cartoon (Haiman, 1990):

| Husband, at TV: | That's over twelve hours of continuous football action! |
| Wife, deadpan: | **Whoopee.** |

[10] Grice (1978, p. 125) argued: "If speaking ironically has to be, or at least to appear to be, the expression of a certain sort of feeling or attitude, then a tone suitable to such a feeling or attitude seems to be mandatory, at any rate for the least sophisticated examples."

On the surface, the wife appears to agree with her husband, but she is betrayed by her monotone. She is staging a scene in which she exclaims "Whoopee!" The husband is to appreciate the contrast between her staged enthusiasm and her actual indifference. As John Haiman (1990) noted, sarcasm is often explicitly marked with a sneering or contemptuous tone, a monotone ("Whoopee"), an exaggerated intonation ("You poor baby!" or "My heart bleeds for you" in feigned compassion), or a singsong. With sarcasm as with irony, what speakers stage is less high drama than melodrama.

TEASING

A tease is a staged communicative act designed to make fun of or playfully mock the addressee. Teasing is sometimes hard to tell from irony or sarcasm, suggesting already that it is a member of the same family. Some teasing is good-humored, and the person teased responds in the same fictional domain as the teaser. In this example, Gerald has just bought a brand-new sports car (Drew, 1987):

Gerald: Hi how are you
Martha: Well, you're late as usual
Gerald: eheh eheh eheh eheh
Lee: **What's the matter couldn't you get your car started?**
Gerald: **hehh That's right. I had to get it pushed, eheh eheh eheh**

Lee pretends he is seriously asking Gerald whether he could get his car started. Gerald shows he appreciates the pretense ("hehh") by staging a response "That's right. I had to get it pushed" as if Lee's question were serious. Lee's utterance has two layers:

Layer 2   Implied Lee asks implied Gerald whether he could get his car started.
Layer 1   Lee and Gerald jointly pretend that the event in layer 2 is taking place.

For the tease to work, Gerald must recognize layer 2 and appreciate Lee's reasons for creating it. Gerald's response, in line with the pretense, has two layers as well.

How does teasing work? One answer has been offered by Paul Drew (1987) for teases that receive serious responses. In this example (p. 227),[11] "Larry has been mildly complaining about a function he and

---

[11] In this notation, "hhh" indicates audible breathing, "(0.5)" indicates pause length in seconds, and "=" indicates that the two adjacent turns are "latched" together with no pause between them.

Alice have to go to that evening and which he knows starts at seven o'clock":

Alice:	Uh::::: Hey try and get home at a decent hour 'cause
Larry:	Yeh I be home by ni:ne,
Alice:	No: (.) get home pretty early okay? (0.5)
Alice:	Please,
Larry:	**Well I can leave right now if you want,=**
Alice:	=No::, hhh
Larry:	khh-hh
Alice:	ih::::hh So:, (0.3) Okay?

After Alice nags Larry about getting home early, he stages an offer to "leave right now if you want"; his utterance has two layers. Alice responds to the offer as if it had been a serious offer ("No::"); her utterance has only one layer. Yet she and Larry mutually establish that she has recognized his pretense when the two of them exchange laughs. Here, then, is a joint pretense, although Alice doesn't respond in a joint pretense.

What is A doing in teasing B? According to Drew, A's tease is a reaction to B's earlier behavior. In Drew's collection of examples, the recipients were always overdoing something – bragging, extolling another person's virtues, complaining in outrage, going on about something, telling a far-fetched story, being overly self-deprecating, or playing innocent. Alice was overdoing her concern about Larry getting home on time. What A does in teasing B is pretend to take B's overdone action one step further. The purpose is to get B to see how overblown his or her action was to evoke such a reaction. Larry creates scene 2, which he intends to be compared with the actual scene 1:

Scene 2	Implied Alice is *so* anxious that implied Larry be home early *that implied Larry is offering to leave right now.*
Scene 1	Alice is *quite* anxious that Larry be home early.

Alice is to appreciate the contrast and, thereby, see that Larry is criticizing her for being overly anxious. It is the criticism that Alice defends herself against with her response.

Teases are staged the same way as irony and sarcasm. A and B jointly pretend that Ai is performing a serious communicative act for Bi. The correspondence function C(2) specifies: A = Ai; B = Bi. The staged act is a normal reaction to something B has overdone, showing B's action to be worthy of ridicule, and A intends B to appreciate this.[12] Like irony, teases get introduced into the conversation sequentially and interactively. And as in irony, A and B are to imagine the events in layer 2 and yet appreciate A's reasons at layer 1 for creating those events.

Not all teasing takes this form. Another form is the *put-on*, as in this example (Philips, 1975):

Several students are working together at a table where a microphone has been placed. One student turns from the group and calls out to the teacher, "Mr. Smith, Charlie's foolin' with the mike." Charlie says, "I am not." The teacher looks up when summoned, but doesn't respond, turning back to his paper work. In this case, Charlie hadn't touched the microphone.

When the first student, let's name him Ben, calls out to Mr. Smith, he is trying to put him on about a classroom infraction by Charlie. What is different here is the participants in the staging. Ben is pretending to tell Mr. Smith about the infraction, but Mr. Smith isn't in on the pretense – at least not at first. Only Charlie is. Ben's put-on has these two layers:

Layer 2   Implied Ben, incensed, tells Smith that implied Charlie is fooling with the mike.

Layer 1   Ben and Charlie jointly pretend that the event in layer 2 is taking place.

The victim of the put-on (here, Mr. Smith) is expected to catch on only later, to the delight of the instigator (Ben) and the others in the know (Charlie). In this example, Ben is putting Mr. Smith on and, simultaneously, teasing Charlie, getting him into trouble. Teasing and put-ons may take a variety of forms, but they all involve layering and an appreciation of that layering.[13]

OVERSTATEMENT, UNDERSTATEMENT, AND RHETORICAL QUESTIONS

Overstatement and understatement – hyperbole and meiosis – are stagings in which the speaker pretends to use an expression that is exaggerated or understated in some way. Here is an example of overstatement (2.22b.658):

---

[12] Drew (p. 232): "Teases are designed to make it very apparent what they are up to – that they are not intended as real or sincere proposals – by being constructed as very obviously exaggerated versions of some action etc.; and/or by being in direct contrast to something they both know or one has just told the other."

[13] For a related phenomenon, see Labov's (1972) "Rules for ritual insults."

Ann: my room at the moment is covered have you seen it since it was covered
        in **millions** of little pots, all growing pips and seeds and things,
Betty: no

Ann isn't claiming to have literally millions of little pots in her room, but only more pots than expected. She is using *millions* in overstatement.

Overstatement is clearly akin to teasing and irony. Ann and Betty, her partner, briefly create two layers:

Layer 2   Implied Ann tells implied Betty that what her room is covered with is
           millions of little pots.
Layer 1   Ann and Betty jointly pretend that the event in layer 2 is taking place.

Ann wants Betty to imagine scene 2 and appreciate the contrast with scene 1:

Scene 2   The room is covered with *millions* of little pots.
Scene 1   The room is covered with, say, *fifty* little pots.

Her purpose is to emphasize just how many little pots there are for the size of her room. As in other stagings, C(2) specifies among other things that A = Ai and B = Bi. Understatement is subject to a similar analysis.

Rhetorical questions are also staged communicative acts. Take this piece of conversation (1.12.1364):

Betty: well you see her grandchildren, don't go to see her,
Calvin: m
Betty: so **why should it matter**, I mean I might have hundreds of them,
         and yet,
Donald: yeah
Betty: they probably would never come to see me,

When Betty says "Why should it matter?" she is pretending to ask why it should matter (to the grandmother what happens around her). She doesn't really want an answer – it is so obvious it isn't needed. Indeed, she goes on to her next utterance without leaving space for an answer. The purpose is clear. At level 2, implied Betty is seriously asking implied Calvin and Donald why it should matter. At level 1, the three of them jointly pretend that she is doing that. They are to imagine Betty asking the question and them answering and, through the contrast with the actual situation, appreciate how obvious its answer is.

Staged communicative acts, then, come in many forms – irony, sarcasm, teasing, overstatement, understatement, rhetorical questions, and others. In each case, A engages B (and perhaps others) in staging a brief scene that blatantly contrasts with the current situation. A intends B to appreciate why A has drawn attention to these contrasts. In irony and sarcasm, it is to point out how unexpected or unwanted the current situation is, or how naive, innocent, or silly certain people are, and thereby to derogate them. In one type of teasing, it is to point out how B has overdone something and thereby to ridicule that action. In overstatement, it is to increase the degree of one feature of the current situation. And in rhetorical questions, it is to point out the obviousness of a current issue. Staged communicative acts are remarkably useful.

Ostensible communicative acts

Some apparent communicative acts have a built-in ambivalence. Suppose Irene asks Jake what he thinks of her new dress, he says "I like it," and she replies "Oh, thanks." Irene has put Jake in an awkward position, and the two of them recognize this. She has asked him to comment on her dress, and, to be polite, he can't very well say he doesn't like it. If he doesn't like it very much, he might say "I like it," but without the appropriate enthusiasm or elaboration. He expects Irene to appreciate that he is only *ostensibly* saying he likes it. What he is actually doing is showing her, not that he likes her dress, but that he holds her in high enough regard to put on a show of liking it. Here we have what Ellen Isaacs and I (1990) have called an ostensible compliment and its ostensible acceptance.

Ostensible communicative acts deserve attention because they help us better understand what it means to make a polite gesture. Polite gestures (like Jake's compliment) are paradoxical. They are performed only for politeness' sake – they are not to be taken seriously – and yet they work. How is that possible? To begin, let us consider ostensible invitations, as described in an investigation by Isaacs and myself (1990).

OSTENSIBLE INVITATIONS

Two Stanford University students, Ross and Cathy, have a date to study one evening, but Ross has a problem. Some old friends of his from Southern California have called to say they are arriving at Stanford that evening and want him to go to a basketball game at Berkeley, about an hour away, and he has accepted. He telephones Cathy, describes the circumstances, explains he is going to the game, and says:

Ross: Do you want to come?
Cathy: That's all right. I'll pass.
Ross: Okay.

As Ross and Cathy each later explained, they recognized that Ross was inviting Cathy only to be polite. He didn't honestly want her to accept, and recognizing this, she didn't. With this maneuver they were both satisfied. On the surface, he had given her the chance to go along and she had declined. At the same time, but below the surface, he showed her that he still cared for her, and she showed him that she understood that. The date dissolved without public rancor or loss of face.

Ostensible invitations have properties that can be accounted for if we assume they have two layers. Ross' utterance has these two layers:

Layer 2 Implied Ross is sincerely inviting implied Cathy to go to the game.

Layer 1 Ross and Cathy jointly pretend that the event in layer 2 is taking place.

Ross intends Cathy to imagine him sincerely making the invitation. This way she will also imagine how much he values her company: He regards her highly enough to invite her along. All this is at layer 2. Ross also intends Cathy to appreciate why he is making the pretense. He is putting on public display an act that shows how highly he regards her. Yet he intends her to see that he doesn't really want her to go along, and to be polite she should decline. So Ross gets Cathy to appreciate that he doesn't want her to go, yet avoids putting that on record, which would lead to loss of face. What he puts on record instead is a display of his regard for her.

Ostensible acts have the same properties as staged acts, but with several differences. If A ostensibly invites B to event E, the invitation has these properties:

1. *Joint pretense.* A engages B in a joint pretense. (Ross and Cathy mutually recognize that Ross is making a pretense.)
2. *Communicative act.* The joint pretense is that Ai is sincerely inviting Bi to E. (Ross and Cathy's joint pretense is that he is sincerely inviting her to go to the game.)
3. *Correspondence.* A is to be taken as Ai, and B as Bi. (In their pretense, Ross is to be taken as implied Ross, and Cathy as implied Cathy.)
4. *Contrast.* A intends A and B to mutually recognize certain contrasts between the demonstrated and actual situations and to see A's reason for highlighting them. (Ross wants Cathy to compare what *could be*, that he really wants her to go, with what is, that he doesn't actually want her to go. She will then see that he would like to have been with her *if circumstances had been different* – that he still enjoyed and wanted her company.)
5. *Ambivalence.* If asked, A couldn't sincerely say he wanted B to go to event E, nor could he sincerely say he didn't. (Ross couldn't honestly say "Yes, I

really want you to come," because he didn't really want Cathy to go. Yet he also couldn't admit to her publicly that he didn't want her to come, for that would imply he didn't regard her highly enough to invite her.)

6. *Collusion.* A expects B to respond to the pretense appropriate to A's wishes. (If Cathy is cooperative, she will decline Ross' invitation.)

It is properties 5 and 6, ambivalence and collusion, that distinguish ostensible from staged acts. If Ross had been sarcastic in asking "Do you want to come?" he would deny he really wanted Cathy to go, and she might respond with equal sarcasm, "Yeah, I just love hanging out with the guys." What makes the invitation ostensible is that he wouldn't deny either that he really wanted Cathy to go, or that he didn't. He displays *ambivalence.* And he wants her to respond by *colluding* with him, by pretending to take the invitation seriously and declining, which she does. Ostensible invitations project ostensible responses.

For ostensible invitations to work, people must engineer the situation to make the ostensibility of the invitations clear. Suppose, again, that A ostensibly invites B to event E. Isaacs and I found that people try to arrange the circumstances in at least these ways:

1. A makes B's presence at E implausible. "I know you are too busy, but..."
2. A extends his or her invitation to B only after B has solicited it.
3. A doesn't motivate the invitation beyond simple social courtesy.
4. A doesn't insist or persist on the invitation – for example, after B has politely declined the first time.
5. A is vague about the arrangements for event E. "Let's have lunch sometime."
6. A hedges the invitation with such expressions as "well," "I guess," "maybe," and "if you want."
7. A delivers the invitation with inappropriate cues – flatter intonation, hesitations, rapid speaking – any sign to show that he or she isn't fully committed to the invitation.

Precisely how A engineers the invitation depends on the circumstances. If it is obvious that B can't attend E, A is free to be as enthusiastic as he or she wants – to show appreciation for B.

Ostensible invitations are risky – which is one of their virtues. When Ross asks Cathy "Do you want to come?" when he doesn't want her to, he faces several risks. First, she may misconstrue his invitation as sincere. If she does, she may accept it. Or she may resent being invited to a basketball game with the guys, something Ross knows she wouldn't enjoy. If Ross has engineered it right, these risks should be slight. At least, they should be smaller than the potential benefits of letting her know he still appreciates her. Or second, Cathy may choose not to collude in her response and put it on record that he doesn't want her to go: "Oh, you don't really want me to go." If this happens, Ross has a ready reply, "But of course I do – that's why I invited you," and he is committed to taking her. In short, A prefers the risks of misconstrual to the benefits of indirection, and has a clear defense against any implied slight.

OTHER OSTENSIBLE COMMUNICATIVE ACTS

Many joint projects besides invitations and their acceptances are also ostensible. Greetings, for example, often consist of ostensible questions and answers, as in this example (3.1c.1030):

Detch: *good morning*
Morris: *good morning Miss* Detch how are you
Detch: **fine thank you**
Morris: **would you like to** take the comfortable chair

When Morris says, "How are you?" he is ostensibly asking Miss Detch how she is, and with "Fine" she is ostensibly answering that question. Morris would be surprised and disappointed if Detch really did say how she was, and she recognizes this (Sacks, 1975).

Morris and Detch make clear the ostensibility of their actions in several ways. When Detch says "thank you," it isn't for Morris' question. Rather, it is for Morris showing he cares enough to display a concern about her health. And Morris considers his display to be all that is needed. He doesn't even wait for Detch's answer before starting the next utterance. So with the exchange "How are you?" "Fine thank you," Morris and Detch imagine an exchange in which a concerned Morris asks Detch about her health, and she tells him sincerely that it is fine. They appreciate that Morris' purpose is to display a personal concern as a preliminary to their talk, and hers is to display a healthy person ready to enter that talk.

Congratulations and apologies can also be ostensible. When the loser of a game congratulates the winner, the congratulations and its acceptance are usually recognized as ostensible. The loser isn't honestly happy that the winner won, and the winner recognizes this. Or when a child is required by a mother or school teacher to apologize to another child for some wrong, that apology and its acceptance are ordinarily ostensible as well. The first child, apologizing under protest, isn't really sorry, and the second child recognizes this. These congratulations and apologies are heard not as insincere but as ostensible. The loser and the child, by asking their partners to imagine the real congratulations and apology, display a sincere regard for the recipients or the system they belong to.

Ostensible projects like this work in two ways. First, the participants agree on idealized communicative acts – what their current joint project would be if the circumstances were ideal. That in itself shows a certain mutual respect. Ross and Cathy, for example, jointly create a picture in which he sincerely invites her to go along to the game, and she sincerely declines. Second, in creating these idealized acts, the participants jointly avoid putting on record troublesome issues that might otherwise come up. Ross and Cathy avoid discussing why he would rather go out with the guys than with her.

POLITE GESTURES

Most ostensible acts are designed to deal with politeness. Recall how people manage face (Chapter 10). They try to maintain both their *self-worth*, to be respected by others, and their *autonomy*, to be unimpeded by others. Ostensible acts help maintain both. When the participants create idealized ostensible acts, like Ross and Cathy's invitation and declination, they deal with self-worth. They display a mutually respectful exchange in a situation that otherwise threatens to reveal the opposite. And when they keep troublesome issues off record, they also deal with autonomy. They avoid discussing the issues explicitly.

These properties suggest a deeper explanation for the politeness of the pre-requests we saw in Chapter 10. Recall this exchange:

Clark: Do you know where Goldberg's Grocery is?
Verona: Yes, it's just around the corner.

In my utterance, I framed the social situation as one in which I was uncertain whether Verona knew where Goldberg's Grocery was, and she was to tell me if she did. In response, she took up the situation as I framed it and answered "yes." Then, without prompting, she went on to tell me the information I wanted ("it's around the corner"). The situation I framed was preparatory to asking Verona where the store was. She saw that and offered me that information.

The question and its first answer can profitably be viewed as ostensible communicative acts. If Verona didn't know where Goldberg's Grocery was, it would be embarrassing to ask her. To avoid that embarrassment, I pretended to ask her only *whether* she knew, and she colluded with me by saying "Yes." Yet she appreciated why I initiated the ostensible question, recognizing that I wanted to find Goldberg's Grocery. So she took up that proposed joint project as well and said, "It's just around the corner." She pretended with me that I was asking her a question, and she colluded with me in answering it. If she had asked me "Did you really want to know if I knew?" I couldn't honestly have said "Yes, I did." Nor could I have admitted "No, I didn't," for that would have implied I didn't care whether I embarrassed her or not.

Recall that many pre-requests (like "Can you?" "Could you?" "Do you know?" "Will you?" "Would you?") are highly conventional, addressing generic obstacles, and are to be taken as *pro forma*. But what does it mean to be "*pro forma*"? Take this example from a telephone call to a local shop (Clark, 1979):

Susan: Could you tell me what time you close tonight?
Manager: Six o'clock.

Susan pretends that perhaps the manager "couldn't" tell her what time they close. The manager recognizes her reasons for the pretense because he gives her the time wanted. But he doesn't collude with her by saying "Yes" first. He takes the pretense to be *pro forma* and not in need of acknowledgment. Still, he could have answered "yes." In another study (Munro, 1977), when people were asked face to face "Could you tell me what time it is?" 45 percent of them said "Yes" before giving the time.

Even though "Could you tell me?" is *pro forma*, it still has a point. The manager can maintain his self-worth and autonomy simply by recognizing Susan's pretense: She has taken the pains to offer him an out, and even if it is a merely ostensible out, that is still deferential. "Could you tell me what time you close?" is judged as more polite than "What time do you close?" (Clark and Schunk, 1980). The manager also realizes that Susan has offered him the option of being polite in return. All he has to do is answer her ostensible question first with "yes," and that is face-saving for her to do too. Indeed, for *pro forma* pre-requests like "Could you tell me?" the response "Yes, we close at six" is judged to be more polite than "We close at six" (Chapter 10).

Ostensible communicative acts like these are often called rituals, habits, mere gestures, and even mindless actions, but the pejorative labels don't do them justice. On closer examination, they turn out to be subtle and effective tools for managing self-worth and autonomy.

Conclusions

In the simplest layering, people perform two joint actions simultaneously. The actions in layer 1 take place in one domain, and those in layer 2 take place in a second domain jointly created by the participants in the first domain. The best examples come from joint pretense. Alan and Beth, in urban San Francisco in 1952, make believe they are Wild Bill and Calamity Jane in the Deadwood gold rush of 1876. When Alan picks up a pebble in San Francisco (layer 1), he and Beth construe his behavior simultaneously as Wild Bill picking up a gold nugget in Deadwood (layer 2).

In joint activities, people use layering when they want to contrast some hypothetical world with the current, real world. With layering, they don't describe the hypothetical world: They demonstrate it. They and their audience imagine the new world without actually having to enter it. They simulate experience at a distance. People exploit these properties for a range of purposes.

Layering is essential to stories. Storytellers and their audiences work together to create elaborate happenings in hypothetical domains, jointly pretending that the happenings are actually taking place. In plays and movies, actors and their audiences jointly create performances with much the same pretense. The primary participants in all these examples are to imagine what is happening in the story world and yet appreciate why the author and actors are creating them.

Speakers also stage individual communicative acts to get addressees to appreciate certain contrasts between the staged and actual situations. With irony, the point is to comment on an unexpected anomaly. With sarcasm, it is to wound the addressee. With one type of teasing, it is to comment on something the addressee has overdone. With hyperbole, it is to stress the extent of some attribute, and with meiosis, to underplay its extent.

A subtler form of layering is found in ostensible communicative acts. In an ostensible invitation, the speaker and addressee jointly pretend that the speaker is inviting the addressee to some event. The two of them recognize that the invitation isn't to be taken seriously, and that the addressee is to collude with the speaker. The point of the speaker's pretense is to show appreciation for the addressee and to keep the half-heartedness of the invitation off record. Ostensible acts – thanks, apologies, congratulations, questions about one's health – are broadly useful in managing face, in keeping social relations equitable.

PART VI

Conclusion

13 | Conclusion

People use language for doing things with each other, and their use of language is itself a joint action. Much of this book has been devoted to these two points. In the course of this examination, I have made three broad arguments. One is that people use language only within broader joint activities. Another is that communicative acts divide into levels, tracks, and layers. And a third is that the very notion of language itself needs to be expanded if we are to account for language use. In this chapter I take a final look at these arguments.

Social action

Language is rarely used as an end in itself. It is primarily an instrument for carrying out broader activities – buying goods, planning parties, playing games, gossiping, exchanging stories, entertaining and being entertained. All of these are *joint* activities in which two or more people, in socially defined roles, carry out individual actions as parts of larger enterprises. Language is simply a device by which they coordinate those individual actions. When I buy a bottle of shampoo in the drugstore – a joint activity – among other things I talk to the clerk. But if I were asked, "What did you do in the drugstore?" I wouldn't say, "I talked to the clerk," even though I did. I would reply, "I bought some shampoo," which describes the larger enterprise. Using language was only a means to that end.

We cannot study language use without studying joint activities, and vice versa. People cannot carry out joint activities without signaling each other, nor do they ordinarily signal each other except in the course of joint activities. Language use – in its broad sense – is an essential ingredient in all joint activities. The tight link between language use and joint activities has been a source of confusion. Many phenomena have been treated as features of language use when they are really features of the joint activities in which the language is being used. These phenomena include coordination, cooperation, conventions, turns, closure, joint projects, opportunistic actions, and the accumulation of common ground.

If the examples in this book are any guide, joint activities range widely. They run the gamut from cooperative to competitive, formal to informal, egalitarian to autocratic, extended to brief. There may be two, or many, participants, and they may be acting at the same place and time (face-to-face conversation), or at great distances in place (telephone conversations) or in time (writing). Most joint activities depend on norms, practices, skills, and expectations that are shared by communities of expertise – Scots, physicians, baseball aficionados – and that cover everything from how to shake hands or deal cards to how to show deference or display emotion. Although there has been some effort to analyze joint activities, we will need more thorough analyses if we are ever to have a proper account of language use.

The word *social* comes from the Latin word *socius* for "partner" or "companion." It is in this sense that language use is a species of social action – perhaps the most basic species there is.

Lines of action

Using language is usually treated as if it were a single line of action – like walking along a trail in the woods. On the trail you avoid rocks and fallen trees, choose to go left or right at each fork in the trail, and wander up, down, and around, but your path is always continuous and coherent – a single unbroken line of movement. Using language is not that way at all. It is composed of separate lines of actions along three distinct dimensions: *levels*, *tracks*, and *layers*. The most basic of these is levels, but we need tracks and layers to account for a variety of things people do with words and gestures.

LEVELS

It is one thing to claim that communicative acts are joint actions, and quite another to specify what that means. When a drugstore clerk says to me, "I'll be right there," she and I are doing things together, but what? I have argued for four levels of joint action in the performance of such an utterance:

Speaker A's actions	Addressee B's actions
4 A is proposing joint project *w* to B	B is considering A's proposal of *w*
3 A is signaling that *p* for B	B is recognizing that *p* from A
2 A is presenting signal *s* to B	B is identifying signal *s* from A
1 A is executing behavior *t* for B	B is attending to behavior *t* from A

At level 1, the clerk is getting me to attend to her voice and gestures. At level 2, she is getting me to identify the English expressions she is presenting – "I'll be right there." At level 3, she is getting me to construe what she is to be taken to mean – that she will serve me in a moment. And at level 4, she is getting me to consider taking up the joint project she is proposing – that I accept her delay. Levels beyond level 4 are needed to account for more extended joint projects, but I haven't considered them much in this book.

Levels of actions form what I have called action ladders, which have the properties of upward causality, upward completion, and downward evidence. If we look at the clerk's and my actions separately, they each form action ladders. But viewing our actions separately misses the fact that they are linked, tied together, at each level as two parts of a single action by the pair of us. We each perform participatory actions at each level that require the other doing his or her part. The result is a ladder of joint actions. It is these ladders that specify how the clerk and I are acting jointly during her utterance.

TRACKS

In joint activities, most talk is about the official business – about the buying of goods, the planning of a party, the playing of a game, etc. Yet there is also talk – in the background – about the communicative acts by which that business is conducted. I have called these two lines of talk primary and secondary tracks – track 1 and track 2. Tracks are recursive, so new tracks can be added indefinitely, although they rarely go beyond track 3 or 4. And there are tracks at each level of joint action. Whereas the communicative acts in track 1 have been well studied – after all, they constitute the conversation proper – those in track 2 have been largely ignored. They have often been viewed as unsystematic noise, or as performance errors, and therefore unworthy of our attention. In fact, they are systematic and essential to the successful use of language.

The communicative acts in track 2 are used for managing conversation at all four levels of action. When people nod, smile, or say "uh huh" during another's utterance, they are saying "I understand you so far," a signal in track 2 to help achieve closure at level 3. When speakers add "uh" or "um" to their utterances, they are signaling breaks in their presentations, also in track 2, in order to deal with problems at level 2. When speakers make repairs, which are also in track 2, they may be dealing with problems at any level. Remarkably, signals such as "uh" and "um" have evolved just for use in track 2, and so have such procedures as repeating a word as part of a repair. It is only by dividing signals into tracks that we fully appreciate the division of labor in the signals people use. Managing talk is truly distinct from carrying out official business, and it comes complete with many of its own techniques and signals.

LAYERS

People sometimes make as if to say things they don't really mean. When Sam tells Reynard "I must go down to the bank" (1.1.423), he really, truly means that he has to go down to the bank. This utterance has a single layer of actions, which I have called layer 1. But when Sam says to Reynard, "A girl went into a chemist's shop," as part of a joke, he doesn't really, truly mean that a girl went into a chemist's shop. Rather, he and Reynard engage in the joint pretense that he really, truly means that a girl went into a chemist's shop. This utterance has two layers of actions. At layer 1, Sam and Reynard make the joint pretense that the events in layer 2 actually occur. At layer 2, a reporter played by Sam is telling a reportee played by Reynard about a woman going into a chemist's shop. Layering is also recursive, and there may be as many as four, five, or six layers in a situation.

Although layering is needed to account for how we create and understand works of fiction – novels, plays, movies, television comedies, jokes, short stories – it is also needed for what I have called *staged* communicative acts. These include verbal irony, sarcasm, teases of all sorts, hyperbole, meiosis, rhetorical questions, and other such tropes. It is also needed for ostensible communicative acts. In an ostensible invitation, for example, speakers and their addressees make as if the speakers were truly inviting their addressees to do something, but recognize all along that the addressees are not expected to accept the invitation. Layering is widespread in everyday talk, imbuing it with a spirit, edge, and sense of imagination it wouldn't otherwise have.

Levels, tracks, and layers are not just figments of the analyst's imagination. They are distinctions people using language appreciate – even if their appreciation is not always explicit. People tacitly know what it is for listeners to attend to a speaker's utterance without identifying it, or to identify it without understanding it, or to understand it without taking up the speaker's proposal. People tacitly know what speakers are doing when they say "um" or "I mean." People tacitly know what speakers and addressees are doing when speakers tease, become sarcastic, or make ostensible invitations. Levels, tracks, and layers are ways of representing these tacit understandings.

What is language?

The study of language is often divided into the study of language structure and the study of language use. To study language structure is to analyze the phonology, morphology, syntax, and semantics of conventional languages like English, Dakota, Japanese, and American Sign Language, but the study of language use hasn't been so easy to characterize. It has often been equated with linguistic pragmatics, a branch of linguistics, but there is little agreement on what that is (Davis, 1991; Gazdar, 1979; Levinson, 1983; Lyons, 1977). Pragmatics generally includes the study of linguistic utterances in context, but excludes nonlinguistic signals and phenomena of "mere" performance. The trouble is that nonlinguistic signals and performance phenomena have figured prominently in the accounts of language use in this book.

The tack I have taken is to identify language use with the use of *signals* – acts by which one person means something for another. There are, I have argued, three basic methods of signaling: describing-as, indicating, and demonstrating (Chapter 6). We *describe* something *as* a fish when we present the word *fish*. We *indicate* an individual fish when we point at it. And we *demonstrate* the size of a fish when we hold our hands so far apart. Most signals are composites of the three methods. The signals created by these methods form a coherent category of human action, whereas linguistic utterances do not.

Almost all so-called linguistic utterances are really composite signals (Chapter 6). When Barbara says "That book is mine" while pointing at a book, her reference to the book is a composite of describing-as and indicating: It requires both her words and her gesture. We cannot account for what she means without appealing to both. And when Alan says "At the baseball game today, one guy got so mad at the umpire that he went [rude gesture] and yelled 'Go back where you came from' [imitating an angry voice and cupping his hands around his mouth]," his utterance contains *as constituents* two demonstrations of what the fan did – the rude gesture and the quotation. We cannot begin to account for what Alan means without appealing to both. Indicating and demonstrating are nonlinguistic methods of signaling, yet most utterances employ indicating, and a great many also employ demonstrating.

Nonlinguistic signals are important in their own right (Chapters 7, 8, 9). When Alan asks Barbara, "Want some coffee?" she can say "yes" or nod, while smiling or not smiling, performed with or without enthusiasm. Because "yes" and the nod are alternatives, Barbara means something by her choice of "yes" over the nod, a point we would miss if we excluded nonlinguistic signals. She also means something by her choice of smile vs. nonsmile, and by the presence vs. absence of enthusiasm. And when Linda says "en I'm getting a sun tan" pointing first at her left cheek and then at her right (Chapter 9), we would fail to account for what she means if we ignored her concurrent gesture. Nods, smiles, gestures – these are all necessary to understanding ordinary *linguistic* communication.

And what about the signals in track 2 (Chapter 9)? Are *uh* and *um* and word elongation part of linguistic utterances? What are we to do with *uh huh*, smiles, and nods as signals of acknowledgment? What about eye gaze, turn restarts, and recycled turn beginnings as signals about attention? No account of language use can be complete without these signals, the linguistic and nonlinguistic together.

The "language" of language use, *language$_u$*, is therefore not the same as the "language" of language structure, *language$_s$*. Traditionally, language$_s$ is the system of symbols of a language like Japanese, Dakota, or American Sign Language, but language$_u$ is the system of signals, both linguistic and nonlinguistic, created by all three methods of signaling. I fear there will always be difficulty in keeping the two straight, and we will have to continue to use the circumlocution "language in its extended sense" for language$_u$. But keep them straight we must. To limit the study of language use to language$_s$ would undermine the enterprise entirely. For language use, we must continue to study language in its extended sense.

References

Albert, S., and Kessler, S. (1976). Processes for ending social encounters: The conceptual archeology of a temporal place. *Journal of Theory of Social Behavior*, 6, 147–170.

(1978). Ending social encounters. *Journal of Experimental Social Psychology*, 14, 541–553.

Argyle, M., and Cook., M. (1976). *Gaze and mutual gaze.* Cambridge University Press.

Atkinson, J. M. (1984). Public speaking and audience responses: Some techniques for inviting applause. In J. M. Atkinson and J. C. Heritage (Eds.), *Structures of social action: Studies in conversational analysis*, pp. 370–409. Cambridge University Press.

Atkinson, J. M., and Drew, P. (1979). *Order in court: The organisation of verbal interaction in judicial settings.* Atlantic Highlands NJ: Humanities Press.

Augarde, T. (1986). *The Oxford guide to word games.* Oxford University Press.

Aumann, R. (1976). Agreeing to disagree. *Annals of Statistics*, 4, 1236–1239.

Austin, J. L. (1962). *How to do things with words.* Oxford University Press.

Bach, K., and Harnish, R. M. (1979). *Linguistic communication and speech acts.* Cambridge MA: MIT Press.

Barwise, J. (1989). *The situation in logic.* Stanford CA: Center for the Study of Language and Information.

Barwise, J., and Etchemendy, J. (1986). *The liar.* London: Oxford University Press.

Bateson, G. (1972). A theory of play and fantasy. In G. Bateson, *Steps to an ecology of mind*, pp. 177–193. New York: Ballantine.

Bavelas, J. B. (1992). Redefining language: Nonverbal linguistic acts in face-to-face dialogue. B. Aubrey Fisher Memorial Lecture, University of Victoria, Victoria, Canada.

(1994). Gestures as part of speech: Methodological implications. *Research on Language and Social Interaction*, 27, 201–221.

Bavelas, J. B., Black, A., Lemery, C. R., MacInnis, S., and Mullett, J. (1986). Experimental methods for studying elementary motor mimicry. *Journal of Nonverbal Behavior*, 10, 102–119.

Bavelas, J. B., Black, A., Lemery, C. R., and Mullett, J. (1986). "I *show* you how you feel": Motor mimicry as a communicative act. *Journal of Personality and Social Psychology*, 50, 322–329.

Bavelas, J. B., Chovil, N., Lawrie, D. A., and Wade, A. (1992). Interactive gestures. *Discourse Processes*, 15, 469–489.

Beattie, G. W. (1981). Interruption in conversational interaction, and its relation to the sex and status of the interactants. *Linguistics*, 19, 15–35.

393

(1982). Look, just don't interrupt! *New Scientist, 95*(1324), 859–860.

(1983). *Talk: An analysis of speech and non-verbal behaviour in conversation.* Milton Keynes: Open University Press.

Beattie, G. W., and Barnard, P. J. (1979). The temporal structure of natural telephone conversations (directory enquiry calls). *Linguistics, 17,* 213–229.

Beattie, G. W., Cutler, A., and Pearson, M. (1982). Why is Mrs. Thatcher interrupted so often? *Nature, 300,* 744-747.

Bell, R. A., and Healey, J. G. (1992). Idiomatic communication and interpersonal solidarity in friends' relational cultures. *Human Communication Research, 18*(3), 307–335.

Bilous, F. R. (1992). The role of gestures in speech production: Gestures enhance lexical access. Ph.D. dissertation, Columbia University.

Blackmer, E. R., and Mitton, J. L. (1991). Theories of monitoring and the timing of repairs in spontaneous speech. *Cognition, 39,* 173–194.

Bock, J. K., and Levelt, W. J. M. (1994). Language production: Grammatical encoding. In M. A. Gernsbacher (Ed.), *Handbook of psycholinguistics,* pp. 945–984. San Diego: Academic Press.

Bolinger, D. (1985). The inherent iconism of intonation. In J. Haiman (Ed.), *Iconicity in syntax,* pp. 97–108. Amsterdam: John Benjamins.

Boomer, D. S. (1965). Hesitation and grammatical encoding. *Language and Speech, 8,* 148–158.

Booth, W. C. (1961). *The rhetoric of fiction.* University of Chicago Press.

(1983). *The rhetoric of fiction.* 2nd edn. University of Chicago Press.

Bower, G. H., Black, J. B., and Turner, T. J. (1979). Scripts in memory for text. *Cognitive Psychology, 11,* 177–220.

Brandenburger, A. (1992). Knowledge and equilibrium in games. *Journal of Economic Perspectives, 6*(4), 83–101.

Bratman, M. E. (1987). *Intention, plans, and practical reason.* Cambridge MA: Harvard University Press.

(1990). What is intention? In P. R. Cohen, J. Morgan, and M. E. Pollack (Eds.), *Intentions in communication,* pp. 15–31. Cambridge MA: MIT Press.

Brennan, S. E. (1990). Seeking and providing evidence for mutual understanding. Ph.D. dissertation, Stanford University.

Brennan, S. E., and Williams, M. (1995). The feeling of another's knowing: Prosody and filled pauses as cues to listeners about the metacognitive states of speakers. *Journal of Memory and Language, 34,* 383–398.

Brown, G., and Yule, G. (1983). *Discourse analysis.* Cambridge University Press.

Brown, P., and Levinson, S. (1978). Universals in language usage: politeness phenomena. In E. Goody (Ed.), *Questions and politeness,* pp. 56–311. Cambridge University Press.

(1987). *Politeness.* Cambridge University Press.

Bruce, B. (1981). A social interaction model of reading. *Discourse Processes, 4,* 273–311.

Brunner, L. J. (1979). Smiles can be back channels. *Journal of Personality and Social Psychology, 37*, 728–734.

Buchler, J. (Ed.). (1940). *Philosophical writings of Peirce.* London: Routledge and Kegan Paul.

Bühler, K. (1982). The deictic field of language and deictic words. In R. J. Jarvella and W. Klein (Eds.), *Speech, place, and action,* pp. 9–30. New York: John Wiley.

Burge, T. (1975). On knowledge and convention. *Philosophical Review, 84*, 249–255.

Butterworth, B., and Beattie, G. (1978). Gesture and silence as indicators of planning in speech. In R. N. Campbell and P. T. Smith (Eds.), *Recent advances in the psychology of language: Formal and experimental approaches,* vol. II, pp. 347–360. New York: Plenum Press.

Cargile, J. (1969/70). A note on "iterated knowings." *Analysis, 30*, 151–155.

Cassell, J., and McNeill, D. (1991). Gesture and the poetics of prose. *Poetics Today, 12*(3), 375–404.

Chafe, W. (1979). The flow of thought and the flow of language. In T. Givon (Ed.), *Syntax and semantics 12: Discourse and syntax,* pp. 159–181. New York: Academic Press.

(1980). The deployment of consciousness in the production of a narrative. In W. Chafe (Ed.), *The pear stories,* pp. 9–50. Norwood NJ: Ablex.

(1992). Intonation units and prominences in English natural discourse. Paper presented at the University of Pennsylvania Prosodic Workshop, Philadelphia.

Chase, W. G., and Simon, H. A. (1973). The mind's eye in chess. In W. G. Chase (Ed.), *Visual information processing,* pp. 215–281. New York: Academic Press.

Chatman, S. (1978). *Story and discourse: Narrative structure in fiction and film.* Ithaca NY: Cornell University Press.

Chovil, N. (1991). Social determinants of facial displays. *Journal of Nonverbal Behavior, 15*, 141–154.

(1991/2). Discourse-oriented facial displays in conversation. *Language and Social Interaction, 25*, 163–194.

Chovil, N., and Fridlund, A. J. (1991). Why emotionality cannot equal sociality: Reply to Buck. *Journal of Nonverbal Behavior, 15*, 163–167.

Cialdini, R. B. (1993). *Influence: Science and practice.* New York: Harper Collins.

Clark, E. V., and Clark, H. H. (1979). When nouns surface as verbs. *Language, 55*, 430–477.

Clark, H. H. (1978). Inferring what is meant. In W. J. M. Levelt and G. B. Flores d'Arcais (Eds.), *Studies in the perception of language,* pp. 259–322. London: Wiley.

(1979). Responding to indirect speech acts. *Cognitive Psychology, 11*, 430–477.

(1983). Making sense of nonce sense. In G. B. Flores d'Arcais and R. Jarvella (Eds.), *The process of language understanding,* pp. 297–331. New York: Wiley.

(1994). Managing problems in speaking. *Speech Communication, 15*, 243-250.

(1996). Communities, commonalities, and common ground. In J. Gumperz and S. Levinson (Eds.), *Whorf revisited*, pp. 324–355. Cambridge University Press.

Clark, H. H., and Brennan, S. A. (1991). Grounding in communication. In L. B. Resnick, J. M. Levine, and S. D. Teasley (Eds.), *Perspectives on socially shared cognition*, pp. 127–149. Washington, DC: APA Books.

Clark, H. H., and Carlson, T. B. (1982a). Hearers and speech acts. *Language, 58*, 332–373.

(1982b). Speech acts and hearers' beliefs. In N. V. Smith (Ed.), *Mutual knowledge*, pp. 1–36. New York: Academic Press.

Clark, H. H., and Clark, E. V. (1977). *Psychology and language: An introduction to psycholinguistics*. New York: Harcourt Brace Jovanovich.

Clark, H. H., and French, J. W. (1981). Telephone goodbyes. *Language in Society, 10*, 1–19.

Clark, H. H., and Gerrig, R. J. (1983). Understanding old words with new meanings. *Journal of Verbal Learning and Verbal Behavior, 22*, 591–608.

(1984). On the pretense theory of irony. *Journal of Experimental Psychology: General, 113*, 121–126.

(1990). Quotations as demonstrations. *Language, 66*, 764–805.

Clark, H. H., and Haviland, S. E. (1974). Psychological processes in linguistic explanation. In D. Cohen (Ed.), *Explaining linguistic phenomena*, pp. 91–124. Washington: Hemisphere Publication Corporation.

(1977). Comprehension and the given-new contract. In R. O. Freedle (Ed.), *Discourse production and comprehension*, pp. 1–40. Hillsdale NJ: Erlbaum.

Clark, H. H., and Marshall, C. R. (1978). Reference diaries. In D. L. Waltz (Ed.), *Theoretical issues in natural language processing*, Vol. II, pp. 57–63. New York: Association for Computing Machinery.

(1981). Definite reference and mutual knowledge. In A. K. Joshi, B. L. Webber, and I. A. Sag (Eds.), *Elements of discourse understanding*, pp. 10–63. Cambridge University Press.

Clark, H. H., and Schaefer, E. F. (1987a). Collaborating on contributions to conversations. *Language and Cognitive Processes, 2*(1), 19–41.

(1987b). Concealing one's meaning from overhearers. *Journal of Memory and Language, 26*, 209–225.

(1989). Contributing to discourse. *Cognitive Science, 13*, 259–294.

(1992). Dealing with overhearers. In H. H. Clark (Ed.), *Arenas of language use*, pp. 248-297. University of Chicago Press.

Clark, H. H., Schreuder, R., and Buttrick, S. (1983). Common ground and the understanding of demonstrative reference. *Journal of Verbal Learning and Verbal Behavior, 22*, 1–39.

Clark, H. H., and Schunk, D. H. (1980). Polite responses to polite requests. *Cognition, 8*, 111–143.

Clark, H. H., and Wilkes-Gibbs, D. (1986). Referring as a collaborative process. *Cognition, 22*, 1–39.

Coates, L. (1992). A collaborative theory of inversion: Irony in dialogue. Paper presented at the International Communication Association, Miami.

Cohen, A. A., and Harrison, R. P. (1973). Intentionality in the use of hand illustrators in face-to-face communication situations. *Journal of Personality and Social Psychology, 28,* 276–279.

Cohen, P. R. (1978). On knowing what to say: Planning speech acts. Ph.D. dissertation, University of Toronto.

Cohen, P. R., and Levesque, H. J. (1990). Persistence, intention, and commitment. In P. R. Cohen, J. Morgan, and M. E. Pollack (Eds.), *Intentions in communication,* pp. 33–69. Cambridge MA: MIT Press.

Cohn, D. (1978). *Transparent minds: Narrative modes for presenting consciousness in fiction.* Princeton University Press.

Cruttenden, A. (1986). *Intonation.* Cambridge University Press.

Crystal, D. (1969). *Prosodic systems and intonation in English.* Cambridge University Press.

Crystal, D., and Davy, D. (1975). *Advanced English conversation.* London: Longman.

Davidson, J. A. (1984). Subsequent versions of invitations, offers, requests and proposals dealing with potential or actual rejection. In J. M. Atkinson and J. Heritage (Eds.), *Structures of social action: Studies in conversation analysis,* pp. 102–128. Cambridge University Press.

(1990). Modifications of invitations, offers and rejections. In G. Psathas (Ed.), *Interaction competence,* pp. 149–180. Washington, DC: International Institute for Ethnomethodology and Conversational Analysis and University Press of America.

Davis, S. (1979). Perlocutions. *Linguistics and Philosophy, 3,* 225–243.

(1991). Introduction. In S. Davis (Ed.), *Pragmatics: A reader,* pp. 3–13. New York: Oxford University Press.

Dawes, R. (1990). The potential nonfalsity of the false consensus effect. In R. M. Hogarth (Ed.), *Insights in decision making,* pp. 179–199. Chicago University Press.

DeLaguna, G. (1927). *Speech: Its function and development.* New Haven CN: Yale University Press.

Downing, P. A. (1977). On the creation and use of English compound nouns. *Language, 53,* 810–842.

Dreckendorff, H. O. (1977). Towards a theory of n-tuple binds. *Sociological Inquiry, 47* (2), 143–147.

Drew, P. (1984). Speakers' reportings in invitation sequences. In J. M. Atkinson and J. Heritage (Eds.), *Structures of social action: Studies in conversation analysis,* pp. 129–151. Cambridge University Press.

(1987). Po-faced receipts of teases. *Linguistics, 25,* 219–253.

DuBois, J. (1974). Syntax in mid-sentence. *Berkeley studies in syntax and semantics,* vol. I, pp. III.1–III.25. Berkeley CA: University of California, Institute of Human Learning and Department of Linguistics.

Duncan, S. D., Jr. (1972). Some signals and rules for taking speaking turns in conversations. *Journal of Personality and Social Psychology, 23,* 283–292.

(1973). Toward a grammar for dyadic conversation. *Semiotica, 9,* 29–47.

Edmonds, P. G. (1993). A computational model of collaboration on reference in direction-giving dialogues. M.Sc. Thesis, Department of Computer Science, University of Toronto.

Efron, D. (1941). *Gesture and environment.* New York: King's Crown Press.

Ekman, P. (1979). About brows: Emotional and conversational signals. In M. V. Cranach, K. Foppa, W. Lepenies, and D. Ploog (Eds.), *Human ethology: Claims and limits of a new discipline,* pp. 169–203. Cambridge University Press.

(1992). An argument for basic emotions. *Cognition and Emotion, 6,* 169-200.

Ekman, P., and Friesen, W. (1969). The repertoire of nonverbal behavior: Categories, origins, usage and coding. *Semiotica, 1,* 49–98.

Ekman, P., Friesen, W. V., O'Sullivan, M., and Chan, A. (1987). Universals and cultural differences in the judgments of facial expressions of emotion. *Journal of Personality and Social Psychology, 53*(4), 712–717.

Engle, R., and Clark, H. H. (1995). Using composites of speech, gestures, diagrams, and demonstrations in explanations of mechanical devices. Paper presented at the American Association of Applied Linguistics, San Diego CA.

Erman, B. (1987). *Pragmatic expressions in English: A study of you know, you see, and I mean in face-to-face conversation.* Stockholm, Sweden: Almqvist and Wiksell International.

Ervin-Tripp, S. (1976). Is Sybil there? The structure of American English directives. *Language in Society, 5,* 25-66.

(1981). How to make and understand a request. In H. Parret, M. Sbisà, and J. Verschueren (Eds.), *Possibilities and limitations of pragmatics: Proceedings of the conference on pragmatics at Urbino, July 8–14, 1979,* pp. 195–210. Amsterdam: Benjamins.

Falk, J. (1979). The conversational duet. Ph.D. dissertation, Princeton University.

Fenster, M., Kraus, S., and Rosenschein, J. (1995). Coordination without communication: Experimental validation of focal point techniques. Paper presented at the International Conference on Multiagent Systems, California.

Fillmore, C. (1975). *Santa Cruz lectures on deixis.* Bloomington IN: Indiana University Linguistics Club.

(1981). Pragmatics and the description of discourse. In P. Cole (Ed.), *Radical pragmatics,* pp. 143–166. New York: Academic Press.

Fowler, H. W. (1965). *A dictionary of modern English usage.* Oxford University Press.

Fox Tree, J. E. (1995). Effects of false starts and repetitions on the processing of subsequent words in spontaneous speech. *Journal of Memory and Language, 34,* 709–738.

Fox Tree, J. E., and Clark, H. H. (1994). Pronouncing 'the' as /thiy/ to signal trouble in spontaneous conversation. Paper presented at the Psychonomics Society, St. Louis MO.

Francik, E. P., and Clark, H. H. (1985). How to make requests that overcome obstacles to compliance. *Journal of Memory and Language, 24,* 560–568.

Freedman, N. (1972). The analysis of movement behavior during the clinical interview. In A. W. Siegman and B. Pope (Eds.), *Studies in dyadic communication*, pp. 153–175. New York: Pergamon.

Fridlund, A. J. (1991). Sociality of solitary smiling: Potentiation by an implicit audience. *Journal of Personality and Social Psychology, 60*, 229–240.

(1994). *Human facial expression: An evolutionary view*. San Diego CA: Academic Press.

Fussell, S. R., and Krauss, R. M. (1991). Accuracy and bias in estimates of others' knowledge. *European Journal of Social Psychology, 21*, 445–454.

(1992). Coordination of knowledge in communication: Effects of speakers' assumptions about what others know. *Journal of Personality and Social Psychology, 62*(3), 378–391.

Galambos, J. A., and Rips, L. J. (1982). Memory for routines. *Journal of Verbal Learning and Verbal Behavior, 21*, 260–281.

Gardner, J. (1983). *The art of fiction: Notes on craft for young writers*. New York: Alfred Knopf.

Garnham, A., Shillcock, R. C., Brown, G. D. A., Mill, A. I. D., and Cutler, A. (1982). Slips of the tongue in the London–Lund corpus of spontaneous conversation. *Linguistics, 19*, 805–817.

Garrod, S., and Anderson, A. (1987). Saying what you mean in dialogue: A study in conceptual and semantic co-ordination. *Cognition, 27*, 181–218.

Gazdar, G. (1979). *Pragmatics: Implicature, presupposition, and logical form*. New York: Academic Press.

Gee, J. P. (1986). Units in the production of narrative discourse. *Discourse Processes, 9*, 391–422.

Geluykens, R. (1987). Tails (right-dislocations) as a repair mechanism in English conversation. In J. Nuyts and G. de Schutter (Eds.), *Getting one's words into line: On word order and functional grammar*, pp. 119–129. Dordrecht: Foris.

(1988). The interactional nature of referent-introduction. *Papers from the 24th regional meeting of the Chicago Linguistic Society*, pp. 151–164. Chicago Linguistic Society.

(1992). *From discourse process to grammatical construction: On left-dislocation in English*. Amsterdam: Benjamins.

Gerrig, R. J. (1989a). Reexperiencing fiction and non-fiction. *Journal of Aesthetics and Art Criticism, 47*, 277–280.

(1989b). Suspense in the absence of uncertainty. *Journal of Memory and Language, 28*, 633–648.

(1993). *Experiencing narrative worlds: On the psychological activities of reading*. New Haven CN: Yale University Press.

Gibbs, R. W., Jr. (1979). Contextual effects in understanding indirect requests. *Discourse Processes, 2*, 1–10.

(1981). Your wish is my command: Convention and context in interpreting indirect requests. *Journal of Verbal Learning and Verbal Behavior, 20*, 431–444.

(1983). Do people always process the literal meanings of indirect requests? *Journal of Experimental Psychology: Learning, Memory and Cognition, 9*, 524–533.

(1986a). On the psycholinguistics of sarcasm. *Journal of Experimental Psychology: General, 115*, 3–15.

(1986b). What makes some indirect speech acts conventional? *Journal of Memory and Language, 25*(2), 181–196.

(1989). Understanding and literal meaning. *Cognitive Science, 13*, 243–251.

(1994). *The poetics of mind: Figurative thought, language, and understanding.* Cambridge University Press.

Gilbert, M. (1981). Game theory and convention. *Synthese, 46*, 41–93.

(1983). Agreements, conventions, and language. *Synthese, 54*, 375–407.

Gleitman, L., and Gleitman, H. (1970). *Phrase and paraphrase: Some innovative uses of language.* New York: Norton.

Goffman, E. (1967). *Interaction ritual: Essays on face-to-face behavior.* Garden City NY: Anchor Books.

(1971). *Relations in public.* New York: Harper and Row.

(1974). *Frame Analysis.* New York: Harper and Row.

(1976). Replies and responses. *Language in Society, 5*, 257–313.

(1978). Response cries. *Language, 54*, 787–815.

(1981a). *Forms of talk.* Philadelphia: University of Pennsylvania Press.

(1981b). Radio talk. In E. Goffman (Ed.), *Forms of talk*, pp. 197–327. Philadelphia: University of Pennsylvania Press.

Goldberg, J. (1975). A system for the transfer of instructions in natural settings. *Semiotica, 14*, 269–296.

Goldberg, L. R. (1993). The structure of phenotypic personality traits. *American Psychologist, 48*(1), 26–34.

Goldman, A. I. (1970). *A theory of human action.* Princeton University Press.

Goodman, N. (1968). *Languages of art.* Indianapolis: Bobbs-Merrill.

Goodwin, C. (1981). *Conversational organization: Interaction between speakers and hearers.* New York: Academic Press.

(1986a). Between and within: Alternative sequential treatments of continuers and assessments. *Human Studies, 9*, 205–217.

(1986b). Gestures as a resource for the organization of mutual orientation. *Semiotica, 62*, 29–49.

(1987). Forgetfulness as an interactive resource. *Social Psychology Quarterly, 50*(2), 115-131.

Goodwin, M. H., and Goodwin, C. (1986). Gesture and coparticipation in the activity of searching for a word. *Semiotica, 62*, 51–75.

Gordon, D., and Lakoff, G. (1971). Conversational postulates. *Papers from the seventh regional meeting of the Chicago Linguistic Society*, pp. 63–84. Chicago Linguistic Society.

Gouldner, A. W. (1960). The norm of reciprocity: A preliminary statement. *American Sociological Review, 25*(2), 161–178.

Green, G. M. (1989). *Pragmatics and natural language understanding*. Hillsdale NJ: Lawrence Erlbaum.

Grice, H. P. (1957). Meaning. *Philosophical Review, 66*, 377–388.

(1968). Utterer's meaning, sentence-meaning, and word-meaning. *Foundations of Language, 4*, 225–242.

(1975). Logic and conversation. In P. Cole and J. L. Morgan (Eds.), *Syntax and semantics 3: Speech acts*, pp. 41–58. New York: Seminar Press.

(1978). Some further notes on logic and conversation. In P. Cole (Ed.), *Syntax and semantics 9: Pragmatics*, pp. 113–127. New York: Academic Press.

(1982). Meaning revisited. In N. V. Smith (Ed.), *Mutual knowledge*, pp. 223–243. London: Academic Press.

Grimes, J. E. (1975). *The thread of discourse*. The Hague: Mouton.

Grimshaw, A. D. (1987). Finishing other's talk: Some structure and pragmatic features of completion offers. In R. Steele and T. Threadgold (Eds.), *Language topics: Essays in honour of Michael Halliday*, pp. 213–235. Amsterdam: John Benjamins.

Grosz, B. (1981). Focusing and description in natural language dialogues. In A. Joshi, B. Webber, and I. Sag (Eds.), *Elements of discourse understanding*, pp. 84–105. Cambridge University Press.

Grosz, B., and Sidner, C. (1986). Attention, intentions, and the structure of discourse. *Computational Linguistics, 12*, 175–204.

(1990). Plans for discourse. In P. R. Cohen, J. Morgan, and M. E. Pollack (Eds.), *Intentions in communication*, pp. 419–444. Cambridge MA: MIT Press.

Haiman, J. (1990). Sarcasm as theater. *Cognitive Linguistics, 1*, 181-205.

Halliday, M. A. K. (1967). Notes on transitivity and theme in English. Part 2. *Journal of Linguistics, 3*, 199–244.

Halliday, M. A. K., and Hasan, R. (1976). *Cohesion in English*. New York: Longman.

Halpern, J. Y., and Moses, Y. (1990). Knowledge and common knowledge in a distributed environment. *Journal of the ACM, 37*(3), 549–587.

Hancher, M. (1979). The classification of cooperative illocutionary acts. *Language in Society, 8*, 1–14.

Hankamer, J., and Sag, I. A. (1976). Deep and surface anaphora. *Linguistic Inquiry, 7*, 391–426.

Harder, P., and Kock, C. (1976). *The theory of presupposition failure*. Copenhagen: Akademisk Forlag.

Harman, G. (1977). Review of *Linguistic behavior* by Jonathan Bennett. *Language, 53*, 417–424.

Hart, J. T. (1965). Memory and the feeling-of-knowing experience. *Journal of Educational Psychology, 56*, 208–216.

(1967). Memory and the memory-monitoring process. *Journal of Verbal Learning and Verbal Behavior, 6*, 685–691.

Heeman, P. (1991). A computational model of collaboration on referring expressions. M.Sc. Thesis, Department of Computer Science, University of Toronto.

Heeman, P., and Hirst, G. (1992). *Collaborating on referring expressions* (TR 435). Department of Computer Science, University of Rochester, Rochester NY.

Heritage, J. (1984). A change-of-state token and aspects of its sequential placement. In J. M. Atkinson and J. Heritage (Eds.), *Structures of social action: Studies in conversation analysis*, pp. 299–345. Cambridge University Press.

Heritage, J., and Greatbatch, D. (1986). Generating applause: A study of rhetoric and response at party political conferences. *American Journal of Sociology, 92*, 110–157.

Hirschberg, J., and Litman, D. (1987). Now let's talk about "now": Identifying cue phrases intonationally. *Proceedings of the Twenty-fifth Annual Meeting of the Association for Computational Linguistics*, pp. 163–171. Stanford CA: Association for Computational Linguistics.

Hirst, G., McRoy, S., Heeman, P., Edmonds, P., and Horton, D. (1994). Repairing conversational misunderstandings and non–understandings. *Speech Communication, 15*, 213–229.

Hobbs, J., and Evans, D. (1980). Conversation as planned behavior. *Cognitive Science, 4*, 349–477.

Hoch, S.J. (1987). Perceived consensus and predictive accuracy: The pros and cons of projection. *Journal of Personality and Social Psychology, 53* (2), 221–234.

Hockett, C. F. (1967). Where the tongue slips, there slip I. *To honor Roman Jakobson: Essays on the occasion of his 70th birthday*, pp. 910–936. The Hague: Mouton.

Holmes, J. (1986). Functions of *you know* in women's and men's speech. *Language in Society, 15*, 1–21.

Homans, G. C. (1950). *The human group*. New York: Harcourt Brace.

(1958). Social behavior as exchange. *American Journal of Sociology, 63*, 597–606.

Hopper, R. (1992). *Telephone conversation*. Bloomington IN: Indiana University Press.

Hopper, R., Knapp, M. L., and Scott, L. (1981). Couples' personal idioms: Exploring intimate talk. *Journal of Communication, 31*, 23-33.

Horn, L. R. (1984). Toward a new taxonomy for pragmatic inference: Q-based and r-based implicature. In D. Schiffrin (Ed.), *Meaning, form and use in context: Linguistic application*, pp. 11–42. Washington: Georgetown University Press.

Houtkoop, H. (1987). *Establishing agreement: An analysis of proposal–acceptance sequences*. Dordrecht: Foris.

Hymes, D. (1974). *Foundations of sociolinguistics: An ethnographic approach*. Philadelphia: University of Pennsylvania Press.

Irvine, J. T. (1974). Strategies of status manipulation in the Wolof greeting. In R. Bauman and J. Sherzer (Eds.), *Explorations in the ethnography of speaking*, pp. 167–191. Cambridge University Press.

Isaacs, E. A., and Clark, H. H. (1987). References in conversation between experts and novices. *Journal of Experimental Psychology: General, 116*, 26–37.

(1990). Ostensible invitations. *Language in Society, 19*, 493–509.

James, D. (1972). Some aspects of the syntax and semantics of interjections. *Papers from the Eighth Regional Meeting of the Chicago Linguistic Society*, pp. 162-172. Chicago Linguistic Society.

(1973). Another look at, say, some grammatical constraints on, oh, interjections and hesitations. *Papers from the Ninth Regional Meeting of the Chicago Linguistic Society*, pp. 242–251. Chicago Linguistic Society.

Jameson, A., Nelson, T. O., Leonesio, R. J., and Narens, L. (1993). The feeling of another person's knowing. *Journal of Memory and Language, 32*(3), 320–335.

Jefferson, G. (1972). Side sequences. In D. Sudnow (Ed.), *Studies in social interaction*, pp. 294–338. New York: Free Press.

(1973). A case of precision timing in ordinary conversation: Overlapped tag-positioned address terms in closing sequences. *Semiotica, 9*, 47-96.

(1978). Sequential aspects of storytelling in conversation. In J. Schenkein (Ed.), *Studies in the organization of conversational interaction*, pp. 219–248. New York: Academic Press.

(1989). Preliminary notes on a possible metric which provides for a "standard maximum" silence of approximately one second in conversation. In D. Roger and P. Bull (Eds.), *Conversation*, pp. 166–196. Clevedon: Multilingual Matters.

Jefferson, G., Sacks, H., and Schegloff, E. A. (1987). Notes on laughter in the pursuit of intimacy. In G. Button and J. R. E. Lee (Eds.), *Talk and social organization*, pp. 152–205. Clevedon: Multilingual Matters.

Johnson-Laird, P. N. (1983). *Mental models*. Cambridge University Press.

Jorgensen, J., Miller, G., and Sperber, D. (1984). Test of the mention theory of irony. *Journal of Experimental Psychology: General, 113*, 112–120.

Karttunen, L., and Peters, S. (1975). Conventional implicature of Montague grammar. Paper presented at the Berkeley Linguistics Society, Berkeley CA.

Kasher, A. (1977). Foundations of philosophical pragmatics. In R. Butts and J. Hintikka (Eds.), *Basic problems in methodology and linguistics*, vol. III, pp. 225–242. Dordrecht: Reidel.

Kaspar, W. (1976). Gemeinsames Wissen: zu einem wissensorientierten Wahrheitsbegriff. *Zeitschrift für germanistische Linguistik, 4*, 17–25.

Kay, P., and Zimmer, K. (1976). On the semantics of compounds and genitives in English. Paper presented at the sixth annual meeting of the California Linguistics Association, San Diego CA.

Keller, R. (1975). *Wahrheit und kollektives Wissen. Zum Begrio der Präsupposition*. Düsseldorf: Pädagogischer Verlag Schwann.

Kendon, A. (1967). Some functions of gaze-direction in social interaction. *Acta Psychologica, 26*, 22–63.

(1980). Gesticulation and speech: Two aspects of the process of utterance. In M. R. Key (Ed.), *Relationship of verbal and nonverbal communication*, pp. 207–227. Amsterdam: Mouton de Gruyter.

(1981). Geography of gesture. *Semiotica, 37*, 129–163.

(1983). Gesture and speech: How they interact. In J. M. Weimann and R. P. Harrison (Eds.), *Nonverbal interaction*, pp. 13–45. Beverly Hills CA: Sage.

Kirshenblatt-Gimblett, B. (1974). The concept and varieties of narrative performance in east European Jewish culture. In R. Bauman and J. Sherzer (Eds.), *Explorations in the ethnography of speaking*, pp. 283–308. Cambridge University Press.

Klapp, R. E. (1956/7). The concept of consensus and its importance. *Sociology and Social Research, 41*, 336-342.

Klein, W. (1982). Local deixis in route directions. In R. Jarvella and W. Klein (Eds.), *Speech, place, and action: Studies in deixis and related topics*, pp. 161–182. Chichester: John Wiley.

Krahé, B. (1992). *Personality and social psychology: Towards a synthesis.* London: Sage.

Kraus, S., and Rosenschein, J. S. (1992). The role of representation in interaction: Discovering focal points among alternative solutions. In Y. Demazeau and E. Werner (Eds.), *Decentralized Artificial Intelligence III*, pp. 147–165. Amsterdam: Elsevier Science Publishers.

Krauss, R. M. (1991). What do conversational gestures tell us? Paper presented at the Society of Experimental Social Psychology, Columbus OH.

Krauss, R. M., and Fussell, S. R. (1991). Perspective-taking in communication: Representations of others' knowledge in reference. *Social Cognition, 9*, 2–24.

Krauss, R. M., and Glucksberg, S. (1977). Social and nonsocial speech. *Scientific American, 236*, 100–105.

Krauss, R. M., Morrel-Samuels, P., and Colasante, C. (1991). Do conversational hand gestures communicate? *Journal of Personality and Social Psychology, 61*(5), 743–754.

Kraut, R. E., and Johnston, R. E. (1979). Social and emotional messages of smiling: An ethnological approach. *Journal of Personality and Social Psychology, 37*, 1539–1553.

Kreuz, R., and Glucksberg, S. (1989). How to be sarcastic: The reminder theory of verbal irony. *Journal of Experimental Psychology: General, 118*, 347-386.

Kumon-Nakamura, S., Glucksberg, S., and Brown, M. (1995). How about another piece of pie: The allusional pretense theory of discourse irony. *Journal of Experimental Psychology: General, 124*, 3–21.

Labov, W. (1972). Rules for ritual insults. In D. Sudnow (Ed.), *Studies in social interaction*, pp. 120–169. New York: Free Press.

Lakoff, R. (1973). The logic of politeness; or, Minding your p's and q's. *Papers from the ninth regional meeting of the Chicago Linguistics Society*, pp. 292–305. Chicago Linguistics Society.

(1977). Politeness, pragmatics and performatives. In A. Rogers, B. Walls, and J. P. Murphy (Eds.), *Proceedings of the Texas conference on performatives, presuppositions, and implicatures*, pp. 79–106. Washington DC: Center for Applied Linguistics.

Langer, E. J., and Abelson, R. (1972). The semantics of asking a favor: How to succeed in getting help without really trying. *Journal of Personality and Social Psychology, 24*, 26-32.

Langer, E. J., Blank, A., and Chanowitz, B. (1978). The mindlessness of ostensibly thoughtful action: The role of "placebic" information in interpersonal interaction. *Journal of Personality and Social Psychology, 37*, 2014–2024.

Latané, B., and Darley, J. (1968). *The unresponsive bystander: Why doesn't he help?* New York: Appleton-Century-Crofts.

Leech, G. N. (1983). *Principles of pragmatics*. London: Longman.

Lerner, G. H. (1987). Collaborative turn sequences: Sentence construction and social action. Ph.D. dissertation, University of California, Irvine.

Levelt, W. J. M. (1983). Monitoring and self-repair in speech. *Cognition, 14*, 41–104.

(1984). Spontaneous self-repairs in speech: Processes and representations. In M. P. R. Van den Broecke and A. Cohen (Eds.), *Proceedings of the Tenth International Congress of Phonetic Sciences*, pp. 105–118. Dordrecht: Foris Publications.

(1989). *Speaking*. Cambridge MA: MIT Press.

Levi, J. (1978). *The syntax and semantics of complex nominals*. New York: Academic Press.

Levinson, S. C. (1979). Activity types and language. *Linguistics, 17*, 365–399.

(1983). *Pragmatics*. Cambridge University Press.

(1987). Minimization and conversational inference. In J. Verschueren and M. Bertuccelli-Papi (Eds.), *The pragmatic perspective*, pp. 61–130. Amsterdam: John Benjamins.

(1992). Activity types and language. In P. Drew and J. Heritage (Eds.), *Talk at work*, pp. 66–100. Cambridge University Press.

Lewis, D. K. (1969). *Convention: A philosophical study*. Cambridge MA: Harvard University Press.

(1979). Scorekeeping in a language game. *Journal of Philosophical Logic, 8*, 339–359.

Litman, D. J., and Allen, J. F. (1987). A plan recognition model for subdialogues in conversations. *Cognitive Science, 11*(2), 163–200.

Lucariello, J. (1994). Situational irony. *Journal of Experimental Psychology: General, 113*, 112–120.

Lyons, J. (1977). *Semantics*, Vol. I. Cambridge University Press.

Macaulay, R. K. S. (1987). Polyphonic monologues: Quoted direct speech in oral narratives. *IPrA Papers in Pragmatics, 1*, 1–34.

Marks, G., and Miller, N. (1987). Ten years of research on the false-consensus effect: An empirical and theoretical review. *Psychological Bulletin, 102*(1), 72–90.

McCarthy, J. (1980). Circumscription: A form of non–monotonic reasoning. *Artificial Intelligence, 13*, 27–39, 171–172.

(1986). Applications of circumscription for formalizing common sense knowledge. *Artificial Intelligence, 19*, 89–116.

(1990). Formalization of two puzzles involving knowledge. In V. Lifschitz (Ed.), *Formalizing common sense: Papers by John McCarthy*, pp. 158–166. Norwood NJ: Ablex Publishing.

McNeill, D. (1992). *Hand and mind*. University of Chicago Press.

Mead, G. H. (1934). *Mind, self, and society*. University of Chicago Press.

Mehan, H. (1979). *Learning lessons: Social organization in the classroom*. Cambridge MA: Harvard University Press.

Merritt, M. (1976). On questions following questions (in service encounters). *Language in Society, 5*, 315–357.

(1984). On the use of okay in service encounters. In J. Baugh and J. Sherzer (Eds.), *Language in use: Readings in sociolinguistics*, pp. 139–147. Englewood Cliffs NJ: Prentice-Hall.

Minsky, M. (1975). A framework for representing knowledge. In P. H. Winston (Ed.), *The psychology of computer vision*, pp. 211–277. New York: McGraw-Hill.

Morgan, J. L. (1978). Two types of convention in indirect speech acts. In P. Cole (Ed.), *Syntax and Semantics 9: Pragmatics*, pp. 261–280. New York: Academic Press.

Morgan, J. L., and Sellner, M. B. (1980). Discourse and linguistic theory. In R. J. Spiro, B. C. Bruce, and W. F. Brewer (Eds.), *Theoretical issues in reading comprehension: Perspectives from cognitive psychology, linguistics, artificial intelligence, and education*, pp. 165–200. Hillsdale NJ: Lawrence Erlbaum.

Morrel-Samuels, P., and Krauss, R. M. (1992). Word familiarity predicts temporal asynchrony of hand gestures and speech. *Journal of Experimental Psychology: Learning, Memory, and Cognition, 18*(3), 615–622.

Morris, D., Collett, P., Marsh, P., and O'Shaughnessy, M. (1979). *Gestures: Their origins and distribution*. New York: Stein and Day.

Morrow, D., Lee, A., and Rodvold, M. (1993). Analyzing problems in routine controller–pilot communication. *International Journal of Aviation Psychology, 3*, 285–302.

Morrow, D., Rodvold, M., and Lee, A. (1994). Nonroutine transactions in controller–pilot communication. *Discourse Processes, 17*(2), 235–258.

Mullen, B., Atkins, J. L., Champion, D. S., Edwards, C., Hardy, D., Story, J. E., and Vanderklok, M. (1985). The false consensus effect: A meta-analysis of 115 hypothesis tests. *Journal of Experimental Social Psychology, 21*, 262–283.

Munro, A. (1977). Speech act understanding in context. Ph.D. dissertation, University of California, San Diego.

Nelson, T. O., Leonesio, R. J., Landwehr, R. F., and Narens, L. (1986). A comparison of three predictors of an individual's memory performance: The individual's feeling of knowing versus the normative feeling of knowing versus base-rate item difficulty. *Journal of Experimental Psychology: Learning, Memory, and Cognition, 12*, 279–287.

Nickerson, R. S., Baddeley, A. D., and Freeman, B. (1987). Are people's estimates of what other people know influenced by what they themselves know? *Acta Psychologica, 64*(3), 245–259.

Norman, D. A. (1988). *The design of everyday things.* New York: Doubleday.

Nunberg, G. (1979). The non-uniqueness of semantic solutions: Polysemy. *Linguistics and Philosophy, 3*, 143–184.

(1981). Validating pragmatic explanations. In P. Cole (Ed.), *Radical pragmatics,* pp. 199-222. New York: Academic Press.

Ono, T., and Thompson, S. A. (1994). Unattached NPs in English conversation. Paper presented at the Berkeley Linguistic Society, Berkeley.

Oreström, B. (1983). *Turn-taking in English conversation.* Lund: Gleerup.

Perry, J. (1979). The problem of the essential indexical. *Nous, 13*, 3–21.

Philips, S. U. (1975). *Teasing, punning, and putting people on* (Working Papers in Sociolinguistics 28). Austin TX: Southwest Educational Developmental Laboratory.

Pierrehumbert, J., and Hirschberg, J. (1990). The meaning of intonational contours in the interpretation of discourse. In P. R. Cohen, J. Morgan, and M. E. Pollack (Eds.), *Intentions in communication,* pp. 271–311. Cambridge MA: MIT Press.

Planalp, S. (1993). Friends' and acquaintances' conversations II: Coded differences. *Journal of Social and Personal Relationships, 10*, 339–354.

Planalp, S., and Benson, A. (1992). Friends' and acquaintances' conversations I: Perceived differences. *Journal of Social and Personal Relationships, 9*, 483–506.

Planalp, S., and Garvin-Doxas, K. (1994). Using mutual knowledge in conversation: Friends as experts on each other. In S. Duck (Ed.), *Dynamics of relationships,* pp. 1–26. Thousand Oaks CA: Sage.

Polanyi, L. (1978). False starts can be true. *Proceedings of the Berkeley Linguistics Society Fourth Annual Meeting,* pp. 628–639. Berkeley Linguistics Society.

(1985). Conversational storytelling. In T. Van Dijk (Ed.), *Handbook of discourse analysis 3: Discourse and dialogue,* pp. 183–202. New York: Academic Press.

(1989). *Telling the American story.* Cambridge MA: MIT Press.

Pomerantz, A. (1978). Compliment responses: Notes on the cooperation of multiple constraints. In J. Schenkein (Ed.), *Studies in the organization of conversational interaction,* pp. 79–112. New York: Academic Press.

(1984). Agreeing and disagreeing with assessments: Some features of preferred/dispreferred turn shapes. In J. M. Atkinson and J. Heritage (Eds.), *Structures of social action: Studies in conversation analysis,* pp. 57–101. Cambridge University Press.

Putnam, H. (1970). Is semantics possible? In H. E. Kiefer and M. K. Munitz (Eds.), *Language, belief, and metaphysics,* pp. 50–63. Albany: State University of New York Press.

Quine, W. V. (1970). Natural kinds. In N. Rescher (Ed.), *Essays in honor of Carl G. Hempel: A tribute on the occasion of his sixty-fifth birthday*, pp. 5–23. Dordrecht: Reidel.

Radford, C. (1966). Knowing and telling. *Philosophical Review, 78*, 326–336.

Récanati, F. (1986). On defining communicative intentions. *Mind and Language, 1*(3), 213–242.

Redeker, G. (1986). Language use in informal narratives: Effects of social distance and listener involvement. Ph.D. dissertation, University of California, Berkeley.

(1990). Ideational and pragmatic markers of discourse structure. *Journal of Pragmatics, 14*, 367–381.

Reichman, R. (1978). Conversational coherency. *Cognitive Science, 2*, 283–327.

Reinhart, T. (1981). Pragmatics and linguistics: An analysis of sentence topics. *Philosophica, 27*, 53–94.

Rimé, B., Schiaratura, L., Hupet, M., and Ghysselinckx, A. (1984). Effects of relative immobilization on the speaker's nonverbal behavior and on the dialogue imagery level. *Motivation and Emotion, 8*, 311–325.

Robert, H. M. (1970). *Robert's rules of order newly revised*. Glenview IL: Scott, Foresman.

Ross, L., Greene, D., and House, P. (1977). The false consensus phenomenon: An attributional bias in self–perception and social perception processes. *Journal of Experimental Social Psychology, 13*, 279–301.

Sachs, J., Bard, B., and Johnson, M. L. (1981). Language learning with restricted input: Case studies of two hearing children of deaf parents. *Applied Psycholinguistics, 2*(1), 33–54.

Sacks, H. (1974). An analysis of the course of a joke's telling in conversation. In R. Bauman and J. Sherzer (Eds.), *Explorations in the ethnography of speaking*, pp. 337–353. Cambridge University Press.

(1975). Everyone has to lie. In M. Sanches and B. Blount (Eds.), *Sociocultural dimensions of language use*, pp. 57–80. New York: Academic Press.

(1987). On the preference for agreement and contiguity in sequences in conversation. In G. Button and J. R. E. Lee (Eds.), *Talk and social organization*, pp. 54-69. Clevedon: Multilingual Matters.

Sacks, H., and Schegloff, E. (1979). Two preferences in the organization of reference to persons in conversation and their interaction. In G. Psathas (Ed.), *Everyday language: Studies in ethnomethodology*, pp. 15–21. New York: Irvington Publishers.

Sacks, H., Schegloff, E. A., and Jefferson, G. (1974). A simplest systematics for the organization of turn-taking in conversation. *Language, 50*, 696–735.

Sadock, J. M. (1978). On testing for conversational implicature. In P. Cole (Ed.), *Syntax and semantics 9: Pragmatics*, pp. 281–297. New York: Academic Press.

Sadock, J. M., and Zwicky, A. (1985). Speech act distinctions in syntax. In T. Shopen (Ed.), *Language typology and syntactic description I: Clause structure*, pp. 155–196. Cambridge University Press.

Sag, I. A. (1981). Formal semantics and extralinguistic context. In P. Cole (Ed.), *Radical pragmatics*, pp. 273–294. New York: Academic Press.

Sag, I. A., and Hankamer, J. (1984). Toward a theory of anaphoric processing. *Linguistics and Philosophy, 7*, 325–345.

Saussure, F. de. (1916/1968). *Cours de linguistique générale*. Paris: Payot.

Schank, R. C., and Abelson, R. P. (1975). *Scripts, plans, goals, and understanding*. Hillsdale NJ: Erlbaum.

Scheff, T. J. (1967). Toward a sociological model of consensus. *American Sociological Review, 32*, 32–46.

Schegloff, E. A. (1968). Sequencing in conversational openings. *American Anthropologist, 70*(4), 1075–1095.

(1972). Notes on a conversational practice: Formulating place. In D. Sudnow (Ed.), *Studies in social interaction*, pp. 75–119. New York: Free Press.

(1979). Identification and recognition in telephone conversational openings. In G. Psathas (Ed.), *Everyday language: Studies in ethnomethodology*, pp. 23–78. New York: Irvington.

(1980). Preliminaries to preliminaries: "Can I ask you a question?" *Sociological Inquiry, 50*, 104–152.

(1982). Discourse as an interactional achievement: Some uses of "uh huh" and other things that come between sentences. In D. Tannen (Ed.), *Analyzing discourse: Text and talk. Georgetown University Roundtable on Languages and Linguistics 1981*, pp. 71–93. Washington, DC: Georgetown University Press.

(1984). On some gestures' relation to talk. In J. M. Atkinson and J. Heritage (Eds.), *Structures of social action: Studies in conversation analysis*, pp. 262–296. Cambridge University Press.

(1986). The routine as achievement. *Human Studies, 9*, 111–152.

(1987). Recycled turn beginnings: A precise repair mechanism in conversation's turn-taking organization. In G. Button and J. R. E. Lee (Eds.), *Talk and social organization*, pp. 70–85. Clevedon: Multilingual Matters.

Schegloff, E. A., Jefferson, G., and Sacks, H. (1977). The preference for self-correction in the organization of repair in conversation. *Language, 53*, 361–382.

Schegloff, E. A., and Sacks, H. (1973). Opening up closings. *Semiotica, 8*, 289–327.

Schelling, T. C. (1960). *The strategy of conflict*. Cambridge MA: Harvard University Press.

(1978). *Micromotives and macrobehavior*. New York: Norton.

Schiffer, S. R. (1972). *Meaning*. Oxford University Press.

Schiffrin, D. (1987). *Discourse markers*. Cambridge University Press.

Schober, M. F. (1995). Speakers, addressees, and frames of reference: Whose effort is minimized in conversations about locations? *Discourse Processes, 20*(2), 219–247.

Schober, M. F., and Clark, H. H. (1989). Understanding by addressees and overhearers. *Cognitive Psychology, 21*, 211–232.

Schourup, L. C. (1982). Common discourse particles in English conversation. Ph.D. dissertation, Ohio State University.

Schweller, K. G. (1978). The role of expectation in the comprehension and recall of direct and indirect requests. Ph.D. dissertation, University of Illinois at Urbana-Champaign.

Searle, J. R. (1969). *Speech Acts*. Cambridge University Press.

(1975a). Indirect speech acts. In P. Cole and J. L. Morgan (Eds.), *Syntax and semantics 3: Speech acts*, pp. 59–82. New York: Seminar Press.

(1975b). The logical status of fictional discourse. *New Literary History, 6*, 319–332.

(1975c). A taxonomy of illocutionary acts. In K. Gunderson (Ed.), *Minnesota studies in the philosophy of language*, pp. 334–369. Minneapolis: University of Minnesota Press.

(1978). Literal meaning. *Erkenntnis, 13*, 207–224.

(1980). The background of meaning. In J. Searle, F. Kiefer, and M. Bierwisch (Eds.), *Speech act theory and pragmatics*, pp. 22–43. Dordrecht: Reidel.

(1990). Collective intentions and actions. In P. R. Cohen, J. Morgan, and M. E. Pollack (Eds.), *Intentions in communication*, pp. 401–415. Cambridge MA: MIT Press.

Shriberg, E. E. (1994). Preliminaries to a theory of speech disfluencies. Ph.D. dissertation, University of California, Berkeley.

Smith, V. L., and Clark, H. H. (1993). On the course of answering questions. *Journal of Memory and Language, 32*, 25–38.

Smullyan, R. M. (1978). *What is the name of this book?* Englewood Cliffs NJ: Prentice-Hall.

Snow, C. E., Arlman–Rupp, A., Hassing, Y., Jobse, J., Joosten, J., and Vorster, J. (1976). Mothers' speech in three social classes. *Journal of Psycholinguistic Research, 5*, 1–20.

Sperber, D., and Wilson, D. (1981). Irony and the use-mention distinction. In P. Cole (Ed.), *Radical pragmatics*, pp. 295–318. New York: Academic Press.

(1986). *Relevance*. Cambridge MA: Harvard University Press.

Stalnaker, R. C. (1978). Assertion. In P. Cole (Ed.), *Syntax and semantics 9: Pragmatics*, pp. 315–332. New York: Academic Press.

Stenström, A. B. (1984). *Questions and responses in English conversation*. Lund: Gleerup.

Sternberg, M. (1982). Proteus in quotation-land: Mimesis and the forms of reported discourse. *Poetics Today, 3*, 107–156.

Strawson, P. F. (1964). Intention and convention in speech acts. *Philosophical Review, 75*, 439–460.

(1974). *Subject and predicate in logic and grammar*. London: Methuen.

Streeck, J. (1980). Speech acts in interaction: A critique of Searle. *Discourse processes, 3*, 133-154.

Svartvik, J. (1980). "Well" in conversation. In S. Greenbaum (Ed.), *Studies in English linguistics: For Randolph Quirk*, pp. 167–177. London: Longman.

Svartvik, J., and Quirk, R. (Eds.). (1980). *A corpus of English conversation*. Lund: Gleerup.

Tannen, D. (1989). *Talking voices: Repetition, dialogue and imagery in conversational discourse*. Cambridge University Press.

Thomason, R. H. (1990). Accommodation, meaning, and implicature: Interdisciplinary foundations for pragmatics. In P. R. Cohen, J. Morgan, and M. E. Pollack (Eds.), *Intentions in communication*, pp. 325–364. Cambridge MA: MIT Press.

Traum, D. (1994). A computational theory of grounding in natural language conversation. Ph.D. dissertation, University of Rochester.

Tuomela, R. (1996). *Importance of us: Philosophical studies in basic social notions*. Stanford CA: Stanford University Press.

Tuomela, R., and Miller, K. (1988). We-intentions. *Philosophical Studies, 53*, 367–389.

Van Dijk, T. (1972). *Some aspects of text grammars*. The Hague: Mouton.
    (1977). *Text and context: Explorations in the semantics and pragmatics of discourse*. London: Longman.

Van Dijk, T. A., and Kintsch, W. (1983). *Strategies of discourse comprehension*. New York: Academic Press.

Van Wijk, C., and Kempen, G. (1987). A dual system for producing self-repairs in spontaneous speech: Evidence from experimentally elicited corrections. *Cognitive Psychology, 19*, 403–440.

Vanderveken, D. (1990). On the unification of speech act theory and formal semantics. In P. R. Cohen, J. Morgan, and M. E. Pollack (Eds.), *Intentions in communication*, pp. 195–220. Cambridge MA: MIT Press.

Verschueren, J. (1980). *On speech act verbs*. Amsterdam: John Benjamins.

Von Savigny, E. (1983). Sentence meaning and utterance meaning: A complete case study. In R. Bäuerle, C. Schwarze, and A. von Stechow (Eds.), *Meaning, use, and interpretation of language*, pp. 423–435. Berlin: Walter de Gruyter.

Walster, E. H., Berscheid, E., and Walster, G. W. (1976). New directions in equity research. In L. Berkowitz (Ed.), *Advances in experimental social psychology*, Vol. IX, pp. 1–42. New York: Academic Press.

Walster, E. H., Walster, G. W., and Berscheid, E. (1978). *Equity: Theory and research*. Rockleigh NJ: Allyn and Bacon.

Walton, K. L. (1973). Pictures and make-believe. *Philosophical Review, 82*, 283–319.
    (1976). Points of view in narrative and depictive representation. *Nous, 10*, 49–61.
    (1978). Fearing fictions. *Journal of Philosophy, 75*, 5–27.
    (1983). Fiction, fiction-making, and styles of fictionality. *Philosophy and Literature, 8*, 78–88.
    (1990). *Mimesis as make-believe: On the foundations of the representational arts*. Cambridge MA: Harvard University Press.

Wilkes-Gibbs, D. (1986). Collaborative processes of language use in conversation. Ph.D. dissertation, Stanford University.

Wilkins, D. P. (1992). Interjections as deictics. *Journal of Pragmatics, 17*, 119–158.

Wilson, D., and Sperber, D. (1992). On verbal irony. *Lingua, 87*, 53–76.

Wittgenstein, L. (1958). *Philosophical investigations*. Trans. G. E. M. Anscombe. 3rd edn. New York: Macmillan.

Wunderlich, D. (1977). On problems of speech act theory. In R. Butts and J. Hintikka (Eds.), *Basic problems in methodology and linguistics*, Vol. III, pp. 243–258. Dordrecht: Reidel.

Ziff, P. (1977). About proper names. *Mind, 86*, 319–332.

Index of names

Subject index

acceptance phase 227, 233
accepted purpose 140
acknowledgments 230, 231, 247, 323
  backgrounded 250
  backgrounding of 231
  overlaps in 231
  scope of 231
acquaintedness 115
act 18
action 18
  coordination of 35
  layers of 16, 24
action ladders 147–148, 224, 389
  joint 151–153
action–response pair 200–201
action tradition 56
actions
  adaptive 61
  autonomous 19, 60
  components of speaking, listening
    21
  coordination of 11, 139
  deceptive 61
  depictive 174
  individual 3, 18, 387
  joint 3, 18, 19, 23
  lines of 388–391
  nonserious 353
  of language 17–25
  participatory 19
activating rules 184

activity 18
activity roles 33, 37
activity type 30
acts, meta-communicative 241
additions 264
addressee-directed illocutionary acts
  151
addressees 11, 14, 151
adjacency 199
adjacency pairs 197–198, 200, 205,
  325, 343
agreement 66
agreements, explicit 98
ambiguity 77
ambivalence 378, 379
anchoring 164
anecdotes 346, 360
animator 20
annotated record 48
anomalous suspense 366
anticipated products 22
aperiodic activities 85
applause 351
appreciation 358–359, 366–367
artificial instruments 167
aspects of demonstrations
  annotative 173
  depictive 173
  incidental 173
  supportive 173
assertion 134